NATIONAL HUMAN RIGHTS INSTITUTIONS IN EUROPE AND LATIN AMERICA

NATIONAL HUMAN RIGHTS INSTITUTIONS IN EUROPE AND LATIN AMERICA

An International and Comparative Study

Edited by
Sebastián López Escarcena
Manuel Núñez Poblete
Jan Wouters

INTERSENTIA
Cambridge – Antwerp – Chicago

Intersentia Ltd
8 Wellington Mews
Wellington Street | Cambridge
CB1 1HW | United Kingdom
Tel: +44 1223 736 170
Email: contact@larcier-intersentia.com
www.larcier-intersentia.com

Distribution for the UK and
Rest of the World (incl. Eastern Europe)
NBN International
1 Deltic Avenue, Rooksley
Milton Keynes MK13 8LD
United Kingdom
Tel: +44 1752 202 301 | Fax: +44 1752 202 331
Email: orders@nbninternational.com

Distribution for Europe
Lefebvre Sarrut Belgium NV
Hoogstraat 139/6
1000 Brussels
Belgium
Tel: +32 (0)2 548 07 13
Email: contact@larcier-intersentia.com

Distribution for the USA and Canada
Independent Publishers Group
Order Department
814 North Franklin Street
Chicago, IL 60610
USA
Tel: +1 800 888 4741 (toll free) | Fax: +1 312 337 5985
Email: orders@ipgbook.com

National Human Rights Institutions in Europe and Latin America.
An International and Comparative Study

ISBN 978-1-83970-384-3
D/2024/7849/13
NUR 820

MIX
Papier | Ondersteunt verantwoord bosbeheer
FSC® C004472

GPRC
Guaranteed Peer Reviewed Content

British Library Cataloguing in Publication Data. A catalogue record for this book is available from the British Library.

CONTENTS

LIST OF ABBREVIATIONS

ACHR	American Convention on Human Rights
AJIL	American Journal of International Law
Am. U. Int'l L. Rev.	American University International Law Review
APF	Asia-Pacific Forum of NHRIs
B.C.L.Rev.	Boston College Law Review
CDDH	Steering Committee on Human Rights
CDDH INST	CDDH drafting group on civil society and national human rights institutions
CERREM	Committee for Risk Assessment and Recommendation of Measures (Colombia)
CESCR	Committee on Economic, Social, and Cultural Rights
CHCDH	Commission nationale consultative des droits de l'homme
CJEU	Court of Justice of the European Union
CHR	Commission on Human Rights
CNDH	Comisión Nacional de los Derechos Humanos
CoE	Council of Europe
COHOM	Council Working Party on Human Rights
CPF	Common Provision Funds
CRPD	Convention on the Rights of Persons with Disabilities
CSO(s)	Civil society organisation(s)
DG NEAR	Directorate-General for Neighbourhood and Enlargement Negotiations
DIMR	Deutsches Institut für Menschenrechte
DROI	Committee on Human Rights of the European Parliament

ECHR	European Convention on Human Rights
ECOSOC	Economic and Social Council
ECRI	European Commission against Racism and Intolerance
ECtHR	European Court of Human Rights
EEAS	European External Action Service
EIDHR	European Instrument for Democracy and Human Rights
EJIL	European Journal of International Law
ELJ	European Law Journal
ENA	École Nationale d'Administration
ENM	École Nationale de la Magistrature
ENNHRI	European Network of National Human Rights Institutions
Equinet	European Network of Equality Bodies
ESC	European Social Charter
EU	European Union
FARC-EP	Revolutionary Armed Forces of Colombia – People's Army
FIO	Federación Iberoamericana del Ombudsperson
FRA	European Union Agency for Fundamental Rights
FREMP	Council Working Party on Fundamental Rights
GAL	Global administrative law
GANHRI	Global Alliance for National Human Rights Institutions
Gonzaga J.I.L.	Gonzaga Journal of International Law
GRETA	Group of Experts on Action against Trafficking in Human Beings
GVP	Preliminary Assessment Group (Colombia)
Harv. Hum. Rts. J.	Harvard Human Rights Journal
HRBA	Human Rights Based Approach
HRC	UN Human Rights Council
HRDTP	Human Rights and Democracy Thematic Programme

Hum.Rts.L.Rev.	Human Rights Law Review
Hum.Rts.Q.	Human Rights Quarterly
Hum. Rts. Rev.	Human Rights Review
IA	Impact assessment
IACHR	Inter-American Commission on Human Rights
IACtHR	Inter-American Court of Human Rights
ICC	International Coordinating Committee of NHRIs
ICON	International Journal of Constitutional Law
IIDH	Instituto Interamericano de Derecho Humanos
ILC	International Law Commission
INDH	Instituto Nacional de Derechos Humanos
INDDHH	Institución Nacional de Derechos Humanos y Defensoría del Pueblo
IN-LAW	Informal International Lawmaking Project
Int'l Org.	International Organization
INTPA	EU Directorate-General for International Partnerships
IPA	International Public Authority
J. Hum. Rts. Pract.	Journal of Human Rights Practice
J. Lat. Am. St.	Journal of Latin American Studies
JORF	Journal officiel de la République française (France)
L.C.P.	Law and Contemporary Problems
LGBTI	Lesbian, gay, bisexual, transgender and intersex people
LIBE	Committee on Civil Liberties, Justice and Home Affairs of the European Parliament
MIPs	Multi-annual indicative programmes
MP	Member of Parliament
NANHRI	Network of African NHRIs
NDICI	Neighbourhood, Development and International Cooperation Instrument
NGO(s)	Non-governmental organisation(s)

NHRI(s)	National Human Rights Institution(s)
Nord. J. Int'l L.	Nordic Journal of International Law
NPM	National Preventive Mechanism
N.Q.Hum.Rts.	Netherlands Quarterly of Human Rights
OAS	Organization of American States
ODIHR	Office for Democratic Institutions and Human Rights
OGF	Official Gazette of the Federation (Mexico)
OHCHR	Office of the High Commissioner for Human Rights
OP-CAT	Optional Protocol to the Convention against Torture and Other Cruel, Inhuman or Degrading Treatment or Punishment
OSCE	Organization for Security and Co-operation in Europe
RAXEN	European Information Network on Racism and Xenophobia
Revista IIDH	Revista Instituto Interamericano de Derechos Humanos
RINDHCA	Network of NHRIs from the Americas
RIOOD	Red Iberoamericana de Organismos y Organizaciones contra la Discriminación
SCA	Sub-Committee on Accreditation of the Global Alliance of National Human Rights Institutions
SCJN	National Supreme Court of Justice (Mexico)
Soc. Forces	Social Forces (journal)
SRHR	EU Special Representative for Human Rights
TEU	Treaty on European Union
Tex.L.Rev.	Texas Law Review
UN	United Nations
UNAM	National Autonomous University of Mexico
UNGA	United Nations General Assembly

ABOUT THE AUTHORS

Paola Acosta
Paola Acosta is professor of constitutional law and researcher at Externado University of Colombia, and former editor of the *Revista Derecho del Estado*. She holds a PhD in law from the Complutense University of Madrid, and an LLM and an LLB from Externado University of Colombia. Paola is currently a member of the Institute of Constitutional Studies Carlos Restrepo Piedrahita.

Heiner Bielefeldt
Heiner Bielefeldt is Professor for human rights and human rights politics at the Friedrich-Alexander University Erlangen-Nürnberg and member of the Centre for Human Rights Erlangen-Nürnberg (CHREN). Between 2003 and 2009 he served as director of the German Institute for Human Rights. From 2010 to 2016 he held the mandate of the UN Special Rapporteur on freedom of religion or belief.

Emmanuel Decaux
Emmanuel Decaux is Professor emeritus of the University of Paris Panthéon-Assas, where he taught public international law and international human rights law. He is currently President of the Court of Conciliation and Arbitration within the OSCE and, since 2021, President of the René Cassin Foundation – International Institute of Human Rights. He has published on topics of public international law and international organisations, with a focus on the peaceful settlement of disputes and human rights. Decaux was a member of the UN Committee on Enforced Disappearances and president between 2011 and 2016. He was a member of the UN Sub-Commission on the Promotion and Protection of Human Rights (2002–2006) and member of the Human Rights Council Advisory Committee (2007–2010). For 30 years he was also a member of the French National Advisory Commission for Human Rights (CNCDH) (1992–2022).

Sebastián Donoso
Sebastián Donoso is a member of the Council of the National Human Rights Institute of Chile. He holds a MSc in Social Policy and Planning in Developing Countries from the London School of Economics and Political Science, and an LLB from the Pontifical Catholic University of Chile, where he teaches indigenous law and is an associate researcher of its Centre for Public Policy. Sebastián has taught at the Diplomatic Academy of Chile, Santiago, the Pontifical Catholic

University of Valparaíso and the Austral University of Chile, Valdivia. He was special advisor on indigenous issues to the Ministry General Secretariat of the Presidency of Chile.

José Julio Fernández
José Julio Fernández is a Professor of constitutional law at the University of Santiago de Compostela and former ombudsperson (*Valedor do Pobo*) of the Autonomous Community of Galicia (2007–2015). José Julio holds a PhD and an LLB from University of Santiago de Compostela, and has been a researcher at the universities of Aix-Marseille, Bayreuth, Bologna, Cologne, Freiburg, Leuven, Lisboa, Mexico (UNAM), Paris 1 (Panthéon-Sorbonne), Pisa, São Paulo, and Strasbourg, as well as the Centre for Political and Constitutional Studies of Madrid and the Max Planck Institute for Comparative Public Law and International Law.

Pablo González Domínguez
Pablo González is staff attorney at the Inter-American Court of Human Rights, and a professor of human rights at the Pan-American University of Mexico. He holds a JSD from the University of Notre Dame, Indiana, an LLM from Georgetown University, Washington D.C., and an LLB from the Pan-American University (Mexico City). Pablo was an advisor to the Justice Studies Center of the Americas (CEJA) in Santiago, and has taught at the Externado University of Colombia, the National Autonomous University of Mexico (UNAM), and the University of La Sabana, Colombia, as well as the Inter-American Institute of Human Rights.

Veronika Haasz
Veronika Haasz obtained her PhD from the University of Vienna in 2020. Her research focused on national institutions for the promotion and protection of human rights, with special regard to the transformation of ombuds-institutions to national human rights institutions. She graduated in Law from the University of Pécs, Hungary and holds an LLM in International Human Rights and Humanitarian Law from the European University Viadrina, Germany. Veronika worked as a researcher with the European Institute for Gender Equality and for the UN as national consultant. Her previous working experiences include the Global Campus of Human Rights in Venice, the EU Agency for Fundamental Rights in Vienna, the German Institute for Human Rights in Berlin, and the Office of the Commissioner for Educational Rights in Budapest.

Markus Krajewski
Markus Krajewski is Professor at the Friedrich-Alexander University of Erlangen-Nürnberg (FAU) and holds the Chair in Public Law and Public International Law. Prof. Krajewski is one of the programme directors of the MA in Human Rights and chairperson of the Centre for Human Rights Erlangen-Nürnberg (CHREN). He also chairs the Board of Trustees of the German

Institute for Human Rights and is Secretary-General of the German Branch of the International Law Association. Before joining FAU, Markus Krajewski taught at King's College London, the University of Potsdam and the University of Bremen.

Michael Krennerich
Michael Krennerich is Professor of political science at the Chair of Human Rights and Human Rights Politics, University Erlangen-Nürnberg. He holds a doctorate in Political Science, Philosophy and Public Law from Heidelberg University and a post-doctoral Habilitation from the University Erlangen-Nürnberg. Since 2007, he is the chairperson of the 'Centre for Human Rights Erlangen-Nürnberg (CHREN), and between 2016 and 2020, he was one of the coordinators of the German NGO-network on human rights *Forum Menschenrechte*. Michael Krennerich is also co-founder and chief-editor of the academic journal *Zeitschrift für Menschenrechte – Journal for Human Rights*, founded in 2007.

Sebastián López Escarcena
Sebastián López is Professor of international law at the Pontifical Catholic University of Chile (UC Chile), and former director of its Department of International Law. He is an associate member of the Centre for Global Governance Studies of the Catholic University of Leuven and of the Research Institute in International and European Law of the University Paris 1 (Panthéon-Sorbonne). He holds a PhD from the University of Edinburgh, an LLM from the University of Leiden, and an LLB and BA from UC Chile. Sebastián has been a guest or visiting fellow or professor at the universities of Amsterdam, Cornell, Edinburgh, Heidelberg, Leuven, Notre Dame, and Paris 1, as well as the Boston College. He has also taught at the Diplomatic Academy, the Judicial Academy and the Military Academy of the Chilean state, the Pontifical Catholic University of Valparaíso, and the University of the Pacific, Peru.

Emilio Maus Ratz
Emilio Maus is Professor of international human rights law at the Pan-American University in Mexico City. He holds a Dr.iur. and an LLM from the University of Cologne, a MSc and an LLB from the Pan-American University (Mexico City), where he is the director of the Master's Programme in Human Rights and Constitutional Law. Formerly, Emilio was a director at the National Human Rights Commission of Mexico.

Katrien Meuwissen
Dr. Katrien Meuwissen is senior human rights officer and team leader at ENNHRI, the European Network of National Human Rights Institutions (NHRIs) in wider Europe. Katrien oversees ENNHRI's work on establishment of NHRIs and their international accreditation, leads European standard-setting on NHRIs, develops strategic engagement of NHRIs with regional counterparts and coordinates ENNHRI's thematic work. In 2023 Katrien was

appointed as member of the Board of the Flemish Human Rights Institute with a six-year mandate. Katrien obtained a PhD in international law at the KU Leuven in 2017, with a dissertation on NHRIs in Europe. Katrien was formerly a teaching assistant and researcher in international law at KU Leuven, and the Leuven Centre for Global Governance Studies.

Manuel Núñez Poblete
Manuel Núñez is Professor of constitutional law and international law at the Pontifical Catholic University of Valparaíso, Chile. He holds a PhD from the University of Santiago de Compostela in Galicia and an LLB from the Pontifical Catholic University of Valparaíso. Manuel was a member of the Council of the National Human Rights Institute of Chile, and currently he is part of its Advisory Council. Formerly, Manuel was the director of the School of Law of the Catholic University of the North, in Antofagasta, and of the School of Law of the Pontifical Catholic University of Valparaíso.

Beate Rudolf
Beate Rudolf, Dr iur., Professor of Law, is Director of the German Institute for Human Rights, the German NHRI (since 2010). From 2016 to 2019, she also chaired the Global Alliance of National Human Rights Institutions (GANHRI). Before joining the Institute, she was junior professor of public law and equality law at the Faculty of Law of Freie Universität Berlin. She also led the project 'International Law Standards for Governance in Weak and Failing States' in the Collaborative Research Center 'Governance in Areas of Limited Statehood'. She was a member of the European Network of Legal Experts in the Field of Gender and Equality of the European Commission and served, *inter alia*, as Vice-President of the European Women Lawyers Association (EWLA).

Eduardo Vio Grossi†
Eduardo Vio Grossi was Professor of international law at the Pontifical Catholic University of Valparaíso and judge at the Inter-American Court of Human Rights. He held a PhD from the University of Grenoble, and a Dr.h.c. and an LLB from the Pontifical Catholic University of Valparaíso. Eduardo was director of legal affairs at the Ministry of Foreign Affairs of Chile and President of the Inter-American Juridical Committee of the Organization of American States (OAS). He taught at the Diplomatic Academy of the Chilean state, and the Central University of Venezuela, among other institutions. Judge Vio passed away in December 2022.

Jan Wouters
Jan Wouters is Full Professor of International Law and International Organizations, Jean Monnet Chair *ad personam*, Director of the Institute for International Law and of the Leuven Centre for Global Governance Studies, and Administrator of the America Europe Fund at KU Leuven. He is Adjunct Professor at Columbia University and Visiting Professor at the College of

Europe, LUISS, Paris2 and SciencesPo. He recently coordinated two large European projects, FRAME ('Fostering Human Rights Among European External and Internal Policies', 2013–2017) and RECONNECT ('Reconnecting Europe with its Citizens through Democracy and Rule of Law', 2018–2022). He provides advice and training to international organisations and governments.

STUDYING NATIONAL HUMAN RIGHTS INSTITUTIONS IN EUROPE AND LATIN AMERICA

Introductory Remarks

Sebastián López Escarcena, Manuel Núñez Poblete
and Jan Wouters

National Human Rights Institutions (NHRIs) currently operate across all five continents, striving to comply with the so-called 'Paris Principles'.[1] As a term of art, NHRI is a widely accepted one. Under its aegis, numerous institutions promote and protect human rights following two basic models: commissions and ombudsman offices, and sometimes hybrid and specialised institutions. NHRIs have been integrated into a network of administrative agencies and judicial courts that deal with human rights at the national and international levels. They provide a valuable example of institutional dialogue and cross-fertilisation between municipal and international law. At least in Europe and Latin America, their presence is so extensive that it could be argued that NHRIs are now part of a common legal tradition, which allows for certain distinctive features in each region.

1. WHY THIS BOOK?

At present, there are quite a few informative monographs and edited books on NHRIs, written from a general or a specific perspective.[2] No publication,

---

1 Adopted by UN General Assembly (GA) Resolution 48/134 of 20 December 1993, National institutions for the promotion and protection of human rights.

2 See e.g., G. de Beco and R. Murray, *A Commentary on the Paris Principles on National Human Rights Institutions*, Cambridge University Press, Cambridge 2014; S. Cardenas, *Chains of Justice: The Global Rise of State Institutions for Human Rights*, University of Pennsylvania Press, Philadelphia 2014; E. Brems, G. de Beco and W. Vandenhole (eds.), *National Human Rights Institutions and Economic, Social and Cultural Rights*, Intersentia, Cambridge 2013; M. Frahm (ed.), *Australasia and Pacific Ombudsman Institutions: Mandates, Competences and Good Practice*, Springer 2013; J. Wouters and K. Meuwissen (eds.), *National Human Rights*

however, has yet contextualised and analysed the similarities and differences between European and Latin American NHRIs, providing case studies on concrete commissions, ombuds offices and institutes from across these two regions.[3] By drawing on the existing literature, this book aims to bridge the European and Latin American experiences on NHRIs, while emphasising the essential international aspect that these institutions have. Filling a gap in the legal literature, this work is aimed at studying NHRIs from an international and

Institutions in Europe: Comparative, European and International Perspectives, Intersentia, Cambridge 2013; R. Goodman and T. Pegram (eds.), *Human Rights, State Compliance, and Social Change: Assessing National Human Rights Institutions*, Cambridge University Press, Cambridge 2012; J. Mertus, *Human Rights Matters: Local Politics and National Human Rights Institutions*, Stanford University Press, Stanford 2009; G. Kucsko-Stadlmayer (ed.), *European Ombudsman-Institutions: A Comparative Legal Analysis regarding the Multifaceted realisation of an Idea*, Springer 2008; B. Burdekin, *National Human Rights Institutions in the Asia-Pacific Region*, Martinus Nijhoff, Leiden 2007; R. Murray, *The Role of National Human Rights Institutions at the International and Regional Levels: The Experience of Africa*, Hart Publishing, Oxford 2007; G. Fellous, *Les institutions nationales des droits de l'homme: acteurs de troisième type*, Documentation française, Paris 2006; A. Pohjolainen, *The Evolution of National Human Rights Institutions: The Role of the United Nations*, Danish Centre for Human Rights, Copenhagen 2006; L. Reif, *The Ombudsman, Good Governance and the International Human Rights System*, Springer 2004; K. Hossain, L.F.M. Besselink, H.S.G. Selassie and E. Völker (eds.), *Human Rights Commissions and Ombudsman Offices: National Experiences throughout the World*, Brill, Leiden 2001; B. Lindsnaes, L. Lindholt and K. Yigen (eds.), *National Human Rights Institutions: Articles and Working Papers. Input to the Discussions on the Establishment and Development of the Functions of National Human Rights Institutions*, Danish Centre for Human Rights, Copenhagen 2000.

3 There are several good articles on NHRIs, but none addressing this issue in depth. See e.g. K. Linos and T. Pegram, 'What Works in Human Rights Institutions?' (2017) 111/3 *AJIL* 628; K. Linos and T. Pegram, 'Architects of their Own Making: National Human Rights Institutions and the United Nations' (2016) 38/4 *Hum.Rts.Q.* 1109; K. Linos and T. Pegram, 'The Language of Compromise in International Agreements' (2016) 70/3 *Int'l Org.* 587; K. Meuwissen, 'NHRIs and the State: New and Independent Actors in the Multi-layered Human Rights System?' (2015) 15/3 *Hum.Rts.L.Rev.* 441; M. Brodie, 'Progressing Norm Socialisation: Why Membership Matters – The Impact of the Accreditation Process of the International Coordinating Committee of National Institutions for the Promotion and Protection of Human Rights' (2011) 80/2 *Nord. J. Int'l L.* 143; R. Carver, 'One NHRI or Many? How Many Institutions Does It Take to Protect Human Rights? – Lessons from the European Experience' (2011) 3/1 *J. Hum. Rts. Pract.* 1; R. Carver, 'A New Answer to an Old Question: National Human Rights Institutions and the Domestication of International Law', (2010) 10/1 *Hum.Rts.L.Rev.* 1; T. Pegram, 'Diffusion Across Political Systems: The Global Spread of National Human Rights Institutions' (2010) 32/2 *Hum.Rts.Q.* 729; J. Koo and F. Ramirez, 'National Incorporation of Global Human Rights: Worldwide Expansion of National Human Rights Institutions, 1966–2004', (2009) 87/3 *Social Forces* 1321; G. de Beco, 'National Human Rights Institutions in Europe' (2007) 7/2 *Hum.Rts.L.Rev.* 331; R. Murray, 'National Human Rights Institutions – Criteria and Factors for Assessing their Effectiveness' (2007) 25/2 *N.Q.Hum.Rts.* 189; F. Uggla, 'The Ombusdman in Latin America' (2004) 36 *J. Lat. Am. St.* 423; S. Cardenas, 'Emerging Global Actors: The United Nations and National Human Rights Institutions' (2003) 9/1 *Global Governance* 23; R. Kumar, 'National Human Rights Institutions: Good Governance Perspectives on Institutionalization of Human Rights' (2003) 19/2 *Am. U. Int'l L. Rev.* 259; L. Reif, 'Building Democratic Institutions: The Role of National Human Rights Institutions in Good Governance and Human Rights Protection' (2000) 13 *Harv. Hum. Rts. J.* 1.

comparative standpoint. As such, it not only includes introductory chapters on the relationship between NHRIs and the United Nations (UN), the European Union (EU) and the Inter-American Court of Human Rights (IACtHR), but also general contributions on European and Latin American institutions, in addition to specific case studies on commissions, ombuds offices and institutes of these regions. For this purpose, we have selected NHRIs that have proven influential in Europe and Latin America and, at times, beyond them. To ensure a synoptic and balanced view on the topic, great care has been taken in the selection of these NHRIs to include the main forms of institutional organisation. Firstly, in order to assess the distinct models they adopt, we have chosen three of the major European NHRIs: Spain's *Defensor del Pueblo*, which is especially relevant to Latin America; France's *Commission nationale consultative des droits de l'homme* (the French Commission), of great tradition in the area, and the younger, and highly interesting, *Deutsches Institut für Menschenrechte* in Germany. Secondly, regarding Latin America, we have decided to study in this book the main institutions which adopt either an ombuds, a commission or an institute model: those of Argentina, Chile, Colombia, Ecuador, Mexico, Paraguay, and Uruguay.

For all the cases examined in this volume, an effort has been made to identify the most important challenges facing NHRIs, in conjunction with their primary organisational patterns, powers and relationships with regional human rights protection systems. Consequently, the case studies included in this book outline the legal basis of each institution, emphasising their structure and mandate, in addition to their role, both as stipulated by national legislation and in terms of their participation in the international monitoring process, led today by the Global Alliance for National Human Rights Institutions (GANHRI). For Latin American institutions, the emphasis has been placed on their interaction with the systems of the UN and of the Organization of American States (OAS), while for European NHRIs the focus of analysis has been broader, encompassing the UN, the EU, the Council of Europe and the Organization for Security and Co-operation in Europe (OSCE). In the NHRIs studied throughout this book, several common challenges can be observed: building or consolidating trust; budgetary cuts; delays in the establishment processes; non-renewal of their membership by state authorities; or an expansion of roles without the necessary support in terms of personnel and infrastructure. In addition, several specific challenges have also been identified, such as the consolidation of pluralism within each institution; competition with other bodies with greater authority and social influence; and a lack of opportunities for regional cooperation.

2. STRUCTURE OF THE BOOK

This work is divided into two parts. The first one addresses the general issues raised by NHRIs under international law, such as the Paris Principles and the regional role played by these institutions, as well as their relationship with the EU, the Council of Europe and the OSCE, on the one hand, and with the IACtHR, on the other. The second part provides the case analyses of the eight European and Latin American NHRIs chosen for this book because of their relevance.

The first chapter is by Sebastián López Escarcena. He analyses the history, legal nature, and purpose of the Paris Principles, and relates them to the rule of law. These principles, which have played a central role in the establishment and internationalisation of NHRIs, were adopted by a resolution of the UN General Assembly (UNGA) in 1993, but were first defined in 1991 at the International Workshop on National Institutions for the Promotion and Protection of Human Rights held in Paris. These principles operate in practice as proper legal rules, at least in the accreditation process led by the competent GANHRI sub-committee, whose general observations supplement their provisions. From a normativist perspective, the Paris Principles can be considered an example of soft law; from a non-normativist standpoint they can be deemed an instance of global administrative law, informal international law-making, or an exercise of public international authority. Regardless of the approach chosen, however, Sebastián López Escarcena claims that the Paris Principles are but one of several cases that illustrate how international law brings the rule of law into domestic law.

In the second chapter, Katrien Meuwissen provides an overview of European NHRIs. In line with the approach of this book, her contribution describes the characteristics of these NHRIs, as well as the challenges and opportunities they encounter at the multiple levels of the human rights system: across the region, at the level of the European Network of NHRIs (ENNHRI), and at the level of NHRIs' engagement with European human rights mechanisms, like the EU, the Council of Europe and the OSCE. Undoubtedly, this composite institutional web of institutions allows for a functional context that is more complex than that of their Latin American counterparts. Katrien Meuwissen's chapter also identifies important challenges that are not exclusive to Europe, including the rise of populism, threats to democracy and minorities, and decreasing budgets. In all, this chapter paints the multi-layered human rights landscape for European NHRIs within which national illustrations, following later in the book, can be situated.

In the third chapter, James Rischbieth and Jan Wouters analyse the relationship between the EU and NHRIs, which, in light of their common objectives, they see as natural partners for human rights, democracy and rule of law. They situate NHRIs in contemporary EU activity, and consider some of the key ways the EU has engaged with and could better engage with NHRIs in both its internal and external action. James Rischbieth and Jan Wouters conclude that EU institutions can, and should, liaise with NHRIs and their regional and international networks when undertaking any human and fundamental rights-based work. From consultation and participation during the development of EU and member state legislation, to the crafting of third-country human rights strategies and development policy; from cooperation during political dialogues, to information sharing during the crafting of the EU's thematic and annual reports; from advice on means of support and coordination during the implementation of human rights policies, to the provision of support for human rights defenders under threat: all EU human rights action should involve NHRIs. Indeed, NHRIs are one of the actors best positioned to ensure that Union policies make a difference 'on the ground': NHRIs know the ins and outs of their national context, what works and what does not work; they are familiar with the interests of local people; they understand local priorities and complexities; and they know how best to approach thorny local and regional issues and conflicts.

The fourth chapter concerns the identity, mission, and authority of NHRIs in Latin America. Manuel Núñez Poblete discusses these key institutional issues, providing an insight into 14 Latin American institutions, from their establishment in the mid-1980s to the present. According to the author, NHRIs are a distinctive feature of the *ius constitutionale commune* of Latin America. However, despite their general constitutional status, NHRIs are not exempt from displaying the same weaknesses as political institutions across the region. In addition to describing the distinct organisational forms of Latin American NHRIs, this chapter discusses their common characteristics and those that distinguish them from their European counterparts. These common features include the internationalisation of constitutionalism, and the effect on institutional identity that certain specific models in the region generate. The chapter then analyses the factors that influence the construction and effectiveness of NHRIs' moral or political authority. Manuel Núñez Poblete concludes by reviewing the role of NHRIs within the Inter-American System for the protection of human rights.

The role of NHRIs within the Inter-American System for the protection of human rights is analysed more closely by an author who had extensive experience of that regional human rights system. In the fifth chapter, Judge Eduardo Vio Grossi (†) discusses the role played by non-governmental organisations (NGOs) and NHRIs in the IACtHR. In the controversies brought before this international tribunal, not only do the ministries of foreign affairs participate as respondents, but also their NHRIs participate as claimants. This chapter briefly analyses the insufficient normative framework that regulates the relationship between the IACtHR, NGOs and NHRIs: mainly, the American Convention on Human Rights and the Rules of Procedure of the IACtHR. It surveys, in addition, the participation of NGOs and NHRIs in cases lodged at the IACtHR against the states to which they belong. This is done by looking at those instances in which NGOs have filed *amicus curiae* briefs and when they have acted as defenders or representatives of complainants, alleged victims, or their families in contentious proceedings before the IACtHR.

The second part of the book is dedicated to the analysis of specific European and Latin American case studies. The sixth chapter, by Emilio Maus and Pablo González Domínguez, analyses the *Comisión Nacional de los Derechos Humanos*, created in 1990 as a response to international demands for a transition of the

Mexican state from an authoritarian to a democratic regime and to address the promotion and protection of human rights as state policy. The chapter examines the evolution, organisation, functioning and growing political relevance of this human rights commission, as well as its role in improving the understanding of these rights, not only at federal level, but also with attention to international and local dimensions. Since its creation, the powers of the Mexican commission, and the mechanisms to allow for a more effective institutional operation, have been gradually strengthened. The normative analysis of this chapter concludes with an in-depth assessment of the regime of accountability, autonomy and fulfilment of the Paris Principles by the Mexican commission, and an evaluation of its effectiveness and the challenges that it confronts, particularly in light of budget reductions and a highly concentrated political system burdened by violence and corruption.

In the seventh chapter, Emmanuel Decaux studies the *Commission nationale consultative des droits de l'homme* (CNCDH), based on what he identifies as the three development stages of the oldest NHRI. Reformed several times since 1947, the areas now covered by the French commission are broad, both domestically and internationally. It issues reports and studies, advisory opinions, and declarations on human rights, but does not directly receive complaints regarding human rights violations. The CNCDH's membership is designed to ensure its independence and pluralism. Its work is carried out by four or five great *pôles*, formerly known as sub-commissions, all of which have their own working groups. The president of the French commission is nominated by the Prime Minister and has a very important role as leader and public representative of this large, collective institution. Currently, the CNDCH faces various challenges, among which are the risk of being merged with other public institutions like the *Défenseur des droits*, the traditional administrative ombuds office in France, and its growing bureaucratisation resulting from a large budget and staff.

Paola Acosta is the author of the eighth chapter, in which she reviews three *defensorías del pueblo* or ombuds offices: those of Argentina, Colombia and Ecuador. These institutions are assessed in the context of the new Latin American constitutionalism. Acosta analyses the organisation, functioning, efficacy, and accountability of the Argentinean, Colombian and Ecuadorian NHRIs by reviewing their respective regimes of autonomy, their compliance with the Paris Principles and their relations with international monitoring bodies and international courts. The author also addresses the institutional pressures these NHRIs face as a result of the proliferation of human rights agencies in the region, but also because of their loss of autonomy and even corruption. The main claim of this chapter is that the institutional efforts expended to implement the NHRIs have not been in vain, but neither have they been sufficient to meet the challenges posed by human rights. The author places special emphasis on the relationship between these ombuds offices and civil society, an important issue in light of the Paris Principles.

The ninth chapter, by Veronika Haász, continues the subject of Latin American NHRIs, discussing the ombuds offices of two neighbouring countries. Paraguay and Uruguay share a similar historical past, but the recovery from authoritarian regimes has worked out differently for each of them. This is reflected in the timing and circumstances of the creation of their ombuds offices, as well as in the form and functioning of these entities. While the Paraguayan *Defensoría del Pueblo* has its roots in the Swedish and Spanish ombuds model, as do most institutions in the continent, and dates back to 1995, the Uruguayan *Institución Nacional de Derechos Humanos y Defensoría del Pueblo* is a combination of the ombudsman and the institute models and is a relatively new institution established in 2008. As such, the latter diverges from the general rule in Latin America and is more similar to the Chilean NHRI, another young institution. The chapter describes the characteristics of the Paraguayan and Uruguayan NHRIs, from their establishment to their autonomy of operation, highlighting not only the similarities and differences between them, but also analysing their effectiveness, compliance with the Paris Principles, and the novel challenges they currently face.

José Julio Fernández Rodríguez is the author of the tenth chapter. He analyses one of the European NHRIs most influential in Latin America, the *Defensor del Pueblo* or ombuds office of Spain, a national-level constitutional organ that interacts with other local-level ombuds offices that operate in the Autonomous Communities of this country. In contrast to the viewpoint provided by Paola Acosta, this chapter argues in favour of the 'persuasion magistracy' or 'magistracy of influence' characteristic of the ombudsman, as the foundation on which its authority is built, and which is the key to its success. The chapter also evaluates the structure and mandate of the Spanish NHRI, characterised by a broad range of themes that are subject to monitoring, with the author placing special emphasis on the complaints procedure. Among the challenges and threats assessed, Fernández Rodríguez studies the economic crisis and the widespread lack of confidence in public institutions that are affecting not only Spain, but also other countries' NHRIs. The overall assessment of the Spanish *Defensor del Pueblo*'s performance is positive. However, this remains dependent on the independence and *auctoritas* of the institution, without which it is meaningless, according to the author.

In the eleventh chapter, Heiner Bielefeldt, Markus Krajewski, Michael Krennerich and Beate Rudolf provide an in-depth analysis of one of the newest NHRIs in Europe: the *Deutsches Institut für Menschenrechte* (DIMR), or German Institute for Human Rights. Overviewing the legal foundations, institutional structure, and main tasks of this NHRI, the chapter offers an insight into the discussions that led to the establishment of the DIMR and its further development, especially the arduous way to a legal status in 2015. The chapter shows how the re-accreditation of the DIMR helped strengthen the institution's role, function, and independence. The authors argue that the development of this NHRI, and the political opposition it partly faced, illustrate that the need for the establishment and the functions of this kind of institute are not always fully understood and accepted by all political players, even in a democratic state based on the rule of law. Finally, this contribution highlights the importance of civil society in the context of the establishment and current work of the DIMR. Until its creation, the legal tradition of human rights protection in Germany had rested on general jurisdictional protection, and on the Federal Constitutional Court in particular. However, the DIMR is still in the consolidation process and the considerable power of this court remains in itself a challenge. Consequently, the authors contend that the DIMR has yet to find its place within German society and abroad.

Sebastián Donoso and Manuel Núñez Poblete are the authors of the twelfth and final substantive chapter, which concerns one of the newest NHRIs in Latin America. The Chilean *Instituto Nacional de Derechos Humanos* (INDH) is a public agency structured as an autonomous body, even though it has no constitutional status. The chapter explains the origins and legal foundations of Chile's NHRI. It studies the collegiate nature of the INDH, key to its credibility, and its main functions, giving special attention to its power to make recommendations to the National Congress and other domestic authorities, through annual reports, *amicus curiae* briefs or other instruments. Finally, this chapter analyses the work of the INDH according to international standards, and its institutional challenges after almost a decade of existence. The latter include strengthening its stature, ensuring presence across all the regions of what is a large country in geographical terms, and the tendency for national legislation to create specialised agencies that divert personal and budgetary resources.

The present book ends with overarching concluding remarks by the editors.

PART I

NATIONAL HUMAN RIGHTS INSTITUTIONS IN EUROPE AND LATIN AMERICA IN CONTEXT

FOSTERING THE RULE OF LAW

The Paris Principles on NHRIs

Sebastián López Escarcena

1. INTRODUCTION

The Principles relating to the Status of National Institutions were first defined at a workshop, held in Paris in 1991, and were formally adopted by the UN General Assembly (UNGA) two years later.[1] Their relevance cannot be overstated, for they put forward the main criteria that NHRIs have to fulfil, including principles as to their role, establishment, composition, and operation.[2] Loosely conceptualised in doctrine, NHRIs embody state self-regulation and accountability in the area of human rights.[3] Following the Paris Principles, the UN has defined them as 'a body which is established by a Government under the constitution, or by law or decree, the functions of which are specifically designed in terms of the

1 See generally UN General Assembly Res. 48/134 (20 December 1993) A/RES/48/134.

2 See generally Principles relating to the Status of National Institutions. Available at: <https://nhri.ohchr.org/EN/AboutUs/Pages/ParisPrinciples.aspx>.

3 See S. Cardenas, *Chains of Justice: The Global Rise of State Institutions for Human Rights*, University of Pennsylvania Press, Philadelphia 2014, pp. 6–8; R. Goodman and T. Pegram, 'National Human Rights Institutions, State Compliance, and Social Change' in R. Goodman and T. Pegram (eds.), *Human Rights, State Compliance, and Social Change: Assessing National Human Rights Institutions*, Cambridge University Press, Cambridge 2012, p. 1; L. Reif, 'The Shifting Boundaries of NHRI Definition in the International System' in R. Goodman and T. Pegram (eds.), *Human Rights, State Compliance, and Social Change: Assessing National Human Rights Institutions*, Cambridge University Press, Cambridge 2012, pp. 52–53. See also K. Linos and T. Pegram, 'What Works in Human Rights Institutions?' (2017) 111/3 *AJIL* 628, 629; K. Linos and T. Pegram, 'The Language of Compromise in International Agreements' (2016) 70/3 *Int'l Org.* 587, 589; M. Novak, 'National Human Rights Institutions in Europe: Comparative, European and International Perspectives' in J. Wouters and K. Meuwissen (eds.), *National Human Rights Institutions in Europe: Comparative, European and International Perspectives*, Intersentia, Cambridge 2013, pp. 13–14; A. Pohjolainen, *The Evolution of National Human Rights Institutions: The Role of the United Nations*, The Danish Institute for Human Rights, Copenhagen, 2006, pp. 1, 6; S. Cardenas, 'Emerging Global Actors: The United Nations and National Human Rights Institutions' (2003) 9/1 *Global Governance* 23, 23.

promotion and protection of human rights'.[4] NHRIs typically adopt the form of a either a commission or ombudsman, the shape and size of which differs from state to state.[5] Beyond such classic models, hybrid and specialised institutions have also been recognised as NHRIs.[6] Since the 1990s, these permanent and independent agencies have multiplied extensively throughout the world. At present, more than 100 states have one of these administrative bodies active in their territory.[7]

The Paris Principles have not only allowed the UN to delineate NHRIs, but have also become the benchmark used for measuring their structural design. For years, these non-binding principles have been applied as legal rules in the now all-important accreditation processes which govern these institutions. However, two questions remain: what exactly is the nature of an NHRI? And what is its main objective? This chapter seeks to answer these questions. NHRIs are the offspring of the UN's fairly well-documented commitment to the promotion and protection of human rights. For this reason, the work that follows considers the historical background within which the Paris Principles appeared, before analysing their legal status and ultimate purpose according to different theoretical perspectives in law.

---

4 United Nations, *National Human Rights Institutions: A Handbook on the Establishment and Strengthening of National Institutions for the Promotion and Protection of Human Rights*, United Nations Press, 1995, para. 39, see also para. 38. On this definition see Goodman and Pegram (n 3) p. 1; Reif, 'The Shifting Boundaries of NHRI Definition' (n 3) p. 54; Pohjolainen (n 3) p. 66–67; B. Lindsnaes and L. Lindholt, 'National Human Rights Institutions: Standard-Setting and Achievements' in B. Lindsnaes, L. Lindholt and K. Yigen (eds.), *National Human Rights Institutions: Articles and Working Papers*, Danish Centre for Human Rights, Copenhagen 2000, p. 11. See also L. Reif, 'Building Democratic Institutions: The Role of National Human Rights Institutions in Good Governance and Human Rights Protection' (2000) 13 *Harv. Hum. Rts. J.* 1, 5–6.

5 See United Nations, *National Human Rights Institutions* (n 1) paras. 41–44, 46–52, 56–62. See also Linos and Pegram, 'What Works in Human Rights Institutions?' (n 3) p. 634; K. Linos and T. Pegram, 'Architects of their Own Making: National Human Rights Institutions and the United Nations' (2016) 38/4 *Hum.Rts.Q.* 1109, 1109; Linos and Pegram, 'The Language of Compromise in International Agreements' (n 3) p. 597.

6 See Cardenas, *Chains of Justice* (n 3) pp. 8–10, 20–23, 70–72; Reif, 'The Shifting Boundaries of NHRI definition' (n 3) pp. 52–53, 58–61, 64–71; Cardenas, 'Emerging Global Actors' (n 3) p. 25; Reif, 'Building Democratic Institutions' (n 4) pp. 5–13. Cf. Novak (n 3) pp. 15–16, 25–26; Pohjolainen (n 3) pp. 1, 16–20. See also United Nations, *National Human Rights Institutions* (n 1) paras. 53–55.

7 See Linos and Pegram, 'What Works in Human Rights Institutions?' (n 3) p. 629; Linos and Pegram, 'Architects of their Own Making' (n 5) p. 1110; Linos and Pegram, 'The Language of Compromise in International Agreements' (n 3) p. 589; Cardenas, *Chains of Justice* (n 3) pp. 2, 6–7; Novak (n 3) pp. 17–18; Goodman and Pegram (n 3) p. 1; Cardenas, 'Emerging Global Actors' (n 3) p. 23. See also J. Wouters and K. Meuwissen, 'National Human Rights Institutions in Europe: An Introduction' in J. Wouters and K. Meuwissen (eds.), *National Human Rights Institutions in Europe: Comparative, European and International Perspectives*, Intersentia, Cambridge 2013, p. 3; J. Koo and F. Ramirez, 'National Incorporation of Global Human Rights: Worldwide Expansion of National Human Rights Institutions, 1966–2004' (2009) 87/3 *Soc. Forces* 1321, 1326.

2. THE UN FACTOR

The UN's involvement in the creation and development of NHRIs has been extensive.[8] As early as 1946, the Nuclear Commission on Human Rights, a group of nine experts entrusted by the Economic and Social Council (ECOSOC) with the task of preparing terms of reference for the future Commission on Human Rights (CHR), proposed that this UN organ should recommend that its member states

> establish information groups or local human rights committees within their countries who would transmit periodic information to the Commission on Human Rights on the observance of human rights in their countries both in their legal systems and their jurisdictional and administrative practice.[9]

Following this proposal, ECOSOC invited these states to consider the desirability of creating such groups and committees, which were envisioned to collaborate in furthering the work of the CHR.[10] This idea was not welcomed enthusiastically at first.[11] Despite this unfavourable context, France took the lead in 1947, by establishing the first NHRI: the *Commission consultative pour la codification du droit international et la définition des droits et devoirs des États et des droits de l'homme* (the French Commission) or *Commission nationale consultative des droits de l'homme*, as it is called today.[12] A few other NHRIs were created before the boom of the 1990s, mostly in Europe and Latin America.[13] Since then, NHRIs have spread to numerous states in Africa, the Americas, Asia, Oceania, and Europe.[14] Moreover, important regional NHRI networks have been created in these continents.[15] Across this entire period, the UN has been actively

---

8 See e.g. G. de Beco and R. Murray, *A Commentary on the Paris Principles on National Human Rights Institutions*, Cambridge University Press, Cambridge 2014, pp. 7–8; Cardenas, 'Emerging Global Actors' (n 3) pp. 24, 28–30, 35; Reif, 'Building Democratic Institutions' (n 4) pp. 3–5.

9 E/38/Rev.1 (1946) 5–6. See Cardenas, *Chains of Justice* (n 3) p. 27; Pohjolainen (n 3) p. 30.

10 ECOSOC Res. 2/9 of 21 June 1946 para 5. See Cardenas, *Chains of Justice* (n 3) pp. 27–30, 37; de Beco and Murray (n 8) note 3 at p. 4; Novak (n 3) fn 4 at p. 14; Pohjolainen (n 3) pp. 30–31; Cardenas, 'Emerging Global Actors' (n 3) p. 28; Lindsnaes and Lindholt (n 4) p. 5.

11 See Pohjolainen (n 3) pp. 31–32.

12 See Cardenas, *Chains of Justice* (n 3) pp. 27–30, 75–78.

13 See Linos and Pegram, 'Architects of their Own Making' (n 5) pp. 1112, 1116; Cardenas, *Chains of Justice* (n 3) pp. 33–39, 78–105; Reif, 'Building Democratic Institutions' (n 4) p. 7.

14 See Cardenas, *Chains of Justice* (n 3) pp. 39–45, 106–309; Reif, 'Building Democratic Institutions' (n 4) p. 7; Pohjolainen (n 3) p. 74.

15 See Cardenas, *Chains of Justice* (n 3) pp. 45–49; Pohjolainen (n 3) p. 75. These are called: Network of African National Human Rights Institutions; Network of National Human Rights Institutions of the Americas; Asia-Pacific Forum of National Human Rights Institution; and European Network of National Human Rights Institutions.

advocating for the establishment and strengthening of NHRIs in every corner of the world.[16]

During the 1950s, UN bodies focused largely on the creation of an international human rights regime, side-lining the development of NHRIs to the point of virtual standstill.[17] Once the CHR had finished drafting the International Covenants on Civil and Political Rights, and Economic, Social and Cultural Rights (the UN Covenants), NHRIs slowly returned to prominence and began to occupy a relevant place in the UN's agenda.[18] In 1962, the CHR provided the first blueprint for NHRIs, entrusted with human rights monitoring activities and with offering advice and education in this area.[19] A year later, the UNGA invited states 'to intensify their domestic efforts in the field of human rights, with the assistance of their appropriate organizations'.[20] The development of the international human rights regime in the 1960s, particularly after the UNGA adopted the UN Covenants in 1966, allowed NHRIs to become a rather recurrent topic of discussion at this international organisation.[21] By the end of the 1970s, the UN Covenants had entered into force, and as part of the preparations for the thirtieth anniversary of the Universal Declaration of Human Rights, the UNGA asked the UN Secretary General to organise a seminar on NHRIs.[22] Seizing this opportunity, the CHR encouraged its member states to set up national institutions 'within the framework of their national legislation and policy and according to their available means' and invited them to an international seminar, which had the aim of 'suggest[ing] certain possible guidelines for the structure and functioning of national institutions'.[23]

The Seminar on National and Local Institutions for the Promotion and Protection of Human Rights was held in Geneva in 1978.[24] Its official report included the first set of international guidelines applicable to a wide range of state and non-state bodies concerned with human rights. According to these guidelines, the functions of NHRIs are broad, covering the provision of

---

16 See Cardenas, *Chains of Justice* (n 3) pp. 37–52; Cardenas, 'Emerging Global Actors' (n 3) p. 24.

17 See Pohjolainen (n 3) pp. 32–33.

18 See Pohjolainen (n 3) p. 34.

19 See generally Commission on Human Rights Res. 9 (XVIII) of 27 March 1962. See also Pohjolainen (n 3) pp. 34–38.

20 UN General Assembly Res. 1961 (XVIII) of 12 December 1963 para 4. See also Pohjolainen (n 3) p. 38.

21 See generally UN General Assembly Res. 2200A (XXI) of 16 December 1966. See also Pohjolainen (n 3) pp. 39–42. Cf. Cardenas, *Chains of Justice* (n 3) pp. 37–39.

22 See generally UN General Assembly Res. 32/123 of 16 December 1977. See also Lindsnaes and Lindholt (n 4) p. 5.

23 Commission on Human Rights Res. 23 (XXXIV) of 8 March 1978, paras. 1, 3.

24 This seminar introduced NHRI as a term of art. See Cardenas, *Chains of Justice* (n 3) p. 39. Cf. Linos and Pegram, 'The Language of Compromise in International Agreements' (n 3) p. 597.

information and the education of public opinion; the analysis of laws, judicial decisions and administrative acts; and advice to governments on human rights. To duly perform these duties, the guidelines recommended that NHRIs publish periodic reports on human rights issues and receive, investigate, and remedy individual complaints of human rights violations.[25] Both the CHR and the UNGA endorsed the results of the seminar and encouraged member states to take appropriate steps for the establishment of NHRIs, bearing its guidelines in mind.[26] The 1978 seminar provided a basis upon which the notion of an independent, permanent, and pluralistic NHRI was developed over the following years.[27] Throughout the 1980s, its guidelines were the implicitly accepted standards on NHRIs.[28] The turning point for these institutions came in the following decade. In 1990, the CHR requested the UN Secretary General to convene a workshop, which had the main purpose of studying the cooperation between NHRIs and the UN, so as to boost the effectiveness of these institutions.[29] The UNGA promptly welcomed the decision to organise this seminar.[30] With support from the French Commission and government and collaboration from the UN Centre for Human Rights (now the Office of the UN High Commissioner for Human Rights or OHCHR), the workshop took place in Paris in 1991.[31]

The International Workshop on National Institutions for the Promotion and Protection of Human Rights was attended by 50 individuals from 35 countries, mostly members of various NHRIs, UN agencies, regional human rights bodies, and NGOs.[32] Few governmental representatives attended the workshop.[33] The debate over the mandate, legal status, structure, and powers of NHRIs was the most relevant contribution of the three-day seminar.[34] Not many of the

---

25 See generally ST/HR/SER.A/2 of 18–19 September 1978.

26 See generally Commission on Human Rights Res. 24 (XXXV) of 14 March 1979; UN General Assembly Res. 34/49 of 23 November 1979. See also Lindsnaes and Lindholt (n 4) p. 6. Cf. Linos and Pegram, 'The Language of Compromise in International Agreements' (n 3) pp. 597–98.

27 See Pohjolainen (n 3) pp. 43–48.

28 See Cardenas, *Chains of Justice* (n 3) p. 39; Pohjolainen (n 3) pp. 48–55.

29 See Commission on Human Rights Res. 1990/73 of 7 March 1990, para. 3.

30 See UN General Assembly Res. 46/124 of 17 December 1991, para. 13.

31 See Pohjolainen (n 3) pp. 58–59. See also de Beco and Murray (n 8) pp. 3–4.

32 For instance, the European Court of Human Rights, the Inter-American Commission and Court of Human Rights, the International Labour Organization (ILO), the Organisation for Economic Co-operation and Development (OECD), the UN Centre for Human Rights, and the United Nations Educational, Scientific and Cultural Organization (UNESCO). NGOs participated as observers in this workshop.

33 See Linos and Pegram, 'The Language of Compromise in International Agreements' (n 3) p. 598. See also de Beco and Murray (n 8) p. 4; C. Sidoti, 'National Human Rights Institutions and the International Human Rights System' in R. Goodman and T. Pegram (eds.), *Human Rights, State Compliance, and Social Change: Assessing National Human Rights Institutions*, Cambridge University Press, Cambridge 2012, pp. 95–96; Pohjolainen (n 3) p. 59.

34 See Pohjolainen (n 3) p. 59. See also de Beco and Murray (n 8) p. 4.

attendees – of what later became known as the First International Workshop on NHRIs – expected a concrete outcome, at least not in the form of a resulting document. The draft principles adopted in Paris therefore came as a surprise to most participants.[35] However, as Katerina Linos and Tom Pegram explain:

> [W]hile individuals from thirty-five countries attended the plenary session, interviews with key participants indicate that a working group of only four NHRI representatives (from Australia, France, Mexico, and the Philippines) drafted a document behind the scenes. Minutes of the meeting and interviews suggest that the first two days of the meeting were devoted to statements about how existing NHRIs worked. Then, the draft Paris Principles prepared by the working group suddenly appeared on the final day and were unanimously adopted in plenary without debate.[36]

These new guidelines further developed the standards introduced in 1978, but not without some differences. For instance, NHRIs were conceptualised more narrowly in 1991 than in the old guidelines. With their new status as the main domestic body holding a general competence to promote and protect human rights, the independence, mandate, and structure of NHRIs were strengthened in Paris, and their functions were adjusted accordingly. Nonetheless, the complaints-handling duty of NHRIs, boldly introduced in 1978, was downgraded to a mere optional task in 1991.[37] Due to the central role played by experts from Australia, France, Mexico, and the Philippines, the seminar favoured the human rights commission model over other types of NHRIs.[38] According to Linos and Pegram:

> The Paris Principles' genesis shaped their content. The absence of a formal diplomatic process with the requisite support and expertise, combined with extreme time pressure, ensured these negotiators made a number of mistakes. Some are simple translation errors, but others are fundamental. Significant mistakes include the relegation of features typical of Latin-American ombudsmen to weak recommendations and to omissions. In Paris, the experts promoted the advisory and quasi-judicial commission models rather than the ombudsman model because human rights ombudsmen from Latin America were severely underrepresented at the Paris meeting, and other participants did not know enough about human rights ombudsmen to promote their features. [...] Moreover, European 'classical' ombudsmen, with a more limited human

---

35 See Linos and Pegram, 'Architects of their Own Making' (n 5) p. 1113; Linos and Pegram, 'The Language of Compromise in International Agreements' (n 3) p. 598.

36 Linos and Pegram, 'The Language of Compromise in International Agreements' (n 3) p. 599. See ibid p. 590.

37 See Pohjolainen (n 3) pp. 59–60.

38 See ibid p. 59. See also Linos and Pegram, 'Architects of their Own Making' (n 5) pp. 1114, 1117.

> rights mandate than Latin American 'human rights' ombudsmen, made statements at the meeting that led some participants to believe that ombudsmen in general were not well suited to address human rights concerns.[39]

First called Principles relating to the Status of Commissions and their Advisory Role, the guidelines adopted in the 1991 workshop were renamed a year later by the CHR as the Principles relating to the Status of National Institutions. They are commonly known today as the Paris Principles.[40] In 1993, the World Conference on Human Rights was organised in Vienna. The UNGA established a preparatory committee for this conference, to which the CHR was invited to make recommendations.[41] In its response, the CHR welcomed the Paris Principles and asked the committee to consider how to promote NHRIs that would conform to the principles.[42] The Final Declaration and Programme of Action of the World Conference, or Vienna Declaration, was adopted by a consensus of 171 states.[43] In it, they noted 'the important and constructive role of national institutions in particular their advisory capacity to the competent authorities, their role in remedying human rights violations, in the dissemination of human rights information, and education in human rights'.[44] Moreover, the Vienna Declaration recognised the Paris Principles as a benchmark for NHRIs, encouraged states to create and develop institutions that correspond with them, and acknowledged 'the right of each state to choose the framework which is best suited to its particular needs at the national level'.[45] Although the Vienna Declaration did not provide a clear notion or agenda for the future development of NHRIs, it nevertheless reaffirmed their importance within the domestic structure of any state committed to the promotion and protection of human rights, and established a set of standards to follow in this regard.[46]

---

39 Linos and Pegram, 'The Language of Compromise in International Agreements' (n 3) p. 599. See Linos and Pegram, 'Architects of their Own Making' (n 5) p. 1113–14. See also Reif, 'The Shifting Boundaries of NHRI definition' (n 3) p. 54; Sidoti (n 33) p. 96; Pohjolainen (n 3) p. 8.

40 The CHR also asked the UN Secretary-General to use the Paris Principles in the manual on NHRIs that the Centre for Human Rights was then preparing. See generally Commission on Human Rights Res. 1992/54 of 3 March 1992.

41 See generally UN General Assembly Res. 45/155 of 18 December 1990. See also Pohjolainen (n 3) pp. 59–60.

42 See generally Commission on Human Rights Res. 1992/54 of 3 March 1992. See also Pohjolainen (n 3) p. 61.

43 See Cardenas, *Chains of Justice* (n 3) p. 41.

44 See A/CONF. 157/24 (1993) Part 1 para. 36.

45 ibid.

46 See Pohjolainen (n 3) p. 64. See also Linos and Pegram, 'Architects of their Own Making' (n 5) p. 1113.

3. PRINCIPLES FROM PARIS

In 1993, the UNGA endorsed the Paris Principles and encouraged governments to create NHRIs in compliance with them.[47] From this year on, a reference to effective, independent, and pluralistic NHRIs, which are compliant with these guidelines, has been an integral part of resolutions adopted by UN policy-making bodies on the issue.[48] In essence, the Paris Principles enumerate the mandate and working methods of NHRIs, while stressing the relevance of the independent and pluralistic nature of these institutions.[49] As characterised within them, NHRIs require: a broadly defined human rights competence; establishment by legislative means; a pluralist representation of civil society in their composition; independence from the correspondent state; an adequate infrastructure and funding; and optional power to handle individual complaints.[50] For this purpose, the text of the Paris Principles is divided into four sections, titled: 'Competence and responsibilities'; 'Composition and guarantees of independence and pluralism'; 'Methods of operation'; and 'Additional principles concerning the status of commissions with quasi-jurisdictional competence'. As Anna-Elina Pohjolainen points out:

> Notwithstanding the fact that the Paris Principles provide only a general outline for national institutions, they propose the creation of a national structure, which was – and still is – in many ways almost revolutionary. For one thing, the whole concept of national institutions is dating only from the early 1990s, and at the time only few experts in a handful of countries were familiar with the utility and nature of this type of institution. Furthermore, the idea that governments should establish and fund agencies, which would develop transnational connections and possess a certain scope of freedom of action at the international level must have appeared strange in the state-centered world which had only recently learned to accept the participation of non-governmental organisations. Finally, the fact that the institutions outlined in

---

47 See generally UN General Assembly Res. 48/134 of 20 December 1993. See also Linos and Pegram, 'Architects of their Own Making' (n 5) p. 1110; Linos and Pegram, 'The Language of Compromise in International Agreements' (n 3) p. 599; de Beco and Murray (n 8) p. 3. The Paris Principles were included without modifications in an annex to this resolution. See Linos and Pegram, 'Architects of their Own Making' (n 5) p. 1113. See also Cardenas, *Chains of Justice* (n 3) p. 42.

48 Including both the CHR and the UNGA. See de Beco and Murray (n 8) pp. 6–7; Sidoti (n 33) p. 94; Pohjolainen (n 3) pp. 64–65. Regarding the UN and NHRIs after 1993, see Linos and Pegram, 'Architects of their Own Making' (n 5) pp. 1127–28; de Beco and Murray (n 8) pp. 6–8; Cardenas, *Chains of Justice* (n 3) pp. 44–45, 50–52; Pohjolainen (n 3) pp. 65–77. See also Sidoti (n 33) pp. 104–122.

49 See de Beco and Murray (n 8) p. 5. See also Pohjolainen (n 3) p. 6.

50 See Cardenas, *Chains of Justice* (n 3) pp. 39–41; Novak (n 3) p. 15; Pohjolainen (n 3) pp. 6–8; Lindsnaes and Lindholt (n 4) pp. 1, 10–11. See also Linos and Pegram, 'Architects of their Own Making' (n 5) pp. 1118–19.

> the Paris Principles did not fit easily in the traditional three-division of state powers but appeared to have a role in both the legislative, judicial and executive field, must have confused many governments. Despite these peculiar characteristics, national institutions have spread to many new places all over the world since the introduction of the Paris Principles in the early 1990s.[51]

The origin of the Paris Principles explains their focus. Written by the NHRIs that attended the Paris workshop, and not by the UN bodies present there, the 1991 guidelines reflect a desire, on one hand, to regulate NHRIs' mandates, status, and relationship with the state, while, on the other, revealing a desire to acknowledge existing differences regarding their structures, operations, and powers.[52] For this reason, the Paris Principles do not impose a particular model of NHRI. As the UNGA expressly recognised when endorsing them, 'it is the right of each State to choose the framework that is best suited to its particular needs at the national level'.[53] This origin also explains why NHRIs opted for a self-accreditation process, through peer-review.[54] To this effect, a coalition of institutions established an International Coordination Committee for National Institutions for the Promotion and Protection of Human Rights (ICC), in 1993, as a loose and informal association, which was later incorporated as a non-profit entity under Swiss law.[55] Aimed at promoting and strengthening NHRIs in accordance with the Paris Principles, the ICC is now called the Global Alliance for National Human Rights Institutions (GANHRI). It is a close collaborator with the OHCHR;[56] in fact, it is physically located at the UN Office in Geneva (UNOG).[57] One of GANHRI's main functions is the accreditation of new members and the periodic re-accreditation of existing members, in conformity with the Paris Principles.[58] Compliance with the Principles is, thus, determined by NHRIs. Accreditation gives these institutions membership of their own international and regional networks and allows them to participate

---

51 Pohjolainen (n 3) p. 8.

52 See de Beco and Murray (n 8) pp. 3, 4–5. See also Linos and Pegram, 'Architects of their Own Making' (n 5) 1113; Goodman and Pegram (n 3) p. 7; Sidoti (n 33) p. 96.

53 UN General Assembly Res. 48/134 of 20 December 1993, para. 12. See de Beco and Murray (n 8) pp. 5–6; Wouters and Meuwissen (n 7) p. 3. See also Cardenas, *Chains of Justice* (n 3) p. 42. Other UN documents on NHRIs generally emphasise this as well. See Cardenas, 'Emerging Global Actors' (n 3) p. 36.

54 See Novak (n 3) p. 16. See also Sidoti (n 33) p. 98.

55 See Sidoti (n 33) note 13 at p. 97. See also de Beco and Murray (n 8) p. 9; Cardenas, *Chains of Justice* (n 3) p. 42; Reif, 'The Shifting Boundaries of NHRI Definition' (n 3) p. 56.

56 See GANHRI's Statute, art 6. Available at: <https://www.ohchr.org/sites/default/files/documents/countries/nhri/ganhri/EN_GANHRI_Statute_adopted_15032023.pdf>. The ICC was renamed GANHRI in 2016. See ibid preamble.

57 See GANHRI's Statute, art 4.

58 See GANHRI's Statute, art 7.

in UN bodies.[59] Originally, accreditation was largely an informal undertaking of the ICC.[60] Today, however, the Sub-Committee on Accreditation of GANHRI (SCA) is in charge of the process, which is governed by the global alliance's statute and the sub-committee's rules of procedure.

NHRIs are now defined as

> an independent national institution established by a member or Observer State of the United Nations with a constitutional or legislative mandate to promote and protect human rights, and which is, or intends to be, accredited by GANHRI in line with the Paris Principles.[61]

These institutions apply for initial accreditation or for re-accreditation every five years.[62] NHRIs that fully comply with the Paris Principles are accredited with 'A-status' and become voting members of GANHRI, while those that are partially compliant with these principles are accredited with 'B-status' and become non-voting members.[63] At present, 89 NHRIs have A status and 31 have B status.[64] The OHCHR is a permanent observer of the SCA and serves as its secretariat.[65]

The SCA consists of one representative from each of the regional NHRI networks: these are Africa, the Americas, Asia and the Pacific, and Europe.[66] To explain the meaning and practical application of the Paris Principles, the SCA issues General Observations.[67] These amount to an evolving jurisprudence: i.e., to an authoritative interpretation not only of GANHRI's membership criteria, but also of NHRIs' functions and design requirements.[68] Because of the General Observations, the Paris Principles may well be described as a living instrument.[69] As such, they have become a template for institutional design that has been largely created and developed by NHRIs themselves, and not the UN member

---

59 See Rules of Procedure for GANHRI SCA, art 3.1. Available at: <https://www.ohchr.org/sites/default/files/Documents/Countries/NHRI/GANHRI/ENG_GANHRI_SCA_RulesOfProcedure_adopted_04.03.2019_vf.pdf>. See also GANHRI's Statute, art 1, 31.1.

60 See Cardenas, *Chains of Justice* (n 3) p. 50. See also Sidoti (n 33) pp. 97–98.

61 GANHRI's Statute, art 1.

62 See ibid section 5, art 15.

63 See ibid, section 6, art 24.1 and 24.2.

64 Only 10 NHRIs have C status, which stands for not compliant with the Paris Principles. See the Chart of the Status of National Institutions accredited by GANHRI as at April 2023. Available at: <https://www.ohchr.org/sites/default/files/Documents/Countries/NHRI/StatusAccreditationChartNHRIs.pdf>.

65 See SCA's Rules of Procedure, section 5.1.

66 See the definition of regional network in GANHRI's Statute, art 1.

67 See SCA's Rules of Procedure, section 2.2. See also GANHRI's Statute, art 1. See generally General Observations of the SCA. Available at: <https://nhri.ohchr.org/EN/AboutUs/GANHRIAccreditation/General%20Observations%201/EN_GeneralObservations_Revisions_adopted_21.02.2018_vf.pdf>.

68 See Cardenas, *Chains of Justice* (n 3) p. 50; Reif, 'The Shifting Boundaries of NHRI Definition' (n 3) p. 57; Sidoti (n 33) p. 98. See also de Beco and Murray (n 8) pp. 9–10.

69 See de Beco and Murray (n 8) pp. 23–24.

states upon which the UNGA called in its 1993 resolution.[70] GANHRI is now the institutional gatekeeper for NHRIs. It reviews them according to the Paris Principles,[71] and, as a result, the design of NHRIs is considerably homogenous, with few regional variations.[72]

Sonia Cardenas defines accreditation as 'the process by which membership in an organization is granted on the basis of having met specific standards or criteria'.[73] These are none other than the Paris Principles, which are generally considered as the touchstone of all NHRIs: that is to say, the international minimum standards or criteria that ultimately define them.[74] As Chris Sidoti indicates, '[t]he Paris Principles do not ensure the effectiveness of a national human rights institution, only that it conforms in law, structure, mandate, and scope of operations with what is the minimum acceptable internationally'.[75] Despite being a set of authoritative standards for NHRIs, the Paris Principles are not legally binding. Originally the outcome of a seminar attended mostly by NHRIs, these principles have, from a formal standpoint, merely received the subsequent endorsement of the CHR and the UNGA.[76] Why, then, have they become so influential? The fact that the Paris Principles were drafted, explained, and somewhat expanded by NHRIs, making them relevant and credible among these institutions, offers a possible answer to the question.[77] Linos and Pegram assert that 'the effectiveness of international agreements does not depend

70 See Linos and Pegram, 'Architects of their Own Making' (n 5) p. 1112. See also Linos and Pegram, 'What Works in Human Rights Institutions?' (n 3) p. 629; Linos and Pegram, 'The Language of Compromise in International Agreements' (n 3) p. 589; Sidoti (n 33) pp. 96–97.

71 See Goodman and Pegram (n 3) p. 8; Sidoti (n 33) pp. 97–98. See also Linos and Pegram, 'Architects of their Own Making' (n 5) pp. 1111, 1123; P. Rosenblum, 'Tainted Origins and Uncertain Outcomes: Evaluating NHRIs' in R. Goodman and T. Pegram (eds.), *Human Rights, State Compliance, and Social Change: Assessing National Human Rights Institutions*, Cambridge University Press, Cambridge 2012, p. 320. Cf. J. Mertus, 'Evaluating NHRIs: Considering Structure, Mandate, and Impact' in R. Goodman and T. Pegram (eds.), *Human Rights, State Compliance, and Social Change: Assessing National Human Rights Institutions*, Cambridge University Press 2012, pp. 78, 79. See de Beco and Murray (n 8) pp. 29–30; Pohjolainen (n 3) p. 14.

72 See Goodman and Pegram (n 3) pp. 10–11. See also Reif, 'The Shifting Boundaries of NHRI definition' (n 3) pp. 53, 72.

73 See Cardenas, *Chains of Justice* (n 3) p. 49.

74 See Cardenas, *Chains of Justice* (n 3) p. 39; Goodman and Pegram (n 3) p. 5; Sidoti (n 33) pp. 95–97; Pohjolainen (n 3) p. 6.

75 Sidoti (n 33) p. 97.

76 In the 2000s, though, the normative status of the Paris Principles was somewhat bolstered by their incorporation into two treaties: the 2002 Optional Protocol to the Convention against Torture and other Cruel, Inhuman or Degrading Treatment or Punishment (OPCAT) and the 2006 Convention on the Rights of Persons with Disabilities (CRPD), in force since 2006 and 2008, respectively. See Linos and Pegram, 'Architects of their Own Making' (n 5) pp. 1128–33; de Beco and Murray (n 8) pp. 3, 8–9, 23, 27–29; Cardenas, *Chains of Justice* (n 3) pp. 51–52; Novak (n 3) pp. 21–23; Sidoti (n 33) p. 95.

77 See Linos and Pegram, 'Architects of their Own Making' (n 5) p. 1113; de Beco and Murray (n 8) pp. 4–5, 12, 18, 20; Sidoti (n 33) pp. 96, 98. See also Goodman and Pegram (n 3) pp. 7–8.

primarily on whether states have legal obligations to comply with particular agreements', since

> two additional dimensions of international agreements are critical components for effectiveness: first, the precision of international agreements, whether the content of the commitment is unambiguously specified; second, and most consequentially, delegation. Delegation refers to whether a third party, independent of the participating states, is entrusted with monitoring and compliance functions.[78]

This is exactly the case with the SCA, which administers the accreditation of NHRIs[79] – a process that grants these institutions access to the UN human rights system.[80]

4. NHRIs AND THE RULE OF LAW

There is little doubt about the Paris Principles' success. Their legal status, however, is less than clear. From a strictly normative perspective, the Paris Principles can be described as a soft law instrument, due to their undeniable influence on the field of NHRs. That is to say, as an instrument that is normative in substance, but not legally binding.[81] However, it is not only the Paris Principles that have

78 Linos and Pegram, 'Architects of their Own Making' (n 5) p. 1111. Concerning the first of these dimensions, Linos and Pegram have an interesting thesis:

> 'When an agreement specifies some tasks firmly, some flexibly, and does not mention others, governments may respond strategically, redirecting efforts toward firmly specified tasks, and away from flexibly specified or omitted tasks. When tasks are specified using precise and unconditional formulations, there is less room for dispute about the adequacy of implementation efforts. If a government ignores a firmly specified task, foreign and domestic monitors can easily spot the discrepancy and withhold agreement benefits. Governments face the strongest incentives to focus on firmly specified tasks when they face tight constraints in an issue area, but want to signal that they are performing at the international standard. Flexible language can therefore induce some states to move in the opposite direction from what an agreement's drafters intended.' (Linos and Pegram, 'The Language of Compromise in International Agreements' (n 3) p. 588). See generally ibid.

79 See Linos and Pegram, 'Architects of their Own Making' (n 5) pp. 1111–12, 1122.

80 See generally Commission on Human Rights Res. 2005/74 of 20 April 2005. See also Linos and Pegram, 'Architects of their Own Making' (n 5) pp. 1127–28. According to these authors:

> 'A status accreditation by the SCA grants a country's NHRI formal speaking rights within the UN Human Rights Council (HRC). In particular, NHRIs have multiple opportunities to participate in the Universal Periodic Review (UPR) procedure. During their review, states are frequently called upon to establish NHRIs and ensure existing structures are strengthened in accordance with the Paris Principles. It also confers a seal of legitimacy that is gaining recognition in other UN forums.'

81 See A. Boyle and C. Chinkin, *The Making of International Law*, Oxford University Press, Oxford 2007, pp. 211–14. See also P. Birnie, A. Boyle, and C. Redgwell, *International Law and the Environment*, Oxford University Press, Oxford 2009, pp. 34–37.

been included in this category. Linda Reif, for instance, describes the General Observations of the SCA as 'a form of soft law to interpret soft law'.[82] Linos and Pegram add that, due to the access to the UN human rights system granted, at present, to accredited NHRIs:

> [t]he SCA has drawn parallels between its function and that of a treaty body. Senior officials within the OHCHR echo this point and suggest that the significant changes we are witnessing in accreditation, especially a new phenomenon of downgrades, are a product of reframing the role of the SCA and a desire to give the Paris Principles the gravitas, if not the status, of an international treaty.[83]

From a non-normativist point of view, the Paris Principles, as well as the General Observations of the SCA, are good examples of global administrative law (GAL).[84] Arguably the most influential doctrine recently proposed as an alternative to international law, the GAL Project essentially affirms that there is a law that is applicable to processes of an administrative character, which involves legal and political structures that exceed those of a purely intra-state nature.[85] Chiefly promoted from North America and Europe, GAL scholarship can also be found, at present, in Africa, Asia, Latin America, and Oceania.[86] GAL was first defined in a landmark journal article of 2005 as

> comprising the mechanisms, principles, practices, and supporting social understandings that promote or otherwise affect the accountability of global administrative bodies, in particular by ensuring they meet adequate standards of transparency, participation, reasoned decision, and legality, and by providing effective review of the rules and decisions they make.[87]

GAL includes subjects and sources that are not among those generally accepted within international law. Thus, it not only recognises public international law

---

82 Reif, 'The Shifting Boundaries of NHRI definition' (n 3) p. 57. On the Paris Principles as soft law see e.g., Linos and Pegram, 'Architects of their Own Making' (n 5) p. 1110; de Beco and Murray (n 8) p. 6.

83 Linos and Pegram, 'Architects of their Own Making' (n 5) p. 1126.

84 See e.g., Linos and Pegram, 'What Works in Human Rights Institutions?' (n 3) p. 629. Regarding GAL, see generally C. Bories (ed.), *Un droit administratif global? / A Global Administrative Law?*, Editions Pedone, Paris 2012; S. Cassese (ed.), *Research Handbook on Global Administrative Law*, Edward Elgar, Cheltenham 2016.

85 See S. López Escarcena, 'Investment Disputes *oltre lo stato*. On Global Administrative Law, and Fair and Equitable Treatment' (2018) 59/8 *B.C.L.Rev.* 2685, 2685–86.

86 See S. López Escarcena, 'Contextualizing Global Administrative Law' (2018) 21/2 *Gonzaga J.I.L.* 57, 58–59.

87 B. Kingsbury, N. Krisch, and R. Stewart, 'The Emergence of Global Administrative Law' (2005) 68/3–4 *L.C.P.* 15, 17. Lorenzo Casini has called this article the GAL manifesto. See L. Casini, 'Global Administrative Law Scholarship' in S. Cassese (ed.), *Research Handbook on Global Administrative Law*, Edward Elgar, Cheltenham 2016, pp. 551, 554–55.

as a source but also: a renewed version of *jus gentium*, described as a type of *lex mercatoria*; a so-called international public law that governs the exercise of this kind of authority; public or administrative national law, from a comparative perspective; and the norms generated by autonomous systems.[88] As to subjects, GAL affirms that the administrative character of an activity can stem from its nature, effects, or objective and even the type of entity that carries it out.[89] Therefore, global administration can come from formal intergovernmental organisations, which are international institutions *par excellence*; from hybrid public-private organisations or purely private entities that exercise public authority; from trans-governmental and transnational networks, which are less structured forms of governance between states, international organisations, and/or other actors; and more complex forms of governance, such as global hybrid, multi-level, or informal regulatory regimes.[90]

GAL insists on the notion of 'publicness': i.e., the public character that a given regulatory regime must have for it to be considered part of GAL, with the understanding being that 'public' originates from the whole society and refers to matters of general interest. The principles that comprise this condition of publicness are, among others: legality, rationality, proportionality, rule of law, and respect for human rights. In this context, legality means that the actors within a system must act in accordance with its rules; rationality is related to reasoned decision-making; rule of law has a procedural nature; and respect for human rights refers to the substantial content that is not covered by the notion of rule of law.[91]

An offshoot of a workshop comprising NHRIs, the Paris Principles have been recognised by the declaration of the Vienna conference on human rights and by a resolution of the CHR, endorsed by a resolution of the UNGA, and have, thereafter, been interpreted by the SCA. Their inclusion in the sources and subjects of GAL is, consequently, indisputable. Nevertheless, the Paris Principles and the General Observations of the SCA might well be categorised as an exercise of public authority or as informal international law-making, depending on the non-normativist approach chosen.

The Project on the Exercise of International Public Authority (IPA) had two phases: one aimed at international institutions in general and the other at judicial institutions in particular.[92] IPA focused on public law and considered itself to be a synthesis of the previous attempts made to fill the normative gaps

---

88 See López Escarcena, 'Contextualizing Global Administrative Law' (n 86) pp. 65–66.

89 See ibid p. 66.

90 See ibid.

91 See ibid.

92 See ibid p. 70. See generally A. von Bogdandy, R. Wolfrum, J. von Bernstorff, P. Dann, and M. Goldmann (eds.), *The Exercise of Public Authority by International Institutions: Advancing International Institutional Law*, Springer, New York 2010; A. von Bogdandy and I. Venzke (eds.), *International Judicial Lawmaking*, Springer, New York 2012.

left by global governance, within which it included GAL.[93] In this project, the exercise of international public authority was defined as 'any kind of governance activity by international institutions, be it administrative or intergovernmental [that] determines individuals, private associations, enterprises, states, or other public institutions'.[94]

The Informal International Lawmaking Project (IN-LAW) started from very similar premises to those of GAL and IPA, and much like them, it analysed law-making beyond the traditional sources and subjects of international law.[95] IN-LAW notes that there is a law that dispenses with certain distinctive formalities that are usually associated with traditional international law-making. This can be observed from the points of view of the output, the process, and the actors involved in cross-border cooperation. Hence, international law-making can be informal, in the sense that:

(i) it does not lead to traditional sources of international law, such as treaties, but to guidelines, standards, declarations, etc. of a normative character, i.e. directing or affecting the conduct of different actors (output);
(ii) it takes place in loosely coordinated networks or forums, rather than in conventional international organisations, which does not prevent the existence of detailed procedural rules, a permanent staff, or physical headquarters, but excludes simple negotiations (process); and
(iii) it does not involve traditional diplomatic actors, such as heads of state, ministers of foreign affairs or ambassadors; instead, it involves other ministries, domestic regulators, agencies, sub-federal entities, other state powers, such as the legislative or judicial branches, and even private actors operating alongside public authorities (actors).[96]

Being academic endeavours, GAL, IPA, and IN-LAW are descriptive and prescriptive in nature, combining bottom-up and top-down solutions to the

---

93 See López Escarcena, 'Contextualizing Global Administrative Law' (n 86) p. 70.

94 A. von Bogdandy, P. Dann, and M. Goldmann, 'Developing the Publicness of Public International Law: Towards a Legal Framework for Global Governance Activities' (2008) 9/11 *German L.J.* 1375, 1376; A. von Bogdandy *et al*, (n 92) p. 5. The approach proposed by IPA sought to offer a more strictly conceptual explanation of the internationalisation of administrative law than the one provided by GAL. According to IPA, international and internal institutions cannot be confused, as is often the case where normative solutions, based on simple domestic analogies, are proposed. See López Escarcena, 'Contextualizing Global Administrative Law' (n 86) p. 70.

95 See ibid, 73. See generally J. Pauwelyn, R. Wessel, and J. Wouters (eds.), *Informal International Lawmaking*, Oxford University Press, Oxford 2012; J. Pauwelyn, R. Wessel, and J. Wouters, 'When Structures Become Shackles: Stagnation and Dynamics in International Lawmaking' (2014) 25/3 *EJIL* 733.

96 See López Escarcena, 'Contextualizing Global Administrative Law' (n 86) pp. 73–74.

perceived problems of international law.[97] The Paris Principles and the General Observations of the SCA have an evident descriptive and prescriptive character and offer a mixture of bottom-up and top-down approaches, even when analysed from a strictly normativist standpoint. Although they originate from and have been developed by NHRIs themselves, these instruments of soft law are yet another example of international law striving to bring the rule of law into municipal law.[98] Otherwise known as *état de droit* or *rechtstaat*, the rule of law is basically aimed at limiting state power.[99] According to Tom Bingham, its minimum content entails 'that all persons and authorities within the state, whether public or private, should be bound by and entitled to the benefit of laws publicly made, taking effect (generally) in the future and publicly administered in the courts'.[100] The rule of law also requires states to comply with their international obligations, human rights commitments included.[101] As domestic counterparts of international organisations like the CHR (now the Human Rights Council, HRC), NHRIs are now an integral part of a law-governed state.[102] Originally established to bridge the chasm that existed in large parts of the world, between the requirements of international human rights law and the actual conditions existing at that moment in several municipal jurisdictions, NHRIs are designed to aid states in complying with their international obligations.[103] Then and now, as Cardenas posits, 'the creation of NHRI is a welcome development, insofar

---

97 See ibid pp. 67, 70, 72–73, 74, 80.

98 Concerning the rule of law, see generally L. Heuschling, *Etat de droit – Rechtsstaat – Rule of Law*, Dalloz, Paris 2002. On international law and the rule of law, see generally C. Villegas, *La preeminencia del derecho en derecho internacional*, Aranzadi, Cizur Menor 2013. In fact, importing the rule of law into the domestic sphere is not only the main purpose of the Paris Principles and the general observations of the SCA but is also the ultimate goal of international human rights law and international investment law, from their own perspectives. See S. López Escarcena, *Indirect Expropriation in International Law*, Edward Elgar, Cheltenham 2014, pp. 203–11.

99 See ibid (López Escarcena) pp. 210–11.

100 T. Bingham, *The Rule of Law*, Penguin, London 2011, pp. 8, 37.

101 See ibid (Bingham) 110–29. In Bingham's view, the minimum content of the rule of law implies fulfilling certain conditions, which can be briefly summarised as follows: accessible law (i.e., intelligible, clear, and predictable), equally applicable to all (except when objective differences justify differentiation); establishing public powers reasonably exercised by state organs (for the purposes for which they were conferred, without exceeding their limits); affording adequate protection to human rights (both national and international); providing means for resolving disputes (without undue delay or costs), through fair adjudicative procedures provided by the state. See pp. 37–109. See also J. Waldron, 'Are Sovereigns Entitled to the Benefit of the International Rule of Law?' (2011) 22/2 *EJIL* 315, 316–17, 325–27; J. Waldron, *The Rule of Law and the Measure of Property*, Cambridge University Press, Cambridge 2012, pp. 6–7, 15–16, 52–58.

102 See Cardenas, *Chains of Justice* (n 3) pp. 27–30.

103 See Linos and Pegram, 'Architects of their Own Making' (n 5) p. 1109; Linos and Pegram, 'What Works in Human Rights Institutions?' (n 3) p. 629; Cardenas, *Chains of Justice* (n 3) pp. 27–30, 49; Reif, 'Building Democratic Institutions' (n 4) p. 3.

as it serves to embed international norms in local structures'.[104] The General Observations of the SCA expressly recognise this important aspect of NHRIs, when they declare that these institutions

> are established by States for the specific purpose of advancing and defending human rights at the national level, and are acknowledged to be one of the most important means by which States bridge the implementation gap between their international human rights obligations and actual enjoyment of human rights on the ground.[105]

The General Observations add that

> [t]he establishment and strengthening of NHRIs pursuant to the Paris Principles falls within the set of international human rights commitments made by States. It is therefore the responsibility of the State to ensure that it has in place a Paris Principle-compliant NHRI.[106]

5. CONCLUSION

Although the Paris Principles are nothing more than the unexpected result of a seminar held in 1991 (later recognised by a resolution of the CHR in 1992 and a conference declaration in 1993 and endorsed by a resolution of the UNGA that same year), they have become the virtually unquestioned yardstick according to which the structural design of NHRIs is measured. This is certainly surprising for an instrument that can only be categorised as 'soft law', when considered from a normativist standpoint: a stance that still articulates and represents the primary theoretical approach to international law. At present, NHRIs play a central role in the implementation of international human rights obligations by states. The whole accreditation process, currently carried out by GANHRI, is pivoted upon compliance with the Paris Principles and the General Observations of the SCA. Because of this, they can be seen as a fitting illustration of how international law can help in fostering the rule of law within domestic jurisdictions. The Paris Principles and the General Observations of the SCA operate, in practice, as proper legal rules, despite their shortcomings and their evident lack of legitimacy, due to their origin and nature. Considering the relevance of the topic, should states themselves not agree, somehow, on the rules governing NHRIs? Negotiating universal treaties, however, is not without its risks. De-codification is one of them. To avoid calling into question well accepted international rules

104 See Cardenas, 'Emerging Global Actors' (n 3) pp. 24–25.
105 Introduction to the General Observations of the SCA of 21 February 2018, para. 2.
106 ibid.

and standards, the sets of articles recently adopted by the International Law Commission (ILC) in important areas, such as international state responsibility, diplomatic protection, and unilateral acts of states, operate as informal legal instruments that offer guidance to judges, state officials, advocates, academics, etc.[107] Interpreted and applied by them, the rules advanced in these articles have subsequently been developed via implementation, much like the Paris Principles, as construed in the General Observations of the SCA. Perhaps this is precisely the role that these authoritative standards are destined to continue playing in the life of NHRIs.

[107] In the case of international state responsibility, the ILC expressly debated the issue. See J. Crawford, *The International Law Commission's Articles on State Responsibility*, Cambridge University Press, Cambridge 2005, pp. 58–60.

EUROPEAN NATIONAL HUMAN RIGHTS INSTITUTIONS AS MULTI-LAYERED ACTORS

Characteristics, Challenges and Opportunities

Katrien MEUWISSEN*

1. INTRODUCTION

In line with the UN Paris Principles, NHRIs are established by constitution or law as permanent, accessible, and specialist human rights access points, for both rights-holders and duty-bearers at national level. They provide information to citizens, cooperate with civil society, deliver advice to government, hold state authorities to account for human rights violations, and inform the international community of the national human rights situation on the ground. Emerging in the 1990s, NHRIs remain a rather novel phenomenon in the human rights landscape, in Europe and beyond. The increasing establishment and role of European NHRIs remains understudied, and, until recently, the unique features of NHRIs were not very familiar to human rights practitioners in the region.[1]

While a number of chapters in this book include case studies addressing the functioning of particular NHRIs, the present chapter provides a bird's eye perspective on the European NHRI landscape. It will describe typical characteristics of NHRIs in the European region, highlighting some important challenges and opportunities for NHRIs across the continent. Following the approach of this edited volume, the chapter will distinctly address characteristics of European NHRIs, across the multiple layers of the human rights system. In the first section, the focus is placed on the characteristics, opportunities, and challenges that are typical for European NHRIs at the national level. The second section will delve further into features common for European NHRIs at the supranational level. Attention will be paid to network cooperation

* The information and opinions expressed are solely attributable to the author and not to ENNHRI.

1 For a regional focus on Europe, see J. WOUTERS and K. MEUWISSEN (eds.), *National Human Rights Institutions in Europe: Comparative, European and International Perspectives*, Intersentia, Cambridge 2013.

amongst European NHRIs as well as the supranational engagement of NHRIs with European human rights organisations and bodies, including those of the Council of Europe (CoE), the Organization for Security and Co-operation in Europe (OSCE), and the European Union (EU).

2. NHRIs ACROSS EUROPEAN COUNTRIES

2.1. CHARACTERISTICS

The European human rights landscape is the densest in the world. This is not only reflected in the variety of regional human rights organisations but also the many domestic mechanisms which play a role in promoting and/or protecting human rights across European countries. There is no single account that gives an overview of all existing public bodies with a human rights-related mandate across European countries. One illustration that reveals the potential density is Belgium. Being a country of merely 11 million inhabitants, the Belgian government has listed seven institutions as 'national institutions for the protection of human rights', including the wide variety of national bodies with a competence relating to specific rights, such as racial discrimination, children's rights, and women's rights.[2] However, none of these institutions equate to the type of body that would be fully compliant with the international standards, as envisaged and set in place by the Paris Principles.[3] What characterises NHRIs that are in compliance with these Principles is their possession of a legal mandate and the competence to independently address the promotion and protection of the full span of human rights in a country; therefore, national bodies with a thematic mandate do not amount to Paris Principles-compliant NHRIs.

The concept of NHRIs, as proclaimed in the Paris Principles, was conceived at the UN level, yet such institutions did not spread throughout the European region until the turn of the twenty-first century.[4] The most prevalent and

---

2 See National Report of Belgium for the Universal Periodic Review (UPR) of the UN Human Rights Council, A/HRC/WG.6/11/BEL/1 of 16 February 2011, paras. 8–14.

3 In its UPR report of 2015, the Belgian government explained its efforts to establish, and the challenges involved in establishing, a NHRI in compliance with the Paris Principles. See A/HRC/WG.6/24/BEL/1, paras. 8–9.
In 2019, a law was adopted by the Belgian government establishing an institution for the promotion and protection of human rights at the federal level. While conceived of as a NHRI, this new institution also has important limitations: in terms of its ability to address all human rights, as required by the Paris Principles because of its residual competence compared to the various pre-existing bodies in Belgium.

4 The list of attendance at the 2002 meeting of European NHRIs refers to five institutions as fully Paris Principles-compliant: the Danish, French, Greek, Spanish, and Swedish NHRIs. See the Summary of the discussion at the Fourth European Meeting of National Institutions, Belfast and Dublin, 14–16 November 2002, available at: <https://nhri.ohchr.org/EN/Regional/Europe/Pages/4th-European-Meeting-of-National-Human-Rights-Institutions.aspx>.

oldest European national body with a mandate related to human rights is probably the ombuds-institution, which dates back to 1809, when the first such body was instituted in Sweden. The ombuds-institution started to diffuse beyond Scandinavia from the 1960s onwards,[5] and it traditionally focused on processing the maladministration complaints of individuals against the state. The establishment of ombuds-institutions, since the 1970s, has been promoted by European organisations.[6] In Central and Eastern European states, the ombudsman is almost omni-present: under external instigation, the Scandinavian model spread across the region after the collapse of the Soviet Union.[7] National equality bodies are another type of domestic, human rights-mandated entity, and they are apparent across the European region. Since the 1990s, the European Commission against Racism and Intolerance (ECRI) has called upon CoE member states to establish equality bodies concerned with racial discrimination.[8] Approximately 10 years later, the establishment of national equality bodies with racism and gender discrimination mandates became a legal obligation for all EU member states.[9] In a context which sees a range of national human rights bodies in place but only some with the competence to address human rights in their entirety, the EU Agency for Fundamental Rights (FRA) has characterised the human rights landscape across European countries as 'fragmented'.[10]

Since the dawn of the new millennium, an ever-increasing number of European governments have started to establish NHRIs in compliance with the Paris Principles. While there is no European regulation requiring the creation of NHRIs, European governments – much like their peers across the globe – receive continuous calls to do so in the context of international and regional monitoring procedures.[11] The establishment of NHRIs fits the well-recognised

---

5 L. Reif, *The Ombudsman, Good Governance and the International Human Rights System*, Martinus Nijhoff, Leiden 2004, pp. 1–2.

6 For instance, as early as 1971, the CoE Parliamentary Conference invited national parliaments to 'consider favourably' the establishment of an ombudsman 'as known in Scandinavian countries'. CoE Parliamentary Conference on Human Rights, 18–20 October 1971, Strasbourg, p. 112, para. 29.

7 R. Carver, 'National Human Rights Institutions in Central and Eastern Europe: The Ombudsman as Agent of International Law' in R. Goodman and T. Pegram (eds.), *Human Rights, State Compliance and Social Change: Assessing National Human Rights Institutions*, Cambridge University Press, Cambridge 2012, pp. 181–209.

8 ECRI General Policy Recommendation No. 2, CRI (97)36 of 13 June 1997.

9 See I. Rorive, 'A Comparative and European Examination of National Institutions in the Field of Racism and Discrimination' in K. Boyle (ed.), *New Institutions for Human Rights Protection*, Oxford University Press, Oxford 2009, pp. 137–73.

10 EU Fundamental Rights Agency, *National Human Rights Institutions in the EU Member States: Strengthening the Fundamental Rights Architecture in the EU* (EU 2010) p. 3.

11 In the context of the UPR, for example, one of the recommendations most frequently received by governments is the establishment of a Paris Principles-compliant NHRI. This information can be retrieved from the database provided by UPR INFO, which provides an overview of all recommendations formulated to states under review during the UPR as well as states' responses to the recommendations. The database is available at: <https://www.upr-info.org/database/>.

need to better bridge the gap between the international human rights standards developed since the end of World War II and national realities in this area. Promoting themselves as human rights frontrunners, European governments do, indeed, appear sensitive to international calls to establish NHRIs. Within the time-span of 20 years, all European governments have accepted international recommendations to establish a NHRI in compliance with the Paris Principles,[12] and about half of the European governments have done so effectively. Currently, among the 46 CoE member states, 28 have a NHRI in compliance with the Paris Principles.[13] Within the EU, 19 of its 27 member states have a Paris Principles-compliant NHRI: Austria, Bulgaria, Croatia, Cyprus, Denmark, Estonia, Finland, France, Germany, Greece, Ireland, Latvia, Lithuania, Luxembourg, the Netherlands, Poland, Portugal, Slovenia, and Spain.[14]

When European governments decide to establish an NHRI in compliance with the Paris Principles, they often opt to transform a pre-existing national body with a human rights-related mandate into an NHRI. In Central and Eastern European countries, governments have generally decided to establish a Paris Principles-compliant NHRI by expanding the mandate of a pre-existing maladministration ombudsman, allocating this national body an explicit role to promote and protect all human rights.[15] In other instances, governments have decided to transform national equality bodies into NHRIs with a mandate covering all human rights.[16] While one specific NHRI typology is generally prevalent in regions beyond Europe,[17] the European NHRI landscape is more

---

12 In 2021, the Committee of Ministers of the Council of Europe has adopted a Recommendation encouraging all Council of Europe Member States to establish and strengthen effective, pluralist and independent NHRIs. Council of Europe Committee of Ministers Recommendation 2021/1 of 31 March 2021.

13 For an overview of the countries with a NHRI in compliance with the Paris Principles, see the GANHRI Chart on Accreditation of National Institutions, which is updated bi-annually. Available at: <https://nhri.ohchr.org/EN/AboutUs/GANHRIAccreditation/Pages/default.aspx>.

14 Based on the accreditation status of NHRIs in December 2022.

15 See Carver (n 7).

16 An example of this is the Dutch NHRI. See Y. Donders and M. Olde-Monnikhof, 'The Newly Established Netherlands Institute for Human Rights: Integrating Human Rights and Equal Treatment' in J. Wouters and K. Meuwissen (eds.), *National Human Rights Institutions in Europe: Comparative, European and International Perspectives*, Intersentia, Cambridge 2013, pp. 83–104.

17 In Africa, as well as the Asia-Pacific region, most NHRIs follow the Commonwealth model of multi-member national human rights commissions. Some countries in Francophone Africa and the Arab world, such as Senegal, Morocco, and Egypt, prefer the French model of advisory commissions. Most countries in Latin America follow the ombuds-institution model, which is similar to the Spanish *Defensor del Pueblo*. See M. Nowak, 'National Human Rights Institutions in Europe: Comparative, European and International Perspectives' in J. Wouters and K. Meuwissen (eds.), *National Human Rights Institutions in Europe: Comparative, European and International Perspectives*, Intersentia, Cambridge 2013, p. 25.

diverse and encompasses the full span of possible NHRI typologies discerned by the UN Office of the High Commissioner for Human Rights (OHCHR).[18] These NHRI typologies include: ombuds-type NHRIs, characterised by their focus on individual complaints-handling; commission-type NHRIs, with a typical focus on inquiries or advisory functions; and institute-type NHRIs, which are generally characterised by their particular emphasis on research-related work.[19]

2.2. OPPORTUNITIES AND CHALLENGES

In the dense European human rights scene, NHRIs have particular added value. Unlike mere complaints-handing mechanisms in Europe, such as judges or maladministration bodies, NHRIs can combine a reactive and proactive approach to the implementation of human rights.[20] NHRIs can react when violations of human rights occur, through their reporting or complaints-handling functions, and they can also work towards the prevention of violations through their awareness-raising and educational functions. Moreover, unlike national bodies with a limited human rights mandate, the mandates of NHRIs encompass rights in their entirety, which allows them to identify and address the most urgent human rights priorities in a country, independently of the governments' political agenda or popular concerns.

Accordingly, NHRIs will often speak up for the rights of the most vulnerable groups, such as persons in detention or migrants and refugees, especially when such groups fall outside of the ambit of specialised national bodies active within a country. By virtue of their broad mandate, NHRIs can address gaps in national human rights protection systems and perform the role of human rights watchdogs for under-represented, vulnerable groups. Moreover, in a fragmented European human rights scene, where various national bodies are often competent for specific (aspects of) human rights, broadly mandated NHRIs can function as one-stop shops, referring rights-holders to the most pertinent human rights access point within a country. The broad mandate also enables NHRIs to address complex human rights problems in their entirety, thereby responding to the indivisible and interdependent nature of universal human rights standards.

NHRIs are regularly referred to as bridge-builders. In view of their broad mandates, these institutions need to build upon and cooperate with the full

---

18 See generally OHCHR, *National Human Rights Institutions: History, Principles, Roles and Responsibilities* (UN 2010).

19 ibid.

20 See generally K. Meuwissen, 'Fundamental Rights Protection in Europe Beyond Individual Complaints: The Potential of National Human Rights Institutions' in L. Violini and A. Baraggia (eds.), *The Fragmented Landscape of Fundamental Rights Protection in Europe*, Edward Elgar, Cheltenham 2018.

spectrum of human rights stakeholders within a country. The Paris Principles require NHRIs to collaborate with other national human rights bodies, advise and make recommendations to state authorities, closely cooperate with civil society, and engage with international human rights mechanisms. From the perspective of human rights NGOs, for example, NHRIs can present an avenue by which to place human rights concerns in a country on the agenda of public authorities. As public bodies, NHRIs enjoy formal access to other state authorities and are required by the Paris Principles to provide, at least annually, a report to their national parliament on the human rights situation in their country.[21] NHRIs in compliance with the Paris Principles are also recognised as reliable sources of information at the UN and European level, and they receive preferential access to international human rights procedures, where they can present information on the human rights situation of a country independent from the information provided by their government.[22]

While their legal mandate to promote and protect human rights in their entirety presents important opportunities for NHRIs, some particular challenges also confront these human rights actors. Unlike judges, parliaments, or governments, NHRIs do not as a rule have binding decision-making powers. About half of the European NHRIs have an individual complaints-handling mandate, but this is primarily geared towards amicable settlement and the formulation of broader policy recommendations, rather than issuing binding decisions with enforceable remedies.[23] By monitoring human rights situations, making public findings, and formulating recommendations, NHRIs can contribute to the respect and promotion of human rights in their country. Yet, even when NHRIs fulfil their functions effectively, i.e., in compliance with the Paris Principles, and provide reliable information and pertinent recommendations, national decision-makers can ultimately decide not to take the NHRIs' findings and recommendations into account.

The typical focus of NHRIs on groups that are in a minority position with regard to the population of a country can also create particular challenges, especially in the current European climate of increasing populism, where threats to democracy and the rule of law are on the rise. A populist climate typically goes together with a negative discourse concerning minority groups in the population

---

21 See Principles relating to the Status of National Institutions, para. 3.a; General Observations of the SCA of 21 February 2018, para. 1.11.

22 See K. Meuwissen, 'NHRI Participation to United Nations Human Rights Procedures: International Promotion Versus Institutional Consolidation?' in J. Wouters and K. Meuwissen (eds.), *National Human Rights Institutions in Europe: Comparative, European and International Perspectives*, Intersentia, Cambridge 2013 and section 3 below.

23 K. Meuwissen, 'National Human Rights Institutions as Bridge-Builders Between the State and the Multi-Layered Human Rights System: An International Legal Analysis from a European Perspective', PhD, KU Leuven 2017, pp. 317–18.

and the restriction of space for actors speaking up for the rights of individuals pertaining to minority groups.[24] The current political climate in Europe provides a more difficult context for human rights work and presents direct challenges for NHRIs, in terms of carrying out their work in an independent and effective manner.[25] When the rule of law and separation of powers are not respected in a country, NHRIs' independent and efficient functioning, which rests upon respect for their mandate entrenched in national law, becomes inherently more difficult. A recent example was the Polish context, where, following a ruling by the government-captured Constitutional Tribunal, the country's independent NHRI had for months no leader in place.[26]

Austerity crises, the impact of COVID-19, the war against Ukraine and the political climate in Europe have, in various instances, led to a reduction in resources allocated to human rights, including to NHRIs.[27] Despite the Paris Principles' requirement for governments to adequately fund NHRIs, to enable the institutions to effectively carry out their mandates, many are facing budget restraints.[28] In a context of tight resources and increasing human rights challenges, balancing the prioritisation of roles and strategising by decision-makers, with the safeguarding of an NHRI's position as a reliable and independent access point for rights-seekers and the general public, poses an important challenge for all European NHRIs.

3. THE EUROPEAN NETWORK OF NHRIs

3.1. CHARACTERISTICS

The international embedment of NHRIs is not only reflected in their strong links with international human rights organisations but also in their cooperation with NHRI peer organisations, who carry out the same mandate in different national

---

24 See e.g., EU Fundamental Rights Agency, *Challenges Facing Civil Society Organisations Working on Human Rights in the EU* (EU 2018).

25 See generally European Network of National Human Rights Institutions, *The Rule of Law in the European Union: Reports from National Human Rights Institutions* (ENNHRI 2019).

26 See further: ENNHRI, Equinet, GANHRI, IOI, OSCE ODIHR and UN OHCHR Joint statement in support of the Office of the Polish Commissioner for Human Rights <http://ennhri.org/wp-content/uploads/2021/05/Joint-Statement-in-Support-of-the-Polish-NHRI_ENG.pdf>; Human Rights Watch, 'Poland's Top Watchdog Removed at Government's Behest', available at: https://www.hrw.org/news/2021/04/15/polands-top-watchdog-removed-governments-behest>.

27 D. Hogan *et al*, *Austerity and Human Rights in Europe: Perspectives and Viewpoints from Conferences in Brussels and Berlin 12 and 13 June 2013*, German Institute for Human Rights and ENNHRI, Berlin 2014.

28 See Principles relating to the Status of National Institutions, para. 2; General Observations of the SCA of 21 February 2018, para. 1.10.

contexts. NHRI networks were being established as early as the elaboration of the Paris Principles: in the early 1990s. Currently, NHRIs from across the world come together under the umbrella of the Global Alliance of National Human Rights Institutions (GANHRI). GANHRI brings together over 120 NHRIs and is composed of four regional NHRI networks: the Network of African NHRIs (NANHRI); the Asia-Pacific Forum of NHRIs (APF); the Network of NHRIs from the Americas (RINDHCA); and the European Network of NHRIs (ENNHRI). While state authorities determine the context in which NHRIs must carry out their work at a national level, network cooperation offers NHRIs the opportunity to learn and exchange experiences across borders, provide each other with mutual support and solidarity, contribute to international and regional human rights mechanisms, and speak with one voice on human rights problems of a transnational nature.

Through its efforts to strengthen, support, and connect European NHRIs, ENNHRI aims to enhance the promotion and protection of human rights in the region. ENNHRI has expanded gradually; it currently incorporates over 40 NHRIs from across Europe, spanning from Norway in the north, to Portugal in the south, and Azerbaijan in the east. Compared to other regional NHRI networks, ENNHRI's membership is one of the largest,[29] and it is the most diverse as far as NHRI typologies are concerned. At the same time, ENNHRI's governance structure is relatively new; up until the 2000s, network cooperation amongst European NHRIs retained an intermittent character and did not result in a clear membership profile or common action plans. The network's functioning depended on the leadership of some particularly active NHRIs – mainly from Western Europe – and cooperation was limited to certain issue areas and actions: for example, third-party interventions brought before the European Court of Human Rights (ECtHR) by European NHRIs. It was only in 2013 that European NHRIs launched ENNHRI's current governance structure, including the setting-up of a permanent secretariat in Brussels. A Statute for ENNHRI was adopted in 2013, which lays down inclusive governance processes. Twice a year, all ENNHRI members gather at its General Assembly, where key decisions are taken on the network's governance and representation. The ENNHRI Board, which is composed of five to six of the network's members from across the region, is responsible for its continuous management. One member of the Board is appointed as Chair and represents the network at the highest political levels.

ENNHRI's strategic plan for the period 2022–2025 prioritises the existence of strong NHRIs across Europe, in compliance with the Paris Principles. The network therefore engenders peer support across its membership and delivers technical advice to governments, parliaments, and other stakeholders on the establishment of NHRIs. While ENNHRI's membership is steadily growing,

[29] NANHRI and ENNHRI both have over 40 members.

only about half of the countries across the Council of Europe currently have an NHRI which fully complies with the Paris Principles. There is, thus, significant potential to further establish these institutions across the region, in compliance with the principles.

A unique feature of the NHRIs' peer networks is the accreditation process, which results in an internationally recognised status indicating that the institution at issue has complied with the Paris Principles. A-status NHRIs are deemed to be in compliance with the Paris Principles, while B-status NHRIs are considered to be only partially compliant. The accreditation process is carried out by the GANHRI Sub-Committee on Accreditation (SCA), which is composed of four A-status NHRIs, one from each region, under the auspices of the OHCHR. A-status NHRIs must undergo a review every five years, while B-status NHRIs and NHRIs without accreditation status may apply at any time to gain recognition of (better) fulfilment of the Paris Principles. ENNHRI currently counts 31 members as being in compliance with the Paris Principles, nine members with B-status, and seven members without accreditation status. Only A-status members can obtain governance positions and have a right to vote, but ENNHRI functions in an inclusive manner and B-status and non-accredited members are involved in network activities, which can also further contribute to their functioning in compliance with the Paris Principles. Because it is carried out under the auspices of the OHCHR, the NHRI network's accreditation process also results in the compliant NHRIs gaining official participation status at the UN.[30] As will be further highlighted in section 3, the accreditation status is also increasingly used as a reference point for engagement by European human rights actors with European NHRIs.

With its focus on enhancing the promotion and protection of human rights in Europe, ENNHRI forges bridges between NHRIs' national work and human rights activity at the regional level. ENNHRI thus: provides a forum for the regional exchange of NHRIs' experiences and data collection; develops reports with recommendations and public statements on critical human rights issues; and engages with the wide spectrum of European human rights stakeholders. Through its engagement with regional actors and mechanisms, ENNHRI aims to engender change and follow-up at a national level, while also contributing to the regional human rights infrastructure and efforts to safeguard it. ENNHRI has established various thematic working groups, which bring together expert staff from across European NHRIs to share their experiences and further build their capacity to tackle thematic human rights concerns. ENNHRI has a legal working group, which has a long-standing focus on engagement with the CoE, including the ECtHR; it also constitutes a focal point for the other legal aspects of NHRIs'

---

30 See Meuwissen, 'NHRI Participation to United Nations Human Rights Procedures: International Promotion Versus Institutional Consolidation?' (n 22).

work, such as the implementation of the EU Charter for Fundamental Rights and the role performed by NHRIs in upholding the rule of law and democracy in European countries. Other thematic areas for which ENNHRI working groups have been established are: economic, social and cultural rights; the rights of migrants and refugees; the rights of persons with disabilities; business and human rights; the rights of older persons; climate change; and artificial intelligence.[31]

In less than 10 years, the ENNHRI Secretariat in Brussels has expanded from one person to a team of about 10. The permanent Secretariat supports the establishment of NHRIs and their accreditation, acts as focal point for support when European NHRIs face threats, facilitates regular communication and peer exchange amongst ENNHRI members, organises capacity-building activities, and functions as an access point for engagement with stakeholders at the regional level. Through the Secretariat, ENNHRI also applies for and manages grants, which allow the network to organise its activities on a regular basis and in an inclusive manner. Some ENNHRI projects target particular human rights themes of regional relevance: between 2015 and 2018, ENNHRI implemented a project addressing the rights of elderly persons in long-term care facilities,[32] while in 2018–2020 a project was conducted which focused on the role of NHRIs in conflict and post-conflict situations.[33]

3.2. OPPORTUNITIES AND CHALLENGES

NHRIs remain a relatively new actor in the European human rights landscape and their added value and complementary role compared to other actors, such as civil society organisations and national bodies with a thematic human rights mandate, is not always known, nor has it yet been consistently recognised. ENNHRI accordingly provides an important forum where the specific added value of NHRIs can be clarified and promoted – through the publication of guidelines on the role of these institutions in particular contexts or in addressing specific human rights issues. ENNHRI has, for example, elaborated a guide on the role of NHRIs concerning the implementation of judgments of the ECtHR; published a study on NHRIs' monitoring of migrant rights at borders; and prepared a guide for NHRIs on ensuring a human-rights-based approach to poverty measurement in Europe.[34]

31 An overview of human rights themes addressed through the network is available at: <http://ennhri.org/our-work/topics/>.

32 All project-outcome documents are available at: <http://www.ennhri.org/-rights4elders->.

33 The webpages dedicated to this project are available at: <https://ennhri.org/nhris-post-conflict/>.

34 All documents are available at the ENNHRI website.

NHRI networks function as catalysts for peer exchange and collective learning amongst these institutions, but they also provide a collective voice for NHRIs on the international scene. As will be seen further in the following section, awareness-raising by ENNHRI has resulted in the allocation of a specific status and role for NHRIs across an increasing number of European human rights procedures. The dense regional European human rights landscape offers many avenues for NHRIs to forge partnerships and receive support. While membership fees are crucial to facilitate ENNHRI's functioning, the network also attracts key resources from European counterparts that allow it to carry out its activities. Without support from European counterparts, the limited resources allocated to NHRIs at a national level would not suffice to allow European NHRIs to maintain an operational and effectively functioning network. ENNHRI also plays an important role in the NHRI accreditation process;[35] in addition to supporting members going through the global accreditation process, ENNHRI also invests in enhancing the transparency, fairness and rigour of the process and its applicable rules. The international standards for NHRIs are conceived as living instruments that can be further specified and amended over time, according to progressing insights and changing circumstances. As a result, the peer review process becomes increasingly stringent over time, and human rights actors across the world increasingly rely on the global NHRI quality-label when identifying reliable human rights counterparts at a national level. Moreover, ENNHRI also engages with regional actors (EU and Council of Europe) to develop regional standards on NHRIs addressed to state authorities, which complement the UN Paris Principles in Europe.[36]

Another important added value of ENNHRI is the fostering of solidarity across NHRIs and between NHRIs and other European human rights actors. This function gains particular relevance in a context of shrinking space for civil society and threats to democracy and the rule of law in Europe. The 2018 ENNHRI annual conference was dedicated to the role of NHRIs as human rights defenders as well as the ways in which support can be provided to human rights defenders who are facing threats in this increasingly challenging context for democracy and the rule of law.[37] ENNHRI has adopted guidelines on the

---

35 See M. Brodie, 'Progressing Norm Socialisation: Why Membership Matters. The Impact of the Accreditation Process of the International Coordinating Committee of National Institutions for the Promotion and Protection of Human Rights' (2011) 80/2 *Nord. J. Int'l. L.* 143.

36 Notably, ENNHRI has engaged with the Council of Europe in the development of the Committee of Ministers Recommendation 2021/1 on NHRIs. See ENNHRI statement, available at: <http://ennhri.org/news-and-blog/european-nhris-prepare-input-for-review-of-council-of-europe-recommendation-on-nhris>.

37 More information on the ENNHRI annual conference of 2018 is available at ENNHRI's website.

network's delivery of support to its members where they are facing threats.[38] These support measures can take different forms, such as undertaking in-country visits to meet relevant stakeholders at a national level or issuing public statements that call on state authorities to respect the independence and functioning of NHRIs in compliance with the Paris Principles. ENNHRI aims to further bolster international support for NHRIs that comply with these principles. It does so, increasingly, through partnerships with regional and international human rights organisations, including the OHCHR Regional Office in Europe, the OSCE Office for Democratic Institutions and Human Rights of the Organization for Security and Co-operation in Europe (ODIHR), the CoE, and the EU. In 2016 and 2021, for example, joint statements were adopted by ENNHRI, ODIHR, the CoE, and the OHCHR Regional Office in support of the Polish NHRI, and a joint country visit was undertaken in 2019.[39]

The broad and diverse ENNHRI membership is a source of richness and inspiration, but it also creates some challenges at the network level. Governance policies are being established which emphasise the inclusive nature of network activities; however, at the same time, resources are not sufficiently available to the extent that they would allow ENNHRI to work on all issues of interest to its members. ENNHRI is also unable to provide the kind of services that would facilitate a truly inclusive environment for NHRI-staff active from Lisbon to Baku, such as translation into languages other than English. Ten years into ENNHRI's existence, processes have been put into place to engage its membership and facilitate internal and external network communication, the exchange of information, and advocacy. After an initial phase of setting up the network, ENNHRI is moving to the next stage of its professional development; in this phase, more focus will be placed on ensuring NHRIs' resilience, representing an influential regional human rights voice and improving impactful support for NHRIs seeking to realise human rights across the European region.

4. NHRI ENGAGEMENT WITH EUROPEAN HUMAN RIGHTS MECHANISMS

4.1. CHARACTERISTICS

In line with the Paris Principles, European NHRIs cooperate with the wide diversity of European human rights mechanisms, and they do so on a bilateral

---

38 The Guidelines on ENNHRI Support to NHRIs under Threat were adopted in March 2016 and are available at: <http://www.ennhri.org/IMG/pdf/guidelines.support.nhris.threat.march16.pdf>.

39 Available at: <http://ennhri.all2all.org/IMG/pdf/joint_statement_concerning_polish_commissioner_for_human_rights_final.pdf>; <http://ennhri.org/wp-content/uploads/2021/05/Joint-Statement-in-Support-of-the-Polish-NHRI_ENG.pdf>.

and collective (network) level. What follows is a short overview of the main mechanisms in place and the engagement of European NHRIs and ENNHRI with these regional mechanisms.

The oldest and most well-known European human rights framework is that of the CoE, which counts 46 member states and encompasses various actors and procedures specifically dedicated to human rights. Engagement between the CoE and NHRIs is long-standing; in fact, it was the CoE which supported the initial meetings of European NHRIs during the 1990s, as the network was emerging. Human rights standard-setting at the CoE is developed within the context of its Steering Committee on Human Rights (CDDH), which prepares human rights standards and statements for adoption by the Committee of Ministers of CoE member states. By 2001, the European network of NHRIs had already obtained observer status in the CDDH, together with a handful of civil society organisations.[40] ENNHRI attends and contributes to CDDH plenary meetings as well as meetings of thematic subcommittees which address ENNHRI's priority themes. Throughout 2017–2020, for example, ENNHRI contributed to the meetings of the CDDH drafting group on civil society and national human rights institutions (CDDH INST), helping to develop strong Committee of Ministers recommendations on civil society space, ombuds-institutions, and national human rights institutions.[41] Currently, ENNHRI engages in the CDDH groups developing European standards on key emerging issues such as the right to a healthy environment,[42] human rights in times of crisis, and artificial intelligence.[43]

The CoE's core human rights instrument is the European Convention on Human Rights (ECHR). All CoE member states are legally bound by the ECHR and must accept the competence of the European Court of Human Rights (ECtHR), which sits in Strasbourg, to render binding judgments concerning the rights listed in the treaty. NHRIs can contribute to the implementation of the ECHR before, during, and after the Strasbourg proceedings.[44] Before cases

[40] For a list of the observers, see the terms of reference of the CDDH and its subordinate bodies for the biennium 2020–2021, as adopted by the Committee of Ministers.

[41] An overview of the work and outcomes of CDDH INST initiatives is available at: <https://www.coe.int/en/web/human-rights-intergovernmental-cooperation/human-rights-development-cddh/civil-society-and-human-rights-institutions>.

[42] See ENHRI's statement addressed to the CDDH -ENV: 'ENNHRI calls on the Council of Europe to adopt a binding instrument on the right to a healthy environment' available at: <https://ennhri.org/news-and-blog/cddh-env-contribution-right-to-healthy-environment>.

[43] See ENHRI's statement addressed to the CoE CAI: 'Ensuring a human rights based-approach to artificial intelligence: NHRIs contribute to Council of Europe draft convention' <https://ennhri.org/news-and-blog/ensuring-a-human-rights-based-approach-to-artificial-intelligence-nhris-contribute-to-council-of-europe-draft-convention>.

[44] On the examination of NHRI contributions to the ECtHR, see A. Buyse, 'The Court's Ears and Arms: National Human Rights Institutions and the European Court of Human Rights' in J. Wouters and K. Meuwissen (eds.), *National Human Rights Institutions in*

are brought to the ECtHR, NHRIs can play an important role in disseminating information to the public and state authorities concerning the Court's case-law and procedures. This can, for example, prevent domestic legislation and measures from contravening the ECtHR's case-law or could prevent individuals from lodging manifestly ill-founded complaints at the Court. In line with Article 36.2 of the ECHR, NHRIs can intervene during the ECtHR's proceedings as *amicus curiae*. European NHRIs have done so in both an individual and collective capacity, while ENNHRI's legal working group envisages the identification of strategic cases, which might be suitable candidates for *amici curiae* briefs to be submitted by the network.[45] The domestic follow-up of ECtHR judgments also lies naturally within the general monitoring and reporting mandates of NHRIs. Accordingly, ENNHRI has published a Guidance for NHRIs to Support Implementation of Judgments from the ECtHR.[46] Notably, NHRIs are granted an explicit right to provide information to the Committee of Ministers on the domestic implementation of ECtHR cases: within the context of the procedure concerning the supervision of the execution of ECtHR judgments.[47] European NHRIs increasingly provide communications to the Committee of Ministers, while ENNHRI organises training for NHRI staff on the execution of ECtHR judgments.[48]

The CoE human rights framework also includes the European Social Charter (ESC) and its monitoring and complaints procedures, which operate under the auspices of the independent experts of the European Committee on Social Rights. Unlike the ECHR, the ratification of the ESC is optional, and the decisions of the European Committee on Social Rights are not binding. In line with the Paris

---

Europe: Comparative, European and International Perspectives, Intersentia, Cambridge 2013, pp. 173–86; G. de Beco, 'La contribution des institutions nationales des droits de l'homme au renforcement de l'efficacité de la Court européenne des droits de l'homme' (2009) 77 *Revue Trimestrielle des Droits de l'Homme* 165.

45 For further elaboration on how cases are identified for interventions by NHRIs, see B. Adamson, 'NHRI and their European Counterparts: Scope for Strengthened Cooperation and Performance towards European Human Rights Institutions' in J. Wouters and K. Meuwissen (eds.), *National Human Rights Institutions in Europe: Comparative, European and International Perspectives*, Intersentia, Cambridge 2013, p. 146; ENNHRI's website also gives information on third party interventions submitted, such as the 2019 cases of *Strøbye v. Denmark* and *Rosenlind v. Denmark*. See: <http://ennhri.org/news-and-blog/ennhri-submits-third-party-intervention-to-european-court-of-human-rights-on-right-to-vote-for-persons-with-disabilities/>.

46 The Guidance is available at: <http://ennhri.org/IMG/pdf/ennhri_guidelines-v2_a4_web.pdf>.

47 Rules of the Committee of Ministers for the Supervision of the Execution of Judgments and of the Terms of Friendly Settlements, adopted on 10 May 2006, Rule 9.

48 Annual reports of the CoE Committee of Ministers on the 'Supervision of the Execution of Judgements and Decisions of the European Court of Human Rights.' These indicate the number of NHRI contributions to the process. They are available at: <https://www.coe.int/en/web/execution/annual-reports>.

Principles, NHRIs encourage their governments to ratify the ESC and adopt the Additional Protocol, which provides for a System of Collective Complaints. In the context of the reporting procedure, NHRIs submit reports to the European Committee on Social Rights; these offer the NHRI's independent assessment of the implementation of the ESC in their country and may counter the reports submitted by governments. NHRIs cannot launch a collective complaints procedure on their own initiative, but they can support NGOs in doing so.[49] Moreover, NHRIs use the recommendations and reports of the European Committee of Social Rights in their work at the national and international level to promote the progressive realisation of economic and social rights.[50] The CoE heads a Platform on Social and Economic Rights, which is co-organised with ENNHRI, the European Network of Equality Bodies (Equinet), and the EU Agency for Fundamental Rights (FRA). The platform partners meet bi-annually to share good practices for the implementation of the Social Charter and other relevant regional instruments and identify how regional and domestic actors can jointly contribute to the further realisation of social rights across Europe.

An overview of the main points of engagement between NHRIs and the CoE must include a reference to the CoE's Commissioner for Human Rights, who represents a high-level independent voice and wields significant political weight in the European human rights landscape. The Commissioner's mandate encompasses in-country visits; cooperation with the domestic human rights structures in Europe, including NHRIs; and encouragement of the establishment of these structures throughout the region.[51] In the context of in-country visits, the Commissioner consistently allocates time to meet with NHRIs, with a view to garnering their assessment of the human rights situation in the given country. The Commissioner also speaks up in support of the effective and independent functioning of European NHRIs and provides support to NHRIs when they face threats in their domestic context.[52] The Commissioner regularly engages at the collective level, with ENNHRI, on human rights topics of common concern, as illustrated by the co-organisation of a roundtable on the right to refugee family reunification in 2017.

The OSCE has a broader territorial scope than the CoE: it counts 57 participating states from across Europe, Central-Asia, and North America.

---

49 This, for example, has been the case in Greece, where the Greek General Confederation of Labour (GSEE) submitted complaint No. 111/2014 at a time when the Greek National Commission for Human Rights was undertaking advocacy efforts on the issue.

50 For a list with national illustrations, see the ENNHRI statement on the Turin process of 2016, which is available at: <http://ennhri.org/IMG/pdf/ennhri_statement_on_turin_process_10_10_16_final.pdf>.

51 See CoE, Committee of Ministers Res. 99(50), art 3(c)–(d) of 7 May 1999.

52 In 2017, for example, the Commissioner issued a statement on political rhetoric in Georgia, which the Commissioner viewed as being harmful to the independence and effectiveness of the Georgian NHRI.

The OSCE emerged during the Cold War, and its 'human dimension' represents one of its three core objectives: with the others encompassing 'politico-military' and 'economic-environmental' dimensions. The OSCE is not a fully-fledged international organisation, and states do not conclude binding treaties under the OSCE's auspices. OSCE 'human dimension commitments' are listed in political declarations and are the subject of regular meetings between the OSCE's participating states. A central actor in the area of the human dimension is the Office for Democratic Institutions and Human Rights (ODIHR): the OSCE expert body accorded advisory and capacity-building functions that aims at fostering the implementation of the human dimension commitments. In practice, cooperation between NHRIs and the OSCE runs mainly through ODIHR, which carries out joint capacity-building initiatives, together with ENNHRI, for NHRI staff across the OSCE region. ENNHRI and ODIHR also co-organise an annual NHRI Academy, which involves a week-long training programme, tailored to the specific needs of NHRI staff, and addresses relevant working methods and human rights themes of particular interest.[53] ODIHR also promotes the establishment and functioning of NHRIs in line with the Paris Principles; it does so through the adoption of legal opinions on NHRI regulatory frameworks and the organisation of activities that promote awareness and implementation of the Paris Principles.[54] NHRIs are also committed supporters of the national implementation of OSCE human dimension commitments; they offer support through both outreach activities at a national level and participation in meetings at the OSCE level, such as its annual Human Dimension Implementation Meeting.

Established after the Second World War, as a project to secure peace through economic integration, the European Union (EU or Union) now has 27 member states. The Union has increasingly incorporated human rights across its internal and external legal frameworks and policies.[55] In the external relations context, various EU policies include human rights as a strategic goal, including in the areas of EU enlargement and development cooperation. It has also adopted a cross-cutting EU Action Plan on Human Rights and Democracy, which sets out a holistic approach to the integration of strategic human rights commitments across the EU's external policy areas. On the internal plane, fundamental rights protection has found its way into the EU legal order, through judgments of the Court of Justice of the EU (CJEU) and legislation concerned with anti-discrimination and data protection. More comprehensive approaches to

53 More information on the NHRI Academy is available at: <http://www.ennhri.org/NHRI-Academy-overview>.

54 In 2016, for example, ODIHR organised an expert meeting on strengthening the independence of NHRIs in the OSCE region. The documentation and outcomes of the meeting are available at: <https://www.osce.org/odihr/289946>.

55 For an extensive analysis of the EU and human rights matters within its internal and external policies, see the FRAME project reports, available at: <http://www.fp7-frame.eu/reports/>.

fundamental rights protection have emerged more recently on the EU's internal plane. The EU Charter for Fundamental Rights has been accepted as primary EU law since 2008, and it is applicable to EU institutions and member states in its implementation. Moreover, the FRA has been set up with the competence to collect data and provide recommendations and advice on the implementation of fundamental rights in the EU. The amalgam of EU actors and policies provides important avenues for both political and financial support for European NHRIs. For their part, NHRIs provide various EU actors with expert information on human rights, and link up EU activities, policies and regulations with local realities. The most relevant EU counterpart for NHRIs will differ, depending on the territorial scope and the theme addressed. With members from the EU and beyond, and its links to the global network of NHRIs, ENNHRI presents a relevant partner for EU actors dedicated to internal or external policies.

Internally, the FRA has been dubbed 'the EU's NHRI'. Its regulatory framework includes an obligation to cooperate with NHRIs across the EU,[56] and cooperation between FRA and NHRIs takes place on a very regular basis. Such cooperation covers a broad diversity of themes, including the implementation of the Charter of Fundamental Rights.[57] NHRIs use the CJEU's case-law in their work at the national level. However, direct engagement with the CJEU is limited because of the complex regulatory framework and the lack of a procedure which might enable NHRIs to bring information directly before the Court, unless NHRIs were previously involved at the domestic level in the case considered by the CJEU. This can be contrasted to the *amicus curiae* procedure available before the ECtHR which is more open to third parties and explicitly refers to NHRIs. ENNHRI maintains regular contacts and cooperates with the European Commission and its various Directorate-Generals (DGs). ENNHRI liaises, on a regular basis, with the relevant Commissioners and DG for Justice and Consumers on a range of issues, including the implementation of the EU Charter and the protection and promotion of the rule of law. Moreover, ENNHRI engages with the European Parliament, including in the context of its resolutions and reports on human rights, democracy and the rule of law.[58]

---

56 For further analysis, see J. Wouters, K. Meuwissen, and A.S. Barros, 'The European Union and National Human Rights Institutions' in J. Wouters and K. Meuwissen (eds.), *National Human Rights Institutions in Europe: Comparative, European and International Perspectives*, Intersentia, Cambridge 2013.

57 Training on the topic was, for example, co-organised by FRA and ENNHRI in 2018, 2020, and 2021. FRA is also following up the implementation of the Charter of Fundamental Rights in EU member states, in cooperation with NHRIs, through the organisation of capacity-building activities at the national level.

58 NHRIs have been recognised in the European Parliament's 2020 resolution on the Establishment of an EU Mechanism on Democracy, the Rule of Law and Fundamental Rights, where the Parliament calls for the establishment of more comprehensive EU monitoring of all EU values, including country-specific recommendations and ensured follow-up by the EU institutions based on an Inter-Institutional Agreement. The adopted proposal calls for NHRIs'

In an EU context in which fundamental rights and the rule of law are facing growing challenges, newly adopted EU policies in these areas tend to focus more on national implementation of rights and values, while recognising and emphasising the need for independent and robust NHRIs in each EU Member State. NHRIs of this nature are seen as being vital when it comes to addressing rights and rule of law challenges at the national level and providing EU institutions with reliable 'on the ground' information.[59] Since 2019, ENNHRI has started annual joint reporting of its members on the situation of the rule of law and submits its findings and recommendations to relevant regional counterparts such as the European Commission.[60] Notably, the European Commission refers to NHRIs in compliance with the Paris Principles as part of healthy checks and balances in EU Member States.[61] In contrast, threats to NHRIs are considered by the European Commission as threats to the rule of law.[62]

ENNHRI also engages with the DG for Employment, Social Affairs and Inclusion in the context of the European Pillar of Social Rights: for example, the bodies mutually exchange information on the rights of persons with disabilities. Externally, regular cooperation takes place between ENNHRI and the DG for International Partnerships (INTPA) and with the DG for Neighbourhood and Enlargement Negotiations (NEAR). Support for NHRIs that are in compliance with the Paris Principles was taken up as a top priority in the EU's 2017–2019 Action Plan on Human Rights and Democracy: this position has been

involvement in the different stages of the EU's mechanism and stresses that an independent NHRI in compliance with the UN Paris Principles can also serve as an indicator of respect for democracy, rule of law and fundamental rights in EU member states. European Parliament resolution of 7 October 2020 on the establishment of an EU Mechanism on Democracy, the Rule of Law and Fundamental Rights (2020/2072(INI)), 7 October 2020.

59 The initial (2020) report of the European Commission on the rule of law, for example, states that NHRIs 'play an important role as rule of law safeguard and can provide an independent check on the system in a rule of law crisis'. It also identifies the work of NHRIs as an indicator of the rule of law and stresses that 'checks and balances rely on … effective independent authorities such as ombudsperson institutions or national human rights institutions'. See <https://ec.europa.eu/info/publications/2020-rule-law-report-communication-and-country-chapters_en>. The 2021 EU Strategy on the Implementation of the Charter of Fundamental Rights describes strong and effective NHRIs as 'critical links between government and civil society insofar as they address the "protection gap" between the rights of individuals and responsibilities of the state'. The Strategy accordingly sets out the EC's support for the establishment of an NHRI in each EU Member State and their capacity-building to further contribute to the implementation of the Charter. See <http://ennhri.org/news-and-blog/european-commission-presents-strategy-on-implementing-charter-of-fundamental-rights-highlighting-role-of-nhris/>.

60 See ENNHRI's webpage: <https://ennhri.org/rule-of-law-report-2022>.

61 European Commission, 2022 rule of law report, available at <https://ec.europa.eu/info/policies/justice-and-fundamental-rights/upholding-rule-law/rule-law/rule-law-mechanism/2022-rule-law-report_en>.

62 ibid.

reiterated in the 2020–2024 Action Plan.[63] In addition, the EU has funded a global capacity-building project for NHRIs and NHRI networks, through the European Instrument for Democracy and Human Rights (EIDHR) and the Neighbourhood, Development and International Cooperation Instrument (NDICI).[64] Increasing attention paid to NHRIs is also apparent at the Council of the EU: The 2021 Council Conclusions on strengthening the application of the Charter highlight the added value and further potential of NHRIs,[65] while ENNHRI has been invited by the Council's Working Party on Human Rights (COHOM) and its Working Party on Fundamental Rights (FREMP) to inform state representatives about NHRIs and the situation of human rights within and outside the EU.[66]

4.2. OPPORTUNITIES AND CHALLENGES

This bird's-eye overview indicates the enormous potential for the creation of synergies between European NHRIs and their wide range of regional human rights counterparts. The uniquely broad mandate of NHRIs, covering human rights in their entirety and including both functions of promotion and protection, entails that these institutions can provide useful information to virtually any actor that is dedicated to improving the enjoyment of human rights across the region. The international accreditation status of NHRIs provides a unique reference point for regional actors who are seeking human rights information from reliable national institutions. Likewise, the varied European human rights frameworks and actors also represent a huge pool of expertise relating to the various functions and human rights themes addressed by European NHRIs. These stakeholders also offer vital sources of political and financial support for NHRIs across the region. In the context of a shrinking space for human rights, democracy, and the rule of law throughout Europe, it becomes increasingly important for human rights defenders to support each other. European actors

63 See <https://ec.europa.eu/info/law/better-regulation/have-your-say/initiatives/12122-Human-rights-and-democracy-in-the-EU-2020-24-action-plan_en>.

64 More information on the project is available at the NHRI-EU website, managed by the Danish Institute for Human Rights, available at: <https://www.humanrights.dk/projects/nhrieu-capacity-project> and at the dedicated webpage of GANHRI.

65 Council of the European Union, Council conclusions on strengthening the application of the Charter of Fundamental Rights in the European Union, 8 March 2021, Brussels, OR. en 6795/21, available at: <https://data.consilium.europa.eu/doc/document/ST-6795–2021-INIT/en/pdf>.

66 See e.g., ENNHRI's 2019 presentation at a joint COHOM-FREMP meeting on NHRIs on the key challenges for fundamental rights in the EU, available at: <http://ennhri.org/news-and-blog/ennhri-highlights-nhris-contributions-to-realising-human-rights-before-council-of-the-eu/>.

can help NHRIs when they face threats at the national level, while NHRIs can speak up when regional human rights frameworks are facing pressure. For instance, in the context of ENNHRI's role in fostering reform of the ECtHR, the body has been actively engaging and consistently highlighting the importance of ensuring the independent functioning of the Court.[67]

Specific hurdles for cooperation between NHRIs and regional human rights frameworks are generally produced by a lack of awareness and the absence of clear institutional structures that might further enable such cooperation. The European mechanisms dedicated to the protection of human rights typically pre-dated the emergence of NHRIs across the region; therefore, they are often not specifically developed to accommodate effective engagement with these institutions. While NHRIs have unique features, they are one amongst various domestic bodies dedicated to human rights in the region; moreover, the specific character and added value of NHRIs is not always recognised regionally. Nevertheless, as NHRIs become increasingly active and organised at the regional level, it is apparent that these actors are also becoming more recognised and embedded in the regulatory and policy frameworks of European human rights organisations. Such recognition facilitates NHRIs' further contribution and their use of regional processes, but it also enhances the insights of regional actors as to how to cooperate most effectively with these institutions in their work.

The establishment of NHRIs in compliance with the Paris Principles is not a legal requirement for European governments. In those countries where these institutions have not been created yet, relevant actors will have to look for other national human rights counterparts to feed information into their work.[68] When European human rights procedures are directed to specific thematic rights, it is important for regional actors to include the voice of different types of national human rights bodies in their work. In the case of discrimination issues, for example, national equality bodies would be natural counterparts, in addition to broadly-mandated NHRIs.[69] The ample opportunities for cooperation between regional human rights frameworks and NHRIs also entail that decisions must be made regarding where engagement is most beneficial. The mandate of NHRIs is to realise the enjoyment of human rights at the national level; engagement with regional counterparts by individual NHRIs is, therefore, also primarily

67 See e.g., ENNHRI's submission relating to the 2018 draft Copenhagen Declaration, available at: <http://ennhri.org/ENNHRI-warns-against-the-weakening-of-the-Convention-system-in-its-submission>.

68 One of the last countries that rejected the need to establish a NHRI in line with the Paris Principles is the USA, which is an OSCE participating state. The lack of political will in this country constitutes an important hurdle for NHRIs to become embedded in OSCE intergovernmental procedures.

69 In about half of the European countries, NHRIs with a broad mandate are also the designated national equality body in the respective country.

directed towards that goal and will be carried out predominantly in the context of country-specific procedures, such as the national implementation of ECtHR judgments or in-country visits by regional human rights mechanisms, such as the Commissioner for Human Rights. The most relevant regional counterpart will vary depending on the situation and the aim to be addressed. NHRIs will need to identify their engagement priorities depending on their national context and needs.

European NHRIs also aim to echo regional voices concerning structural problems across the region. Various tools have been developed at the level of ENNHRI to do just this, including collective *amicus curiae* interventions in ECtHR procedures, and ENNHRI reports and statements submitted in the context of regional procedures such as the European rule of law monitoring and reporting procedures.[70] While ENNHRI interventions and reports aim to weigh in on structural policies and regulations, this often requires substantial investment in resources and follow-up actions. Moreover, the impact of collective interventions remains generally unpredictable and will only be measurable in the medium- to long-term. Some tools are already in place to prioritise ENNHRI's limited resources, and to pool the expertise and resources across ENNHRI's members, such as in the context of *amici curiae*. More comprehensive strategic approaches for engagement with regional mechanisms are being developed; identifying the most important entry points and ensuring better access and participation rights in regional processes, for ENNHRI and its members to effectively contribute to the enjoyment of human rights, democracy and rule of law across Europe.

5. CONCLUSION

This chapter has given a bird's-eye perspective of European NHRIs, including their domestic, regional, and international levels of engagement. It offers insights into the multi-layered human rights landscape in which NHRIs operate – using their domestic expertise to feed into regional mechanisms –, build on regional instruments, and lean on actors to trigger change at the national level. NHRIs are independent public institutions established by domestic law. States, however, are not obliged to create NHRIs, and their emergence is due, mostly, to strong support from human rights mechanisms at the UN and regional level. Important initial support for NHRIs in Europe came from the CoE, at the beginning of the 1990s. Gradually, this support has resonated across other

70 ENNHRI's report on the rule of law in Europe, which covers 51 countries and feeds NHRIs' information into regional and international rule of law procedures, is available at: <http://ennhri.org/rule-of-law-report/>.

European human rights frameworks, including the OSCE and the EU. Situated in the densest regional human rights arena in the world, European NHRIs have ample opportunities to build on regulations, policies, and practices deriving from regional human rights actors to engender change at the domestic level. Nevertheless, NHRIs are relatively young actors in the European human rights landscape. Accordingly, the regional human rights infrastructure has not been specifically devised to accommodate effective engagement with them. The recognition of the specific characteristics and added value of NHRIs is still emerging. With a legal mandate that allows NHRIs to independently address any human rights issue, these institutions can respond to important gaps in a densely populated but fragmented European human rights landscape.

The rather recent integration of European NHRIs into the regional human rights framework is also reflected in the relatively novel development of ENNHRI. It was only in 2013 that the decision was taken by European NHRIs to establish ENNHRI's Secretariat in Brussels: a decade later than analogous regional bodies in the Asia-Pacific and Africa. After an initial phase of setting-up its new governance structures, ENNHRI now aims to develop more tailored and pro-active tools to strengthen, support, and connect NHRIs across the European region. Many of these institutions are built in Europe on pre-exiting domestic bodies, such as ombuds offices or national equality bodies. Within their broad mandate to promote and protect human rights, European NHRIs will often be allocated more specific mandates and can be referred to as multi-mandated domestic bodies. While all European NHRIs operate within the framework of the Paris Principles, the NHRI landscape is very diverse. This chapter has flagged some overall challenges for NHRIs, which are visible across European countries. These include: the shrinking space for democracy and the rule of law; the rise of populism and negative human rights discourses; and a decrease in the resources allocated to human rights in the European region, including to NHRIs. In a context of ample challenges and limited resources, it is clear that building bridges between European human rights actors is of crucial importance. Strong and independent NHRIs carry crucial added value in such a context, and deserve more support for doing so.

THE EUROPEAN UNION AND NATIONAL HUMAN RIGHTS INSTITUTIONS

Towards a Stronger Partnership for Human Rights, Democracy and Rule of Law

James RISCHBIETH and Jan WOUTERS

1. INTRODUCTION

Since the adoption of the Charter of Fundamental Rights of the European Union (the Charter) in 2000 – and even more so since the Treaty of Lisbon in 2009 elevated the Charter's legal status to a position of parity *vis-à-vis* the European Union's (EU or Union) founding Treaties – the EU's commitment to the promotion and protection of and respect for fundamental rights in its internal policies and action has grown exponentially. In its internal law, policy, and action the Union seeks to ensure that its institutions and Member States acting within the scope of EU law proceed in compliance with citizens' fundamental rights, as enshrined in the Charter. EU external action tells a similar story of exponential growth in human rights activity, with the Treaty of Lisbon at the apex of strong exhortations requiring the Union to advance 'the universality and indivisibility of human rights and fundamental freedoms' in the wider world.[1] The Union has shown itself to be a staunch defender of human rights worldwide, not least through its dealings with third countries and engagement with human rights protection mechanisms at the UN and beyond.[2]

Given this context, it is hardly surprising that the EU has become increasingly interested in and supportive of the work of National Human Rights Institutions (NHRIs). After all, NHRIs, given their intimate knowledge and experience of national (human rights) contexts, their unique roles and capabilities, and (usually) independent nature, provide a natural ally as the EU seeks to promote rights both internally and externally. Recognition of the importance the EU

---

1 Article 21(1) TEU.

2 See F. GÓMEZ, C. CHURRUCA MUGURUZA and J. WOUTERS (eds.), *EU Human Rights and Democratization Policies: Achievements and Challenges*, Routledge, London 2018.

places on NHRIs is visible in a series of documents released by a wide variety of EU actors over the past few years.

The post-2015 period has seen the recognition of NHRIs grow significantly in the EU's external action. The Union's last two Action Plans on Human Rights and Democracy (2015 and 2020) and the 2021–2027 Thematic Programme on Human Rights and Democracy have all paid significant attention to the importance of 'supporting the capacity of (NHRIs)' and working with them in various aspects of EU external action. The importance of NHRIs has also been consistently recognised in the Annual Reports on Human Rights and Democracy in the World, published, since 2022, by the High Representative of the Union for Foreign Affairs and Security Policy (High Representative) and prior to that (2009–2021) by the European External Action Service (EEAS). The extent to which the EU actually engages with NHRIs, however, is not all that clear.

While lagging behind its external action slightly, the period since 2019 has seen EU attention to the critical work of NHRIs develop at a lightning pace in its internal action. The European Commission, Council, and European Parliament have all contemplated and emphasised the important roles NHRIs play in fundamental rights and rule of law protection, defence, and promotion. The EU Agency for Fundamental Rights (FRA) has engaged consistently with NHRIs and cooperates both with Member State NHRIs and the European Network of National Human Rights Institutions (ENNHRI).

Like many human rights developments, however, there is a concern that rhetoric has leapt ahead of reality on the ground: the EU lacks the concrete frameworks and guidelines that might ensure effective and efficient collaboration and cooperation with NHRIs in both its internal and external action. This is the next step for the Union, turning nascent attention and rhetoric into consistent and fruitful cooperation in practice.

This chapter highlights the natural partnership that should emerge given the EU and NHRI's common objectives, situates NHRIs within contemporary EU activity, and considers some of the key ways the EU has engaged with and could better engage with NHRIs in both its internal and external action. It builds upon a book chapter authored by Wouters, Meuwissen, and Barros, published in 2013,[3] by offering a window into the development of the EU-NHRI relationship across the intervening years. In terms of EU recognition of NHRIs, change has been significant: several arenas for potential collaboration have arisen since 2013, concerning both the EU's internal and external action; the international human rights landscape has also changed significantly, both within and outside the EU; and NHRIs now seem to have caught the Union's attention.

---

3 J. Wouters, K. Meuwissen and A.S. Barros, 'The European Union and National Human Rights Institutions' in J. Wouters and K. Meuwissen (eds.), *National Human Rights Institutions in Europe: Comparative, European and International Perspectives*, Intersentia, Cambridge 2013, 187–220.

However, it is unclear if there has been much of a change when it comes to actual EU engagement with individual NHRIs. It seems to be the case that the Union's interactions with regional NHRI networks have proliferated, including, most notably, its collaboration, cooperation, and communication with ENNHRI, but it still engages relatively infrequently with individual NHRIs – although this seems to be changing in country-specific procedures.[4]

The chapter opens by contemplating the EU's human rights culture as well as the natural place for NHRIs within this context. It then proceeds by outlining the contemporary situation of NHRIs within the EU and contemplates the ways in which the Union has considered NHRIs and called for increased collaboration with and support for them in both its internal policy and action. Next, the chapter contemplates several areas where collaboration might be better fostered, making an argument for clarification and concretisation of EU-NHRI interactions. This exercise is repeated in the context of EU external action. In conclusion, some brief recommendations are set out, including a call to encourage the Union to engage in and fund future institutional and academic research aimed at ascertaining an empirical understanding of EU-NHRI interactions.

2. THE EU'S HUMAN RIGHTS CULTURE

Respect for human rights and fundamental freedoms stands at the very core of the EU's identity and objectives. For this reason, it should come as no surprise that human rights action is part of the Union's core business, and this is true in both its internal and external action spheres. Indeed, the protection and promotion of human and fundamental rights has been described as 'a silver thread running through all EU action both at home and abroad'.[5] This is all based on the Union's establishment and maintenance as a bastion of democracy, rule of law, and human rights. Following the entry into force of the Treaty of Lisbon, the Treaty on European Union (TEU), one of the Union's founding Treaties, it was made clear that 'respect for human rights' is one of the fundamental values upon which the Union is founded.[6] The Treaty emphasises that the EU shall contribute

4 E.g. the annual Rule of Law Report of the European Commission (DG JUST) and the EU Enlargement Packages (DG NEAR).

5 European Commission and High Representative of the European Union for Foreign Affairs and Security Policy, 'Joint Communication to the European Parliament and the Council. Human Rights and Democracy at the Heart of the EU External Action – Towards a More Effective Approach', Brussels, 12 December 2011, COM(2011) 886 final, 12 December 2011, p. 4.

6 The full list of values is as follows: 'respect for human dignity, freedom, democracy, equality, the rule of law and respect for human rights, including the rights of persons belonging to minorities.' Article 2, Consolidated Version of The Treaty on European Union, 7 June 2016,

to the 'protection of human rights' in its relations with the wider world.[7] It also stipulates that the Union 'recognises the rights, freedoms and principles' set out in the Charter and that the latter 'shall have the same legal value as the Treaties'.[8] To further underline the EU's commitment to human rights, the TEU lays out that the Union shall accede to the European Convention of Human Rights;[9] however, as is well known, the achievement of this objective has faced complications, not least due to Opinion 2/13 of the Court of Justice of the EU (CJEU), which held the then draft accession agreement to be incompatible with the EU Treaties.[10] Negotiations in this respect are ongoing, having resumed in 2019, and seem close to a new draft agreement.[11] As the EU is yet to accede to the ECHR, its cooperation with NHRIs in this space is not yet relevant in the context of this chapter; however, it may become a topic of significant interest and a breeding ground for meaningful EU-NHRI cooperation in the future, especially given NHRIs' robust record when it comes to working with and at the ECtHR in Strasbourg.[12]

In line with its objectives and values, the EU has cultivated a 'human rights culture', which permeates both its internal and external action. The Union's human rights laws, rules, policies, and action are vast, multi-faceted, and complex. They interweave with Member State, third-state, regional, and international human rights mechanisms and activities, and constitute a significant part of the work of many Union organs, including the Commission; Council; Parliament; CJEU, FRA; EEAS; and the Office of the EU Special Representative for Human Rights (SRHR), who has acted as the EU's leading voice on human rights since 2012.[13]

As emphasised by the current High Representative, Josep Borrell, the EU's 'commitment to upholding the universality, indivisibility and interdependence of human rights and democratic values [has been] continuous'.[14] Still, implementation gaps persist. It is vital that the Union continues to work to ensure

O.J. C 202/13. On these values, see *inter alia* J. Wouters, 'From an Economic Community to a Union of Values: the Emergence of the EU's Commitment to Human Rights' in J. Wouters, M. Nowak, A.-L. Chané and N. Hachez (eds.), *The European Union and Human Rights: Law and Policy*, Oxford University Press, Oxford 2020, 11; J. Wouters, 'Revisiting Article 2 of the TEU: A True Union of Values?' (2020) 5:1 *European Papers* 255.

7 Article 3(5) TEU.

8 Article 6(1), first paragraph, TEU.

9 Article 6(2) TEU.

10 Opinion 2/13 of The Court (Full Court) 18 December 2014, Opinion Pursuant to Article 218(11) TFEU, ECLI:EU:C:2014:2454.

11 Council of Europe, 'EU accession to the ECHR' (CoE 2022), available at: <https://www.coe.int/en/web/human-rights-intergovernmental-cooperation/accession-of-the-european-union-to-the-european-convention-on-human-rights>.

12 On this see Chapter 2 by K. Meuwissen in this volume.

13 For the current SRHR, Eamon Gilmore, see Council of the European Union, Council Decision (CFSP) 2019/346 of 28 February 2019 O.J. L 62/12, 1 March 2019.

14 J. Borrell, 'Foreword by HR/VP Josep Borrell' in 'Report of the EU High Representative for Foreign Affairs and Security Policy 2021 Annual Report on Human Rights and Democracy in the World'. EEAS, Brussels 2022, p. 8.

fundamental rights are guaranteed within the EU and that its external action correlates with its core values. This necessitates a constant quest for improved approaches to rights protection and promotion.

Fortunately, it seems that the protection and promotion of rights has never been viewed with more importance at the EU level. This is due to the growing threats to human rights and democracy which have characterised recent years. Democratic backsliding, threats to the rule of law, the rise of extremist populism and nationalism, a worldwide authoritarian turn, the narrowing of civic space, and a pandemic which has torn at the societal fabric, have all threated core EU values.[15] Faced with these threats, the EU has doubled down on the importance of human rights as guarantors of freedom, democracy, liberty, and good governance.[16] Rights are, after all, a bastion against illiberalism, authoritarianism, and totalitarianism. In a world where democratic space is shrinking, 'the need for effective, coherent, [and] strong collective action on human rights and democracy is even more imperative'.[17] It is, therefore, no surprise that the EU has begun to pay more and more attention to its potential partners, including human rights defenders, civil society, and NHRIs.

3. NHRIs AS BRIDGES AND NATURAL EU ALLIES

The UN High Commissioner for Human Rights has, rightly, described NHRIs as 'cornerstones of the protection of human rights'.[18] As the Sub-Committee on Accreditation (SCA) of the Global Alliance of National Human Rights Institutions (GANHRI) made clear in 2018:

> NHRIs are established by States for the specific purpose of advancing and defending human rights at the national level, and [they] are acknowledged to be one of the most important means by which States bridge the implementation gap between their international human rights obligations and actual enjoyment of human rights on the ground.[19]

---

15 European Commission, 'International Partnerships: Human Rights and Fundamental Values', available at: <https://international-partnerships.ec.europa.eu/policies/peace-and-governance/human-rights_en#human-rights-and-democracy-action-plan-2020-2024> ('European Commission, International Partnerships, Human Rights & Fundamental Values').

16 J. Borrell, 'Foreword' in EU Action Plan on Human Rights and Democracy 2020–2024; E. Gilmore, European Union's Special Representative for Human Rights, 'Introduction' in EU Action Plan on Human Rights and Democracy 2020–2024; see also Conclusions 3 and 4, Council of the European Union, Council Conclusions on the EU Action Plan on Human Rights and Democracy 2020–2024, 18 November 2022, 12848/20; Borrell (n 14) p. 7.

17 ibid, Gilmore.

18 UN OHCHR, 'NHRIs: History, Principles, Roles and Responsibilities' (Professional Training Series No. 4 (Rev. 1) 2010) p. 13.

19 See Observation 2, GANHRI, General Observations of the Sub-Committee on Accreditation, 21 February 2018, Geneva, p. 1 (General Observations, SCA).

As discussed throughout this volume, NHRIs provide the key and independent link – the bridge – between rights-holders and governments. With the EU we see the addition of a supranational actor, which constitutes an extra dimension when it comes to NHRIs and their 'bridging' role.

In 2013, Wouters, Meuwissen, and Barros noted the importance of this bridging role in the supranational EU context, by suggesting that 'NHRIs can constitute important bridges across the multiple layers of the EU internal and external human rights architecture.'[20] The bridge metaphor reflects the ways in which NHRIs can provide a connection between the Union's laws, policies, and principles, on the one hand, and individual rights-bearers located within national contexts, on the other. Such 'rights-bearers' include both citizens affected by internal action and third nationals influenced by external EU actions. In such capacities, NHRIs act as human rights promoters, protectors, watchdogs, reporters, communicators, complaints handlers, and educators, in relation to EU human rights laws and policies.[21]

However, NHRIs can also play a broader bridging role, connecting the scattered dimensions of the complex and multi-layered EU human rights architecture with its density of stakeholders, legal instruments, and policy areas. This includes the facilitation of crucial connections between different EU institutions and bodies and Member States, and the EU and external partners. It includes the promotion of direct EU-NHRI dialogue and information sharing and tangible cooperation between NHRI and EU representatives across a range of areas, including policy advice, cooperation in the crafting of legislation, and oversight of EU and Member State authorities when implementing rights. All such activities have the potential to facilitate better EU human rights policies and practices.

The bridge metaphor is apt, but, given the expansive roles of NHRIs, it is now too narrow to suffice on its own. While NHRIs are certainly bridges, they are active human rights players in and of themselves. The EU should view them as such, as allies in the protection, promotion, and implementation of fundamental rights within the Union and of human rights in the EU's external action. After all:

> NHRIs are established with the explicit mandate to promote and protect human rights in a national setting, and as they are increasingly involved in regional and international human rights promotion and protection across the globe, they seem to be natural partners for the EU in its … human rights policy.[22]

The possibilities for EU-NHRI collaboration and cooperation are broad and offer opportunities for each to bolster the work of the other. NHRIs have the

---

20 J. Wouters, K. Meuwissen, and A.S. Barros (n 3).

21 Depending on the mandate of a given NHRI.

22 See Wouters, Meuwissen, Barros (n 3).

potential to contribute both proactively and reactively to EU processes.[23] Proactively, they have the capacity to contribute significantly to EU policy- and law-making and the rights-compliant distribution of EU funds; they can provide country-specific information, which is especially important in third-country contexts in the EU's external action; they also have significant scope to assist Member States as they seek to comply with the Charter when acting within the scope of EU law; and they have a unique capacity to connect citizens with EU laws and policies through public outreach and education. Reactively, they play roles as watchdogs, reporters, investigators, and complaints handlers; can independently monitor the influence and effectiveness of EU policies in their countries; have the capacity to provide independent and reliable information and experience to EU actors on local issues; and can connect citizens with mechanisms designed to enforce fundamental rights, even acting as complaints mechanisms themselves, as *amici curiae*, or as victims' supporters or representatives in strategic litigation. The Union can play a vital role in supporting, funding, building the capacity of, and protecting NHRIs. The Union is becoming increasingly aware of the fact that without partners on the ground, its rights-based agenda cannot succeed; as such, robust support of NHRIs maintains links to human rights developments 'on the ground' and has the potential to consolidate a human rights culture.

NHRIs are both potential bridges and potentially useful allies in the EU's stated goal of protecting and promoting human and fundamental rights; however, the extent to which the EU recognises this is not immediately clear. The following sections outline the reality of the EU's relationship with NHRIs in different contexts. It is based on a review of the literature, policy documents, reports, and laws. Before proceeding, however, it is necessary to clarify the situation of NHRIs in the EU.

4. SITUATION OF NHRIs IN THE EU

Twenty-two EU Member States have NHRIs. The exceptions are the Czech Republic, Italy, Malta, Romania, and Sweden. Of these, Romania is awaiting the results of two accreditation applications before the SCA;[24] Italy has two draft

[23] NHRIs combine reactive and proactive approaches to the promotion, protection, and implementation of human rights. See K. Meuwissen, 'European NHRIS as Multi-Layered Actors: Characteristics, Challenges and Opportunities' (Chapter 2 in this volume); see also K. Meuwissen, 'NHRI Participation to United Nations Human Rights Procedures: International Promotion Versus Institutional Consolidation?' in J. Wouters and K. Meuwissen (eds.), *National Human Rights Institutions in Europe: Comparative, European and International Perspectives*, Intersentia, Cambridge 2013, 263–86.

[24] Romania: the *People's Advocate* and the *Romanian Institute for Human Rights*. See ENNHRI, Annual Report 2021, ENNHRI, Brussels August 2022, p. 11 (ENNHRI Annual Report 2021);

laws under examination by its Parliament proposing the creation of an NHRI;[25] January 2022 saw the commencement of the work of a Swedish NHRI, which is yet to apply for SCA accreditation;[26] and an NHRI proposal is 'under discussion in Parliament' in Malta.[27] Nineteen Member States have NHRIs that are fully compliant with the Paris principles. Another three have NHRIs that are not fully compliant: Belgium, Hungary, and Slovakia.[28] Of the five Member States without NHRIs, all are working toward Paris Principles-compliant NHRIs, and two of the NHRIs which are not currently fully compliant are actively striving towards A-status.[29] The promotion of Paris Principles-compliant NHRI's is not just an expressly stated EU goal, but it is also a core commitment made by states under international human rights law.[30]

In some Member States, NHRIs have overlapping mandates and cover different topic areas, for example Belgium;[31] Bulgaria;[32] Finland;[33] Romania;[34] and, as of 2022, Sweden.[35] As for recent developments, 2021 saw Ireland's NHRI reaccredited (i.e., confirmed) with A-status, while 2022 has witnessed the *Volksanwaltschaft* (Austrian Ombudsman Board) reaccredited with A-Status, the *Federaale Instituut Mensenrecht* FIRM (Belgian Federal Institute for the Protection and Promotion of Human Rights) apply for SCA accreditation,[36] the A-status of Cyprus' NHRI,[37] and the commencement of work for a

FRA, 'NHRI accreditation status and mandates: 2022 Update of data in report 'Strong and effective NHRIs – challenges, promising practices and opportunities'' (FRA 2022) (FRA, 2022 update: NHRI accreditation status).

25 See European Commission, '2020 Rule of Law Report: The rule of law situation in the European Union', 30 September 2020, UN Doc. COM(2020) 580 final, p. 24 ('Rule of Law Report 2020').

26 The *Institut för mänskliga rättigheter* (Institute for Human Rights). See ENNHRI, Annual Report 2021, p. 11; FRA, 2022 update: NHRI accreditation status.

27 European Commission, Rule of Law Report 2020, p. 24.

28 European Union Agency for Fundamental Rights, 'Strong and Effective (NHRIs): Challenges, Promising Practices, and Opportunities', FRA, Brussels, 2020, p. 10 (FRA NHRI Report 2020).

29 See ENNHRI, Annual Report 2021.

30 'The establishment and strengthening of NHRIs pursuant to the Paris Principles falls within the set of international human rights commitments made by States. It is therefore the responsibility of the State to ensure that it has in place a Paris Principle-compliant NHRI.' See Observation 2, General Observations, SCA, p. 1.

31 The Federal Institute for the Protection and Promotion of Human Rights (FIRM) is not yet accredited, although it has applied for SCA accreditation, and the Interfederal Centre for Equal Opportunity and the fight against racism and discrimination (UNIA) has B-Status.

32 The Ombudsman of the Republic of Bulgaria (A-Status) and the Commission for Protection against Discrimination (B-Status).

33 Both A-Status.

34 Both awaiting the results of SCA accreditation applications.

35 The Equality Ombudsman (B-Status) and the new Institute for Human Rights (yet to launch a SCA application).

36 FRA, 2022 update: NHRI accreditation status.

37 See 'Ombudswoman's status upgraded', *Cyprus Mail*, 19 October 2022. <http://www.ombudsman.gov.cy/ombudsman/ombudsman.nsf/All/D63ED79BB4AFA6A7C22588E2003D7580?OpenDocument>.

Swedish NHRI.[38] ENNHRI has also 'advised Belgian authorities on the applicable international standards in view of plans to establish a human rights institute in Flanders.'[39] In less promising developments, Hungary's *Alapvető Jogok Biztosának Hivatala* (Office of the Commissioner for Fundamental Rights) was reaccredited and demoted from A-Status down to B-Status in 2021.[40]

Research conducted by the EU's Fundamental Rights Agency suggests that within the EU,[41] 'sixty-eight percent of people have heard of the NHRI in their country.'[42] While this awareness varies significantly from country-to-country (from 96 per cent in Slovenia and 93 per cent in Finland and Poland, to 27 per cent in Belgium and 34, 35, and 41 per cent in France, Luxembourg, and Germany respectively), it seems that citizens are relatively well aware of the national institutions that play a key role in protecting, promoting, and implementing their rights.

This picture suggests that the EU's NHRI landscape is nascent and trending in a positive direction. However, the relationship between the EU itself and individual NHRIs is still in a very early stage of development. The Union has lagged behind other international organisations (e.g., the UN,[43] the Council of Europe[44]) in its efforts to concretely work with NHRIs to achieve common objectives. The FRA has observed that '[t]he EU has never legislated on issues dealing with NHRIs'.[45] However, the Paris Principles are referenced in the

---

38 ENNHRI, Annual Report 2021, p. 11; see also, ibid.

39 ENNHRI, Annual Report 2021, p. 11.

40 FRA, 2022 update: NHRI accreditation status.

41 The survey included EU Member States, the Republic of North Macedonia, the Republic of Serbia, and the United Kingdom.

42 FRA NHRI Report 2020, p. 8.

43 See Meuwissen (n 23) 'NHRI Participation to UN Human Rights Procedures'; See e.g., Principle 22, UN HRC, Guiding principles on human rights impact assessments of economic reforms, 19 December 2018, UN doc. A/HRC/40/57 (HRC, Guiding principles on HRIAs); United Nations Human Rights Special Procedures, 'How to make Economic Reforms Consistent with Human Rights Obligations: Guiding Principles on Human Rights Impact Assessment of Economic Reforms' (UN and University of Pretoria 2020) p. 14; United Nations Development Program and United Nations Office of the High Commissioner for Human Rights, 'UNDP-OHCHR Toolkit for collaboration with NHRIs' (2010). Available at: <https://www.ohchr.org/sites/default/files/Documents/Countries/NHRI/1950-UNDP-UHCHR-Toolkit-LR.pdf> ('UNDP-OHCHR Toolkit for collaboration with NHRIs'). In terms of the UN system, mention can also be made of the World Bank, 'Human Rights Impact Assessments: A Review of the Literature, Differences with other forms of Assessments and Relevance for Development' (The World Bank 2013) pp. 11–12 ('World Bank, HRIAs, 2013').

44 See, in relation to the Lanzarote Convention (i.e., the Council of Europe Convention on the protection of children against sexual exploitation and sexual abuse of 25 October 2007), 'National human rights institutions', <https://www.coe.int/en/web/children/national-human-rights-institutions>. See recently 'Committee of Ministers adopts Recommendation to strengthen national human rights institutions', 31 March 2021, <https://www.coe.int/en/web/portal/-/committee-of-ministers-adopts-recommendation-to-strengthen-national-human-rights-institutions>.

45 FRA NHRI Report 2020, p. 10.

Regulation establishing FRA,[46] and recently Regulation (EU) 2021/1060, which includes fundamental rights as an 'enabling condition' for all stages of the EU funding cycle, considers NHRIs, albeit indirectly and not by name (see below, section 6.3).[47]

Beyond this, up until the late 2010s, only a smattering of EU references to NHRIs existed across Union policy documents, reports, and practice guidelines.[48] However, the period since 2015, in external action, and 2019, in internal action, has marked two slightly different but closely related shifts, which have seen NHRIs consistently referred to in EU documents. The rest of this chapter considers these shifts. The focus here is on providing an overview of developments and an analysis of some of the areas where cooperation could be more robustly encouraged or even formalised. The overview will consider a few key areas where cooperation is said to be important or where it has been expressly encouraged. Ultimately, the chapter seeks to promote more structure and clarity in EU-NHRI cooperation and encourage further research into this developing area, which sits at the intersection of EU action; supranational cooperation; and the implementation, protection, and promotion of human rights on the ground.

5. NHRIs AND EU INTERNAL ACTION

In 2019, the Finnish EU Presidency stressed that:

> [NHRIs], Equality Bodies, Ombuds institutions, professional and other networks, civil society, academia, citizens and media play a crucial role [in human rights protection and promotion]. They should be more closely involved [in EU human rights actions] in order to create a Union of values for all.[49]

If this statement did not mark the start of a shift towards greater recognition of NHRIs in EU internal action, it certainly marked the beginning of a period

---

46 Council Regulation (EC) No. 168/2007 of 15 February 2007 establishing a European Union Agency for Fundamental Rights, O.J. 2007 L53/1, as amended by Council Regulation (EU) 2022/555 of 5 April 2022, O.J. 2022 L108/1.

47 Regulation (EU) 2021/1060 of the European Parliament and of the Council of 24 June 2021 laying down common provisions on the European Regional Development Fund, the European Social Fund Plus, the Cohesion Fund, the Just Transition Fund and the European Maritime, Fisheries and Aquaculture Fund and financial rules for those and for the Asylum, Migration and Integration Fund, the Internal Security Fund and the Instrument for Financial Support for Border Management and Visa Policy, O.J. 2021 L231/159.

48 See e.g., FRA, 'National Human Rights Institutions in EU Member States, Strengthening the fundamental rights architecture in the EU', Luxembourg, EU 2010.

49 Finnish Presidency of the Council of the European Union, 'Presidency conclusions' at the conference 'How to Ensure the Resilience of our Societies in a Changing European Landscape', Helsinki, 10–12 September 2019.

where references to cooperation with NHRIs increased exponentially. In terms of the EU's internal action, various EU actors have emphasised the role to be played by NHRIs in helping the Union conduct its fundamental rights work and bolster democracy and the rule of law.

5.1. EU INTERNAL ACTION AND THE IMPORTANCE OF THE CHARTER

The Charter was initially adopted on 18 December 2000.[50] Although it was not legally binding for another nine years, it soon gained the status of an authoritative catalogue of fundamental rights and had a transformative impact on the working culture and practices of EU institutions.[51] From 1 December 2009, the Treaty of Lisbon updated the Charter's legal status, placing it on par with the EU's founding Treaties and emphasising the importance of promoting and protecting fundamental rights within the Union.

The Charter acts as a legally binding means to protect the fundamental rights of individual EU citizens. According to Article 51(1), the Charter's provisions:

> are addressed to the institutions, bodies, offices and agencies of the Union with due regard for the principle of subsidiarity and to the Member States only when they are implementing Union law. They shall therefore respect the rights, observe the principles and promote the application thereof.[52]

The Charter, thus, applies to the actions of the EU's various 'institutions, bodies, offices and agencies' (according to Article 51(1) of the Charter) including, most importantly, the crafting and passing of EU legislation, formulation of EU policy, disbursement of EU funds, and implementation of all three. Moreover, the provisions of the Charter are applicable in relation to EU Member States where they act to implement and enforce EU law and policy. This includes, *inter alia*, Member State action relating to EU regulations, the transposition of EU directives into national legislation, and Member State action in response to EU decisions. It is worth noting that the European Commission's 2020 Strategy to strengthen the application of the Charter in the EU makes a very strong reference to the role of NHRIs in implementing the Charter:

> Strong and effective national human rights institutions ('NHRIs') are critical links between government and civil society insofar as they address the 'protection gap' between the rights of individuals and the responsibilities of the State. Their overarching

[50] Charter of Fundamental Rights of the European Union, 18 December 2000, O.J. C364/1.
[51] Wouters, Meuwissen, Barros (n 3).
[52] Article 51(1) of the Charter.

> function is to address discrimination in all its forms and to promote the protection of the full range of fundamental rights. NHRIs monitor the application, implementation and promotion of the Charter on the ground, provide information and support to victims of fundamental rights violations and cooperate with the national institutions to improve their use and awareness of the Charter.[53]

The Strategy also includes an explicit reference to Commission support for ensuring that all Member States have Paris Principles-compliant NHRIs.[54]

5.2. THE FRA AND NHRIs

Of all EU bodies, the FRA is most intimately connected with Member State NHRIs. The FRA was established in 2007 with the objective to:

> provide the relevant Union institutions, bodies, offices and agencies of the Union and its Member States when implementing Union law with assistance and expertise relating to fundamental rights in order to support them when they take measures or formulate courses of action within their respective spheres of competence to fully respect fundamental rights.[55]

Although this is a wordy provision, the FRA was essentially tasked with providing assistance, support, and expertise to both EU bodies and Member States to help ensure their compliance with the Charter. Article 8 of the FRA's constituent document governs the Agency's '[c]ooperation with organisations at Member State and international level'.[56] It states that '[t]o help it carry out its tasks, the Agency shall cooperate with … governmental organisations and public bodies competent in the field of fundamental rights in the Member States, including [NHRIs].'[57]

In this respect, the FRA works closely with ENNHRI (Europe's NHRI network) as well as individual Member State NHRIs on a variety of matters, most notably in the promotion and implementation of the Charter in the EU's

---

53 European Commission, Communication to the European Parliament, the Council, the European Economic and Social Committee and the Committee of the Regions, 'Strategy to strengthen the application of the Charter of Fundamental Rights in the EU', 2 December 2020, COM(2020) 711 final, at p. 11.

54 ibid: 'The European Network of National Human Rights Institutions (ENNHRI) can, with the support of the Commission, assist Member States in establishing and promoting Paris principles' complaint [sic] A-status NHRIs.' On the same page, the Commission 'invites (…) Member States in which NHRIs have been established, to ensure they are given the tools and means to comply with the Paris principles and refer to the Charter in their mandate.'

55 Article 2, Council Regulation (EC) No. 168/2007 (n 45).

56 Article 8, ibid.

57 Article 8(2)(a), ibid.

internal activities as well as Member States' implementation of EU law and policy. NHRIs play a crucial role in contributing to the FRA's work, through the provision of country information to FRA reports and opinions on fundamental rights problems across the EU: not least its annual reports on the implementation of the Charter. The FRA also works with NHRIs to collect data, consider topical issues, and disseminate information about fundamental rights.

The FRA is consistently espousing the importance of NHRIs,[58] with the most notable example being FRA's 2020 report on NHRIs, 'Strong and Effective National Human Rights Institutions: Challenges, Promising Practices, and Opportunities'.[59]

This watershed report noted that '[t]here is a very clear consensus that NHRIs are key agents to ensure a vibrant implementation and application of the Charter at national and local levels.'[60] It surveyed and analysed NHRI engagement with the Charter and laid out several recommendations and opinions for future EU cooperation and collaboration with NHRIs in its internal action. The most notable of these can be divided between two categories: (A) EU processes that could be considered for regular NHRI contributions and (B) ways in which the EU should support NHRIs.

5.2.1. *EU Processes that could be Considered for Regular NHRI Contributions*

The FRA noted both specific processes and more general areas where NHRIs have the capacity to contribute.[61] At the specific end of the scale, it recommended NHRI participation in the European Parliament's annual resolution on the situation of fundamental rights in the EU and the European Commission's annual report on the application of the Charter. In more general terms it recommended a role for NHRIs as providers of advice to EU legislators when preparing and implementing policies and legislation, noting that NHRIs 'are the natural "advocates of the Charter" at national and local levels'[62] and raisers of 'arguments relevant to the EU Charter of Fundamental Rights when Member States are adopting EU legislation into national law'. The FRA also noted the added value of NHRIs in independent fundamental rights and rule of law monitoring in Member States[63] and suggested that 'EU institutions could establish a more regular exchange with NHRIs.'[64] The FRA recommended that EU bodies include

58 FRA NHRI Report 2020, p. 1.
59 FRA NHRI Report 2020.
60 ibid, p. 80.
61 ibid, p. 85.
62 ibid, p. 80.
63 ibid, pp. 12–13. See also FRA Opinion 3.
64 ibid, p. 14.

NHRIs more formally as participants in EU debates, strategies, frameworks, and actions concerned with the rule of law,[65] noting that:

> The EU can draw further inspiration from the practice of the UN, whereby Paris Principles-compliant NHRIs are granted particular status in terms of participation and contribution to a number of bodies, mechanisms and processes, including the Human Rights Council and treaty bodies. Such opportunities are far reaching in the UN, involving input into country assessments, follow-up procedures, development of standards and the complaints procedures.[66]

5.2.2. Ways in which the EU can Support NHRIs

As for ways the EU can support NHRIs, the FRA emphasised the importance of ensuring NHRIs and ENNHRI have the financial and human resources necessary to operate effectively and independently.[67] The report stressed the importance of ongoing EU financial support, suggesting that 'the European Commission could consider more funding opportunities to help NHRIs develop expertise on the Charter's application at national level.'[68] EU austerity, the impact of COVID-19, climate change, and the changing political climate in Europe have led to a general reduction in resources allocated to human rights. In this context, many NHRIs are facing budgeting issues.[69] The economic fallout from the 2022 Russian invasion of Ukraine may very well have worsened this situation.

The FRA emphasised the importance of ensuring that Member States play their part in maintaining NHRIs resources 'at a level that enables operational capacity to deliver their mandates effectively and independently', as per the Paris Principles.[70] This goes beyond financial considerations, and indeed the FRA emphasised that '[a]s underlined by the Council of the European Union, EU Member States should ensure a safeguarding and enabling environment for NHRIs and civil society, so that NHRIs are free from threats and harassment.'[71] In terms of NHRI's institutional make-up, the FRA highlighted both the importance of ensuring that NHRI memberships reflect the 'diverse nature' and 'plurality' of society, including the inclusion of civil society and marginalised groups in decision-making,[72] and the necessity of ensuring transparency in 'selection and appointment process[es]' relating to NHRI members, including ensuring that processes are 'open to the widest possible range of applicants.'[73]

---

65 ibid, p. 10.
66 ibid, p. 15.
67 FRA Opinion 3, ibid.
68 ibid, p. 14.
69 See the Chapter 2 by K. Meuwissen in this volume.
70 FRA NHRI Report 2020, FRA Opinions 14 and 15, pp. 21–22.
71 FRA Opinion 11, ibid, p. 19; see also European Commission (n 53), p. 12.
72 FRA Opinion 12, ibid, p. 20.
73 FRA Opinion 10, ibid, p. 19.

In particular, the Agency opined that '[s]uch processes could include independent expert committees and parliamentary involvement.'[74]

While all these points are important, only a handful will be considered here in more detail. First, however, it is important to note the NHRI-related commentary of the Council, European Parliament, and European Commission, all of which have echoed the sentiments of the FRA report. Indeed, the period 2020–21 marked something of a watershed year for EU recognition of the importance of NHRIs in its internal action context, with all three major EU institutions emphasising the importance of partnering with NHRIs in the promotion and protection of fundamental rights and the rule of law.

5.3. RECOGNITION OF NHRIs BY THE COUNCIL, EUROPEAN PARLIAMENT AND EUROPEAN COMMISSION

5.3.1. *Council*

The Council recognised 'that independent NHRIs and equality bodies play a crucial role in the protection and promotion of fundamental rights' and noted that they 'are key for the implementation of the Charter, given their broad and horizontal fundamental rights mandate and their proximity to citizens.'[75] It also specifically recognised the important role of NHRIs in 'awareness-raising' as well as their key 'contribut[ion] to ensuring compliance of national policies with the Charter.'[76] Furthermore, the Council 'encourage[d] Member States that have not yet established independent NHRIs … to do so',[77] and it called on Member States with established NHRIs to 'ensure that they are provided with sufficient resources and staff to fulfil their mandate', underlining that 'securing an enabling environment and adequate funding is essential to unlocking the potential of NHRIs.'[78] Perhaps most importantly, the Council was clear that 'there is room to enhance the impact of the work of NHRIs', and it

> encourage[d] Member States, the Commission, and other Union institutions, bodies, offices and agencies to further strengthen mutual cooperation with [NHRIs], namely by ensuring their regular and substantiated involvement in exchange of views with the government and in reporting exercises.[79]

---

74 ibid.

75 Conclusion 27, Council of the European Union, Council conclusions on strengthening the application of the Charter of Fundamental Rights in the European Union, 8 March 2021, Brussels, OR. en 6795/21, p. 10.

76 ibid.

77 ibid, Conclusion 29.

78 ibid.

79 ibid., Conclusion 30.

The Council conclusions also touched on five key areas where NHRIs play critical parts in fundamental rights protection, noting: (1) the importance of their proximity to citizens; (2) their role in awareness-raising and (3) ensuring compliance of EU Member State policies with the Charter; (4) their crucial involvement in regular dialogues and 'exchange of views'; and (5) their essential role as oversight and reporting bodies.[80] Focusing on these areas is, indeed, key to 'unlocking the potential of NHRIs.' These five areas resemble not only those mentioned in the FRA report but also some of the key areas noted by Meuwissen, Wouters and Barros in 2013,[81] indicating a permeation of academic observations into the work of policy-makers at the highest levels. This is encouraging for the development of NHRIs as critical actors in fundamental rights protection.

In terms of the Council's direct interaction with NHRIs, it is rather limited. However, both the Council's Working Party on Human Rights and Working Party on Fundamental Rights have liaised with ENNHRI.[82]

5.3.2. European Parliament

The European Parliament also weighed in on the importance of NHRIs in 2021, dedicating two paragraphs of its Resolution of 24 June 2021 on the Commission's 2020 Rule of Law Report to recognising the important roles played by NHRIs 'in preserving EU citizens' rights and being able to defend the rule of law at national, regional and local levels'. Like the Council, it emphasised the importance of supporting NHRIs' independence, noting that 'the diminishing independence of some Member States' [NHRIs] … constitutes an immediate threat to the fundamental rights of citizens.'[83] The Parliament also

> call[ed] on the Commission to pay more attention in the next annual cycle to the activities of [NHRIs] by looking in greater depth at how they function, their degree of independence and their real contribution in ensuring that adequate safeguards are in place.[84]

Furthermore, it '[c]alled on the Commission to strengthen the regular, inclusive and structured dialogue' with several human rights actors, including '[NHRIs], ombudspersons, [and] equality bodies.'[85]

---

80 ibid, Conclusions 27–30 (note: there was no Conclusion 28), p. 10.

81 Wouters, Meuwissen, Barros (n 3).

82 ENNHRI, 'Partners' (ENNHRI, 2022) available at: <https://ennhri.org/about-us/partners/#eu> ('ENNHRI, Partners, 2022'); Meuwissen, Chapter 2 of this volume.

83 Paragraph 30, European Parliament, Resolution of 24 June 2021 on the Commission's 2020 Rule of Law Report (2021/2025(INI)), EU Doc. P9 TA(2021)0313, p. 14.

84 ibid.

85 ibid, para. 43, p. 17.

Much like the Council, specialised committees of the European Parliament have consulted with ENNHRI. Indeed, ENNHRI regularly participates in hearings and discussions on human rights matters in both the Committee on Human Rights of the European Parliament (DROI) and the Committee on Civil Liberties, Justice and Home Affairs (LIBE) 'to ensure that NHRI expertise is taken into account.'[86] As long ago as 2013, Wouter, Meuwissen, and Barros were noting that the Parliament's '[s]ubcommittees would benefit from a more structured EU cooperation with NHRIs.'[87] This point remains largely valid today, although NHRIs have been invited to participate in country-specific procedures of LIBE.

5.3.3. *European Commission*

The European Commission has touched on NHRI issues in several policy documents, many of which are discussed in this chapter. It has also relied on their information and advice during its annual reporting on the rule of law in the EU. As for concrete collaboration, much like the European Parliament, the Commission liaises regularly with ENNHRI. For example, ENNHRI meets with the Directorate-General for Justice and Consumers (DG JUST); the Directorate-General for International Co-operation and Development (DG DEVCO); the Directorate-General for Employment, Social Affairs and Inclusion; and the Directorate-General for European Neighbourhood Policy and Enlargement Negotiations.[88]

Aspects of ENNHRI's work are funded by the Commission: DG JUST provides an operational grant for ENNHRI in the context of its work to encourage 'mutual learning, exchange of good practices and cooperation … in relation to European law and policy' and DG DEVCO funds ENNHRI's project on the Role of NHRIs in Situations of (Post-)Conflict.[89]

5.4. TEMPERED ASSESSMENT

The recognition of NHRIs at the aforementioned levels indicates that EU actors are finally recognising their potential as bridges and human rights allies. However, the actual work performed by NHRIs in support of the Charter should not be overstated.

The FRA's 2020 report emphasised that, despite a number of the NHRIs it surveyed suggesting that 'the use of the Charter appears to be increasing … in

86 ENNHRI, Partners, 2022.
87 ibid.
88 ibid.
89 ibid.

their legal and political systems' (16 of 33),[90] only four of the respondent NHRIs were 'currently using the Charter systematically, whereas the others indicate[d] that they are not yet making full use of its potential'.[91] According to FRA's data, 18 of the respondent NHRIs suggested that the 'Charter's limited scope' constrained its use in their activities, while 16 respondent NHRIs suggested that use of the Charter was undermined because international rights instruments presented more 'added value' than the Charter in the context of their work: 13 said the same for national instruments.[92]

Importantly, the FRA's research also suggests that 'relatively few NHRIs engage in direct exchange and cooperation with EU institutions', in large part because of their existing engagement with international human rights mechanisms at the Council of Europe and the UN,[93] where they enjoy more formal and substantial rights of participation.[94] This pattern does not extend to ENNHRI, which 'has played an important role in improving NHRIs' connection to regional policies and processes, including at (the) EU level'.[95]

There seems to be little doubt that EU-NHRI cooperation could be bolstered in the EU's internal action sphere. Indeed, '[s]trong, independent NHRIs with a broad human rights mandate [can act as] "multipliers" of the Charter'.[96] The main challenge in this respect seems to be developing EU statements and sentiments into tangible avenues, structures, and procedures that facilitate direct cooperation with NHRIs in EU processes.

While it is promising to see the EU considering these issues, detail is sorely lacking. Collaboration with NHRIs in the internal action context is seen as a 'potential', but it is ambiguous, and, as the FRA has made very clear, it is fragmented and lacks any kind of guidance *vis-à-vis* the 'hows', 'whys', 'whens', 'wheres' and 'whats' of EU-NHRI coordination. What is plainly needed is a detailed in-depth study of the ways in which different EU actors interact with NHRIs. The FRA report is a good start: it provides analysis of NHRI perceptions

---

90 See FRA NHRI Report 2020, pp. 13 and 79. 18 NHRI respondents 'felt that the role of (the Charter) has increased before national courts over the last 10 years, while 14 also identified such a trend in … law making, 11 in … policy making and seven in … political and public debate. When asked whether the role of the Charter has increased over the last 10 years in the work of the NHRI itself, … 16 [NHRIs] said that the role has increased, whereas 13 denied such an increase in the Charter's relevance for their work', at p. 79.

91 Thirteen of the NHRI respondents 'did not see such an increase in the Charter's relevance for their work'. See ibid, p. 13.

92 Note: four respondent NHRIs did not make greater use of the Charter due to restrictions in their mandate. Ibid, pp. 13 and 79.

93 ibid., p. 14.

94 See Meuwissen (n 23) 'NHRI Participation to UN Human Rights Procedures'; See e.g., Principle 22, HRC, Guiding principles on HRIAs; United Nations Human Rights Special Procedures (n 43), p. 14; See UNDP-OHCHR Toolkit for collaboration with NHRIs.

95 ibid, p. 14.

96 FRA NHRI Report 2020.

of the Charter and their work in relation to it and offers some suggestions for improvement, but a far more in-depth study (or probably studies) is necessary. From this, detailed practice guidelines and best practices as well as concrete means of structural and formal EU-NHRI cooperation might emerge.

6. FRAMEWORK FOR FUTURE EU-NHRI INTERACTION AND COOPERATION

There are several areas where increased EU-NHRI interaction and cooperation could and should be formally fostered. For brevity's sake, we focus on three issues: NHRI participation in (i) EU protection of the rule of law, (ii) EU and Member State human rights impact assessments (IAs), and (iii) EU funding disbursement.

6.1. EU-NHRI COOPERATION ON RULE OF LAW PROTECTION

European NHRIs, through ENNHRI, have already demonstrated their value in the rule of law context. For the past three years ENNHRI has published 'a regional report on the state of the rule of law in Europe'.[97] The latest version contemplated views from across the membership and included 40 national perspectives, identifying both national concerns and Europe-wide trends.[98] The rigour and quality of the report as well as its wide dissemination culminated in recognition, by both the EU and Council of Europe, of the important roles that NHRIs play in rule of law monitoring, oversight, and protection. The report's quality led the European Parliament to call on the Commission to consult further with NHRIs on rule of law issues and, along with the FRA report, should be considered as one of the reasons for the concrete recognition of NHRIs in subsequent EU policy instruments. The EU has acknowledged that NHRIs are not only key partners and guardians of the rule of law in Member States, but their health, in terms of their independence and adequacy of resources and staff, are also indicators of the health of the rule of law in particular Member States.[99]

In the current context, dominated as it is by democratic and rule of law backsliding, NHRIs seem to have demonstrated their value and their real scope to contribute to EU rule of law monitoring. NHRIs have an intimate understanding of local and national issues and, provided they are independent, have the potential to keep EU actors abreast of rule of law issues. NHRIs can

---

97 ibid, ENNHRI, p. 13.
98 ibid.
99 ibid, p. 3.

provide counter-narratives relating to Member State communications with the EU, and, in this respect, the Polish NHRI – the *Rzecznik Praw Obywatelskich* 'Commissioner for Human Rights' – has exhibited stellar practice, by standing up to political pressure and maintaining its independence and robust protection of fundamental rights in what has been described as 'a very adverse environment.'[100] Such action must be supported by the EU politically, through ongoing financial support and through the creation of more structured avenues for EU-NHRI collaboration *vis-à-vis* rule of law monitoring, reporting, and data collection. The Commission's Rule of Law review cycle and annual Rule of Law Report are actions in which NHRIs should play a significant and formalised role. Recent calls by other EU bodies for the Commission to interact more formally with NHRIs are promising, but the need for a formalised means to guide concrete collaboration is obvious. Important in this respect will also be timely and consistent engagement. One of the practical challenges is that neither ENNHRI nor national NHRIs are aware when and with which NHRIs the European Commission is engaging bilaterally. Moreover, the Rule of Law reporting cycle is very short and resource-intensive. The Commission increasingly engages in bilateral meetings with NHRIs before and after the reporting cycle.[101]

The Commission's inaugural Rule of Law Report (2020) itself, notes that '[NHRIs] play an important role as rule of law safeguard and can provide an independent check on the system in a rule of law crisis.'[102] Attention to the role of NHRIs in maintaining national checks and balances, however, is not elaborated upon: the report details three Member States that are yet to establish an NHRI but goes no further; it fails to contemplate the ways in which EU actors should or could engage with NHRIs; and, in fact, the Commission's 'targeted stakeholder consultation' for the report included ENNHRI but no individual NHRIs.[103]

The Commission's 2020 Strategy to strengthen the application of the Charter in the EU offers some slightly more concrete suggestions, although it lacks the kind of detail necessary to guide robust and systematic EU-NHRI collaboration.[104] The Strategy classifies NHRIs amongst a group that it calls 'rights defenders', which includes 'independent authorities protecting rights, such as [NHRIs], equality bodies, Ombuds institutions, data protection authorities, etc'.[105] It sets out support for the establishment of an NHRI in each EU Member State and notes the importance of protecting NHRIs from threats, providing them with

---

100 ENNHRI, Equinet, GANHRI, International Ombudsman Institute, and OHCHR, 'Joint Statement in Support of the Polish Commissioner for Human Rights' (GANHRI 2019).

101 The Commission has just started (with the FRA) a pilot on multi-stakeholder roundtables to follow-up Rule of Law reporting at national level, including NHRIs (as well as state authorities and NGOs).

102 European Commission, Rule of Law Report 2020 (n 33), p. 23.

103 ibid, pp. 5 and 20.

104 Charter Strategy (n 53).

105 ibid, p. 3, fn 18.

adequate resources, and building their capacity to further contribute to the implementation of the Charter. It also describes 'strong and effective NHRIs' as 'critical links between government and civil society insofar as they address the "protection gap" between the rights of individuals and responsibilities of the State', noting the key role they play in

> monitor[ing] the application, implementation and promotion of the Charter on the ground; provid[ing] information and support to victims of fundamental rights violations; and cooperat[ing] with [other] national [bodies] to improve their use and awareness of the Charter.[106]

Although the way in which links between the EU and NHRIs might be enhanced is not spelled out in great detail, some promising points must be noted. The Strategy expressly recognises that 'upholding EU fundamental rights and values is a shared responsibility and requires a collective effort from all concerned, [including NHRIs]'.[107] It also notes 'the importance of cooperation and communication' between 'different levels of government', ... the EU institutions, rights defenders [including NHRIs] and civil society organisations'. In this respect, the Strategy

> encourages Member States to appoint a *Charter focal point* to ease the flow of information and best practice on the Charter and coordinate capacity building efforts in the country. The focal point could also pass information to and from the EU institutions (emphasis added).[108]

The Strategy lists NHRIs as a respected source of 'factual information' and suggests that information could be gathered from NHRIs and through the new Charter focal points.[109] Last but not least, the Strategy has set in place annual thematic reporting on the Charter. NHRIs contribute to this annual reporting, both through ENNHRI and invidually.[110]

6.2. NHRIs AND IMPACT ASSESSMENTS

The 2020 FRA report notes NHRIs' key role as advisers and oversight bodies and contemplates their potential as a central actor in the context of impact

---

106 ibid, p. 11.
107 ibid, p. 3.
108 ibid, p. 6.
109 ibid, p. 7.
110 See, e.g., https://ennhri.org/news-and-blog/ennhri-calls-for-stronger-protection-rights-defenders-eu-charter-report-submission/. Unlike for the Rule of Law reporting (with follow-up trough annual inter-institutional dialogues and national dialogues), the Charter annual reporting has no country-specific recommendations nor country-specific follow-up.

assessments (IAs) relating to EU and Member State laws and policies and their consistency with the Charter. Similarly, the Commission's 2020 Strategy to strengthen the application of the Charter in the EU notes that 'in preparing initiatives the Commission draws on input by key stakeholders (and) open and constructive dialogue with civil society organisations in the interests of supporting the Commission's efforts to mainstream the Charter into all its policies and legislative proposals.'[111] It adds that:

> Consultations are launched to inform Commission initiatives under its Better Regulation rules. The Commission draws on the data provided by the EU Agency for Fundamental Rights, rights defenders such as NHRIs and equality bodies and information collected by international organisations.[112]

This is hardly surprising. After all, NHRIs are human rights experts, experts on their national situations, and have access to unrivalled national information: they are founts of quality and independent information and expertise.

Wouters, Meuwissen, and Barros have gone into detail about the important role NHRIs could play in IAs, both in relation to EU legislation and policies and the legislation and policies of Member States when they are 'acting within the scope of EU law'.[113] In this respect, NHRIs have scope to support the EU in ensuring both Charter-compliant EU law-making and the quality of transposition of EU law into domestic settings.

While it is encouraging to see some permeation of academic arguments into the actions of the Commission and the 2021 Strategy, the Strategy does not lay out how NHRIs are or should be consulted in the IA context. Moreover, none of the Interinstitutional Agreement on Better Law-Making (2016), Commission Staff Working Document on Better Regulation Guidelines (2021), or Commission Better Regulation Toolbox (2021) make any reference to NHRIs.[114] As such, no formalised role is contemplated for NHRIs. They are described as valued partners and 'respected sources of information' and it is suggested that they should be involved in IAs in some unclear way, but the idea that they could

---

111 Charter Strategy (n 53), p. 14; European Commission, 'Better Regulation, "have your say"' (Commission 2022), available at: <https://ec.europa.eu/info/law/better-regulation/have-your-say_en>.

112 ibid, p. 14, fn 93.

113 Article 51(1) of the Charter; For an understanding of what it means to 'act within the scope of Union law', see K. Lenaerts and P. Van Nuffel, *European Union Law*, Sweet and Maxwell, London 2011, pp. 834–35.

114 See the Interinstitutional Agreement on Better Law-Making, 12 May 2016, Brussels, O.J. L123/1 (Interinstitutional Agreement on Better Law-Making 2016); European Commission, Commission Staff Working Document: Better Regulation Guidelines, 3 November 2021, Brussels, EU Doc. SWD(2021) 305 final (Commission Staff Working Document); European Commission, 'Better regulation toolbox – November 2021 Edition' (2021).

play a formal role in IA processes is absent. This is a significant shortcoming, as both EU and Member State IA processes would benefit from the inclusion of structured avenues for NHRIs' contribution.

6.2.1. *EU Impact Assessments*

The Commission launched IAs in 2002,[115] as a means to 'examine whether there is a need for EU action' in a particular area and to 'analyse the possible impacts of available solutions.'[116] IAs are carried out during the Commission's 'preparation phase' relating to new 'legislative proposals, non-legislative initiatives, implementing and delegated acts'.[117] IAs aim at delivering on 'the Union's policy objectives in the simplest, most efficient and effective way possible', in a way that 'is designed to facilitate its transposition and practical application' in Member States.[118] IAs are intended to provide for the gathering and analysis of evidence which might inform and guide the Commission's decision-making process in line with the EU's principles and objectives.

Fundamental rights were not initially prioritised in IAs; however, since the Charter's change in legal status post-Lisbon, the Commission has ensured a concrete focus on fundamental rights assessments within IAs;[119] indeed, IAs are viewed by the Union as 'the main means for the EU to ensure compatibility of legislative proposals with fundamental rights.'[120] Fundamental rights must always be considered in EU IAs.[121] However, the way in which NHRIs might be formally included in the process is not so clear. The Commission's 'Better Regulation Toolbox'[122] is a highly detailed 608-page document which guides EU actors through IAs in different contexts. Despite a detailed section on fundamental rights and the Charter, NHRIs are not considered at any point.

In comparison to the lack of formal NHRI involvement in EU IAs, the UN 'singles out NHRIs as one of the actors that should be responsible for carrying

115 European Commission 'Communication from the Commission: "Impact Assessment"', 5 June 2002, Brussels, EU Doc. COM(2002) 276 final.

116 European Commission, 'Impact Assessments', available at: <https://ec.europa.eu/info/law/law-making-process/planning-and-proposing-law/impact-assessments_en>.

117 ibid.

118 Interinstitutional Agreement on Better Law-Making 2016; Commission Staff Working Document (n 114); European Commission, 'Better regulation toolbox – November 2021 Edition' (2021).

119 IA process findings must be summarised in an IA report, which must, itself, include an 'explanatory memorandum' covering several issues, including its 'conformity with (the Charter)' and 'impacts on fundamental rights'. See Commission Staff Working Document (n 114) p. 35–36; Commission, Impact Assessments (n 107).

120 Interinstitutional Agreement on Better Law-Making 2016.

121 Commission Staff Working Document (n 114) pp. 33 and 35.

122 'Better regulation toolbox' (n 114).

out human rights impact assessments.'[123] It also emphasises the 'importance of independent and empowered NHRIs' in such processes.[124] Similarly, the World Bank has set up mechanisms to include NHRIs in human rights IAs.[125] As the Bank has made clear, the past 10 to 15 years have witnessed an

> increasing demand for various actors to undertake human rights impact assessments before adopting and implementing policies, projects, agreements and programs, … to evaluate the extent to which the elaboration, implementation and monitoring of the[se actions] are consistent with human rights norms.[126]

The Bank is adamant that such 'assessments should involve [all] relevant human rights actors in the particular context, including [NHRIs], NGOs and UN human rights experts.'[127] Such a view is not unique; after all, NHRIs are 'obvious and well equipped' entities for the Commission to consult with formally.[128] NHRIs are intimately familiar with the fundamental rights issues at stake within their national contexts; possess the information, expertise, insight, and data that IAs require; and, provided they are independent,[129] they stand as obvious allies for the EU.

As Meuwissen has emphasised:

> NHRIs in compliance with the Paris Principles [are] recognised as reliable sources of information at the UN and CoE level and receive preferential access to international human rights procedures: where they can present information on the human rights situation of a country independent from the information provided by government.[130]

There is no reason why they should not perform the same formal role in the context of Commission IAs. The FRA has come to a similar conclusion, noting that 'NHRIs could play an important role in impact assessments and inter-institutional agreements on better law making at an EU level.'[131] It has made the following concrete proposal:

> One possibility would be to give [Paris Principles-compliant] NHRIs a privileged role during consultation with stakeholders in the preparation of impact assessments.[132]

---

123 Principle 22, HRC, Guiding principles on HRIAs; United Nations Human Rights Special Procedures (n 43).

124 ibid, HRC.

125 World Bank, HRIAs, 2013.

126 World Bank, HRIAs, 2013, pp. v, ix, 1, and 11.

127 ibid, pp. 11–12.

128 It is interesting to compare how similar the language used by the FRA NHRI Report 2020 (at p. 83) is to the language used by Wouters, Meuwissen, Barros (n 3).

129 i.e., they hold an A-Status from the SCA.

130 Meuwissen, Chapter 2 of this volume; see also Meuwissen (n 23) 'NHRI Participation to UN Human Rights Procedures'.

131 ibid.

132 ibid.

While this sounds simple in theory, it would require the opening of new avenues of communication between specific NHRIs and the Commission. FRA has pointed out that key 'EU institutions and bodies dealing with policies and legislation are increasingly consulting ENNHRI, but there is still no formalised, structured or systematic interaction or engagement of individual NHRIs with the EU institutions.'[133] While it should not be overly difficult to open such lines of communication, the fact remains that a structure facilitating EU-NHRI collaboration on IAs requires concretisation.

Updating the Commission's 'Better Regulation Toolbox' offers an avenue in this respect. However, FRA's 2020 recommendation, quoted above, pre-dated the Toolbox's latest update. The Commission has thus missed an opportunity to formalise NHRI-EU collaboration on IAs. This is a significant oversight; however, it can be rectified in the next version of the Toolbox.

6.2.2. Member State Impact Assessments

As the FRA has observed, '[n]early all EU legislation is adopted into national law and implemented by national authorities.'[134] For this reason, a significant portion of the laws and policies passed and implemented by Member States must also comply with the Charter.[135] NHRIs therefore have a significant role to play in the EU's protection of fundamental rights through their competence to perform national human rights IAs. What is more, the Paris Principles clarify that 'NHRIs have the responsibility to examine legislative proposals and make recommendations to ensure that they are in conformity with the fundamental principles of human rights.'[136]

In this light, the FRA has also recommended that:

> when transposing and implementing EU legislation, Member States should consider inviting NHRIs to contribute to relevant procedures. This could be in relation to, for example, compatibility checks and impact assessments.[137] To reinforce the impact of NHRIs, EU Member States could invite such institutions to make recommendations on the fundamental rights implications of draft legislation and policies to improve … compliance … Parliaments could also have a formalised relationship with NHRIs and ensure that reports by NHRIs addressed to parliament are properly presented and discussed … EU Member States could ensure that there is a systematic tracking and

---

133 ibid.

134 FRA NHRI Report 2020, p. 79.

135 Article 51(1) of the Charter.

136 See 'Competences and responsibilities', Art 3(a)(i), UN Principles Relating to the Status of National Institutions, Annex to UNGA Res. 48/134 (20 December 1993) UN Doc. A/RES/48/134.

137 Opinion 6, ibid, p. 15.

> public reporting of the follow-up and implementation of NHRIs' recommendations. This could include reporting on which recommendations are still pending and at which stage, as well as which recommendations have explicitly been rejected or left without reaction by competent national authorities. If NHRIs' recommendations are not acted on, there could be effective formal ways for NHRIs to have these addressed by parliament.[138]

This extensive suggestion represents the kind of approach that the EU should be considering when seeking to formalise its interactions with NHRIs. It will be interesting to see how Member States, EU institutions, and NHRIs respond to this suggestion.[139]

6.3. NHRI PARTICIPATION IN DISBURSEMENT OF EU FUNDS

Recent updates to the EU's funding disbursement rules offer a window into a way in which the Union could formally include NHRIs in other areas of fundamental rights monitoring. Regulation (EU) 2021/1060 lays down common provisions on the disbursement of EU funds under eight key EU funding instruments.[140] The development is significant, as the Regulation seemingly includes NHRIs as key actors in monitoring the disbursement and use of EU Common Provision funds (CPFs). However, the new rules are not entirely concrete in terms of the role they (seem to) reserve for NHRIs.

Regulation (EU) 2021/1060 sets out 'fundamental rights conditionality', which 'include[s] the Charter … as a horizontal "enabling condition" for accessing EU funds'.[141] In simpler terms: for Member States to access EU CPFs, they must ensure '[e]ffective application and implementation of the Charter.'[142]

---

[138] ibid.

[139] ENNHRI's 2022 'State of the Rule of Law in Europe' report (<https://ennhri.org/rule-of-law-report-2022/>) includes additional information on NHRIs' 'enabling space', teasing out key gaps, including follow-up of NHRI recommendations and suggestions on bridging these gaps. In its 2022 Rule of Law Report: (<https://ec.europa.eu/info/publications/2022-rule-law-report-communication-and-country-chapters_en>), the European Commission has made country-specific recommendations on NHRIs in three countries (Poland, Lithuania and Croatia); amongst these country-specific recommendations features follow-up to NHRI recommendations.

[140] Regulation (EU) 2021/1060 (n 46). The eight funds covered by this common regulation are: the European Regional Development Fund; the European Social Fund Plus; the Cohesion Fund; the Just Transition Fund; the European Maritime, Fisheries and Aquaculture Fund; the Asylum and Migration Fund; the Internal Security Fund; and the Border Management and Visa Instrument.

[141] FRA NHRI Report 2020, p. 81. As indicated above, the enabling condition is applicable throughout the funding cycle, and is not only a pre-condition for initially accessing the funds.

[142] Art 15(1) and Annex III, Regulation (EU) 2021/1060.

Compliance with the Charter, thus, acts a pre-condition for receipt of EU funding. As part of this requirement, Member States must ensure that '[e]ffective mechanisms are in place to ensure compliance with [the Charter]' at all stages of programmes covered by CPFs.[143]

The reason this is potentially so significant from a NHRI-EU cooperation perspective centres around the listing of NHRIs as potential members of 'oversight committees': in their capacity as 'bodies responsible for promoting social inclusion, fundamental rights, rights of persons with disabilities, gender equality and non-discrimination.'[144] 'Oversight committees' are vested with significant responsibilities *vis-à-vis* the monitoring of CPF programmes: beyond oversight competences, committee members have important decision-making powers.[145] This has the potential to place NHRIs in an impactful position *vis-à-vis* Charter protection; however, ambiguity regarding the role of NHRIs arises from Article 39 of the Regulation, read in conjunction with Article 8(1).

Article 39 clarifies that the 'monitoring committee ... shall ensure a balanced representation of the relevant Member State authorities and intermediate bodies and of representatives of the partners referred to in Article 8(1).' Article 8(1) clarifies that such 'partners' include the following:

(a) regional, local, urban and other public authorities;
(b) economic and social partners;
(c) relevant bodies representing civil society, such as environmental partners, non-governmental organisations, and bodies responsible for promoting social inclusion, fundamental rights, rights of persons with disabilities, gender equality and non-discrimination; [and]
(d) research organisations and universities, where appropriate.[146]

NHRIs are covered by Article 8(1)(c); however, they are only one of several potential 'monitoring committee' members. While this throws an element of uncertainty into play, signs suggest that both the EU and civil society actors expect Member States to include NHRIs on monitoring committees.[147] This provides a possible, albeit imperfect, model for the future formal inclusion of NHRIs in other fundamental rights processes, for example Commission IAs and EU rule of law actions.

143 See Annex III, Regulation (EU) 2021/1060.
144 See Arts 8(1)(c), 8(2), 38, and 39, Regulation (EU) 2021/1060.
145 ibid, Art 39.
146 Articles 8(1) and 39, Regulation (EU) 2021/1060.
147 See FRA NHRI Report 2020, p. 14; FRA, ENNHRI, and Equinet, 'Virtual seminar on the role of the Charter of Fundamental Rights of the European Union in the work of Equality Bodies and NHRIs, 20–22 October 2021' (FRA, ENNHRI, Equinet Virtual seminar); Charter Strategy (n 53), pp. 8–9; Maëva Roulette, 'The Charter conditionality in the new Common Provisions Regulation: Enabling conditions in the new Common Provisions Regulation', at FRA, ENNHRI, Equinet Virtual seminar, p. 7.

The importance of this development should not be overstated; however, it also should not be denied. The funding instruments at issue are significant, and the fact that at least some NHRIs will be able to play a part – however small – in using EU hard law to ensure Charter compliance by their Member States is a meaningful development. Of course, questions should be asked as to whether NHRIs have the capacity to perform their role on 'monitoring committees'. In this respect, it becomes all the more important that NHRIs are properly supported and funded, in line with the Paris Principles.[148]

The involvement of NHRIs in EU internal fundamental rights action clearly requires formalisation. In many ways, the EU's internal fundamental rights action has been overshadowed by human rights actions undertaken in the Union's external relations; however, as will be seen across the following sections, many of the issues surrounding formal NHRI involvement in EU activities are as relevant in the external action context as they are in the internal action sphere.

7. NHRIs AND EU EXTERNAL ACTION

As indicated above, Article 3(5) TEU provides that, '[i]n its relations with the wider world', the EU 'shall contribute to … the protection of human rights, in particular the rights of the child'. Article 21(1), first paragraph, TEU confirms and elaborates this, emphasising that:

> The Union's action on the international scene shall be guided by the principles which have inspired its own creation, development and enlargement, and which it seeks to advance in the wider world, [including] the universality and indivisibility of human rights and fundamental freedoms.

The further paragraphs of Article 21 TEU stipulate that within its external action the 'Union shall seek to develop relations and build partnerships with third countries, and international, regional or global organisations which share the[se] principles'[149] and that

> [t]he Union shall define and pursue common policies and actions, and shall work for a high degree of cooperation in all fields of international relations in order to … consolidate and support democracy, the rule of law, human rights and the principles of international law.[150]

---

148 It may be noted that ENNHRI has published an ENNHRI position flagging the challenges and opportunities for NHRIs in this context: <https://ennhri.org/news-and-blog/nhris-monitoring-eu-funds/>.

149 Article 21(1), second para. TEU.

150 Article 21(2), introduction and subpara. (b) TEU.

The Treaty, thus, leaves no doubt that human rights are a clear priority in external policy and action, and the Union has, indeed, invested a great deal of attention and resources to the task of promoting and protecting human rights beyond the EU's borders, including through the elaboration of a raft of instruments and policies across its broad scope of external action.

EU external action covers several key subject areas beyond human rights and democracy.[151] However, the Union has been clear in its assertions that 'human rights are universal, indivisible and interdependent ... [and] are always and everywhere applicable, including at times of conflict or crisis.'[152] In this respect, the Union's external action is underpinned by a Human Rights Based Approach (HRBA), which 'is a working methodology that puts human rights and the rights-holders at the centre of EU external action.'[153] This means that all external action policy areas overlap constantly with human rights concerns: not least Enlargement and Neighbourhood; Development; Security, Defence, and Crisis Response; Migration and Forced Displacement; Climate, Environment and Energy; Sanctions; Trade; and Humanitarian and Emergency Response policy areas.[154]

This has relevance because the Commission, Council, and the High Representative, assisted by the EEAS, must cooperate to ensure human rights are paid their due attention during all instances of the Union's external action.[155]

7.1. A DECADE OF HUMAN RIGHTS ACTION PLANS, STRATEGIC FRAMEWORKS, THEMATIC PROGRAMMES, AND FUNDING INSTRUMENTS

The past decade has seen the Union take significant strides in its efforts to promote, protect, and defend human rights in its dealings with third countries and regional and international governance fora. In particular, the Union has prepared and continually updated specific human rights strategies for third countries since 2011; worked continuously in partnership with like-minded third countries and international and regional fora on advancements in human rights law, policy, and practice; released three successive Action Plans

151 Article 21(2) TEU; European External Action Service, 'What we do'. Available at: <https://www.eeas.europa.eu/en>.

152 ibid.

153 See European Commission, International Partnerships, Human Rights & Fundamental Values (n 15).

154 Article 21(3) TEU confirms this, clarifying that 'the Union shall ensure consistency between the different areas of its external action'.

155 ibid.

on human rights,[156] which shape the EU's approach to its external action; produced a series of massive funding instruments to support human rights programmes; and published the 2021–2027 Thematic Programme on Human Rights and Democracy.[157]

Close analysis of these actions reveals the significantly enhanced attention paid by EU actors, as the period has worn on, to local human rights stakeholders and civil society. In recent years this has seen the Union's attention turn increasingly to local human rights defenders, implementers, and allies, including individual human rights defenders and advocates; civil society organisations (CSOs); NGOs; and, crucially, NHRIs. This reveals a slow shift from top-down EU efforts to promote and protect rights across the wider world, to a more collaborative effort, which recognises the key roles played by local actors in bringing EU values, principles, policies, and approaches to a point where they can bear fruit and make a tangible difference 'on the ground'.

This shift correlates with a period of democratic backsliding, which has witnessed the consistent undermining of rights and the rule of law and a turn toward authoritarianism and anti-liberalism in many parts of the world. The increasing focus on the 'nitty-gritty' of human rights appears to be a recognition both that standard setting alone is not enough to facilitate rights protection and that action must be fostered at local and national levels to properly promote and protect human rights; furthermore, to encourage such developments requires the protection and support, by the EU and its human rights allies, of local human rights actors, including NHRIs.

7.1.1. 2012 Strategic Framework and Action Plan on Human Rights and Democracy

The release of the Union's 2012 Strategic Framework and Action Plan on Human Rights and Democracy was a major milestone in both the EU's external action and the 75+ year history of international efforts to protect and promote universal human rights. The Action Plan laid the groundwork for the mainstreaming of human rights across all areas of the EU's external action. Despite its significance, the 2012 Action Plan made no mention of NHRIs. As this volume clarifies, NHRIs were well established across the globe by 2012, not least in Europe

156 Council of the European Union, EU Strategic Framework and Action Plan on Human Rights and Democracy, Luxembourg, 25 June 2012, EU Doc. 11855/12; Council of the European Union, EU Action Plan on Human Rights and Democracy (2015–2019) and Council Conclusions on the Action Plan on Human Rights and Democracy 2015–2019, 20 July 2015; Council of the European Union, Council Conclusions on the EU Action Plan on Human Rights and Democracy 2020–2024, 18 November 2022, 12848/20.

157 European Commission, Thematic Programme on Human Rights and Democracy Multi-Annual Indicative Programming 2021–2027 (EU 2021).

and Latin America; the Paris Principles were then 21 years old;[158] and other international organisations, including the UN and World Bank, had already established concrete guidelines for cooperation with NHRIs. NHRIs were, thus, conspicuous by their absence in the 2012 Action Plan.

7.1.2. EU Action Plan on Human Rights and Democracy (2015–2019)

The release of the 2015 Action Plan on Human Rights and Democracy (2015–2019) marked a significant turning point for NHRIs. The Action Plan implicitly recognised the shortcomings of its previous approach, emphasising the importance of 'more focused action, [the] systematic and coordinated use of the instruments at its disposal, and enhanced impact of its policies and tools on the ground.' In this context, it was little surprise that the Plan announced that '[t]he EU will put special emphasis on ownership by, and co-operation with, local institutions and mechanisms, including [NHRIs].'[159] The first of the 2015 Action Plan's 34 objectives was, in fact, aimed at '[s]upporting the capacity of [NHRIs].'[160] It directed EU actors, in particular Commission Services, the EEAS, and Member States to include the following concrete action in their activities:

(i) Recognise and support the crucial role of NHRIs as independent institutions and affirm the EU commitment to support and engage in particular with those institutions which are in line with the Paris Principles;
(ii) Work to strengthen the involvement of such NHRIs in consultation processes at country level, in particular regarding Human Rights Dialogues and third countries' reforms;
(iii) Strengthen, in the context of the NHRIs' International Coordinating Committee, the capacities of those with an 'A-status', support the upgrade of those with a 'B-status' to 'A-status', and cooperate with their regional and international networks;
(iv) Facilitate cooperation between NHRIs in EU Member States and NHRIs in partner countries.[161]

This call for increased coordination with and attention to NHRIs provided EU actors with clear priorities for action in respect of NHRIs, and the Action Plan stipulated that 'work on these issues should feed into the next

158 See generally Principles relating to the Status of National Institutions (Workshop on the Status of National Institutions, Paris, 1991); See also UNGA Res. 48/134 (20 December 1993) UN Doc. A/RES/48/134.

159 Council Conclusion 3, EU Action Plan on Human Rights and Democracy (2015–2019) and Council Conclusions, p. 7.

160 ibid, p. 16.

161 EU Action Plan on Human Rights and Democracy (2015–2019) and Council Conclusions, p. 16.

mid-term programming period of the EU External Financing Instruments.'[162] The Multiannual Indicative Programme (2018–2020) for the 2014 Instrument for Democracy and Human Rights duly delivered,[163] with the Commission setting out

> five specific objectives: (1) Support to human rights and human rights defenders in situations where they are most at risk; (2) Support to other EU human rights priorities; (3) Support to democracy; (4) EU election observation; and (5) Support to targeted key actors and processes, including international and regional human rights instruments and mechanisms.[164]

Ultimately, objectives 1, 2, 3, and 5 were financed through the European Instrument for Democracy and Human Rights,[165] with EUR 404,738,000 allocated to these programmes over a three-year period.[166] Action 11 of this funding arrangement, titled 'Capacity development of [NHRIs]', aimed at promoting 'improved capacities and outreach of targeted [NHRIs], GANHRI, and the four Regional Networks.'[167] This action was implemented by a grant of €3.75 million in 2019.[168] Part of Action 9 was also directed at NHRIs,[169] with an indicative amount of €0.75 million allocated to the Asia-Pacific Forum of National Human Rights Institutions in 2020.

While these developments are a significant positive from the perspective of those interested in promoting robust NHRIs, details of the specific funding provided and the influence of the funding on tangible outputs is absent. Numerous questions which are relevant for various EU organs, not least the Commission's Directorate-General for International Partnerships (INTPA), arise in this context, including: where did the money end up? how did it influence NHRIs? which concrete actions and programmes did the funding enable? which benefits arose for NHRIs? how were distributive decisions made? and, could the process be improved? Such questions necessitate robust empirical research into the effects of EU funding on NHRI independence and performance.

---

162 ibid, p. 16.

163 European Commission, The Multiannual Indicative Programme (2018–2020) for the Instrument for Democracy and Human Rights Worldwide, Commission Implementing Decision, EU Doc. C(2018) 6409.

164 ibid.

165 See Regulation (EU) No. 235/2014.

166 European Commission, Commission Implementing Decision of 19 October 2018 on the Multi-Annual Action Programme 2018–2020 for the European Instrument for Democracy and Human Rights (EIDHR) to be financed from the general budget of the Union, Brussels, 19 October 2018, C(2018) 6798 final.

167 ibid.

168 European Commission, Summary: Multi-Annual Action Programme 2018–2020 for the European Instrument for Democracy and Human Rights to be financed from the general budget of the European Union, pp. 5 and 8.

169 ibid.

7.1.3. EU Action Plan on Human Rights and Democracy (2020–2024)

The 2020 Action Plan on Human Rights and Democracy (2020–2024) has 'recommitted the EU and its Member States to use the full range of instruments for the protection and promotion of human rights and democracy in all areas of external action.'[170] This iteration of the EU's human rights action plan has emphasised even more strongly the importance of 'local circumstances and specificities' and 'local needs'.[171] As noted by High Representative Josep Borrell, '[the] new Action Plan is about specific, actionable priorities to advance human rights and democracy around the world.'[172] The EU's Special Representative for Human Rights, Eamon Gilmore, also emphasises the importance of the local and specific:

> The Action Plan is a framework, one of purpose and direction, with a broad range of policies, tools and political and financial instruments at our disposal to implement it. It will be up to the more than 140 EU Delegations and Member State Embassies across the world to translate the Action Plan from paper into practice, through a range of actions tailored for local needs and circumstances.[173]

The Plan can be commended for its recognition that bottom-up action is as important in the context of human rights protection and promotion as top-down policy-making and standard-setting. Its focus on the specific and local is commendable and its objectives are ambitious. In this respect, it reflects observations from 'the field' and academia that 'effective' human rights action 'requires the coordinated action of all actors and stakeholders',[174] including the facilitation of an 'independent civil society, enabling civic space and the support and protection of human rights defenders' as 'essential elements'.[175] The challenge will be ensuring the Action Plan can live up to these lofty objectives, and in a context where so much is promised, a focus on encouraging local actors to craft actions and facilitate implementation and adequate monitoring of EU policy is vital. In this respect, the involvement of NHRIs, with the local expertise and knowledge they hold and independence and critical eye they exude, is not only understandable and valuable: it is essential.

---

170 European External Action Service, '2021 Annual Report on Human Rights and Democracy in the World'. EEAS, Brussels 2022, p. 9.

171 See European Commission, International Partnerships, Human Rights & Fundamental Values (n 15); Borrell (n 14).

172 Borrell (n 14).

173 Gilmore (n 12).

174 Conclusion 7, Council Conclusions on the EU Action Plan on Human Rights and Democracy 2020–2024.

175 Conclusion 6, ibid.

The latest Action Plan incorporates five strategic lines of action.[176] These lay out ostensibly 'concrete objectives',[177] to be pursued through all means of external action activity, through 'the systematic, and coordinated use of the full range of instruments at the EU's disposal' and 'implemented at country, regional and multilateral level', taking into consideration 'local needs and specificities'.[178] They reflect the focus on local circumstances and the inclusion of specific, national, and community-based actors. They are set out as follows:

1. Protecting and empowering individuals
2. Building resilient, inclusive, and democratic societies
3. Promoting a global system for human rights and democracy
4. New technologies: harnessing opportunities and addressing challenges
5. Delivering by working together.

Two of these lay out 'concrete objectives' relating to NHRIs: Action Line 3 and Action Line 5. Action Line 3 is promoted in the Action Plan as being 'at the core of the EU's commitment to strengthening multilateralism.' The objective is to make

---

176 European Commission, International Partnerships, Human Rights & Fundamental Values (n 15).

177 EU Action Plan on Human Rights and Democracy 2020–2024.

178 'The EU will leverage the broad range of policies, tools and political and financial instruments at its disposal to implement [the policy], such as: political, human rights and sectoral policy dialogues; EU trade policies, including the EU's generalised scheme of preferences; thematic and geographical instruments under the 2021–2027 multiannual financial framework; actions in multilateral and regional human rights fora; communication activities and awareness-raising campaigns; public statements, *démarches*; observing trials of human rights defenders; the implementation of 13 EU human rights guidelines; election observation and its follow-up; dialogue with civil society, human rights organisations and the business sector.' See European Commission, 'Q&A: The EU Action Plan for Human Rights and Democracy' (EU 25 March 2020) available at: https://ec.europa.eu/commission/presscorner/detail/en/qanda_20_490 ('European Commission, Q&A: Action Plan for Human Rights and Democracy'); See also EU Action Plan on Human Rights and Democracy 2020–2024, 5.2 'Implementation, Monitoring, and Evaluation' p. 30: 'The following means will be used to implement the actions contained in the present Action Plan: political dialogues; human rights dialogues; sectoral policy dialogues; GSP+/'everything but arms' (EBA) monitoring missions; election missions and their follow-up; common security and defence policy (CSDP) civilian and military missions and operations; use of the relevant EU human rights guidelines with specific tools to achieve thematic objectives; Council conclusions; resolutions in the UN Human Rights Council and the UN General Assembly (UNGA) Third Committee; thematic and geographical financial instruments (relevant programmes and projects); flexible human rights and democracy support; direct support for human rights defenders; monitoring of trials; advocacy for ratification and implementation of key UN human rights treaties, core ILO conventions, main instruments of international humanitarian law, and other relevant conventions and optional protocols; statements on human rights abuses and violations; targeted training sessions for EU staff in Delegations; public diplomacy and targeted campaigns, conferences and other events; dialogue with civil society and other relevant stakeholders; restrictive measures.'

sure that 'the EU's strategic response to the changing international environment is to strengthen its coherence and unity in multilateral fora, to widen and deepen bilateral partnerships, and to build new cross-regional coalitions.'[179] As part of this aim, Action Line 3.4, titled 'Civil Society and [NHRIs]' seeks to:

> 3.4.b. Support independent (NHRIs) and commissions, ombudspersons and equality bodies, in line with the Paris and Venice principles, and engage with them including in the context of human rights dialogues.
>
> 3.4.c. Promote structured and regular dialogues … and maintain focus on follow-up.

Action Line 5.2 focuses on 'working together' to facilitate 'implementation, monitoring and evaluation'. In this respect, one can see the added value that NHRIs could provide. While the hint at formalised inclusion of NHRIs in human rights dialogues and in other forms of cooperation is promising, much like in the internal action context, it remains ambiguous.

7.2. CLARIFYING THE EU'S RELATIONSHIP WITH NHRIs: THE HUMAN RIGHTS AND DEMOCRACY THEMATIC PROGRAMME

2021 saw the release of The Human Rights and Democracy Thematic Programme (2021–2027) (HRDTP), which is one of four EU multi-annual indicative programmes (MIPs) that cover the Union's external action activities.[180] Its value in the current context is twofold: (1) it clarifies the EU's perceptions *vis-à-vis* the place of NHRIs in its external action, including the various roles they can play and the added value they bring; and (2) the Programme acts as the avenue to funding for EU external action activities involving NHRIs, replacing the European Instrument for Democracy and Human Rights (EIDHR),[181] and allowing the Action Plan Framework to be put into action.[182]

Echoing the 2021–2024 Action Plan the Programme identifies 'five key priorities.'[183] Priority 3, which aims at '[p]romoting a global system for human rights and democracy', is of relevance to NHRIs as it directs EU actors 'to work together with' and forge 'strategic partnerships [with] … all key actors, including … [NHRIs] [and] global and regional networks of [NHRIs]'.[184] The

179 EU Action Plan on Human Rights and Democracy 2020–2024, p. 22.

180 Human Rights and Democracy; Civil Society Organisations; Peace, Stability and Conflict Prevention; Global Challenges.

181 EEAS, 2021 Annual Report on Human Rights and Democracy in the World, p. 9.

182 Borrell (n 14), p. 8.

183 Thematic Programme on Human Rights and Democracy 2021–2027, p. 1.

184 ibid, pp. 2–3.

Programme describes NHRIs as 'a vital part of the country-level human rights protection system',[185] emphasising their essential roles in identifying 'country-specific human rights issues' and 'interven[ing], as appropriate, before national, regional, and international authorities.'[186]

The Programme also notes that NHRIs should be 'supported' in EU external action to enable them to fulfil their role as 'independent and effective interlocutors *vis-à-vis* national public authorities and their own citizens.' EU actions, it is suggested, should aim at strengthening NHRIs' capacity in various areas, many of which echo those raised in the 'internal action' section of this chapter: human rights education; awareness-raising; monitoring; reporting; individual complaints handling; and 'making recommendations to harmonise national laws, policies and practices with the international human rights standards.'[187] The Programme also echoes Wouters, Meuwissen, and Barros by referring to 'NHRIs as bridge-builders between civil society, human rights defenders, national authorities and regional and international human rights bodies.'[188]

Beyond this, the Programme offers context regarding the objectives of the 2020 Action Plan, noting that EU action should seek to 'strengthen NHRIs' independence [and] facilitate their access to and engagement with regional and international human rights mechanisms'. The Programme also notes the potential for and value of information exchange between EU actors and NHRIs, including the value of 'exchanging experiences and identifying promising practices.'[189]

The context that the Programme provides is highly valuable, as is the EEAS' 2021 Annual Report on Human Rights and Democracy in the World. The EEAS notes that:

> in most of its human rights dialogues in 2021, the EU called on third countries to ensure that NHRIs are independent, receive the necessary human and financial resources, and are systematically consulted in all relevant policymaking and legislative processes. Emphasis was placed on ensuring that NHRIs and their staff are protected from threats, harassment, and attacks.'[190]

The report also described the EU's engagement with GANHRI and regional NHRI networks in Europe, Africa, Asia, and the Americas, and makes mention of the EU's financial assistance provided to (unnamed) NHRIs.[191] Yet, again,

[185] ibid, p. 23.
[186] ibid.
[187] ibid.
[188] ibid.
[189] ibid, pp. 23–24.
[190] EEAS, 2021 Annual Report on Human Rights and Democracy in the World, pp. 189–90.
[191] EEAS, 2021 Annual Report on Human Rights and Democracy in the World, pp. 188–90.

there is little information offered in both the Programme and the Annual report about *how* cooperation with NHRIs is to be conducted.

EU-third country NHRI cooperation undoubtedly occurs. Communications with EU officials suggest that it is quite country-specific in terms of content, formality, and the avenues of interaction relied upon.[192] A number of common points of cooperation between EU actors and third-country NHRIs have been identified, including: ongoing EU political and funding support for NHRIs, especially in support of active human rights promotion and protection and relevant thematic work; encouragement from the EU for NHRIs to act as independent rights watchdogs; support of NHRIs in their function as National Preventative Mechanisms under the Optional Protocol to the Convention Against Torture and Other Cruel, Inhuman or Degrading Treatment or Punishment (OP-CAT) (where applicable); support of NHRIs as national human rights complaint mechanisms (where applicable); support and encouragement of NHRIs *vis-à-vis* their role in Universal Periodic Review implementation; and the provision of encouragement and support when it comes to promoting interactions with and protection of human rights defenders.[193]

While such engagement undoubtedly occurs, and sometimes on a significant scale, we are – yet again – unable to get to the crux of *how* such cooperation is actually conducted. This uncertainty results from the lack of formal avenues for EU-NHRI communication and elaboration. It is clear that (i) EU-NHRI relations are country-specific, and (ii) completely uniform and formalised means and avenues for communication are not practical or realistic. However, this does not restrict the elucidation, by the EU, of a set of best practices and recommended approaches to interaction and cooperation.

7.3. FUNDING EU EXTERNAL ACTION INVOLVING NHRIs

Like the three other MIPs, the Human Rights and Democracy Thematic Programme is covered by the Global Europe: Neighbourhood, Development and International Cooperation Instrument (NDICI): a €79.5 billion funding instrument which covers the EU's 2021–2027 external action agenda.[194] The NDICI allocates €1.562 billion for the implementation of the Programme, which represents a significant bolstering of the EU's commitment to human rights in its

---

192 Personal correspondence between the authors and EEAS officials. Correspondence on file with the authors.

193 ibid.

194 European Commission, International Partnerships, Human Rights & Fundamental Values (n 15).

external action.[195] Funding is specifically directed to support 'targeted key actors and processes, including … [NHRIs].'[196] When compared to the EIDHR, NHRIs have been allocated a significant increase in funding under the Programme: €33,767,000.[197] NHRIs, therefore, enjoy significant financial attention in the latest EU external action funding, indicating the value ascribed to them by the Commission.[198] The Programme is intended to offer 'independence of action': 'it foresees direct cooperation with human rights defenders and local civil society organisations without the need for approval of national authorities.'[199] This will, of course, offer a direct EU source of funding for NHRIs; it should also facilitate dialogue and information exchange between NHRIs and EU actors.

7.4. IMPLEMENTATION AND EVALUATION OF THE EU'S EXTERNAL ACTION ON HUMAN RIGHTS[200]

As the EU's human rights-based external action has developed over three Action Plans, two major funding instruments, and the 2021 Human Rights and Democracy Thematic Programme (2021–2027), there has been a clear development towards an approach that centres 'local needs and specificities', through 'the adoption of tailored-made strategies at a local level' and 'regular dialogue with civil society, human rights defenders, [NHRIs], the business sector and other relevant stakeholders'.[201] This focus on 'the local' and 'the specific' is reflected repeatedly, and, given the broad human rights mandates and local expertise held by NHRIs, it is easy to see why they would be attractive partners in a context in which the EU seems to so highly value local knowledge, priorities, and experience 'on the ground'.

The EU's focus on fostering and building bottom-up partnerships is quite clear; however, the way in which NHRIs might contribute, beyond being 'supported', 'engaged with', and included in 'structured dialogue', 'implementation, monitoring

---

195 Compared to the funding allocated through the EIDHR (2014–2020), the allocation to the HRDTP offers 'an approximate increase of 17%'. European Commission, International Partnerships, Human Rights & Fundamental Values (n 15).

196 ibid.

197 Albeit for a longer period. 2021–2027.

198 This allocation complements country-specific funding. European Commission, International Partnerships, Human Rights & Fundamental Values (n 15), p. 31.

199 ibid.

200 See the common guidance which ENNHRI, with GANHRI and other regional networks, has developed for EU external action on engagement with NHRIs: <http://ennhri.org/wp-content/uploads/2020/12/Guide-on-engagement-with-NHRIs-in-EU-external-action.pdf>. This is referred to in the EU's 2020 'Annual Report on Human Rights and Democracy', p. 167: <https://www.eeas.europa.eu/sites/default/files/documents/eeas_annual_report_humanity_2021_web.pdf>.

201 European Commission, Q&A: Action Plan for Human Rights and Democracy (n 178).

and evaluation,' is ambiguous. Due to their relative lack of specificity, both the 'Action Lines' of the Action Plan and the text of the Thematic Programme can be interpreted in many and different ways. Without accompanying guidelines on cooperation with, and support for, NHRIs there is no way to consistently bring the EU's objectives to fruition through formal mechanisms, nor is there a set of criteria against which performance can be evaluated.

The EU Human Rights Guidelines, which the 2020 Action Plan,[202] the Thematic Programme, and Commission commentary all refer to, might seem to offer some hope for guidance. Building on human rights norms, lessons learned from experience, and information garnered from academia, the 13 thematic documents that make up the Guidelines offer thematic 'instruments and tools for EU Delegations and Member State Embassies to advance EU human rights policies.'[203] They also offer instructions on how to use the various foreign policy tools available within the EU toolkit for the protection and promotion of human rights. As emphasised in one of the most recent documents, the Guidelines are primarily aimed at informing

> officials and staff members of the EU Institutions, EU Member States and delegations across the world. The guidance is meant for political and operational work in and towards third countries and in multilateral fora, as well as in exchanges with other stakeholders, including civil society. In addition, the guidelines can be a reference for further policy development in the field of human rights.[204]

Included in these stakeholders, one might expect to see NHRIs, and indeed NHRIs are explicitly mentioned in seven of the documents;[205] however, across

---

202 5.2 Monitoring and evaluation (e) 'EU Human Rights Guidelines: Review the EU human rights guidelines, if and when necessary, in particular the EU Guidelines on Human Rights Dialogues with third countries … as required.' EU Action Plan on Human Rights and Democracy 2020–2024, 7.

203 EU Action Plan on Human Rights and Democracy 2020–2024, 7. For a critical assessment, see J. Wouters and M. Hermez, 'EU Guidelines on Human Rights as a Foreign Policy Instrument: An Assessment' in S. Poli (ed.), *Protecting Human Rights in the European Union's External Relations*, CLEER Papers 2016/5, Centre for the Law of EU External Relations, The Hague, 2016, pp. 63–81.

204 European External Action Service and Council of the European Union, EU Guidelines on Safe Drinking Water and Sanitation (EU 2021) p. 4.

205 Council of the European Union, Guidelines to promote and protect the enjoyment of all human rights by lesbian, gay, bisexual, transgender and intersex (LGBTI) Persons, 24 June 2013, Brussels, EU Doc. 11492/13; Council of the European Union, Guidelines on EU Policy Towards Third Countries on Torture and Other Cruel, Inhuman or Degrading Treatment or Punishment, 16 September 2019, Brussels (OR. en) EU Doc. 12107/19; Council of the European Union, EU Human Rights Guidelines on Non-discrimination in External Action, 18 March 2019, Brussels, 6337/19; Council of the European Union, 'Revised EU Guidelines on Human Rights Dialogues with Partner/Third Countries', 22 February 2021, Brussels, 6279/21; European External Action Service and Council of the European Union, EU Guidelines for the Promotion and Protection of the Rights of the Child (EU 2021); European

the other Guidelines, NHRIs are conspicuous by their absence.[206] This being said, there is a clear pattern: over time, the EU has placed more emphasis on the value and importance of cooperation with and protection of NHRIs in the Guidelines. Guidelines from 2008 to 2014 all failed to mention NHRIs;[207] however, those published after 2014 all discuss NHRIs. Moreover, in earlier documents, NHRIs are merely noted as sources of information, while in latter sources, their value is typically laid out more thoroughly. That being said, some recent guidelines have little to say about NHRIs: for example, the Revised EU Guidelines on Human Rights Dialogues with Partner/Third Countries merely state that '[t]he presence of the country's [NHRI] is encouraged [at] … the human rights dialogue.'[208] The EU Guidelines for the Rights of the Child are slightly more generous in the attention they pay to NHRIs; they note that '[t]he EU should support and encourage partner countries to … develop independent institutions on the rights of the child, including [NHRIs]' and emphasise the role played by NHRIs in oversight, as complaint mechanisms, and as information and advice providers *vis-à-vis* the rights of the child.[209] Similarly, the EU Guidelines on Human Rights Defenders include among the EU's practical support 'encouraging and supporting the establishment, and work, of national bodies for the promotion and protection of human rights, established in accordance with the Paris Principles, including, [NHRIs]', while also noting the practical role that NHRIs can play in the protection of human rights defenders.[210] The EU Human Rights Guidelines on Non-discrimination in External Action are more generous still: they not only identify NHRIs as sources of information, *vis-à-vis* assessment, analysis, and reporting, but also offer information on, *inter alia*, the roles, objectives, and functions of NHRIs.[211]

The EU Anti-Torture Guidelines are by far the most detailed when it comes to the discussion of NHRIs. It is worth noting the special connection in many

External Action Service and Council of the European Union, EU Guidelines on Human Rights Defenders (EU 2021); and the EU Guidelines on Safe Drinking Water and Sanitation.

206 See, *inter alia*, Council of the European Union, 'EU Guidelines on promoting compliance with International Humanitarian Law (IHL)', 1 December 2009, Brussels, EU Doc. 16841/09; Council of the European Union, 'EU Guidelines on violence against women and girls and combatting all forms of discrimination against them', 24 November 2008, Brussels, 16173/08; Council of the European Union, 'EU Guidelines on the promotion and protection of freedom of religion or belief', 24 June 2013, Brussels; Council of the European Union, 'EU Guidelines on Death Penalty', 12 April 2013, Brussels, 8416/13; Council of the European Union, 'EU Human Rights Guidelines on Freedom of Expression Online and Offline', 12 May 2014, Brussels.

207 With the exception of the EU Guidelines to promote and protect the enjoyment of all human rights by LGBTI Persons (2013), which lists NHRIs as an important source of information for EU representatives.

208 The EU Guidelines on Human Rights Dialogues with Partner/Third Countries (n 205), p. 15.

209 EU Guidelines for the Rights of the Child (n 205), p. 17.

210 EU Guidelines on Human Rights Defenders (n 205), p. 7.

211 See EU Non-Discrimination Guidelines, pp. 17–18 and 21.

national systems between NHRIs and National Preventive Mechanisms set up under OP-CAT. Guideline 19 to EU actors makes clear that 'the EU promotes and supports the work of NHRIs.'[212] The document also includes so-called 'concrete measures' which the 'the EU will urge third countries to take in order to prohibit torture and other ill-treatment in law and in policy'. These include measures to

> strengthen the role and mandate of [NHRIs] in combating torture; establish national institutions for the prevention of torture ... and consider creating and operating and, where appropriate, strengthening independent national institutions (e.g. human rights ombudspersons or human rights commissions) that can effectively address torture and other ill-treatment[213] and foster 'efficient detention monitoring and oversight mechanisms' by, *inter alia*, allowing 'visits by representatives of civil society and other independent bodies such as ... [NHRIs].'[214]

Although the Guidelines mention NHRIs, they also lack detail about any concrete avenue or forum for EU cooperation with NHRIs. At best, the Guidelines lay out the context-specific value of NHRIs, but they go no further than this.

The Guidelines are mentioned as part of the Action Plan's suggested 'progress monitoring model', which foresees more robust EU monitoring of external EU human rights action, policy, and implementation.[215] This model, thus, offers a potential mode of oversight and review of EU-NHRI activities and cooperation as well as EU policy, programmes, and implementation tools regarding NHRIS. Unfortunately, the Guidelines' lack of specificity is not remedied by the Action Plan's alternative monitoring models. For example, the Council Conclusions on the Action Plan suggest that '[t]he Council will ensure effective follow-up and monitor progress on a regular basis'.[216] However, how the Council will achieve this is not made clear. Alternatively, the Commission has suggested that '[t]he public EU annual report on Human rights and democracy in the world is another effective tool to monitor the progress' of the Action Plan; furthermore, it notes that a 'mid-term review of the [Plan's] implementation is foreseen'.[217] However, neither of these options counter the issues of ambiguity and a lack of specific targets, fora, or structures for EU-NHRI collaboration. Given the absence of alternative monitoring avenues, some kind of review under the Action Plan's progress monitoring model offers a possible, albeit imperfect, mode of oversight. Until a more appropriate and robust approach

---

212 Guideline 19, the EU Anti-Torture Guidelines (n 205), p. 10.
213 Concrete measure 1.2, ibid, p. 22.
214 Concrete measure 2.3, ibid, p. 22.
215 See section 5, EU Action Plan on Human Rights and Democracy 2020–2024.
216 Conclusion 8, Council Conclusions on the EU Action Plan on Human Rights and Democracy 2020–2024.
217 European Commission, Q&A: Action Plan for Human Rights and Democracy.

to monitoring emerges, some kind of oversight under the Action Plan model is 'better than nothing'.

For these reasons, these authors encourage the EU to consider more robust and concrete oversight alternatives, for example, by funding detailed empirical research into the implementation of its external human rights action. In the absence of independent oversight and studies of the Action Plan's implementation, there is a valid concern that rhetoric focused on local, grassroots engagement might fade away in the process of implementation, leaving the external action context with policy documents replete with buzzwords that are not reflected in effective action 'on the ground'.

We call, in particular, for a study into the way in which the Action Plan influences the relationship between the EU and NHRIs in the Union's external action. How are NHRIs actually supported? Where does the money go? How can NHRIs be included in structured dialogue, consultation, implementation, monitoring, and evaluation?

8. CONCLUSION

EU institutions can and should liaise with NHRIs and their regional and international networks when undertaking any human and fundamental rights-based work. From consultation and participation during the development of EU and Member State legislation, to the crafting of third-country human rights strategies and development policy; from cooperation during political dialogues, to information sharing during the crafting of the EU's thematic and annual reports; from advice on means of support and coordination during the implementation of human rights policies, to the provision of support for human rights defenders under threat: all EU human rights action should involve NHRIs. Indeed, NHRIs are one of the actors best positioned to ensure that Union policies make a difference 'on the ground'. NHRIs know the ins and outs of their national context, what works and what does not work; they are familiar with the interests of local people; they understand local priorities and complexities; and they know how best to approach thorny local and regional issues and conflicts. Provided NHRIs are independent, they are interested in fulfilling their mandate to protect and promote human rights, in line with the objectives of the Paris Principles. This puts their objectives in line with EU goals: they are natural allies.

The EU should lean on such allies to better tailor its human rights approaches. While the Union may have been a little slower than other international organisations to publicly espouse the relevance and importance of NHRIs, the past few years have witnessed great change. NHRIs have never before enjoyed such significant public attention at the EU level, but this is not a time to stop. Instead, it is a time to formalise EU-NHRI engagement. This observation does not seek to undervalue years of fruitful informal EU-NHRI cooperation, nor does it ignore the crucial situational support offered by the EU to certain NHRIs. Instead, it is a recognition of how much more could be done. The EU's important groundwork regarding NHRIs must be seen for what it is: a barrel of insufficiently tapped potential which should be directed towards more concrete policy and action aimed at formalising EU-NHRI interactions.

These authors therefore recommend that the EU brings more structure to its cooperation with NHRIs. This should involve concrete and formal mechanisms for EU-NHRI dialogue across a range of topic areas where collaboration might be appropriate. Some of these areas have been discussed in this chapter. However, many other 'areas of collaboration' must be identified. Concrete mechanisms for EU-NHRI collaboration should be procedurally formalised for each area.

Of course, realities and difficulties on the ground,[218] as well as the often unique country-specific relationships that the EU has built with particular NHRIs, cannot be ignored. As such, beyond formal dialogues, the word 'formalisation' is used in a relatively soft sense here. What is required are flexible formalisations, which allow EU delegations and expert external EU actors to identify the best approaches to take when it comes to EU-NHRI interactions. This 'soft formalisation' should take the form of EU policy documents, EU guidelines, and EU toolboxes. These will provide a formal framework for EU-NHRI meetings, practical advice for EU actors taking part in them, and sets of informal guidance and best practices for EU actors engaging with NHRIs in varied situations.

We are thus calling for detailed, clear, and flexible mechanisms for collaboration. To structure such reforms properly, it is imperative that the EU gains a more concrete understanding of the extent to which it actually deals with NHRIs in its daily internal and external action practice. Analysis must take account of similarities and differences in EU-NHRI engagement in both internal and external action as well as different country contexts. Lessons learnt in different contexts have the potential not only to shape general approaches but may also provide inspiration for new strategies and courses of action in other specific contexts. In this respect, it is recommended that the EU direct the FRA to conduct more empirical analysis of EU engagement with NHRIs in its internal relations. We also recommend that the EU sets up analogous EU-led studies in the external relations context.

Beyond this, it is essential that independent eyes also consider NHRI-EU interactions. Our final recommendation therefore centres on funding of independent empirical research into EU-NHRI interactions. The scope for such research is very broad, but it is essential: without it, neither the EU nor NHRIs will benefit from what should be a fruitful relationship.

---

218 Not least a lack of NHRI independence, including NHRI dependence on government and government interference and intervention in NHRI appointments, agendas, and activities.

IN HOC SIGNO VINCES

Identity, Mission and Authority of National Human Rights Institutions in Latin America

Manuel Núñez Poblete

1. INTRODUCTION

Since the mid-1980s, one of the common characteristics of Latin American constitutional design has been the incorporation of autonomous bodies, generally with a parliamentary mandate, that are responsible for promoting knowledge of and respect for human rights by means other than administrative or jurisdictional powers.[1] Normally, these institutions are single-person ombudsmen based on the European model. As Carlos Constenla notes, NHRIs initially followed the 'Iberian model' of Spain and Portugal, in line with the proposals of the Latin American Ombudsman Institute.[2] They subsequently began to adopt their own formats, as a natural consequence of the characteristics of Latin American constitutional and administrative law. At present, it could be claimed that these ombudsmen now constitute the fourth most prevalent branch of state government in the region: ahead of the comptroller generals. Indeed, not even the constitutional courts, which are absent from the three largest countries in the region, enjoy such a widespread presence in Latin America. According to certain legal historians, the 'negative power' of Latin American ombudsmen can trace its roots back to non-sovereign Roman institutions, such as the Tribune of the People, which Jean-Jacques Rousseau described as

1 Rodrigo Uprimny places the start of the wave of constitutional reforms in the mid-1980s and links the general tendency to establish ombudsmen with other circumstances, such as the consolidation of the separation between the Church and the state; the recognition of minorities and indigenous peoples; the incorporation of collective rights; the transformation of the sources of rights; the internationalisation of human rights; the recognition of multiculturalism; and the commitment to equality and non-discrimination, among other factors. See generally R. Uprimny, 'The Recent Transformation of Constitutional Law in Latin America: Trends and Challenges' (2011) 89/7 *Tex.L.Rev.* 1587.

2 See C. Constenla, 'El defensor del pueblo en América Latina' (2015) 12 *Visioni Latinoamericani* 59, 61.

a figure that although 'unable to do anything, is able to prevent everything'.[3] In contrast to the traditional European ombudsman model, which focuses on the submission of complaints filed against deficient state administration, Latin American *defensorías* are vested, from the outset, with the express mandate to protect and promote human rights. Therefore, they are entities that primarily follow the model of the human rights ombudsman.[4]

For comparative purposes, Latin American NHRIs do not differ significantly in age from their European counterparts. They began to appear in the mid-1980s, with the *Procurador de los Derechos Humanos de Guatemala*, or Guatemalan Human Rights Ombudsman, and spread quickly during the 1990s. In contrast to the experiments observed in Canada, Guyana, and Hawaii,[5] which followed the classical ombudsman model, the trend in Latin America has been to establish these institutions as human rights defenders. The reasons behind this vary: from the peace processes that followed bloody civil wars, as is the case in El Salvador and Guatemala, to the transitions to democracy that occurred after the numerous dictatorships elsewhere in the region. The oldest is the Guatemalan NHRI, established in 1985, while the newest is the *Instituto Nacional de Derechos Humanos de Chile*, or National Human Rights Institute of Chile, of 2009. All are characterised by their presence in a region that, with few (albeit notable) exceptions, has confidently ascribed to the move towards universal human rights and that presents high rates of ratification of international treaties, both at the level of the Organization of American States (OAS) and of the UN and the International Labour Organization.

In Latin America, NHRIs have been consolidated with democracy. This stands in contrast to Europe, where the general reluctance to establish these institutions can be explained by doubts about whether there is a genuine need for them: especially in situations where state institutions that already guarantee the rule of law are stable.[6] In numerical terms, there are 14 NHRIs in Central and South America. They are primarily single-person and autonomous entities with a mandated legitimacy that stems from the Congress by which they were constituted; they perform functions of education and of promotion and protection of human rights. The majority are also affiliated to and accredited by the Global Alliance for National Human Rights Institutions (GANHRI).

---

3 P. Catalano, 'Introducción. Poder negativo y Defensor del pueblo' in C. Constenla and R. Pinto Lyra (eds.), *Defensorías del pueblo y ouvidorías en Iberoamérica. Nuevos conceptos y perspectivas*, UFPB, João Pessoa 2012, p. 15.

4 See T. Pegram, 'Diffusion Across Political Systems: The Global Spread of National Human Rights Institutions' (2010) 32/2 *Hum.Rts.Q.* 729, 736; J. Koo and F. Ramírez, 'National Incorporation of Global Human Rights: Worldwide Expansion of National Human Rights Institutions, 1966–2004' (2009) 87/3 *Soc. Forces* 1321, 1325.

5 See L. Reif, *Ombuds Institutions, Good Governance and the International Human Rights System*, Brill, Leiden 2020, p. 524.

6 See G. De Beco, 'National Human Rights Institutions in Europe' (2007) 7/2 *H.R.L.Rev.* 331, 339–40.

The notable exceptions are Cuba, which for decades has not enjoyed an easy relationship with the OAS General Assembly or with the Inter-American Commission on Human Rights (IACHR), and Brazil, which does, however, have two institutions that function in a similar way to the other *defensorías* in the region: one was created in 1964, more than 20 years prior to the current Constitution, and the other in 1993, although this latter entity forms part of the Federal Public Prosecutor's Office.[7]

Table 1. NHRIs in Latin America: Year created, composition type, and GANHRI accreditation

Country	Institution	Year	Composition		GANHRI Accreditation Status
			Single-person	Collegial	
Argentina	*Defensor del Pueblo de la Nación*	1994	X		A
Bolivia	*Defensoría del Pueblo*	1994	X		A
Brazil	*Procuradoria Federal dos Direitos do Cidadão*	1993	X		–
	Conselho de Defesa dos Direitos da Pessoa, now *Conselho Nacional dos Direitos Humanos* (2014)	1964		X	–
Chile	*Instituto Nacional de Derechos Humanos*	2009		X	A
Colombia	*Defensoría del Pueblo*	1991	X		A
Costa Rica	*Defensoría de los Habitantes*	1992	X		A
Dominican Republic	*Defensor del Pueblo*	2001	X		–
Ecuador	*Defensoría del Pueblo*	1998	X		A
El Salvador	*Procuraduría para la Defensa de los Derechos Humanos*	1991	X		A
Guatemala	*Procurador de los Derechos Humanos*	1985	X		A
Honduras	*Comisionado Nacional de Derechos Humanos*	1992	X		B
Mexico	*Comisión Nacional de Derechos Humanos*	1990	X		A
Nicaragua	*Procuraduría para la Defensa de los Derechos Humanos*	1995	X		A
Panama	*Defensor del Pueblo*	1997	X		A
Paraguay	*Defensor del Pueblo*	2001	X		–

(continued)

7 See T. Pegram and N. Herrera, 'Bridging the Gap: National Human Rights Institutions and the Inter-American Human Rights System' in P. Engstrom (ed.), *The Inter-American Human Rights System. Studies of the Americas*, Palgrave, London 2019, p. 169; Reif (n 5) p. 524.

Table 1 *continued*

Country	Institution	Year	Composition		GANHRI Accreditation Status
			Single-person	Collegial	
Peru	*Defensor del Pueblo*	1993	X		A
Uruguay	*Institución Nacional de Derechos Humanos y Defensoría del Pueblo*	2008		X	A
Venezuela	*Defensoría del Pueblo*	1999	X		B

Source: Compiled by the author.

Among the non-accredited institutions are those from Brazil, Paraguay, and the Dominican Republic. Regarding the case of Brazil, the *Procuradoria Federal dos Direitos do Cidadão*, or Federal Ombudsman for the Citizen's Rights, forms part of the Federal Public Prosecutor's Office. It is therefore not autonomous and lacks complete financial independence. Furthermore, no form of civil society participation is envisaged in its structure. Conversely, as of March 2019, the *Defensor del Pueblo*, or People's Defender of Paraguay was recommended for B status by the GANHRI Sub-Committee on Accreditation (SCA).[8] The Dominican Republic initiated negotiations with GANHRI in 2017 regarding its own *Defensor del Pueblo*, but no significant progress has been made to date.

2. BASIC STRUCTURAL ASPECTS

Latin American NHRIs are characterised, in the majority of cases, by their constitutional status. In functional terms, this status evinces their institutional commitment to the promotion and defence of human rights, in a field that goes beyond the traditional jurisdictional guarantees of contemporary constitutionalism. Their ubiquitous presence within the regional doctrine ensures that NHRIs constitute a part of the Latin American *ius constitutionale commune*.[9] In formal terms, this implies that they cannot be replaced or suppressed without a process of constitutional reform, designed to substitute the

---

8 SCA, Report and Recommendations of the Session of the Sub-Committee on Accreditation (SCA), Geneva, 11–15 March 2019. See also the Report and Recommendations of the Session of the Sub-Committee on Accreditation, Geneva, 11–15 March 2019, of the Global Alliance of National Human Rights Institutions, available at: <https://nhri.ohchr.org/EN/AboutUs/GANHRIAccreditation/Documents/SCA%20Report%20March%202019%20-%20EN%20.pdf>.

9 See C. Hakanson, 'Una aproximación al constitucionalismo latinoamericano, características principales y nuevas tendencias' (2017) 100 *Revista de Derecho Político* 1239, 1261. The term '*ius constitutionale commune*' is borrowed from Armin von Bogdandy. See A. von Bogdandy, '*Ius constitutionale commune* en América Latina: una mirada a un constitucionalismo transformador' (2015) 34 *Revista Derecho del Estado* 3.

exercise of ordinary legislative power with that of constitutional power. Thus, their rank within their respective legal system enables a NHRI to enjoy a certain autonomy from the legislative branch.

Table 2. Legal and constitutional status of NHRIs

Country	Legal status	Constitutional status
Argentina		X
Bolivia		X
Brazil	X	
Chile	X	
Colombia		X
Costa Rica	X	X
Cuba		
Dominican Republic		X
Ecuador		X
El Salvador		X
Guatemala		X
Honduras		X
Mexico		X
Nicaragua		
Panama		X
Paraguay		X
Peru		X
Uruguay	X	
Venezuela		X

Source: Compiled by the author.

Constitutional status, however, does not guarantee either the efficacy or the continuity of a NHRI. Indeed, delays by the bodies responsible for making institutional appointments can impede the implementation of a NHRI's mandate, as was the case with the delayed appointment of the ombudsmen to the *Defensorías del Pueblo* of both Paraguay and the Dominican Republic. Moreover, inactivity by Congress in appointing an ombudsman may alter the way in which the existing institution functions, as has been the case in Argentina since 2008.

With the exception of Brazil and Chile,[10] all ombudsmen are appointed by the legislative branch, even if they do not form part thereof, or, in a technical

10 In the case of the National Human Rights Institute of Chile, the number of Council members appointed by both houses of Congress does not reach half that of the total that makes up the senior management body.

sense, do not act on its behalf. Indeed, despite the appointment of ombudsmen by Congress, the *defensorías* do not exercise legislative or jurisdictional functions and can therefore be described as autonomous administrative bodies. This characteristic, which does not dissipate even if legislation assigns them to the sphere of influence of the legislative branch, is also manifested in their power to establish their own internal legal system. While this power does not enable them to alter their functions or composition, it does enable the *defensorías* to administer their own organisation, internal management, and the fulfilment of their functions. From a structural point of view, an additional common feature of the *defensorías* relates to their nature as single-person entities. In the case of Mexico, the NHRI is called the 'Commission' (*Comisión Nacional de Derechos Humanos*) to enhance the fulfilment of its functions. Even though it consists of a Council that is directed by the Commission Chair, the entity is headed by a Chair who is appointed by Congress, while the institution's Council is more consultative than executive in nature. Conversely, the Chilean 'Institute' (*Instituto Nacional de Derechos Humanos*) is entirely collegial or collective, and its senior management consists of a Council, the decisions of which are made by simple majority or, in more significant cases, by qualified majority. The 'Institute and Ombudsman' (*Institución Nacional de Derechos Humanos y Defensoría del Pueblo*) of Uruguay is similar in this respect to its Chilean counterpart, and it has a management Council that is entrusted by law to carry out the main functions of the institution.

Table 3. Composition types

Single-person	Single-person
	Advisory or consultative council (Mexico)
Collegial	Exclusive senior management bodies (Chile and Uruguay)

Source: Compiled by the author.

The management of a NHRI is radically different when its leadership resides in a single authority, rather than in a collegial-type Council. In the former, decisions are made by the head of the institution, while in the latter they are taken by majorities, which may even be responsible for the election and tenure of the Director, as is the case in Chile. This phenomenon, while allowing for greater participation by civil society,[11] may delay the ability of the entity to react in a timely manner and could promote the formation of cliques that strain the functioning of the institution as a whole.

11 When it is permitted to elect at least part of the senior management body.

3. THE FUNDAMENTAL MANDATE OF NHRIs

To promote and protect human rights is the basic function fulfilled by all NHRIs in Latin America: essentially by means of their ability to inform public opinion and denounce human rights violations, disseminate knowledge and education regarding those rights, and process complaints. The sole exception is Chile's NHRI, which was not legislatively designed to receive and process complaints in a systematic or integrated manner. In certain cases, Latin American legislative designs have been concerned with emphasising that the mission of protection is especially important when situations of rights violations are serious, systematic, or cause social upheaval.[12] From among the plurality of forms of mandate design, it is interesting to highlight certain phenomena. This section will refer to two: (i) the coupling of constitutional rights with rights contained in international treaties as the substance of the protection mandate; and (ii) the incorporation of new rights as a sign of the constitutional identity of certain states, which may also lead to changes in the identity of their respective NHRIs.

3.1. NHRIs AS STATE DRIVERS FOR THE INTERNATIONALISATION OF CONSTITUTIONALISM

An important characteristic of Latin American constitutionalism is its fragmentation when it comes to the sources of recognised fundamental rights. Human rights no longer rest exclusively on a single source, i.e., the national Constitution, but are rather built upon a plurality of sources: national Constitutions, international treaties, *jus cogens*, and the jurisprudence of the Inter-American Court of Human Rights (IACtHR), among others. The design of NHRIs has not been immune from this phenomenon of internationalisation of constitutionalism;[13] as a consequence, their mandate to promote and protect rights covers not only domestic but also international rights.

Furthermore, this institutional characteristic is based on the Paris Principles on NHRIs, which expressly consider the duties to encourage the harmonisation

---

12 This is the case with Argentina, Brazil, and Ecuador. See Law Nr. 24,284 of the Republic of Argentina, art 15; Law Nr. 12,986 of the Federal Republic of Brazil, art 2; and Organic Law of the *Defensoría del Pueblo* of Ecuador, art 6. The Ecuadorian law provides:

> 'For the purposes of this law, generalised situations shall be understood as acts that are directed against multiple victims; systematic acts shall be understood as those committed as part of a preconceived plan or policy; and social relevance as acts that, due to the political, social, economic or cultural context in which they occur, generate a high level of concern and impact on human rights and nature, on society or on a specific group, and demand an opportune response.' (Organic Law of the *Defensoría del Pueblo* of Ecuador, art 7.).

13 See J. Kabbler, 'International Constitutionalism' in R. Masterman and R. Schütze (eds.), *Cambridge Companion to Comparative Constitutional Law*, Cambridge University Press, Cambridge 2019, p. 498.

of domestic legislation 'with international human rights instruments' and 'the ratification of these instruments'. While the latter function does not, in itself, lead to an improvement in the overall human rights situation in a country, 'it can create leverage to achieve this'.[14]

International human rights law serves as a major authority for all NHRIs, which act not only as conveyor belts of rules but also of recommendations and interpretations contained in the reports of treaty bodies or in the judgments of courts such as the IACtHR. Thus, international law becomes the invincible authority that makes it possible to justify purely moral opinion, to defeat domestic practices and norms that are contrary to human rights. As a consequence, an interesting relationship emerges here between state Constitutions and international human rights law, where it is possible to observe how the constitutional identity of states becomes diluted by or confronted with this law. Express reference to international treaties can be found in the organic statutes of the NHRIs of Argentina,[15] Bolivia,[16] Chile,[17] Colombia,[18] Costa Rica,[19] the Dominican Republic,[20] El Salvador,[21]

---

14 G. de Beco and R. Murray, *A Commentary on the Paris Principles on National Human Rights Institutions*, Oxford University Press, Oxford 2014, p. 46.

15 The Constitution of the Argentine Nation declares: 'Its mission is the defence and protection of human rights and other rights, guarantees and interests protected by this Constitution and laws'.

16 The Political Constitution of the Plurinational State of Bolivia provides that it is responsible for ensuring the 'validity, promotion, dissemination and fulfilment of individual and collective human rights, as established in the Constitution, laws and international instruments'.

17 Law Nr. 20,405 of the Republic of Chile entrusts the National Human Rights Institute with the promotion and protection of the rights recognised by the Political Constitution and 'the international treaties ratified by Chile and which are in force'.

18 Decree 25 of 2014 of the President of the Republic of Colombia expressly entrusts the Office of the Ombudsman with the responsibility to 'promote compliance with international humanitarian law'.

19 Law Nr. 7,319 of the Republic of Costa Rica defines the Office of the Ombudsman as 'the body responsible for protecting the rights and interests of the inhabitants of the country. This body shall ensure that the operation of the public sector conforms to morality, justice, the Political Constitution, laws, conventions, treaties, covenants signed by the government, and general principles of law'.

20 Law Nr. 19-01 of the Dominican Republic provides:

> 'The essential objective of the Office of the Ombudsman is to safeguard the personal and collective prerogatives of citizens, as enshrined in the Constitution, in the event that these are violated by public administration officials. Likewise, the Office shall safeguard the correct functioning of public administration, so that it conforms to morality and the laws, conventions, treaties, covenants and general principles of law; Among its principal powers, the Office of the Ombudsman will also be responsible for dissemination and education from the perspective of human rights and other prerogatives established in the Constitution of the Republic and the laws, international covenants and other regulations. In this respect, it may act as mediator in well-founded collective complaints and operate in areas where important humanitarian work and entities that provide public services are required'.

21 Decree Nr. 183 of 1992 of the Republic of El Salvador declares that:

> '[F]or the purposes of this law, human rights are understood to be civil and political, economic, social and cultural rights and those of the third generation contemplated in

Guatemala,[22] Honduras,[23] Nicaragua,[24] Panama,[25] Paraguay,[26] and Uruguay.[27] As can be seen, this type of reference is another common characteristic of Latin American ombudsmen. In addition, NHRIs in Latin America are often empowered to recommend the signing or ratification of human rights treaties. This has two important consequences: first, NHRIs are constituted, at the domestic level, as entities that monitor the international obligations of states; second, an innate enthusiasm for the international human rights movement forms part of their institutional DNA. As such, NHRIs are subject to a dual legality: national legality and international legality. Since they are subject to both systems, which may indeed contradict one another, NHRIs must often choose which legality to obey. Usually, it is the international rule that will take precedence, even though the correct doctrine should be to opt for the rule that affords greater protection. This issue is also interesting from the perspective of administrative law, since, although the advisory function must be subject to this same legality, the fact the NHRIs are empowered to suggest the signature or ratification of new treaties drives the advisory role to a level that could be referred to as non-legality, or as being against legality with regards to domestic law, and towards potential international legality.

At this point, this author would like to share a personal experience as a former member of the Council of the Chilean National Human Rights

---

the Constitution, laws and treaties in force; as well as those contained in declarations and principles approved by the United Nations or the Organization of American States'.

22 In 2013, a new duty was added by law to the Human Rights Ombudsman: the responsibility of defending the rights 'defined in international treaties or conventions accepted and ratified by Guatemala'.

23 Decree Nr. 153-95 of the Republic of Honduras provides: 'The National Commissioner for Human Rights is a national institution, established to guarantee the validity of the rights and freedoms recognised in the Constitution of the Republic and the international treaties and conventions ratified by Honduras'.

24 Law Nr. 212 of the Republic of Nicaragua declares: 'The rights included in Section IV of the Constitution and those set forth in Articles 46 and 71 of the same body of law and in other international human rights instruments that may be ratified by the Nicaraguan State in the future are considered protected rights'.

25 Law Nr. 7 of 1997 of the Republic of Panama states that:

> '[t]he Office of the Ombudsman shall safeguard the protection of the rights established in Section III and other rights enshrined in the Political Constitution of the Republic of Panama, as well as the rights provided for in international human rights conventions and the law, by means of overseeing the activities, acts or omissions of public servants and those who provide public services, and shall act in such a way as to ensure they are respected, in line with the terms established by the present law'.

26 According to Law Nr. 631/95 of the Republic of Paraguay, the Office of the Ombudsman 'receives and investigates complaints and claims in relation to the human rights recognised in the Constitution, international treaties and laws'.

27 Law Nr. 18,446 of the Oriental Republic of Uruguay provides that the National Human Rights Institution and Ombudsman is responsible for 'the defence, promotion and protection, in all their extension, of the human rights recognised by the Constitution of the Republic and in the international law'.

Institute. When this NHRI was established, it was necessary to discuss what the institutional focus of its observations would be. The law that created it gave the Institute a dual mission: to protect and promote the rights set forth in the Political Constitution of the Republic of Chile as well as those enshrined in the international treaties ratified by Chile. By 2010, the Constitution was already arousing suspicions in this regard. The act of taking on the task of promoting all the rights established in it, which contains rights of an economic-business nature which are not prevalent in other Constitutions, was not a mission that convinced the entire Council, despite what the law said. The option that the Council chose was to articulate its work on international law and to favour, more often than not, 'international standards' over national prescriptions of rights, thereby rapidly transforming 'international standards' into a common currency of institutional discourse.

3.2. CONSTITUTIONAL AND INSTITUTIONAL IDENTITIES OF NHRIs

An interesting phenomenon that occurs as a result of the internationalisation of constitutional law is the potential dissolution of the legal identity of each state into a common *acquis* tradition: as a result of the penetration of international language into domestic systems.[28] In certain cases, the constitutional identity of domestic legal systems may have more or less depth, but the common denominator tends to make the language of rights a kind of *lingua franca* that does not recognise cultural or political differences between states or which, at least, due to its claim of universality, can reduce the capacity of human rights to shape the constitutional identity of states. In Latin America, however, certain examples remain that show how the trend towards homogenisation is limited through the emergence of new rights paradigms and, consequently, new identities for NHRIs. Indeed, in addition to cases in which these institutions are endowed with powers related to 'public ethics and administrative morality'[29] or

---

28 Scholarship on constitutional identity has been reinvigorated in the 21st century. A study of this concept and its relationship with international human rights law, from a Latin American perspective, can be found in M. Núñez Poblete, 'Introducción al concepto de identidad constitucional y su función frente al derecho supranacional e internacional de los derechos de la persona' (2008) 14/2 *Ius et Praxis* 331. See also C. Calliess and G. van der Schyff (eds.), *Constitutional Identity in a Europe of Multilevel Constitutionalism*, Cambridge University Press, Cambridge 2019; A. Saiz and C. Alcoberro, *National Constitutional Identity and European Integration*, Intersentia, Cambridge 2013; M. Tushnet, 'How do Constitutions Constitute Constitutional Identity?' (2010) 8/3 *ICON* 671; F. Fabbrini and A. Sajó, 'The Dangers of Constitutional Identity' (2019) 25/4 *ELJ* 457.

29 According to the Constitution of the Bolivarian Republic of Venezuela, the Office of the Ombudsman forms part of the bodies that exercise 'citizen power', which are responsible for: '[P]reventing, investigating and sanctioning acts that contravene public ethics and administrative morality; safeguarding good management and legality in the use of public

'morality'[30] – which are not worth exploring here – there are NHRIs that have been mandated to protect collective rights and the rights of nature. For example, the Office of the Ombudsman of Bolivia is responsible for 'promoting the defence of the rights of indigenous and native small-holding farmer nations and peoples, urban and intercultural communities, and Bolivians abroad'.[31] Similarly, the Office of the Ombudsman of the Dominican Republic also contributes to safeguarding the 'collective and general interests established in the Constitution and by law'.[32] In certain cases, such as Bolivia and Ecuador, where legislation recognises the existence of indigenous peoples, the 'intercultural approach' is added as a principle of action of the respective NHRI.

The most interesting case is that of the emerging land and nature ombudsman, which is associated with the 'rights of mother nature'.[33] In Bolivia, the Office of the Ombudsman has made calls to be complemented by the *Defensoría de la Madre Tierra*, or Ombudsman for Mother Nature, created by Law Nr. 71 of 2010[34] and Law Nr. 300 of 2012, which forms part of a 'Plurinational Council to live well in harmony and equilibrium with mother nature'. Ten years after its legal creation, the Ombudsman for Mother Nature is yet to commence its operations: in fact, it was not until 16 September 2019 that a Bill was introduced before the Plurinational Legislative Assembly to enable its establishment.[35] In Ecuador, the country opted to design its NHRI directly as an Office of the Ombudsman responsible for the protection and promotion of human rights 'and the rights of nature'. In effect, the organic law of the Office of the Ombudsman of 2019 requires the implementation of a national mechanism for the prevention, precaution, protection, promotion, and restoration of the rights of nature, or *Pachamama*, with emphasis on the biodiversity of the Amazon, insular, and border regions. In contrast to its Bolivian counterpart, the Office of the Ombudsman of Ecuador has already received complaints and opinions in cases such as the *Bananeras*, *Pacayacu* and *Corridas de Toro*,[36] even prior to the creation of the national mechanism. While it remains premature to pass judgment about the impact of this 'nature-centred' dimension of these

assets, compliance with and application of the principle of legality in all administrative activities of the State, and also promoting education as a process that creates citizenship, as well as solidarity, freedom, democracy, social responsibility and work'.

30 See Law Nr. 7,319 of the Republic of Costa Rica, art 1; Law Nr. 19-01 of the Dominican Republic, art 2.

31 Political Constitution of the Plurinational State of Bolivia, art 218.

32 Constitution of the Dominican Republic, art 191.

33 See M. Tanasescu, *Environment, Political Representation and the Challenge of Rights. Speaking for Nature*, Springer, New York 2016, p. 85. See generally C. Barié, 'Nuevas narrativas constitucionales en Bolivia y Ecuador: el buen vivir y los derechos de la naturaleza' (2014) 59 *Latinoamérica* 9.

34 On the 'Rights of Mother Nature'.

35 Bill Nr. 438/2019–2020.

36 See Resolutions 10-2012, 15-2012 and 1-2013, of the Office of the Ombudsman of Ecuador.

defensorías, here lies a power that undoubtedly separates Latin American NHRIs from their European ombudsmen counterparts. Clearly, the consolidation of this new modality of *defensorías* will depend primarily on the diffusion and influence of the new category of 'the rights of nature' in the region.

3.3. BUILDING *AUCTORITAS*

Another common element of NHRIs in Latin America is the purely moral power of their recommendations and decisions. As the Office of the Ombudsman of Colombia points out, 'the force of the opinions, reports and recommendations stem from the national Constitution, society, its independence, its moral qualities, and its high standing within the State'.[37] NHRIs may not invalidate actions or force the incumbent government to act. At most, their reports can generate a mere obligation to respond, as is the case in Mexico.[38] In short, the force of their opinions is a matter of an 'ethical'[39] or 'persuasive'[40] mandate, endowed with a socially recognised moral power, more akin to *auctoritas* than to *potestas*.[41] This 'authority' is the second tool of persuasion possessed by the NHRIs. Unlike international human rights law, however, *auctoritas* depends entirely on domestic factors. The most sensitive and volatile asset of NHRIs is, thus, their moral authority; accordingly, an interesting game ensues between this and their other major asset, which is the very language of human rights. In effect, if the mission of NHRIs is to build trust in institutions, by promoting accountability through human rights, the success of this mission depends on the very confidence that citizens place in their work. In other words, in order to help rebuild trust in public institutions, NHRIs must be able to generate trust in themselves. As I have heard Roberto Garretón, the 2020 winner of the Chilean National Human Rights Award, say on more than one occasion, 'trust is the only asset that human rights defenders have. Just one mistake is enough for the institution to lose credibility in the eyes of the public'. Clearly, if an NHRI lacks credibility, it becomes extremely difficult to build trust in other institutions.

Building *auctoritas* is, without a doubt, a very slow process. It depends on external factors, such as general confidence in public institutions, which is at historically low levels across the region; the domestic value attributed to GANHRI accreditations;[42] and, above all, internal factors. Among these internal factors, it is necessary to distinguish organic aspects – such as NHRIs'

37 Law Nr. 24 of 1992 of the Republic of Colombia, art 7.

38 See Political Constitution of the United Mexican States, art 102.

39 Organic Law of the *Defensoría del Pueblo* of Ecuador, art 3.

40 Organic Law of the *Defensoría del Pueblo* of Venezuela, art 9.

41 References in the Spanish-speaking world to this distinction are based on the research of Alvaro d'Ors. See A. d'Ors, 'Auctoritas, ΑΥΘΕΝΤΙΑ, Authenticum' (1984) 88 *Estudios clásicos* 375.

42 The importance of this accreditation is not widely understood in the region.

independence, accountability, distance from interest groups (including NGO agendas), proximity to civil society, and compliance with the Paris Principles – from functional aspects. Among the latter, the methodological rigour applied in the construction of standards and in fact-finding processes is a major issue in terms of ensuring that opinions and recommendations are not the result of chance or prejudice. Expressions or actions that may denote ideological biases that are not broadly shared have contributed, rightly or wrongly, to a reduced trust in NHRIs. For example, when the Mexican National Human Rights Commission decided to challenge the constitutionality of Mexico City's regulations on the decriminalisation of abortion, or when the Paraguayan Office of the Ombudsman opposed the 'ideology of gender', criticism arose in favour of the neutrality of the entity, and the consequent threat of a potential crisis of confidence emerged. In Chile, during the initial years of its operations, a lawsuit was filed against the National Human Rights Institute for alleged non-compliance with labour standards. Clearly, this generated a wave of criticism towards the very entity that is not expected to commit errors in the area of human rights. Years later, the fact that its Director declared himself Catholic and against abortion generated even stronger reactions in certain sections of society.

The salaries of staff members, the political bias of its officials or of its focus of attention during monitoring processes, the poor quality of reports, and budget increases not associated with good management results, are just some of the factors that can generate an erosion of trust in NHRIs. On the other hand, it is important to recall that NHRIs are state agencies that are targets, albeit in an indirect manner, of the broader sentiments of distrust that are directed towards public institutions across the region. Indeed, according to data from the Latinobarómetro 2018,[43] confidence in national congresses does not surpass an average of 21 per cent across the region, which is worrying considering that these congresses are responsible for nominating the vast majority of the ombudsmen in Latin America. A fundamental component for the consolidation of trust, in addition to the autonomy of these institutions, is methodological consistency. Invalidated opinions on follow-up or monitoring methodologies will end up as the most resounding institutional failures. Therefore, certain pioneering examples should be noted, such as the Programme for Monitoring and Evaluation of Public Policies on Human Rights;[44] the design of indicators for economic, social and cultural rights, including the rights to health and work;[45] and the steps taken by the Iberoamerican Federation of Ombudsmen

---

43 See Report 2018 of Latinobarómetro Corporation, p. 375. Available at: file:///Users/sebastianlopeze/Downloads/INFORME_2018_LATINOBAROMETRO.pdf.

44 'ProSeDHer' of the Office of the Ombudsman of Colombia, adopted in 2003.

45 See those designed by the Chilean National Human Rights Institute in 2012.

to promote a culture of indicators, these indicators themselves being used to monitor compliance with their recommendations.[46]

At present, Latin American NHRIs are still at the stage of consolidating their domestic authority. Accordingly, no single institution has managed to transcend state borders and become a point of reference in the same way that the Colombian Constitutional Court and the Argentine Supreme Court achieved in their respective times by way of their judgments, which have widely circulated in academic texts as well as the judicial decisions of other high courts throughout the region. Whether NHRIs continue to remain purely domestic authorities, or whether they will assume greater international influence, remains to be seen.

4. NHRIs IN THE INTER-AMERICAN HUMAN RIGHTS SYSTEM

In accordance with the Paris Principles, NHRIs are tasked to cooperate with the UN and the organisations that constitute its human rights system as well as with regional institutions and those from other countries. As interpreted by the SCA,[47] this task includes contributing to the national reports required by regional institutions and international treaty bodies and committees as well as expressing independent opinions on matters, including the submission of shadow reports to states. The importance of the powers assumed by NHRIs in Latin America has been repeatedly emphasised by the IACHR: whether by recommending their assimilation into the ranks of non-state human rights defenders for the purposes of protection,[48] or by positively assessing their

---

46 To be fair, the design of indicators for monitoring compliance with human rights rules is an assessment technique with a short history in national and international practice; indeed, the time when these indicators began to become widespread generally coincided with the boom in Latin American NHRIs. See G. de Beco, 'Human Rights Indicators for Assessing State Compliance with International Human Rights' (2008) 77/1–2 *Nord.J.Int'l L.* 23, 25.
The Office of the UN High Commissioner for Human Rights (OHCHR) offered guidance on this issue in 2012, when almost all NHRIs in the region had been established. See United Nations, *Human Rights Indicators: A Guide to Measurement and Implementation* (UN 2012).

47 See General Observations of the SCA of 21 February 2018, para. 1.4.

48 According to the IACHR:

'The criterion that determines who should be considered a human rights defender is the activity itself. In this sense, those individuals working in State institutions whose functions relate to the promotion and protection of human rights and who, in the exercise of those duties, are victims of acts that directly or indirectly prevent or hamper their work, should receive the same protection as members of civil society who are working in the defense of human rights. This is the case insofar as such acts affect the enjoyment of human rights by society as a whole. Moreover, the Commission takes into account that, in general, public officials working in entities such as human rights offices, ombudsperson's and procurator's offices [*defensorías, personerías, procuradurías*], special human rights prosecutors offices, and the like, who are constantly working to verify the proper functioning of the State and

interventions and follow-ups to the decisions of the Inter-American system.[49] The IACHR has requested provisional measures in favour of human rights defenders;[50] has signed cooperation agreements with the ombudsmen offices of Ecuador (7 January 2020), Colombia (10 December 2018), Guatemala (14 November 2018), and Panama (7 December 2017); and has entered into similar agreements with certain local-level ombudsmen offices, such as those in Oaxaca, Mexico (4 September 2017). Similarly, in the case of the *Human Rights Defender et al v. Guatemala*, the IACtHR emphasised the importance of the role of these defenders, both those which pertain to public institutions and those which act as private parties.[51]

Based on recent practice before the IACHR and the IACtHR, doctrine has recognised that several of the functions of NHRIs are within the area of influence of the Inter-American system.[52] First, it has been observed that, due to their non-jurisdictional status, NHRIs are not to be considered entities that satisfy the right to a legal remedy;[53] nevertheless, it could be said that domestic remedies are exhausted through NHRIs and, therefore, this right becomes activated before the IACHR. Procedurally, the participation of NHRIs, as complainants, representatives of victims, applicants for provisional measures, informants, or witnesses before the IACHR is noteworthy. For such purposes, it is irrelevant whether the entity is a national or local-level institution, where the state is federal in its composition. Given the procedural limitations of the American Convention on Human Rights and the Rules of Procedure of the IACtHR, an NHRI's role before this tribunal is evinced in the submission of *amicus curiae* briefs, its representation of the victims, or in its role as informant in the case of supervision of compliance with judgments

the performance of the authorities in fulfilling their human rights obligations, are more vulnerable to falling victim to hostile acts'.

(Report on the Situation of Human Rights Defenders in the Americas of the IACHR, OAS/Ser. L/V/II.124 Doc. 5 rev.1, 7 March 2006, para. 19.).

49 See: '[The IACHR] is gratified to observe that in exercise of that function, some national institutions have played active roles as driving forces behind decisions taken by the inter-American system and have even intervened as petitioners in filing requests seeking precautionary measures, individual complaints, and as participants in the public hearings held by the Inter-American Commission. The IACHR would encourage ombudspersons in the region to play a more active role in overseeing the international commitments undertaken by their respective States, in accordance with the Paris Principles. It also urges them to increase their participation in and coordination with the inter-American system for the protection of human rights'.
(Second Report on the Situation of Human Rights Defenders in the Americas of the IACHR, OAS/Ser. L/V/II. Doc. 66, 31 December 2011, para. 536.).

50 See e.g., Resolution 67/19 MC 1127/19 of 25 December 2019 of the IACHR.

51 See *Human Rights Defender et al v. Guatemala*, IACtHR, Judgment, 28 August 2014, Series C No. 154, paras. 128–29.

52 See e.g., Pegram and Herrera (n 7) p. 171; Reif (n 5) p. 528.

53 See *Bamaca Velásquez v. Guatemala*, IACtHR, Judgment, 25 November 2000, Series C No. 70.

and advisory opinions.[54] Beyond its normative framework, the possibility of acting within the Inter-American system depends on the domestic regulations of each NHRI, since neither the IACHR nor the IACtHR have power over their respective mandates.

At the international level, whether of investigation before the IACHR or of contentious and advisory proceedings before the IACtHR, regional NHRIs play a role that is no less important than their role played before the UN system. Considering that NHRIs are state entities (and therefore they could potentially be active agents in human rights violations),[55] these regional institutions act in the areas mentioned by providing data and valuable information and context that complainants cannot offer.[56] Clearly, the latter objective is only achieved if the information so provided is truly independent and supported by an appropriate methodology; therefore, when an NHRI represents a victim, whether litigating before the IACHR or the IACtHR,[57] its impartiality will be markedly reduced.

5. CONCLUSION

This chapter is an attempt to characterise the Latin American NHRIs in a general manner. Several common aspects can be seen. These include their parliamentary origins, their normally single-person nature, and their broad mandates to protect and promote human rights. Such common identity traits have allowed NHRIs in Latin America, on the whole, to achieve a level of accreditation that, at a certain point in time, produced even better overall results than their European counterparts. Nevertheless, it should be noted that the incipient phenomenon of the proliferation of thematic or specialised agencies, with a focus on non-discrimination, transparency, indigenous peoples, and children, among other

54 In its advisory opinion 24/17 of 24 November 2017, the participation of several NHRIs and the interesting role of the Office of the Ombudsman of Costa Rica in assisting the Costa Rican state can be observed. See *Gender Identity, and Equality and Non-Discrimination of Same-Sex Couples*, IACtHR, Advisory Opinion 24/17, 24 November 2017.

55 See Reif (n 5) pp. 544–45.

56 A. Buyse, 'The Court's Ears and Arms: National Human Rights Institutions and the European Court of Human Rights' in J. Wouters and K. Meuwissen (eds.), *National Human Rights Institutions in Europe: Comparative, European and International Perspectives*, Intersentia, Cambridge 2013, pp. 173, 177.

57 The Rules of Procedure of the IACtHR provide, in art 37, that the tribunal may appoint an 'Inter-American defender' *ex officio* for alleged victims without legal representation. Since the *Furlán and Family v. Argentina* case of 2011, more than 10 defenders have been appointed in this manner. In 2003, the Inter-American Association of Public Defender Offices was established in Rio de Janeiro, Brazil, to bring together the majority of the criminal justice defence institutions, with the exception of the Office of the Ombudsman of Colombia, which is an NHRI within the terms explained herein. See *Furlán and Family v. Argentina*, IACtHR, Judgment, 31 August 2012, Series C No. 246.

issues, could at some point constitute a threat to the institutional and territorial strength of NHRIs in the region. In comparative terms, there are certain trends in the region that could lead to the appearance of new identities and generations of NHRIs. Although these institutions have an undeniably European origin, the emergence and spread of new rights, such as collective rights or the rights of nature, may generate a fourth category of NHRIs, where the 'h' for 'human' rights is perhaps suppressed or accompanied by an 'n' for 'nature'. As noted previously, this is not so much a reflection of internationalisation as it is a consequence of the particularisation that these institutions undergo, due to the strengthening of the constitutional identity of states.

This chapter has also briefly described the position of Latin American NHRIs *vis-à-vis* the Inter-American Human Rights System. It is at the domestic level that NHRIs can best serve as conveyor belts for international human rights law. Similarly, it is at the domestic level that NHRIs can most readily and effectively contribute to rectify internal practices that may hinder full compliance with national and international human rights obligations. Given that some NHRIs in the region have the power to submit Bills before Congress, as is the case in Bolivia, Colombia, and Peru, or at least to recommend draft BSills, as in Panama, the capacity of these institutions to intervene in the domestic sphere is not insignificant. Therefore, it is no coincidence that the literature attributes to these state actors the function of 'filling' or 'bridging' the gap between the national and international systems.[58]

However, in a context of confrontation between the national and international spheres, NHRIs need to sharpen their hearing and keep a keen lookout to discern which system of rules best recognises and protects human rights in a particular case. In this role, NHRIs are in a better position than the IACHR or the IACtHR: as the two latter institutions merely obey one layer of legality, while NHRIs obey two. In a region that has long suffered the onslaught of dictatorships and where, from time to time, there are reminders that democracy can always be lost, NHRIs are becoming an indispensable instrument.

---

58 K. Meuwissen and J. Wouters, 'Conclusion: Towards a Better Understanding of European NHRIs in a Multi-Layered Human Rights System' in J. Wouters and K. Meuwissen (eds.), *National Human Rights Institutions in Europe: Comparative, European and International Perspectives*, Intersentia, Cambridge 2013, p. 303. See generally Pegram and Herrera (n 7).

(NOTES ON) THE INTER-AMERICAN COURT OF HUMAN RIGHTS, NON-GOVERNMENTAL ORGANISATIONS AND NATIONAL HUMAN RIGHTS INSTITUTIONS

Eduardo Vio Grossi†

1. INTRODUCTION

Three bodies compose the Inter-American Human Rights System, as established by the American Convention on Human Rights (ACHR):[1] the Inter-American Commission on Human Rights (IACHR), the Inter-American Court of Human Rights (IACtHR),[2] and the General Assembly of the Organization of American States (OAS).[3] While the IACHR is mandated to promote the observance and defence of human rights,[4] the IACtHR is granted both contentious and advisory, or non-contentious, jurisdiction,[5] and the General Assembly is tasked with considering the annual report submitted to it by the IACtHR.[6] For the exercise of these powers, the ACHR views the aforementioned bodies in a context in which, due to the period when this treaty was concluded, international society was essentially made up of sovereign states that were and are obliged to respect and ensure respect for the human rights enshrined therein.[7] This is particularly

1 This treaty was signed on 22 November 1968 and entered into force on 22 July 1978. There are currently 23 state parties to the ACHR, 20 of which have accepted the contentious jurisdiction of the Inter-American Court of Human Rights. These are: Argentina, Barbados, Bolivia, Brazil, Chile, Colombia, Costa Rica, the Dominican Republic, Ecuador, El Salvador, Guatemala, Haiti, Honduras, Mexico, Nicaragua, Panama, Paraguay, Peru, Surinam, and Uruguay.

2 See ACHR, art 33.

3 See ibid, art 65.

4 See ibid, art 41.

5 See ibid, arts 62.3 and 64, respectively.

6 See ibid, art 65.

7 See ibid, art 1.1.

the case concerning Articles 1.1, 2, and 35 of the ACHR, among other articles, and, in more specific relation to the IACtHR, Articles 61.1, 65, and 68. Given this context, the treaty provides that only states and the IACHR may be parties to cases in which the IACtHR exercises its contentious jurisdiction.[8]

The Rules of Procedure of the IACtHR (Rules of the Court), however, introduced the possibility for alleged victims of human rights violations to appear before the Court, giving them the opportunity to assert their rights and opinions, and present petitions in an autonomous manner.[9] Subsequently, NGOs began providing support to complainants, or their families, regarding their pleadings, arguments, and evidence. NHRIs of accused states have also provided complainants with support that is similar to that offered by NGOs, including cooperation with the alleged victims or their families. It is this new operational reality at the IACtHR that frames this chapter: a contribution which aims, essentially, to identify and delve into contentious cases submitted to the Court,[10] in particular those that involve the appearance of distinctly domestic entities, such as NGOs and NHRIs. As a consequence, the chapter does not address advisory opinions issued by the Court in the exercise of its non-contentious jurisdiction.[11] Furthermore, it does not assess provisional measures passed in relation to cases, decisions on the supervision of compliance with judgments, or decisions on their interpretation.[12] The Inter-American Defender has also been excluded, as this institution does not constitute an NGO, nor is it a state organ.[13]

---

8 See ibid, arts 62 and 57, respectively.

9 The 1980 version of the Rules of the Court determined that the delegates of the IACHR could be assisted 'by any persons of their choice' (art 21). The 1991 version reiterated this (art 22.1) and added that if those persons assisting the delegates 'include lawyers designated by the original complainant, by the alleged victim or his/her family members', this must be communicated to the IACtHR (art 22.2). The 1996 version stipulated that '[a]t the stage of reparations, the representatives of the victims or their families may present their own motions and evidence autonomously' (art 21). The 2000, 2003, and 2009 versions established that '[a]fter the application has been admitted, the alleged victims, their families or their duly accredited representatives may present their pleadings, motions and evidence autonomously throughout the proceedings' (art 23.1). The current Rules of the Court, approved by it in 2009, state that '[o]nce notice of the brief submitting a case before the Court has been served, in accordance with Article 39 of the Rules of Procedure, the alleged victims or their representatives may submit their brief containing pleadings, motions, and evidence autonomously and shall continue to act autonomously throughout the proceedings' (art 25.1).

10 The case-law of the IACtHR is available at: <https://www.corteidh.or.cr/cf/Jurisprudencia2/busqueda_casos_contenciosos.cfm?lang=en>.

11 For a general overview of NHRI participation in the Inter-American system, see T. Pegram and N. Herrera, 'Bridging the Gap: National Human Rights Institutions and the Inter-American Human Rights System' in P. Engstrom (ed.), *The Inter-American Human Rights System: Impact Beyond Compliance*, Palgrave, London 2019, pp. 171–73.

12 See ACHR, art 63.2; Rules of the Court, art 69; and ACHR, art 67, respectively.

13 Rules of the Court, art 37 states: 'In cases where alleged victims are acting without duly accredited legal representation, the Tribunal may, on its own motion, appoint an Inter-American defender to represent them during the processing of the case'.

Likewise, *amicus curiae* briefs submitted in a personal or individual capacity have not been considered here.

The intention of the chapter is, simply, to provide a general overview of the subject matter, showing, mostly in quantitative terms, the important role that NHRIs and NGOs play in contentious cases adjudicated by the IACtHR. Hopefully, the contribution may be useful for future in-depth studies considering the issue.

2. INTERVENTION OF NGOs

According to the Paris Principles on NHRIs, NHRIs constitute a particular form of civil society participation in the highly significant social issue that is the promotion and protection of human rights. If effective, civil society can rely on NHRIs, as well as NGOs, to reduce any gaps in a government's human rights protection and promotion efforts.[14] Given the close relationship between NHRIs and NGOs, the latter's intervention before the IACtHR sheds some light on how the former may participate in the forum.[15] In contentious proceedings, this can occur in two instances: where an NGO files an *amicus curiae* brief and where it acts as a defender or representative of complainants, alleged victims, or their families.

Amici curiae are covered in Articles 2.3 and 44 of the Rules of the Court.[16] Due to their nature, briefs are filed by third parties to the dispute. Several NGOs have submitted *amici curiae* before the IACtHR, including in the following cases: *Loayza v. Peru*;[17] *Cesti v. Peru*;[18] *Baena et al v. Panama*;[19]

---

14 See G. de Beco and R. Murray, *A Commentary on the Paris Principles on National Human Rights Institutions*, Cambridge University Press, Cambridge 2014, p. 66.

15 The role of civil society before international human rights courts is highlighted in T. Treves *et al* (eds.), *Civil Society, International Courts and Compliance Bodies*, TMC Asser, The Hague 2005.

16 Rules of the Court, art 2.3 says:

> '[T]he expression "*amicus curiae*" refers to the person or institution who is unrelated to the case and to the proceeding and submits to the Court reasoned arguments on the facts contained in the presentation of the case or legal considerations on the subject-matter of the proceeding by means of a document or an argument presented at a hearing'.

17 Ecumenical Foundation for Development and Peace (FEDEPAZ). See generally *Loayza v. Peru*, IACtHR, Judgment, 17 September 1997, Series C Nr. 33. Note: the acronyms used throughout this chapter correspond to the Spanish names of the NGOs mentioned.

18 Center for Legal and Social Studies (CELS) and Center for Justice and International Law (CEJIL). See generally *Cesti v. Peru*, IACtHR, Judgment, 29 September 1999, Series C Nr. 56.

19 Labour Advice Centre of Peru; Economic and Social Rights Center (CDES); CELS; and Colombian Commission of Jurists (CCJ). See generally *Baena et al v. Panama*, IACtHR, Judgment, 2 February 2001, Series C Nr. 72.

Mayagna (Sumo) Awas Tingni Community v. Nicaragua;[20] *Five Pensioners v. Peru;*[21] *Plan de Sánchez Massacre v. Guatemala;*[22] *Herrera v. Costa Rica;*[23] *Canese v. Paraguay;*[24] *Yakye Axa Indigenous Community v. Paraguay;*[25] *Girls Yean and Bosico v. Dominican Republic;*[26] *Mapiripán Massacre v. Colombia;*[27] *Claude et al v. Chile;*[28] *Nogueira de Carvalho et al v. Brazil;*[29]

---

20 Organization of Indigenous Syndics of the Nicaraguan Caribbean (OSICAN) and International Human Rights Law Group.
See generally *Mayagna (Sumo) Awas Tingni Community v. Nicaragua*, IACtHR, Judgment, 31 August 2001, Series C Nr. 79.

21 Human Rights in the Americas and CELS. See generally *Five Pensioners v. Peru*, IACtHR, Judgment, 28 February 2003, Series C Nr. 98.

22 Institute of Comparative Studies in Criminal Sciences of Guatemala (ICCPG) and Center for Research on Justice and Participation (CEJIP). See generally *Plan de Sánchez Massacre v. Guatemala*, IACtHR, Judgment, 29 April 2004, Series C Nr. 105.

23 Independent Journalism Defense Association (PERIODISTAS), Inter-American Press Association (SIP), Global Campaign for Free Expression, and CEJIL. See generally *Herrera v. Costa Rica*, IACtHR, Judgment, 2 July 2004, Series C Nr. 107.

24 Civil Rights Association (ADC) and SIP. See generally *Canese v. Paraguay*, IACtHR, Judgment, 31 August 2004, Series C Nr. 111.

25 National Indigenous Organization of Colombia (ONIC). See generally *Yakye Axa Indigenous Community v. Paraguay*, IACtHR, Judgment, 17 June 2005, Series C Nr. 125.

26 Centre on Housing Rights and Evictions (COHRE), Community Centers of Learning (CECODAP), Latin American and Caribbean Committee for the Defense of Women's Rights (CLADEM), Minority Rights Group International (MRG), Extended Secretariat of the Haitian-Dominican Meeting Network Jacques Viau (REDH) – composed of the Dominican-Haitian Cultural Center (CCDH), Socio-Cultural Movement for Haitian Workers (MOSCTHA), Jesuit Refugee and Migrant Service (SRJM-RD), Dominican Center for Legal Advice and Research (CEDAIL), Association for the Development of Women and the Environment (APRODEMA) – Argentinian Commission for Refugees and Migrants (CAREF), and CELS. See generally *Girls Yean and Bosico v. Dominican Republic*, IACtHR, Judgment, 23 November 2006, Series C Nr. 156.

27 International Center for Transitional Justice (ICTJ) and International Federation for Human Rights (FIDH). See generally *Mapiripán Massacre v. Colombia*, IACtHR, Judgment, 7 March 2005, Series C Nr. 122.

28 ADC, CELS, Access Info Europe, Freedom of Information – Mexico (LIMAC), Impact Litigation Project, and CEJIL. See generally *Claude et al v. Chile*, IACtHR, Judgment, 19 September 2006, Series C Nr. 151. .

29 CEJIL, Front Line – International Foundation for the Protection of Human Rights Defenders, World Organisation Against Torture (OMCT), National Human Rights Movement (MNDH), Organization Una Ventana a la Libertad, José Alvear Restrepo Lawyers' Collective (CCAJAR), Robert F. Kennedy Memorial Center for Human Rights, Miguel Agustín Pro Juárez Human Rights Center (Center PRODH), Committee of Families of the Detained-Disappeared, CDES, Segundo Montes Mozo S.J. Human Rights Documentation Centre (CSMM), Organization Casa Alianza Honduras, Centre for Human Rights Legal Action (CALDH), Venezuelan Programme of Action and Education on Human Rights (PROVEA), Standing Committee for the Defence of Human Rights in Orellana, Interdisciplinary Group for Human Rights (GIDH), Mexican Commission for the Defence and Promotion of Human Rights (CMDPDH), Centre for Democratic Initiatives (CIDEM), Legal Defence Institute (IDL), Association for Human Rights (APRODEH), National Coordinator for Human Rights (CNDDHH), Organization Terra de Direitos, CCJ, Human Rights Coordinating Committee of Paraguay (CODEHUPY), Centre for Human Rights and Environment, Lawyers from Northwest Argentina in Human

La Cantuta v. Peru;[30] *Cantoral and García Santa Cruz v. Peru;*[31] *Kimel v. Argentina;*[32] *Ríos et al v. Venezuela;*[33] *Perozo et al v. Venezuela;*[34] *González et al ('Cotton Field') v. Mexico;*[35] *Usón v. Venezuela;*[36] *Radilla v. Mexico;*[37] *Fernández Ortega et al v. Mexico;*[38] *Rosendo et al v. Mexico;*[39] *Cabrera and Montiel v. Mexico;*[40] *Atala and Daughters v. Chile;*[41]

Rights and Social Studies (ANDHES), CELS, Movement of Dominican-Haitian Women (MUDHA), Human Rights Without Frontiers International (HRWF), Human Rights Network International, and International Association of Lawyers (UIA). See generally *Nogueira de Carvalho et al v. Brazil*, IACtHR, Judgment, 28 November 2006, Series C Nr. 161.

30 IDL. See generally *La Cantuta v. Peru*, IACtHR, Judgment, 26 November 2006, Series C Nr. 162.

31 Flora Tristán Peruvian Women's Centre, Aurora Vivar Association, and the Research and Training Institute for Family and Women (INCAFAM). See generally *Cantoral and García Santa Cruz v. Peru*, IACtHR, Judgment, 10 July 2007, Series C Nr. 167.

32 World Press Freedom Committee and ADC. See generally *Kimel v. Argentina*, IACtHR, Judgment, 2 May 2008, Series C Nr. 177.

33 ADC; World Association of News Publishers; New York City Bar Association; World Press Freedom Committee; and Center of Studies on Law, Justice and Society (Dejusticia). See generally *Ríos et al v. Venezuela*, IACtHR, Judgment, 28 January 2009, Series C Nr. 194.

34 International Association of Broadcasting (IAB), Ibero-American Observatory of Democracy (OID), SIP, New York City Bar Association, and IDL. See generally *Perozo et al v. Venezuela*, IACtHR, Judgment, 28 January 2009, Series C Nr. 195.

35 CEJIL, TRIAL-Track Impunity Always, OMCT, Women's Link Worldwide, Red de Mujeres de Ciudad Juárez Civil Association, Human Rights Watch, International Commission of Jurists, Amnesty International, ICTJ, and REDRESS. See generally *González et al ('Cotton Field') v. Mexico*, IACtHR, Judgment, 16 November 2009, Series C Nr. 205.

36 ADC. See generally *Usón v. Venezuela*, IACtHR, Judgment, 20 November 2009, Series C Nr. 207.

37 Mexican Institute of Human Rights and Democracy (IMDHD), World Association of Community Radios (AMARC-México), Catholics for the Right to Decide (CDD), National Center of Social Communication (CENCOS), Center PRODH, Tlachinollan Mountain Human Rights Centre (Tlachinollan), Centre for Social and Cultural Studies Antonio de Montesinos (CAM), Fundar Centre of Analysis and Research, National Network of Civilian Human Rights Organizations 'Todos los Derechos para Todas y Todos' (RedTDT), Supportive Network Decade Against Impunity, Human Rights Centre Brother Bartolomé de las Casas (FrayBa), and CEJIL. See generally *Radilla v. Mexico*, IACtHR, Judgment, 23 November 2009, Series C Nr. 209.

38 Centro PRODH, Women's Link Worldwide, Argentinian Forensic Anthropology Team (EAAF), and Fundar Centre of Analysis and Research. See generally *Fernández Ortega et al v. Mexico*, IACtHR, Judgment, 30 August 2010, Series C Nr. 215.

39 Fundar Centre of Analysis and Research, Bar Human Rights Committee, Solicitors International Human Rights Group, Lawyers Rights Watch Canada, Women's Link Worldwide, and International Litigation Programme of CLADEM. See generally *Rosendo et al v. Mexico*, IACtHR, Judgment, 31 August 2010, Series C Nr. 216.

40 Association for the Prevention of Torture, CMDPDH, Mexican Centre for Environmental Law (CEMDA), Inter-American Association for Environmental Defense (AIDA), International Forensics Program of Physicians for Human Rights, EarthRights International, and Environmental Defender Law Center. See generally *Cabrera and Montiel v. Mexico*, IACtHR, Judgment, 26 November 2010, Series C Nr. 220.

41 Ombudsgay and Nueva Política civil association. See generally *Atala and girls v. Chile*, IACtHR, Judgment, 24 February 2012, Series C Nr. 239.

Fornerón and Daughter v. Argentina;[42] *Artavia et al v. Costa Rica*;[43] *Santo Domingo Massacre v. Colombia*;[44] *Mendoza et al v. Argentina*;[45] *García Lucero et al v. Chile*;[46] *Operation Genesis v. Colombia*;[47] *Expelled Dominicans and Haitians v. Dominican Republic*;[48] *Gonzáles Lluy et al v. Ecuador*;[49] *López Lone et al v. Honduras*;[50] *Duque v. Colombia*;[51]

---

42 Adoptar Foundation. See generally *Fornerón and Daughter v. Argentina*, IACtHR, Judgment, 27 April 2012, Series C Nr. 242.

43 Center for Reproductive Rights, Group in Favor of IVF, the Associazione Luca Coscioni per la Libertà di Ricerca Cientifica, Catholics for Choice, Institute for Solidarity and Human Rights (ISDEH), International Centre for the Legal Protection of Human Rights INTERIGHTS, International Commission of Jurists, Derecho a Decidir Collective, Dejusticia, Heartland Alliance for Human Needs and Human Rights, AKAHATÁ Working Group on Sexuality and Gender, Promujer y Derechos Humanos civil association, and Equal Rights Trust. See generally *Artavia et al v. Costa Rica*, IACtHR, Judgment, 28 November 2012, Series C Nr. 257.

44 Coalition Against the Involvement of Children and Young Persons in the Armed Conflict in Colombia (COALICO). See generally *Santo Domingo Massacre v. Colombia*, IACtHR, Judgment, 30 November 2012, Series C Nr. 259.

45 ADC, Amnesty International, and Collective for the Rights of Children and Young Persons. See generally *Mendoza et al v. Argentina*, IACtHR, Judgment, 14 May 2013, Series C Nr. 260.

46 Union of Former Political Prisoners of Chile (UNExPP). See generally *Garcia Lucero et al v. Chile*, IACtHR, Judgment, 28 August 2013, Series C Nr. 267.

47 ICTJ; Confesión Voluntariado Misionero Cristiano MANOS UNIDAS; Colombia-Europe-United States Coordination Group (CCEEU) – composed of CCAJAR, GIDH, Corporation for Judicial Freedom (CJL), Yira Castro Legal Corporation (CJYC), REINICIAR Corporation, Association for Alternative Social Promotion (MINGA), Humanidad Vigente Legal Corporation (HVCJ), and member organisations of the Working Group on Extrajudicial Executions of CCEEU; CCJm; and Impact Litigation Project. See generally *Operation Genesis v. Colombia*, IACtHR, Judgment, 20 November 2013, Series C Nr. 270.

48 RFK International Strategic Litigation Unit, CELS, Fundar Centre of Analysis and Research, Latin American Council of Students of International and Comparative Law Dominican Republic Chapter (COLADIC-RD), Caribbean Institute for Human Rights, Centre for Agricultural Training and Social Action (CEFASA), Solidaridad Fronteriza, and Jesuit Migration Network. See generally *Expelled Dominicans and Haitians v. Dominican Republic*, IACtHR, Judgment, 28 August 2014, Series C Nr. 282.

49 Dejusticia, Human Rights for All Lawyers' Association and Equality and Justice Civil Association (ACIJ). See generally *Gonzáles Lluy et al v. Ecuador*, IACtHR, Judgment, 1 September 2015, Series C Nr. 298.

50 Corporación Fundamental centre for justice and human rights, ADC, ACIJ, and Ibero-American Network of Judges (REDIJ). See generally *López Lone et al v. Honduras*, IACtHR, Judgment, 5 October 2015, Series C Nr. 302.

51 International Gay and Lesbian Human Rights Commission, Alliance Defending Freedom, Colombia Diversa, Heartland Alliance for Human Needs and Human Rights, Venezuela Diversa civil association, United and Strong Inc., Promoción de la Mujer / Taller de Comunicación Mujer Corporation, Society Against Sexual Orientation Discrimination (SASOD), Mujer y Salud Collective, Aireana Group for Lesbian Rights, United Belize Advocacy Movement, Latin American Space for Sexuality and Rights (MULABI), AKAHATÁ Working Group on Sexuality and Gender, Ovejas Negras Collective, Centre for the Promotion and Defence of Sexual and Reproductive Rights (PROMSEX), National Network of Black LGBT Persons (RENAF), Latin American and Caribbean Network of Transgender People (REDLACTRANS), Red Trans Peru, Jamaica Forum of Lesbians, All-Sexuals and Gays (J-FLAG), Panamanian Association of Trans People, Panambí association, and ALFIL

Pollo et al v. Peru;[52] *Yarce et al v. Colombia*;[53] *Gómez Murillo et al v. Costa Rica*;[54] *Chichupac Village and Neighboring Communities of Rabinal v. Guatemala*;[55] *Acosta et al v. Nicaragua*;[56] *Vereda de la Esperanza v. Colombia*;[57] *San Miguel et al v. Venezuela*;[58] *Carvajal et al v. Colombia*;[59] *Herzog et al v. Brazil*;[60] *López Soto et al v. Venezuela*;[61] *Isaza et al v. Colombia*;[62] *Alvarado et al v. Mexico*;[63] and *Women Victims of Sexual Torture in Atenco v. Mexico*.[64]

---

association. See generally *Duque v. Colombia*, IACtHR, Judgment, 26 February 2016, Series C Nr. 310.

52 PROMSEX and Latin American Consortium against Unsafe Abortion (CLACAI). See generally *Pollo et al v. Peru*, IACtHR, Judgment, 21 October 2016, Series C No. 319.

53 International Commission of Jurists, CEJIL, Earth Rights International, and REINICIAR Corporation. See generally *Yarce et al v. Colombia*, IACtHR, Judgment, 22 November 2016, Series C Nr. 325.

54 Group in Favor of IVF. See generally *Gómez Murillo et al v Costa Rica*, IACtHR, Judgment, 29 November 2016, Series C Nr. 326.

55 Impunity Watch and REINICIAR Corporation. See generally *Members of the Chichupac Village and Neighboring Communities of the Rabinal Municipality v. Guatemala*, IACtHR, Judgment, 30 November 2016, Series C Nr. 328.

56 Group of organisations referred to as 'Communal and Territorial Authorities of the Indigenous and Afro-descendant Peoples of the Northern and Southern Autonomous Regions of the Nicaraguan Caribbean Coast'. See generally *Acosta et al v. Nicaragua*, IACtHR, Judgment, 25 March 2017, Series C Nr. 334.

57 Colombian Interdisciplinary Team for Forensic Work and Psychosocial Assistance (EQUITAS). See generally *Vereda de la Esperanza v. Colombia*, IACtHR, Judgment, 31 August 2017, Series C Nr. 341.

58 Human Rights Watch. See generally *San Miguel et al v. Venezuela*, IACtHR, Judgment, 8 February 2018, Series C Nr. 348.

59 Colombian Association of News Publishers (ANDIARIOS), Argentinian Press Association (ADEPA), IAB, Chilean National Press Association (ANP), Peruvian Press Council (CPP), Press and Society Institute (IPYS), and International Freedom of Expression Exchange (IFEX). See generally *Carvajal et al v. Colombia*, IACtHR, Judgment, 13 March 2018, Series C Nr. 352.

60 ARTICLE 19. See generally *Herzog v. Brazil*, IACtHR, Judgment, 15 March 2018, Series C Nr. 353.

61 Observation and Action Network for Women's Right to a Life Free of Violence (Red Naranja), Organization Equivalencias en Acción, Venezuelan Association for Alternative Sex Education (AVESA), Center for Justice and Peace (CEPAZ), Hispanic American Center for Women (FREYA), Mujeres en Línea Civil Association, Affirmative Union (UNAF), PROVEA, CIVILIS Derechos Humanos, Research and Gender Studies Unit (Bella Carla Jirón Camacaro), Escuela de Formación Obrera (Priscila López), Venezuelan Observatory for Women's Human Rights, PROMSEX, OMCT, and Women's Link Worldwide. See generally *López Soto et al v. Venezuela*, IACtHR, Judgment, 8 February 2018, Series C Nr. 348.

62 National Trade Union School (ENS). See generally *Isaza et al v. Colombia*, IACtHR, Judgment, 20 November 2018, Series C Nr. 363.

63 Washington Office on Latin America (WOLA), Amnesty International, Centre PRODH, and Movement for Our Disappeared in Mexico. See generally *Alvarado et al v. Mexico*, IACtHR, Judgment, 28 November 2018, Series C Nr. 370.

64 Women's Link Worldwide, ARTICLE 19 (Office for Mexico and Central America), Fundar Centre of Analysis and Research, CELS, WOLA, Amnesty International, and Association to Stop Kidnapping. See generally *Women Victims of Sexual Torture in Atenco v. Mexico*, IACtHR, Judgment, 28 November 2018, Series C Nr. 371.

NGOs have also assumed representative and defence roles on behalf of complainants, alleged victims, or their families in numerous cases. Three periods can be distinguished, depending on the applicable regulatory standard: 1995–2000, 2001–2010, and 2011–2020. Examples of NGO representation and defence in the first period (1995–2000) include the following cases: *El Amparo v. Venezuela*;[65] *Castillo v. Peru*;[66] *Caracazo v. Venezuela*;[67] and *Durand and Ugarte v. Peru*.[68] The case-law was more extensive during the second period (2001–2010) and included: *'The Last Temptation of Christ' v. Chile*;[69] *Barrios Altos v. Peru*;[70] *Las Palmeras v. Colombia*;[71] *Five Pensioners v. Peru*;[72] *Bulacio v. Argentina*;[73] *Mack v. Guatemala*;[74] *Urrutia v. Guatemala*;[75] *Plan de Sánchez Massacre v. Guatemala*;[76] *19 Tradesmen v. Colombia*;[77] *Carpio et al v. Guatemala*;[78] *Serrano Sisters v. El Salvador*;[79] *Huilca v. Peru*;[80] *Yakye Axa Indigenous Community v. Paraguay*;[81]

65 PROVEA, Americas Watch, and CEJIL. See generally *El Amparo v. Venezuela*, IACtHR, Judgment, 18 January 1995, Series C Nr. 19.

66 IDL. See generally *Castillo v. Peru*, IACtHR, Judgment, 3 November 1997, Series C Nr. 34.

67 Committee of Relatives of Victims of the Events of February/March 1989 (COFAVIC), CEJIL, and Human Rights Watch. See generally *Caracazo v. Venezuela*, IACtHR, Judgment, 11 November 1999, Series C Nr. 58.

68 IDL and CEJIL. See generally *Durand and Ugarte v. Peru*, IACtHR, Judgment, 16 August 2000, Series C Nr. 68.

69 Association of Lawyers for Public Liberties A.G. and CEJIL. See generally *'The Last Temptation of Christ' (Olmedo et al) v. Chile*, IACtHR, Judgment, 5 February 2001, Series C Nr. 73.

70 National Human Rights Coordinator. See generally *Barrios Altos v. Peru*, IACtHR, Judgment, 30 November 2001, Series C Nr. 87.

71 CCJ and CEJIL. See generally *Las Palmeras v. Colombia*, IACtHR, Judgment, 6 December 2001, Series C Nr. 90.

72 Labour Advisory Center (CEDAL) and CEJIL. See generally *Five Pensioners v. Peru*, IACtHR, Judgment, 28 February 2003, Series C Nr. 98.

73 Coordinator against Police and Institutional Repression (CORREPI), CELS, and CEJIL. See generally *Bulacio v. Argentina*, IACtHR, Judgment, 18 September 2003, Series C Nr. 100.

74 Lawyers Committee for Human Rights and CEJIL. See generally *Mack v. Guatemala*, IACtHR, Judgment, 25 November 2003, Series C Nr. 101.

75 CALDH. See generally *Urrutia v. Guatemala*, IACtHR, Judgment, 27 November 2003, Series C Nr. 103.

76 CALDH. See generally *Plan de Sánchez Massacre v. Guatemala*, IACtHR, Judgment, 29 April 2004, Series C Nr. 105.

77 CCJ and CEJIL. See generally *19 Tradesmen v. Colombia*, IACtHR, Judgment, 5 July 2004, Series C Nr. 109.

78 CEJIL. See generally *Carpio et al v. Guatemala*, IACtHR, Judgment, 22 November 2004, Series C Nr. 117.

79 Association for the Search of Disappeared Children (Pro-Búsqueda) and CEJIL. See generally *Serrano Sisters v. El Salvador*, IACtHR, Judgment, 1 March 2005, Series C Nr. 120.

80 Peruvian Human Rights Commission (COMISEDH) and CEJIL. See generally *Huilca v. Peru*, IACtHR, Judgment, 3 March 2005, Series C Nr. 121.

81 Tierraviva a los Pueblos Indígenas del Chaco ('Tierraviva') and CEJIL. See generally *Yakye Axa Indigenous Community v. Paraguay*, IACtHR, Judgment, 17 June 2005, Series C Nr. 125.

Moiwana Community v. Surinam;[82] *Yatama v. Nicaragua*;[83] *Acosta v. Ecuador*;[84] *Girls Yean and Bosico v. Dominican Republic*;[85] *Blanco et al v. Venezuela*;[86] *Gómez Palomino v. Peru*;[87] *Pueblo Bello Massacre v. Colombia*;[88] *López Álvarez v. Honduras*;[89] *Sawhoyamaxa Indigenous Community v. Paraguay*;[90] *Baldeón v. Peru*;[91] *Montero-Anguren (Detention Center of Catia) v. Venezuela*;[92] *Goiburú et al v. Paraguay*;[93] *Vargas Areco v. Paraguay*;[94] *Nogueira de Carvalho et al v. Brazil*;[95] *Rochela Massacre v. Colombia*;[96] *Zambrano et al v. Ecuador*;[97] *Escué v. Colombia*;[98] *Cantoral and García Santa Cruz v. Peru*;[99] *Kimel v. Argentina*;[100] *Neptune v. Haiti*;[101]

---

82 Moiwana '86, Association Moiwana, and Forest Peoples Programme. See generally *Moiwana Community v. Surinam*, IACtHR, Judgment, 15 June 2005, Series C Nr. 124.

83 Nicaraguan Centre for Human Rights (CENID) and CEJIL. See generally *Yatama v. Nicaragua*, IACtHR, Judgment, 23 June 2005, Series C Nr. 127.

84 Ecumenical Human Rights Commission (CEDHU). See generally *Acosta v. Ecuador*, IACtHR, Judgment, 24 June 2004, Series C Nr. 129.

85 MUDHA and CEJIL. See generally *Girls Yean and Bosico v. Dominican Republic*, IACtHR, Judgment, 8 September 2005, Series C Nr. 130.

86 APRODEH. See generally *Blanco et al v. Venezuela*, IACtHR, Judgment, 28 November 2005, Series C Nr. 138.

87 COFAVIC and CEJIL. See generally *Gómez Palomino v. Peru*, IACtHR, Judgment, 22 November 2005, Series C Nr. 136.

88 Association of Relatives of the Detained and Disappeared (ASFADDES), CCJ, and CEJIL. See generally *Pueblo Bello Massacre v. Colombia*, IACtHR, Judgment, 31 January 2006, Series C Nr. 140.

89 Honduran Black Fraternal Organisation (OFRANEH). See generally *López Álvarez v. Honduras*, IACtHR, Judgment, 1 February 2006, Series C Nr. 141.

90 APRODEH. See generally *Sawhoyamaxa Indigenous Community v. Paraguay*, 29 March 2006, IACtHR, Judgment, Series C Nr. 146.

91 'Tierraviva' (n 81). See generally *Baldeón v. Peru*, IACtHR, Judgment, 6 April 2006, Series C Nr. 147.

92 COFAVIC and CEJIL. See generally *Montero (Detention Center of Catia) v. Venezuela*, IACtHR, Judgment, 5 July 2006, Series C Nr. 150.

93 Committee of Churches for Emergency Assistance (CIPAE) and Global Rights Partners for Justice. See generally *Goiburú et al v. Paraguay*, IACtHR, Judgment, 22 September 2006, Series C Nr. 153.

94 Paraguayan Peace and Justice Service (SERPAJ PY) and CEJIL. See generally *Vargas Areco v. Paraguay*, IACtHR, Judgment, 26 September 2006, Series C Nr. 155.

95 Centre for Human Rights and Popular Memory (CDHMP) and Global Justice. See generally *Nogueira de Carvalho et al v. Brazil*, IACtHR, Judgment, 28 November 2006, Series C Nr. 161.

96 CCAJAR and CEJIL. See generally *Rochela Massacre v. Colombia*, IACtHR, Judgment, 11 May 2007, Series C Nr. 163.

97 CEDHU. See generally *Zambrano et al v. Ecuador*, IACtHR, Judgment, 4 July 2007, Series C Nr. 166.

98 CCAJAR. See generally *Escué v. Colombia*, IACtHR, Judgment, 4 July 2007, Series C Nr. 165.

99 APRODEH. See generally *Cantoral and García Santa Cruz v. Peru*, IACtHR, Judgment, 10 July 2007, Series C Nr. 167.

100 CELS and CEJIL. See generally *Kimel v. Argentina*, IACtHR, Judgment, 2 May 2008, Series C Nr. 177.

101 Institute for Justice and Democracy in Haiti. See generally *Neptune v. Haiti*, IACtHR, Judgment, 6 May 2008, Series C Nr. 180.

Tiu v. Guatemala;[102] *Valle et al v. Colombia;*[103] *Acevedo et al (Discharged and Retired Employees of the Office of the Comptroller) v. Peru;*[104] *Escher et al v. Brazil;*[105] *Anzualdo v. Peru;*[106] *Garibaldi v. Brazil;*[107] *González et al ('Cotton Field') v. Mexico;*[108] *Radilla v. Mexico;*[109] *Las Dos Erres Massacre v. Guatemala;*[110] *Cepeda v. Colombia;*[111] *Xákmok Kásek Indigenous Community v. Paraguay;*[112] *Fernández Ortega et al v. Mexico;*[113] *Rosendo et al v. Mexico;*[114] *Gómes Lund et al v. Brazil;*[115] and *Cabrera and Montiel v. Mexico.*[116]

As for the third period (2011–2020), NGO representation and defence of complainants, alleged victims, or their families occurred in the following cases:

---

102 CALDH. See generally *Tiu v. Guatemala*, IACtHR, Judgment, 26 November 2008, Series C Nr. 190.

103 GIDH and CCJ. See generally *Valle et al v. Colombia*, IACtHR, Judgment, 27 November 2008, Series C Nr. 192.

104 CEDAL. See generally *Discharged and Retired Employees of the Comptroller v. Peru*, IACtHR, Judgment, 1 July 2009, Series C Nr. 198.

105 Pastoral Land Commission (CPT), Global Justice, Landless Workers Movement (MST), National Network of People's Lawyers (RENAP), and Terra de Direitos. See generally *Escher et al v. Brazil*, IACtHR, Judgment, 6 July 2009, Series C Nr. 200.

106 APRODEH and CEJIL. See generally *Anzualdo v. Peru*, IACtHR, Judgment, 22 September 2009, Series C Nr. 202.

107 MST, CPT, Global Justice, and Organization Terra de Direitos. See generally *Garibaldi v. Brazil*, IACtHR, Judgment, 23 September 2009, Series C Nr. 203.

108 National Association of Democratic Lawyers (ANAD), Centre for the Comprehensive Development of Women (CEDIMAC), CLADEM, and Citizens' Network for Non-Violence and Human Dignity (Red Ciudadana). See generally *González et al ('Cotton Field') v. Mexico*, IACtHR, Judgment, 16 November 2009, Series C Nr. 205.

109 CMDPDH and Association of Relatives of Disappeared Detainees and Victims of Violations of Human Rights in Mexico. See generally *Radilla v. Mexico*, IACtHR, Judgment, 23 November 2009, Series C Nr. 209.

110 CEJIL and Association of Relatives of the Detained-Disappeared of Guatemala (FAMDEGUA). See generally *Las Dos Erres Massacre v. Guatemala*, IACtHR, Judgment, 24 November 2009, Series C Nr. 211.

111 CCAJAR and Manuel Cepeda Vargas Foundation. See generally *Cepeda v. Colombia*, IACtHR, Judgment, 26 May 2010, Series C Nr. 213.

112 'Tierraviva' (n 81). See generally *Xákmok Kásek Indigenous Community v. Paraguay*, IACtHR, Judgment, 24 August 2010, Series C Nr. 214.

113 'Tlachinollan', Organization of Tlapaneco/Me'phaa Indigenous People, and CEJIL. See generally *Fernández Ortega et al v. Mexico*, IACtHR, Judgment, 30 August 2010, Series C Nr. 215.

114 'Tlachinollan', Organization of Tlapaneco/Me'phaa Indigenous People, and CEJI. See generally *Rosendo et al v. Mexico*, IACtHR, Judgment, 31 August 2010, Series C Nr. 216.

115 Torture Never Again group from Rio de Janeiro, Commission of Relatives of the Politically Deceased and Disappeared Persons of the Institute of Studies on State Violence, and CEJIL. See generally *Gómes Lund et al v. Brazil*, IACtHR, Judgment, 24 November 2010, Series C Nr. 219.

116 Center PRODH and Tlachinollan. See generally *Cabrera and Montiel v. Mexico*, IACtHR, Judgment, 26 November 2010, Series C Nr. 220.

Vera et al v. Ecuador;[117] *Mejía v. Ecuador*;[118] *Torres et al v. Argentina*;[119] *Contreras et al v. El Salvador*;[120] *Barrios Family v. Venezuela*;[121] *Fontevecchia and D'Amico v. Argentina*;[122] *García and Family Members v. Guatemala*;[123] *Fornerón and Daughter v. Argentina*;[124] *Díaz Peña v. Venezuela*;[125] *Palma et al v. Ecuador*;[126] *Uzcátegui et al v. Venezuela*;[127] *Río Negro Massacre v. Guatemala*;[128] *Dorzema et al v. Dominican Republic*;[129] Gudiel et al *(Military Dossier) v. Guatemala*;[130] *Santo Domingo Massacre v. Colombia*;[131] *Afro-Descendant Communities Displaced from the Cacarica River Basin (Operation Genesis) v. Colombia*;[132] *Gutiérrez and Family v. Argentina*;[133] *Osorio and Family Members v. Peru*;[134] *García Cruz and Sánchez Silvestre v. Mexico*;[135] *Véliz et al v. Guatemala*;[136]

---

[117] CEDHU. See generally *Vera et al v. Ecuador*, IACtHR, Judgment, 19 May 2011, Series C Nr. 226.

[118] CEDHU. See generally *Mejía v. Ecuador*, IACtHR, Judgment, 5 July 2011, Series C Nr. 228.

[119] AMICIS Legal and Social Clinic of Patagonia. See generally *Torres et al v. Argentina*, IACtHR, Judgment, 26 August 2011, Series C Nr. 229.

[120] Pro-Búsqueda and CEJIL. See generally *Contreras et al v. El Salvador*, IACtHR, Judgment, 31 August 2011, Series C Nr. 232.

[121] COFAVIC, CEJIL, and Justice and Peace Commission. See generally *Barrios Family v. Venezuela*, IACtHR, Judgment, 24 November 2011, Series C Nr. 237.

[122] CELS. See generally *Fontevecchia and D'Amico v. Argentina*, IACtHR, Judgment, 29 November 2011, Series C Nr. 238.

[123] Mutual Support Group (GAM). See generally *García and Family Members v. Guatemala*, IACtHR, Judgment, 29 November 2012, Series C Nr. 258.

[124] Centre for Social and Political Human Development Studies (CESPPEDH). See generally *Fornerón and Daughter v. Argentina*, IACtHR, Judgment, 27 April 2012, Series C Nr. 242.

[125] Venezuela Awareness Foundation. See generally *Díaz Peña v. Venezuela*, IACtHR, Judgment, 26 June 2012, Series C Nr. 244.

[126] CEDHU. See generally *Palma et al v. Ecuador*, IACtHR, Judgment, 3 September 2012, Series C Nr. 247.

[127] COFAVIC and CEJIL. See generally *Uzcátegui et al v. Venezuela*, IACtHR, Judgment, 3 September 2012, Series C Nr. 249.

[128] Association for the Comprehensive Development of Victims of Violence in the Verapaces – Maya Achí (ADIVIMA). See generally *Río Negro Massacre v. Guatemala*, IACtHR, Judgment, 4 September 2012, Series C Nr. 250.

[129] Myrna Mack Foundation. See generally *Dorzema et al v. Dominican Republic*, IACtHR, Judgment, 24 October 2012, Series C Nr. 251.

[130] Support Group for Refugees and Repatriates and CCDH. See generally *Military Dossier v. Guatemala*, IACtHR, Judgment, 20 November 2012, Series C Nr. 253.

[131] CCAJAR, HVCJ, Joel Sierra Human Rights Foundation, and MINGA. See generally *Santo Domingo Massacre v. Colombia*, IACtHR, Judgment, 30 November 2012, Series C Nr. 259.

[132] Inter-Church Justice and Peace Commission. See generally *Operation Genesis v. Colombia*, IACtHR, Judgment, 20 November 2013, Series C Nr. 270.

[133] CELS. See generally *Gutiérrez and Family v. Argentina*, IACtHR, Judgment, 25 November 2013, Series C Nr. 271.

[134] APRODEH. See generally *Osorio and Family Members v. Peru*, IACtHR, Judgment, 26 November 2013, Series C Nr. 274.

[135] Lawyers for Justice and Human Rights (AJDH), Legal Services and Research and Juridical Studies (SLIEJ), and CEJIL. See generally *García Cruz and Sánchez Silvestre v. Mexico*, IACtHR, Judgment, 26 November 2013, Series C Nr. 273.

[136] Network of Non-Violence against Women in Guatemala (REDNOVI) and CEJIL. See generally *Véliz et al v. Guatemala*, IACtHR, Judgment, 19 May 2014, Series C Nr. 277.

Expelled Dominicans and Haitians v. Dominican Republic;[137] *Rochac et al v. El Salvador*;[138] *Kuna of Madungandí and Emberá of Bayano and their Members v. Panama*;[139] *Tarazona et al v. Peru*;[140] *Disappeared from the Palace of Justice v. Colombia*;[141] *Espinoza v. Peru*;[142] *Cruz et al v. Peru*;[143] *Canales et al v. Peru*;[144] *Garífuna Community of Punta Piedra and its Members v. Honduras*;[145] *García Ibarra et al v. Ecuador*;[146] *Quispialaya v. Peru*;[147] *Duque v. Colombia*;[148] *Tenorio et al v. Peru*;[149] *Herrera et al v. Ecuador*;[150] *Yarce et al v. Colombia*;[151] *Valencia et al v. Ecuador*;[152] *I.V. v. Bolivia*;[153] *Chichupac Village and Neighboring Communities of Rabinal v. Guatemala*;[154] *Vásquez Durand et al v. Ecuador*;[155]

---

137 National Coalition for Haitian Rights (NCHR), MUDHA, Repatriates and Refugees Support Group (GARR), and CEJIL. See generally *Expelled Dominicans and Haitians v. Dominican Republic*, IACtHR, Judgment, 28 August 2014, Series C Nr. 282.

138 Pro-Búsqueda. See generally *Rochac et al v. El Salvador*, IACtHR, Judgment, 14 October 2014, Series C Nr. 285.

139 People's Legal Assistance Center (CEALP). See generally *Kuna of Madungandí and Emberá of Bayano Indigenous Peoples and their Members v. Panama*, IACtHR, Judgment, 14 October 2014, Series C Nr. 284.

140 APRODEH. See generally *Tarazona et al v. Peru*, IACtHR, Judgment, 15 October 2014, Series C Nr. 286.

141 CCAJAR, Inter-Church Justice and Peace Commission, and CEJIL. See generally *Rodriguez Vera et al ('Disappeared from the Palace of Justice') v. Colombia*, 14 November 2014, Series C Nr. 287.

142 APRODEH and CEJIL. See generally *Espinoza v. Peru*, IACtHR, Judgment, 20 November 2014, Series C Nr. 289.

143 APRODEH and CEJIL. See generally *Cruz et al v. Peru*, IACtHR, Judgment, 17 April 2015, Series C Nr. 292.

144 Association for the Promotion of Education in Peru (APE PERÚ). See generally *Canales et al v. Peru*, IACtHR, Judgment, 24 June 2015, Series C Nr. 296.

145 OFRANEH. See generally *Garífuna Community of Punta Piedra and its Members v. Honduras*, IACtHR, Judgment, 8 October 2015, Series C Nr. 304.

146 CEDHU. See generally *García Ibarra et al v. Ecuador*, IACtHR, Judgment, 17 November 2015, Series C Nr. 306.

147 COMISEDH. See generally *Quispialaya v. Peru*, IACtHR, Judgment, 23 November 2015, Series C Nr. 308.

148 CCJ. See generally *Duque v. Colombia*, IACtHR, Judgment, 26 February 2016, Series C Nr. 310.

149 APRODEH. See generally *Tenorio et al v. Peru*, IACtHR, Judgment, 22 June 2016, Series C Nr. 314.

150 CEDHU. See generally *Herrera et al v. Ecuador*, IACtHR, Judgment, 1 September 2016, Series C Nr. 316.

151 GIDH. See generally *Yarce et al v. Colombia*, IACtHR, Judgment, 22 November 2016, Series C Nr. 325.

152 CEDHU. See generally *Valencia et al v. Ecuador*, IACtHR, Judgment, 29 November 2016, Series C Nr. 327.

153 Rights in Action. See generally *I.V. v. Bolivia*, IACtHR, Judgment, 30 November 2016, Series C Nr. 329.

154 Popular Law Firm Association. See generally *Members of the Chichupac Village and Neighboring Communities of the Rabinal Municipality v. Guatemala*, IACtHR, Judgment, 30 November 2016, Series C Nr. 328.

155 APRODEH. See generally *Vásquez Durand et al v. Ecuador*, IACtHR, Judgment, 15 February 2017, Series C Nr. 332.

Acosta et al v. Nicaragua;[156] *Gutiérrez Hernández et al v. Guatemala;*[157] *Lagos v. Peru;*[158] *Vereda de la Esperanza v. Colombia;*[159] *Pacheco et al v. Honduras;*[160] *Xucuru Indigeous People and its Members v. Brazil;*[161] *Ramírez Escobar et al v. Guatemala;*[162] *Carvajal v. Colombia;*[163] *Herzog et al v. Brazil;*[164] *Amrhein et al v. Costa Rica;*[165] *Munárriz et al v. Peru;*[166] *Xamán Massacre v. Guatemala;*[167] *Cuscul et al v. Guatemala;*[168] *Terrones et al v Peru;*[169] *Escaleras et al v. Honduras;*[170] *López Soto et al v. Venezuela;*[171] *Isaza et al v. Colombia;*[172] *Villamizar et al v. Colombia;*[173] *Omeara et al v. Colombia;*[174]

---

156 Committee of the Families of Detained-Disappeared Persons in Honduras (COFADEH). See generally *Acosta et al v. Nicaragua*, IACtHR, Judgment, 25 March 2017, Series C Nr. 334.

157 Centre for Legal Assistance for Indigenous People (CALPI), Centre for Justice and Human Rights of the Atlantic Coast of Nicaragua (CEJUDHCAN), and CENID. See generally *Gutiérrez Hernández et al v. Guatemala*, IACtHR, Judgment, 24 August 2017, Series C Nr. 339.

158 GAM. See generally *Lagos v. Peru*, IACtHR, Judgment, 31 August 2017, Series C Nr. 340.

159 APRODEH. See generally *Vereda de la Esperanza v. Colombia*, IACtHR, Judgment, 31 August 2017, Series C Nr. 341.

160 CJL and CEJIL. See generally *Pacheco et al v. Honduras*, IACtHR, Judgment, 15 November 2017, Series C Nr. 342.

161 MNDH/Northeast Region, Legal Advisory Office for Popular Organisations (GAJOP), Indigenous Missionary Council (CIMI), and Global Justice. See generally *Xucuru Indigeous People and its Members v. Brazil*, IACtHR, Judgment, 5 February 2018, Series C Nr. 346.

162 Refugio de la Niñez in Guatemala and CEJIL. See generally *Ramírez Escobar et al v. Guatemala*, IACtHR, Judgment, 9 March 2018, Series C Nr. 351.

163 SIP. See generally *Carvajal Carvajal v. Colombia*, IACtHR, Judgment, 13 March 2018, Series C Nr. 352.

164 CEJIL. See generally *Herzog et al v. Brazil*, IACtHR, Judgment, 15 March 2018, Series C Nr. 353.

165 Factum Consorcio and Inter-American Services of Human Rights Professionals (SIPDH) (in addition to Inter-American Defenders). See generally *Amrhein et al v. Costa Rica*, IACtHR, Judgment, 25 April 2018, Series C Nr. 354.

166 COMISEDH. See generally *Munárriz et al v. Peru*, IACtHR, Judgment, 20 August 2018, Series C Nr. 355.

167 GAM. See generally *Xamán Massacre v. Guatemala*, IACtHR, Judgment, 22 August 2018, Series C Nr. 356.

168 CEJIL, National Network for Persons Living with HIV/AIDS, Association for People United, Life Project, Fernando Iturbide Foundation for the Prevention of AIDS, and Comprehensive Health Association. See generally *Cuscul et al v. Guatemala*, IACtHR, Judgment, 23 August 2018, Series C Nr. 359.

169 APRODEH, COMISEDH, and IDL. See generally *Terrones et al v Peru*, IACtHR, Judgment, 26 September 2018, Series C Nr. 360.

170 CEJIL and Reflection, Research, and Communication Team of the Society of Jesus (ERIC). See generally *Escaleras et al v. Honduras*, IACtHR, Judgment, 26 September 2018, Series C Nr. 361.

171 CEJIL and COFAVIC. See generally *López Soto et al v. Venezuela*, IACtHR, Judgment, 8 February 2018, Series C Nr. 348.

172 ASFADDES and CCJ. See generally *Isaza et al v. Colombia*, IACtHR, Judgment, 20 November 2018, Series C Nr. 363.

173 HVCJ and CCAJAR (to certain victims). See generally *Villamizar et al v. Colombia*, IACtHR, Judgment, 20 November 2018, Series C Nr. 364.

174 CCJ and CEJIL. See generally *Omeara et al v. Colombia*, IACtHR, Judgment, 21 November 2018, Series C Nr. 368.

Trueba et al v. Mexico;[175] *Alvarado et al v. Mexico*;[176] and *Women Victims of Sexual Torture in Atenco v. Mexico*.[177]

3. AUTONOMOUS INTERVENTION OF NHRIs

NHRI participation in legal proceedings before the IACtHR can be divided into two categories, depending on whether the NHRI supported the defendant state or entirely contradicted it. The latter situation should be highlighted; it has occurred either through the NHRI's submission of an *amicus curiae* brief or through its appearance before the IACtHR on behalf of complainants, alleged victims, or their families. The first alternative has occurred in *Baena et al v. Panama*;[178] *Yatama v. Nicaragua*;[179] *Acevedo et al v. Peru*;[180] *Fornerón and Daughter v. Argentina*;[181] *Massacres of El Mozote and Nearby Places v. El Salvador*;[182] *Artavia et al v. Costa Rica*;[183] *Gonzáles Lluy et al v. Ecuador*;[184] *Favela Nova Brasilia v. Brazil*;[185] and *Xucuru Indigenous People and their Members v. Brazil*.[186] As for the second alternative, namely cases where an NHRI has participated through representation and defence of complainants, alleged victims, or their families, these include *(Fermín) Ramírez v.*

175 Commission for Solidarity and Defence of Human Rights (COSYDDHAC) and CEJIL. See generally *Trueba et al v. Mexico*, IACtHR, Judgment, 27 November 2018, Series C Nr. 369.

176 Women's Human Rights Center (CEDEHM), COSYDDHAC, Justice for Our Daughters (JPNH), and Paso del Norte Human Rights Center (CDHPN). See generally *Alvarado et al v. México*, IACtHR, Judgment, 28 November 2018, Series C Nr. 371.

177 Center PRODH and CEJIL. See generally *Women Victims of Sexual Torture in Atenco v. Mexico*, IACtHR, Judgment, 28 November 2018, Series C Nr. 371.

178 Office of the Ombudsman of Panama. See generally *Baena et al v. Panama*, IACtHR, Judgment, 2 February 2001, Series C Nr. 72.

179 Office of the Ombudsman of Nicaragua. See generally *Yatama v. Nicaragua*, IACtHR, Judgment, 23 June 2005, Series C Nr. 127.

180 Office of the Ombudsman of Peru and Metropolitan Municipality of Lima. See generally *Acevedo Jaramillo et al v. Peru*, IACtHR, Judgment, 7 February 2006, Series C Nr. 144.

181 Provincial Commission for Memory of Buenos Aires. See generally *Fornerón and Daughter v. Argentina*, IACtHR, Judgment, 27 April 2012, Series C Nr. 242.

182 Office of the Ombudsman of El Salvador. See generally *Massacres of El Mozote and Nearby Places v. El Salvador*, IACtHR, Judgment, 25 October 2012, Series C Nr. 252.

183 Office of the Ombudsman of Costa Rica. See generally *Artavia et al v. Costa Rica*, IACtHR, Judgment, 28 November 2012, Series C Nr. 257.

184 Office of the Ombudsman of Ecuador. See generally *Gonzáles Lluy et al v. Ecuador*, IACtHR, Judgment, 1 September 2015, Series C Nr. 298.

185 Office of the Ombudsman of Brazil and Ombudsman of the State of São Paulo. See generally *Favela Nova Brasilia v. Brazil*, IACtHR, Judgment, 16 February 2017, Series C Nr. 333.

186 Office of the Ombudsman of Brazil. See generally *Xucuru Indigenous People and their Members v. Brazil*, IACtHR, Judgment, 5 February 2018, Series C Nr. 346.

Guatemala;[187] *Raxcacó v. Guatemala*;[188] *Ticona v. Bolivia*;[189] and *Mendoza et al v. Argentina*.[190]

4. SOME PERSONAL OBSERVATIONS

Three main ideas guide this author's comments on the issue of NHRI and NGO participation in contentious cases before the IACtHR: firstly, the manner in which these entities take part in cases depends on their normative design; secondly, the involvement of NHRIs in a capacity in which they either support the defendant state or act as a third party expressing different or even opposing views to those exposed by the complainant is a legal novelty for the Inter-American system; and, thirdly, the emergence of certain features within IACtHR proceedings appears to replicate those of domestic jurisdictions.

Regarding the first point, by strengthening the role of victims in contentious cases, the reforms of the Rules of the Court have restricted the role of the IACHR in these cases, at least with regards to public hearings,[191] and have encouraged the increased involvement of NHRIs and NGOs. This would seem to have introduced certain procedural settlement formulas that exist in domestic jurisdictions of the Inter-American system, thereby altering the classic international judicial structure adopted by the ACHR, in which the individual has practically no procedural capacity and lacks sufficient active legitimation. The clear trend towards an increased participation of NHRIs and NGOs in these legal proceedings not only manifests in the presentation of *amicus curiae* briefs but also in the representation and defence of complainants, alleged victims, or their families. This has occurred through application of the Rules of the Court. With regards to the period 1995–2000, it should be recalled that the rules in force at the time provided that '[a]t the stage of reparations, the representatives of the victims or their families may present their own motions and evidence autonomously'.[192] This may explain the low number of cases involving victim

---

187 Institute of Public Criminal Defence of Guatemala. See generally *(Fermín) Ramírez v. Guatemala*, IACtHR, Judgment, 20 June 2005, Series C Nr. 126.

188 Institute of Public Criminal Defence of Guatemala. See generally *Raxcacó v. Guatemala*, IACtHR, Judgment, 15 September 2005, Series C Nr. 133.

189 Office of the Ombudsman of Bolivia. See generally *Ticona v. Bolivia*, IACtHR, Judgment, 27 November 2008, Series C Nr. 191.

190 Office of the Ombudsman of Argentina and Deputy Ombudsman before the National Criminal Appeals Chamber. See generally *Mendoza et al v. Argentina*, IACtHR, Judgment, 14 May 2013, Series C Nr. 260.

191 See Rules of the Court, art 51.

192 See 1996 Rules of the Court, art 23.

representatives during this period. By contrast, in the period 2001–2010, the rules in force provided that '[a]fter the application has been admitted, the alleged victims, their families or their duly accredited representatives may present their pleadings, motions and evidence autonomously throughout the proceedings'.[193] Consequently, the number of cases during this period in which entities intervened in proceedings on behalf of the victims increased considerably.

Since 2010, this phenomenon has extended even further, as a result of the current rules, which stipulate that:

> [o]nce notice of the brief submitting a case before the Court has been served, in accordance with Article 39 of the Rules of Procedure, the alleged victims or their representatives may submit their brief containing pleadings, motions, and evidence autonomously and shall continue to act autonomously throughout the proceedings.[194]

Consequently, it could be argued that the greater the procedural role for victims, the more common the participation of NHRIs and NGOs in contentious proceedings before the IACtHR. It should not be forgotten that, in many cases, such participation was required so that victims could gain access to indispensable professional advice and representation. In short, the ability of NHRIs and NGOs to intervene is not independent of the normative design of contentious proceedings. As such, a state-centred design offers few possibilities for intervention, while one that is more open to the participation of victims provides greater possibilities for NHRIs and NGOs to play a role in proceedings.

As to the second point, the independent or autonomous participation of NHRIs in these cases, in parallel with defendant states or even in open contradiction to them, is not expressly provided for in the ACHR or in the Rules of the Court. Therefore, NHRI participation has ultimately depended on whether or not it is permitted under the domestic law of each state. This is the most novel aspect of the participation of NGOs and NHRIs in cases lodged at the IACtHR against the states to which these bodies belong. However, it still remains an incipient phenomenon and does not represent a clear trend that might be difficult to revert. As a consequence, its development and consolidation will depend on what each defendant state at the IACtHR allows in this respect within its own internal, domestic sphere. The independent or autonomous participation of NHRIs, however, may impact the effectiveness of state representation in contentious proceedings before this court, to the extent that there could be, at

193 See 2000, 2003, and 2009 Rules of the Court, art 23.
194 See Rules of the Court, art 25.1.

least partially, a confrontation or contradiction between two organs of the same state. Ultimately, this could be classified as an alteration of the principle of the unity or sole representation of the interests of the state at the international level. If this situation arises, it may also lead to a change in the traditional structure of international legal hearings before courts and tribunals, to the extent that the same structure prevailing in domestic litigation, whereby it is common practice for two State bodies to disagree and maintain opposing claims, is applied in disputes at the IACtHR.

In summary, it can be argued that the current participation of NGOs and NHRIs in legal proceedings before this court is a consequence of the alteration of the structure originally conceived for them. The subjects of this structure were initially the IACHR, on the one hand, which acted as the representative of all OAS member states, and the defendant state, on the other. Contentious cases are currently pursued between the alleged victims of human rights violations of the ACHR, or their families, and these states.

Finally, concerning the third point: both the growing participation of NGOs in legal proceedings before the IACtHR and the new, albeit limited, independent or autonomous participation of NHRIs (undertaken in a manner which diverges from that of defendant states) indicate the emergence of a clear peculiarity in such proceedings in terms of their participants, particularly the alleged victims and their families. This emerging trend has brought the proceedings closer to those conducted in the domestic spheres of states parties to the ACHR and indicates that contentious cases brought before the IACtHR are ultimately no more than an extension, into the Inter-American sphere, of confrontations of legal claims that have arisen in internal or national systems,[195] the difference being that these claims have eventually led to the apportionment of international responsibility where the state in question has been declared to have violated one or more human rights.[196]

195 See ACHR, art 46.1.

196 See ibid., art 68.

PART II

CASE STUDIES

Functioning, Effectiveness and Accountability of National Human Rights Institutions in Europe and Latin America

COMISIÓN NACIONAL DE LOS DERECHOS HUMANOS (MEXICO)

Emilio Maus and Pablo González Domínguez*

1. INTRODUCTION

Since the colonial era, Mexico has had various mechanisms and officials in charge of protecting the country's most vulnerable people. The recognition of the dignity and rights of indigenous people gave rise to the development of different institutions as well as the corresponding doctrinal apparatus for the protection of indigenous peoples. Examples include Francisco de Vitoria's (1538–1539) *Relectiones de indis* and *Relectio de iure belli*, the appointment of Bartolomé de las Casas (1484–1558) as Universal Procurator and Protector of Indians, and the Ordinances for the Good Treatment of Naturals, issued by Emperor Charles V of Spain (1500–1558) in 1528.[1]

After the Mexican Independence War (1810–1821), small efforts, such as the establishment of the Office of the Procurator for the Poor in San Luis Potosí (1847), could not prevent the effective protection of human rights from going into oblivion, due to different social and cultural factors prompted by armed conflicts and political instability as well as the one-party dictatorship instituted after the Mexican Revolution (1910–1921). This period was marked by constant internal disputes, both violent and social, and severe human rights abuses. The most relevant examples were the Cristero War (1926–1929), an armed conflict between civilians, who were defending their religious liberties, and the military, which was enforcing anti-religious legislation that resulted in thousands of deaths; and the Dirty War (1960s–1970s), which was the name given to the military repression aimed at dissolving or suppressing political opposition movements.

By 1980, the Mexican state had become a party to important human rights treaties, including the International Covenant on Civil and Political

* The authors would like to thank Isabela María Echavarría for her assistance in the elaboration of this chapter.

1 See generally O. Cruz Barney, 'Introducción Histórica; Artículo 102' in E. Ferrer Mac-Gregor and L. Guerrero Galván (eds.), *Derechos del pueblo mexicano: Mexico a través de sus constituciones*, Miguel Angel Porrua, Mexico City 2016, vol. X.

Rights; the International Covenant on Economic, Social and Cultural Rights; and the American Convention on Human Rights (ACHR). Nevertheless, it was not until 1989 that the modern Mexican state took on the responsibility of protecting human rights. After a challenged electoral process in 1988, the government decided to establish a human rights protection body, in view of the need to promote the social peace and democratisation of the country and within the framework of the negotiations for a free trade agreement with the USA and Canada. As a result, the Ministry of the Interior created a Directorate-General of Human Rights in 1989, the primary role of which was to develop and implement a national human rights policy. In June 1990, a presidential decree established the *Comisión Nacional de los Derechos Humanos* (CNDH), or National Human Rights Commission, as a decentralised body of the Ministry of the Interior.[2] Its head was appointed directly by the President of the Republic, and its main duties were to propose and monitor compliance with national human rights policy, establish programmes to assist the population, and implement mechanisms to prevent human rights violations.

In 1992, a constitutional reform incorporated the CNDH into the Political Constitution of the United Mexican States.[3] This amendment transferred the responsibility of establishing a federal human rights protection body, as well as the task of appointing its President, to the General Congress of the United Mexican States; mandated that each state of the federation should establish equivalent local bodies; and broadened the scope of the powers of the CNDH, expressly granting it the competence to investigate human rights violations, make public recommendations, and file disciplinary and criminal complaints. However, electoral, labour, and jurisdictional matters were excluded from its jurisdiction.[4] A law enacted that same year provided that the President of the CNDH should be appointed by the President of the Republic, with the approval of the Senate of the Republic.[5]

Subsequent reforms have expanded and strengthened the CNDH's functions and powers and fostered the mechanisms that make its work more effective. A 1999 amendment granted the Commission the status of an autonomous constitutional body, with management, budgetary and decision-making autonomy, legal personality, and control over its own assets; established an Advisory Council; set out an obligation to report annually to the three branches of government; and provided that the President of the CNDH must be elected by the Senate of the Republic. Mexico's President

2 It was published on 6 June 1990, in the Official Gazette of the Federation or *Diario Oficial de la Federación* (OGF).

3 See Political Constitution of the United Mexican States, art 102-B. The original decree was published on 5 February 1917 in the OGF, and was last amended on 18 November 2022.

4 The relevant decree was published on 28 January 1992 in the OGF.

5 See Law of the National Commission on Human Rights, art 10. The respective decree was published on 29 June 1992 in the OGF.

of the Republic could, thus, no longer intervene in the designation of the head of the Commission. Moreover, it was prescribed that, after his or her appointment, the Commission head can only be removed by impeachment of two-thirds of the members present in the Senate at any given time.[6] A 2006 reform granted the CNDH additional standing to file applications for the abstract review of statutes;[7] this is probably one of the most relevant and transcendent powers granted to the Commission.

In 2011, a major reform of the Mexican Constitution raised human rights provisions contained in international treaties to constitutional status. It also sought to strengthen the powers of the CNDH, establishing the obligation of public officials to respond to the recommendations made by the CNDH; its power to request the Senate of the Republic to summon a public servant who refuses to comply with a recommendation; the obligation to guarantee the autonomy of State human rights commissions in State constitutions; its jurisdiction on labour issues; the power to investigate serious human rights violations; and the intervention of civil society in the process of appointing the President of the CNDH.[8] This is the CNDH as we know it today.

The present chapter is divided into eight sections, which examine the institution's main features. Of special note is the hybrid nature of the Commission: it is a domestic institution that functions both as a quasi-jurisdictional organ and as a body for the promotion of human rights, while also playing a role in the global protection of human rights. The contribution will also explore the CNDH's internal organisation, functions, powers, and procedures, as well as questions concerning the body's accountability and its challenges for the future: especially those connected with the strengthening and maintenance of its budgetary and functional autonomy. Some concrete examples of the different types of recommendations issued by the CNDH are given below; they emphasise efforts to fight against serious human rights violations, both those that have occurred in the past and those that are, unfortunately, still happening in Mexico. Finally, the chapter will explore the relationship between the CNDH and international monitoring bodies, with an emphasis on its relationship with the Inter-American Court of Human Rights (IACtHR).

1.1. CLASSIFICATION

The CNDH represents a hybrid model: with both administrative oversight and human rights protection functions, it exists as a hybrid between a classical

---

6 The relevant decree was published on 13 September 1999 in the OGF.

7 The respective decree was published on 30 June 2006 in the OGF.

8 The relevant decree was published on 10 June 2011 in the OGF.

ombudsman and a human rights ombudsman.[9] On the one hand, it receives complaints about the legality of the actions of the administration, while, on the other hand, it ensures the safeguarding of human rights; thus, it constitutes both an administrative control body and a mechanism for preserving the Political Constitution.

Due to its hybrid nature, the CNDH has influenced a third model of ombudsman: the Latin American model. The promotion of human rights is an essential aspect of the functions of any institution fitting this model. Acting free of charge, the Latin American ombudsman is invested with institutional autonomy and issues non-binding recommendations.[10] Because of the ombudsman's itinerant character, its agents hold the powers to conduct visits to and inspect detention centres, migrant stations, etc.

The CNDH's jurisdiction is broad; it covers a variety of governmental agencies, corporations, and officials, including detention centres, immigration and customs officers, police and military forces, public health institutions, etc.[11] Some branches of government have, however, traditionally been excluded from its competence: mainly electoral and judicial activities of the courts. Although the CNDH cannot investigate complaints against private persons or entities, it does have jurisdiction over state authorities where they tolerate offences committed by individuals or other social agents and when they unjustifiably refuse to exercise their powers to prevent them.[12]

1.2. LEGAL FRAMEWORK

The CNDH's creation, structure, and basic powers are regulated by a solid legal framework, which is distributed across different instruments: the Mexican Constitution;[13] the Law of the National Human Rights Commission (1992), which has undergone several reforms, and grants the CNDH the power to

---

[9] See L. Reif, *The Ombudsman, Good Governance and the International Human Rights System*, Springer, New York 2004, p. 11.

[10] See generally H. Fix-Zamudio and J. Luis Soberanes, 'Comentario al Artículo 102' in E. Ferrer Mac-Gregor and L. Guerrero Galván (eds.), *Derechos del pueblo mexicano: Mexico a través de sus constituciones*, Miguel Angel Porrua, Mexico City 2016, vol. X.

[11] See Reif (n 9) p. 3.

[12] See Law of the National Commission on Human Rights, art 6.II.b.

[13] Especially art 102-B, but see also arts 41.c and 105.g. Of all the provisions regulating the CNDH, the most important is art 102-B of the Political Constitution, which is worth quoting at length:

> 'The Congress of the Union and the legislatures of the states, within the scope of their respective powers, will establish bodies for the protection of those human rights enshrined by the Mexican legal order; they will hear complaints against acts or omissions of an administrative nature coming from any authority or public servant – except those attributable to the Federal Judicial Power –, in violation of these rights.

create the Internal Regulation of the National Human Rights Commission, which were initially published in 1992 and replaced in 2003.[14]

The bodies referred to in the preceding paragraph shall make public, non-binding recommendations, as well as complaints and claims to the respective authorities. All public servants are obliged to respond to the recommendations submitted to them by these bodies. When the issued recommendations are not accepted or complied with by the authorities or public servants, the latter must make their refusal public and explain the reasons and legal grounds for it; in addition, the Senate or, during its recesses, the Permanent Commission, or the legislatures of the states, as appropriate, may, at the request of these bodies, call on the authorities or responsible public servants to appear before those legislative bodies to explain the reason for their refusal.

These bodies shall not have competence in electoral and jurisdictional matters.

The body to be established by the Congress of the Union shall be called the National Human Rights Commission; it shall be vested with autonomy – both regarding its management and budget –, legal personality and be endowed with its own patrimony.

The constitutions of the federative states shall establish and guarantee the autonomy of the human rights protection bodies.

The National Human Rights Commission shall have an Advisory Council composed of ten councillors, who shall be elected by a two-thirds vote of the members of the Senate present or, in their absence, by the Permanent Commission of the Congress of the Union, with the same qualified vote. The law shall determine the procedures to be followed for the presentation of proposals by the House itself. The two councillors with the greatest seniority in office shall be replaced annually, unless they are proposed and ratified for a second term.

The President of the National Human Rights Commission, who shall also be the President of the Advisory Council, shall be elected under the same terms as in the preceding paragraph. He shall serve for five years, may be re-elected only once and may only be removed from office under the terms of Title IV of this Constitution.

The election of the head of the National Human Rights Commission, as well as the members of the Advisory Council, and the heads of the human rights protection agencies of the states, will be subject to a public consultation procedure, which must be transparent, under the terms and conditions determined by law.

The President of the National Human Rights Commission shall submit an annual report on its activities to the powers of the Union. To that end, he shall appear before the Houses of Congress under the terms of the law.

The National Human Rights Commission shall hear any complaints regarding the recommendations, agreements or omissions of the equivalent bodies in the states.

The National Human Rights Commission may investigate acts that constitute serious human rights violations, when it deems it appropriate or when requested by the Federal Executive, one of the Chambers of Congress, the holders of executive powers of the states or their Legislatures.'

The other constitutional provisions, mentioned above, grant different powers to the CNDH, such as participation in the designation of the Technical Evaluation Committee, which is responsible for the selection of the Counsels and President of the National Electoral Institute, or the power to file claims for the abstract review of statutes, respectively.

14 The Internal Regulation of the National Human Rights Commission was issued by the Commission according to art 6-X of the Law of the National Human Rights Commission. The

Some laws establish specific regulations and obligations for the CNDH, while others expand its scope of competence or grant it advisory or full status in monitoring committees, through protection mechanisms, and the development and implementation of public policy regarding the human rights of vulnerable groups. These laws and regulations include those that cover: transparency and access to information; protection of personal data; torture and cruel, inhuman, or degrading treatment; victims of crime; human trafficking; violence against women; rights of children and adolescents; care, treatment, and integral development of children; discrimination; equality between women and men; inclusion of persons with disabilities; senior citizens' rights; linguistic rights of indigenous peoples; development of indigenous peoples; care and protection of persons with autism spectrum disorders; protection of human rights defenders and journalists; immigration; civilian awards, incentives and rewards; cultural rights; and criminal justice system for adolescents.[15]

2. ORGANISATION

The CNDH has an executive body composed of its President, Advisory Council, Executive Secretariat, and Technical Secretariat. Its powers cover substantive areas, such as the investigative units (known as *visitadurías* or Visitorships) and auxiliary or administrative areas, which will be discussed below. The President performs various roles: it exercises the legal representation of the CNDH; formulates general guidelines; appoints, directs, and coordinates the officers and personnel; dictates specific measures; allocates functions; submits an annual report of activities to the powers of the Mexican state; celebrates collaboration agreements with authorities, NGOs, and academic institutions; issues public recommendations resulting from the CNDH's investigations; formulates general proposals and reports; and requests the Senate of the Republic to summon authorities or public servants who refuse to accept or comply with recommendations issued by the CNDH. The President also has standing to file a request for *acciones de inconstitucionalidad*: that is to say, for the abstract judicial review of statutes.[16]

The CNDH has six *visitadurías generales*, or General Visitorships, which are investigative units that receive complaints about alleged human rights violations; initiate and carry out investigations concerning human rights violations, at

decrees containing the Commission's internal rules were published on 12 November 1992 and 29 September 2003, respectively, in the OGF.

15 An extensive compilation of the rules concerning the CNDH is available at: <http://appweb.cndh.org.mx/biblioteca/archivos/pdfs/Normatividad-CNDH_2.pdf>. The updated version of these laws is available at: <http://www.diputados.gob.mx/LeyesBiblio/index.htm>.

16 See Law of the National Commission on Human Rights, art 15.

the request of the complainant or on their own initiative; procure, through conciliation between complainants and authorities, immediate solutions to human rights violations; and draft recommendations or agreements to help determine cases and make rulings on the merits.[17] These investigative units are staffed with Deputy Inspectors and professional and technical experts in medicine, forensic medicine, criminology, psychology, and other areas. General Inspectors also have powers to request all kinds of information, documents, and reports from agencies and individuals; physically inspect locations; call-in authorities and witnesses; and request the implementation of precautionary measures.[18]

Administrative units assist the President in handling matters that fall directly under his or her responsibility.[19] The most relevant are: the General Administrator's Office; the Legal Affairs Department; the Office for the Monitoring and Follow-up of the Compliance with Recommendations; the Communications Department; the General Office of Complaints and Orientation; the Transparency Unit; the Planning and Analysis Department; the Automated Information Unit; the National Centre of Human Rights, which is an entity for academic research, training, and the promotion of said rights; and the Internal Auditing Body, which is appointed by Congress.[20]

In Mexico, there is a national commission at the federal level and one in each of the 32 States of the federation. The headquarters of the CNDH are in Mexico City, and it has established 16 regional offices in zones with a higher incidence of human rights violations, such as San Cristóbal de las Casas, to deal with indigenous conflicts. Other offices have also been established at both the northern and southern borders of Mexico, namely in Tijuana, Ciudad Juárez, Chihuahua, Nogales, Reynosa, Tapachula, and along the routes used regularly by migrants, particularly in Villahermosa, Veracruz, Ixtepec, Mérida, San Luis Potosí, and Aguascalientes. In more recent times, offices have also been established in relevant conflict areas, including Acapulco, Morelia, Torreón, and La Paz. These are regions with a high presence of organised crime, and where incidences of human rights violations committed by the military are significant. State commissions can receive complaints against federal authorities and refer them to the CNDH.

The CNDH has also created assistance programmes to address specific issues and promote and protect the rights of vulnerable groups, including journalists and human rights defenders; migrants; women (including attention to women's issues and equality with men); indigenous peoples and communities; children

17 See ibid, art 24.
18 See ibid, arts 39–40.
19 See Internal Regulation of the National Human Rights Commission, art 21.
20 See Law of the National Commission on Human Rights, art 24-bis.

and family affairs; persons with disabilities; sexuality; persons with health issues and HIV; etc. Each programme is incorporated into the structure of a Visitorship.

3. FUNCTIONING

The Mexican Constitution establishes, in Article 1, that 'all authorities, within the scope of their competence, have the obligation to promote, respect, protect and ensure human rights'.[21] Consequently, the state 'shall prevent, investigate, punish and repair' human rights violations.[22] In this context, the various functions and activities of the CNDH can be grouped under two main headings: the *promotion* of human rights and their *protection*. The first of these roles aims to prevent human rights violations, mainly through awareness campaigns, courses, training of public officers, academic research, inter-institutional agreements, the development of public policy, etc. Although their impact might be difficult to assess, these activities consume a large part of the CNDH's resources and are indispensable for the fulfilment of the state's obligations to avoid the occurrence of human rights violations. The CNDH's protection of human rights, particularly in the face of specific violations, embodies the state's obligation to prevent, investigate, punish, and repair human rights violations. This is the Commission's most characteristic function. In this context, the CNDH plays an important role: usually, its investigations, actions, agreements, pronouncements, and particularly its recommendations, are the basis for the reparation and sanctioning of violations. To this end, the CNDH has the power to receive complaints of alleged violations as well as initiate *ex officio* investigations; both activities are undertaken in an effort to lead to a resolution. Proceedings before the Commission are, thus, of two types: first a *queja*, or complaint, whereby a person reports human rights violations by a federal authority (complaints constitute CNDH's essential and original competence);[23] and secondly, *inconformidades*, or disagreements,[24] whereby the CNDH is requested to intervene, as a second instance procedure, against acts or omissions of State human rights commissions, either through the remedies of complaint (*recurso de queja*),[25] or appeal (*impugnación*).[26]

---

21 Political Constitution of the United Mexican States, art 1.

22 ibid.

23 See Law of the National Commission on Human Rights, art 25.

24 See ibid, art 55.

25 See ibid, arts 56–60.

26 See ibid, arts 61–66. While a complaint proceeds when no final decision has been issued, an objection requires the issuance of such a decision.

A third function, outside and beyond its traditional role, consists in safeguarding the constitutional order. In this respect, the Political Constitution grants the CNDH the power to file a complaint for the abstract judicial review of legislation before the Supreme Court of Justice, so as to challenge statutes and norms that violate human rights.

3.1. COMPETENCE

Different criteria determine the CNDH's competence. From a territorial point of view, the Commission has jurisdiction over the entire national territory.[27] This competence also extends to actions or violations that may be committed by federal public servants abroad, such as those at consulates and embassies. The CNDH also receives complaints from abroad regarding events in the national territory.

The CNDH has also issued pronouncements and recommendations about human rights violations committed abroad against Mexican citizens: for instance, pronouncements on the treatment of undocumented immigrants in the USA, compelling Mexican authorities to exercise their powers to protect their nationals abroad; and recommendations pertaining to particular human rights violations.[28] In 1993, the CNDH created a programme to defend Mexicans facing the death penalty in the USA.[29]

From a substantive perspective, the Commission has competence in relation to all kinds of human rights violations; however, there are some exceptions: it cannot investigate complaints which relate to two matters that are expressly excluded from the CNDH's competence, namely electoral affairs and judicial decisions.[30] This means that the Commission cannot review the substantive merits of a judicial decision; however, it is worth noting the Commission's competence to consider complaints regarding acts or omissions of an administrative nature committed by most judicial authorities.[31] For example, the Commission issued a 2014 recommendation against court clerks, for violence and discrimination

27 See Law of the National Commission on Human Rights, art 3.

28 This occurred in a case in which consular authorities were negligent in protecting and assisting Mexican workers, victims of human trafficking and forced labourers in The Bahamas. See Recommendation 1/2009 of the CNDH.

29 See J. Madrazo, 'La CNDH: una mirada retrospectiva' in National Human Rights Commission (ed.), *Comisión Nacional de los Derechos Humanos. 20 aniversario 1990–2010* (CNDH, Mexico City 2010) p. 40.

30 See Political Constitution of the United Mexican States, art 102-B; and Law of the National Commission on Human Rights, art 7.

31 Those of the federal judiciary are excluded. See Law of the National Commission on Human Rights, art 8; see also J. Carpizo, 'Análisis del artículo 102, apartado B, de la Constitución' in *Comisión Nacional de los Derechos Humanos. 20 aniversario 1990–2010* (CNDH, Mexico City 2010) p. 26.

against women, denial of justice, and lack of impartiality, in a case where a mother of two disabled children demanded child support from their father, a retired Supreme Court Justice.[32]

The legal framework regulating the CNDH establishes a system of subsidiarity for the protection of human rights. While the Commission has competence to investigate alleged human rights violations by federal administrative authorities, breaches committed by local authorities are, in principle, investigated by State commissions. Nevertheless, the Political Constitution grants the CNDH the power to investigate complaints arising from the actions, recommendations, agreements, or omissions of State human rights commissions. If local and federal authorities are involved in the same case, the CNDH has exclusive jurisdiction to investigate.[33] The Political Constitution even allows the Commission to investigate complaints against local authorities. The epitome of this competence is its power of attraction, which can be exercised in the case of particularly serious human rights violations, namely those transcending the interests of the state and affecting national public opinion; at the request of a local body; or when the head of a State commission is prevented from dealing with the matter.[34]

As mentioned above, the CNDH cannot investigate violations committed by individuals, at least in principle;[35] however, it does investigate the acts or omissions of authorities in relation to those acts. This is particularly relevant in environmental matters, when human rights violations are committed by companies and corporations, or where authorities have failed to investigate, prosecute, and punish crimes. In this context, the CNDH has issued recommendations regarding the operation of private shelters for victims, schools, trade unions, etc.

The CNDH can investigate alleged human rights violations committed against all kinds of persons, regardless of their sex, nationality, migration status, etc. It pays particular attention to vulnerable groups. It can also investigate human rights violations committed against legal entities, such as companies, unions, foundations, and collectives, including indigenous peoples and communities.[36]

As a result of the 2011 constitutional reforms, the CNDH is expressly authorised to investigate serious human rights violations. This gives the federal executive, the chambers of the Mexican Congress, governors, and State legislatures the power to request the Commission to investigate grave

---

32 See Recommendation 32/2014 of the CNDH.

33 See Law of the National Commission on Human Rights, art 3.

34 See Law of the National Commission on Human Rights, art 60; Internal Regulation of the National Human Rights Commission, art 14; see also Carpizo (n 31) 30.

35 See Law of the National Commission on Human Rights, art 6.II.b.

36 See SCJN P/J1/2015 (10a), *Semanario Judicial de la Federación* 10–12 (2015), vol. I, at 117.

violations. Although this possibility already existed before the reforms, the mechanism extends the scope of subjects that can request an investigation. Prior to the reform, it was unclear whether an authority could request the CNDH's intervention: as this competence was then conferred on the Supreme Court of Justice. It is worth noting that some scholars expressed doubts about the convenience of transferring the power to the CNDH, as it might erode the Commission's authority and alter its nature.[37]

3.2. PROCEDURES

According to the CNDH's legal framework, any person can present a complaint or *queja* relating to human rights violations committed by a federal authority.[38] This is contrasted to the 'appeal remedies of complaint and objection' procedure, which may only be submitted by the complainants within the context of the original procedure before the State commission.[39] Claims can be brought within a year of the occurrence of the respective human rights violation, or from the time when the affected party gained knowledge of the circumstances. Exceptionally, this period of time can be extended in cases of serious human rights violations, such as attacks on life, torture, forced disappearance, or when relevant circumstances justify such an extension. In cases of crimes against humanity, a claim can be presented at any time: no limitation applies in such cases.[40]

According to the Internal Regulation of the National Human Rights Commission, CNDH procedures should be short and simple, with any shortcomings or deficiencies in arguments remedied by the Commission. To achieve speed and effectiveness, formalities should be avoided, and investigations should be carried out as quickly and simply as possible, avoiding unnecessary actions.[41] It should be noted that all the actions of the CNDH are free of charge.[42] The investigations, reports and documentation must be handled in a strictly confidential manner.[43] The complaint can be presented orally, in writing, in Mexican sign language, and by any means of communication – even

---

37 See generally J. Carpizo, '¿Es acertada la probable transferencia de la función de investigación de la Suprema Corte a la Comisión Nacional de los Derechos Humanos?' in M. Carbonell and P. Salazar (eds.), *La reforma constitucional de derechos humanos. Un nuevo paradigma* (UNAM, Mexico City 2011).

38 See Law of the National Commission on Human Rights, art 25.

39 See ibid, arts 56 and 64.

40 See Law of the National Commission on Human Rights, art 26; Internal Regulation of the National Human Rights Commission, art 88.

41 See Internal Regulation of the National Human Rights Commission, art 76.

42 See ibid, art 77.

43 See ibid, art 78.

in a language other than Spanish, for instance where the complainant belongs to an indigenous group. The complaint must contain minimum identification data, including, the name, surname, address, telephone number and signature of the *quejoso*, or complainant, or of the person who is presenting the complaint, and – whenever possible – of the *agraviado*, or affected person; as well as a narrative of the facts and all relevant information necessary to identify the responsible authority.[44] In principle, anonymous complaints will not be investigated,[45] although the CNDH has a wide discretion to investigate human rights violations *ex officio*.[46]

When the Commission receives a written complaint, the first step is to determine whether its admissibility requirements and competences are met. If there is a *prima facie* case of a human rights violation, the writ is sent to one of the general investigative units, which will carry out an investigation. The CNDH must immediately contact the authority identified as being responsible for the alleged human rights violation, to try to achieve an immediate solution to the conflict.[47] To develop the investigation effectively, the General Visitor is vested with the power to: ask the accused authorities to submit reports or documentation; request various documents and reports from other authorities, including judicial bodies, or individuals;[48] carry out visits and inspections, either personally or through technical or professional personnel; summon persons as experts or witnesses; and carry out all other actions that it deems appropriate,[49] including requesting the implementation of precautionary measures.[50] If an accused authority fails to respond to an information request, the facts invoked by the complainant will be presumed to be true.[51] The submission of false information will be criminally prosecuted.[52]

Once the investigation is concluded, the General Visitor will analyse the facts, arguments, evidence, and results of his own research, in order to determine whether or not the authorities have participated in a human rights violation. The evidence presented shall be evaluated as a whole by the General Visitor, according to the principles of logic, experience, and, if necessary, of legality, so that they are sufficiently convinced about the facts that are the subject of the complaint.[53] A violation of human rights should be affirmed where officials participate in unlawful, unreasonable, unjust, inadequate, or erroneous acts and

44 See ibid, art 80.
45 See ibid, art 82.
46 See ibid, art 89.
47 See Law of the National Commission on Human Rights, art 36.
48 See Internal Regulation of the National Human Rights Commission, art 106.
49 See Law of the National Commission on Human Rights, art 39.
50 See ibid, art 40.
51 See Law of the National Commission on Human Rights, art 58.
52 See ibid, art 73.
53 See ibid, art 41.

omissions, or if they acted negligently. In such cases, the General Visitor may formulate a draft recommendation, indicating appropriate measures for the effective restoration of the fundamental rights of the persons concerned and for the reparation of damage; this draft will be submitted to the President of the CNDH for final consideration.[54]

The general practice is that not all human rights violations lead to a public recommendation; instead, only those that are deemed to be matters of a certain significance attract this attention. For example, where there is a public interest in highlighting the wrongs committed by the authorities, when public restoration of rights is deemed necessary to influence the implementation of a public policy, or to prevent future human rights violations by the same authority or similar institutions. Recommendations are the *ultima ratio* of the CNDH, a strong request to the authority to give adequate attention to the victim, so that his or her rights can be properly restored. They represent the most severe expression of the work of the Commission.[55] For less severe situations, the CNDH's legal framework encourages it to resort to other methods of settlement, such as conciliation and the resolution of complaints during the procedure.[56]

3.3. PRONOUNCEMENTS

The CNDH issues different types of opinions, recommendations, proposals, and reports on matters concerning the promotion and protection of human rights. There is a wide range of pronouncements, varying in severity, effect, and scope.

3.3.1. Recommendations for Specific Violations

When the Commission determines that an act or omission constitutes a human rights violation, it can issue a public, autonomous, and non-binding recommendation. Although these decisions are of a declaratory nature,[57] they differ from a court judgment in that the recommendations do not change the legal situation *per se*, and do not revoke or annul a legal act. These decisions,

---

54 See ibid, art 44.

55 See L. de la Barreda, 'Los desafíos del ombudsman' in E. Ferrer Mac-Gregor (ed.), *Derecho procesal constitucional*, Porrúa, Mexico City 2006, vol. 2, p. 1421. See generally the 2019 annual report of the activities of the CNDH, available at: <http://informe.cndh.org.mx/menu.aspx?id=30088>.

56 See Law of the National Commission on Human Rights, art 36; Internal Regulation of the National Human Rights Commission, art 125.

57 See J. Luis Soberanes, 'Artículo 3 (Competencia de la CNDH)' in J. Luis Soberanes, L. García López-Guerrero, and J. Mena (eds.), *Ley de la Comisión Nacional de los Derechos Humanos comentada y concordada* (CNDH, Mexico City 2005) p. 38.

however, constitute a sufficient legal basis for claiming compensation: once accepted, they become mandatory. In its 32 years of existence, the CNDH has issued about 3,300 recommendations on specific violations.[58]

After the 2011 reform, the Commission was expressly granted the power to investigate gross human rights violations. Although this sort of breach had always fallen within its competence, the reform now allows the CNDH to exert greater pressure through the issuance of so-called 'recommendations on gross violations'. From 2011 to 2022, the Commission issued 77 recommendations of this sort, in cases of forced disappearance, deprivation of life, torture, illegal searches, denial of access to justice, sexual violence, illegal detention, excessive use of force, and arbitrary execution.[59] In addition, the National Mechanism for the Prevention of Torture, which is attached to the CNDH, issues recommendations on specific cases relating to this crime. Following a recent reform, these are accounted for independently, and, so far, 13 recommendations of this kind have been published.[60]

More often, complaint proceedings can be concluded through conciliation between the complainant and the responsible authorities, according to the principles of immediacy and effectiveness,[61] and the mandate established by law.[62] Conciliation consists of the recognition of the human rights violation by the authority and the commitment to remedy it;[63] it is prohibited to resolve a complaint in such a way in cases of serious violations of human rights: these being, breaches of the right to life, of the prohibition of torture, enforced disappearances, and crimes against humanity.[64]

3.3.2. General Recommendations and Reports

The CNDH issues pronouncements on general human rights violations, either through general recommendations or special reports. Among the powers granted to the Commission are those of promoting the observance of human rights in Mexico and of making proposals to Mexico's authorities to encourage changes and modifications of legislative and regulatory provisions, as well as administrative practices, that result in better protection of human

58 These recommendations are available at <www.cndh.org.mx/tipo/1/recomendacion>.

59 These recommendations are available at: <www.cndh.org.mx/index.php/tipo/225/recomendacion-por-violaciones-graves>.

60 These recommendations are available at: <www.cndh.org.mx/tipo/227/recomendaciones-del-mecanismo-nacional-de-prevencion-de-la-tortura>.

61 See Law of the National Commission on Human Rights, art 4.

62 See ibid, arts 6.VI, 24.III and 36.

63 See V. Martínez Bullé-Goyri, 'El procedimiento ante los organismos autónomos protectores de los derechos humanos' in E. Ferrer Mac-Gregor (ed.), *Derecho procesal constitucional*, Porrúa, Mexico City 2006, vol. 2, p. 1463.

64 See Law of the National Commission on Human Rights, arts 88 and 119.

rights.[65] These contributions go beyond the resolution of specific cases and, therefore, cannot be carried out through individual recommendations:[66] by contrast, individual recommendations are issued at the request of a complainant and refer to the specific case at issue.[67] For this reason, and in order to comply with the Paris Principles on NHRIs, which establish the need for these institutions to have the broadest possible mandate, the CNDH's Advisory Council approved amendments to the Internal Regulation of the National Human Rights Commission,[68] to grant it the power to issue general recommendations.[69]

These general recommendations seek to expose conduct, contexts, and widespread practices which are the subject of repeated complaints about similar events and may lead to findings of human rights violations. They are also aimed at proposing preventive and corrective measures, especially of an administrative and legislative nature. Such recommendations do not accuse a particular authority of violating human rights;[70] instead, they act as a warning and advice, providing information about more effective ways to protect and promote human rights. For this reason, they do not require formal acceptance by the authorities to whom they are addressed, and their implementation is assessed and verified through general studies and reports.[71]

To date, 47 general recommendations have been issued.[72] These have addressed various topics, including rights pertaining to: people with HIV/AIDS; decent work; violence against women; children's health and obesity; prisoners and their contact with the outside world; human rights in the framework of business; agricultural workers; the cultural heritage of indigenous peoples; minimum wage; health and air pollution; obstetric violence; equal marriage; clinical records; irregular detention in prisons; consultation of indigenous peoples and communities; natural resources; aggression against human rights defenders and journalists; freedom of expression; sexual violence against children in educational centres; violations against journalists; illegal searches; victims of crime; illegitimate use of force; torture; mentally ill prisoners; religious

---

65 See ibid, arts 6.VII and 6.VIII.

66 See R. Plascencia, *Comisión Nacional de los Derechos Humanos, recomendaciones generales 1/2001 a 18/2010* (CNDH, Mexico City 2010) p. 7.

67 See Law of the National Commission on Human Rights, art 49.

68 See ibid, art 129-bis. The respective decree was published on 17 November 2000 in the OGF.

69 See H. Fix-Zamudio and H. Fix-Fierro, *Las recomendaciones generales de la Comisión Nacional de los Derechos Humanos* (UNAM-CNDH, Mexico City 2018) p. 50. On 12 August 2003, the CNDH's Advisory Council approved new internal regulations. Art 140, therein, broadens the power to issue general recommendations. The corresponding decree was published on 29 September 2003 in the OGF.

70 See Plascencia (n 66) p. 8.

71 See Internal Regulation of the National Human Rights Commission, art 140.

72 These recommendations are available at: <www.cndh.org.mx/index.php/tipo/226/recomendaciones-generales>.

discrimination; forced sterilisation in indigenous communities; arbitrary arrests; and humiliating or degrading body searches of persons visiting detention centres. These topics can be classified into three groups, which concern: public safety and the criminal justice system; the rights of vulnerable groups, such as children, migrants, indigenous peoples, women, journalists, human rights defenders; and rights under construction, such as health, economic, social, cultural, and environmental rights, etc.[73]

3.3.3. *Abstract Judicial Review of Statutes*

In 1994, the Mexican Constitution established a procedure for the abstract judicial review of statutes by the Supreme Court of Justice.[74] This procedure involves the review of a statute's constitutionality, regardless of any specific legal dispute or whether the applicant is affected. The group of authorities who have standing in such actions is subject to the *numerus clausus* principle. In 2006, a constitutional reform vested the CNDH with the competence to file such claims, against federal and State laws as well as international treaties, which violate human rights 'enshrined in the Constitution'. In turn, this allows the CNDH to further contribute to safeguarding the legal order.[75] State human rights commissions are also allowed to challenge State legislation passed in violation of human rights. This is probably one of the CNDH's, and State commissions', most important and far-reaching powers.

This power was first exercised in 2007 against the reform of the Federal District Criminal Code, which legalised abortion in that State (Mexico City). The Supreme Court of Justice determined that the CNDH lacked the competence to invoke violations of human rights contained in international treaties.[76] This, despite the fact that, according to Article 133 of the Mexican Constitution, international treaties constitute the 'Supreme Law of the Union', along with the Constitution itself and federal laws.[77] This interpretation placed the CNDH in an awkward position, as it could only resort to this mechanism of judicial control when the law in question allegedly violated human rights as established in the Political Constitution; this, consequently, limited its mandate to protect human rights.

---

73 See Fix-Zamudio and Fix-Fierro (n 69) p. 59.

74 See Political Constitution of the United Mexican States, art 105. The respective decree was published on 31 December 1994 in the OGF.

75 The relevant decree was published on 14 September 2006 in the OGF. See C. Astudillo, 'Las comisiones de derechos humanos y la acción de inconstitucionalidad: perfiles procesales' in C. Astudillo and M. Carbonell (eds.), *Las comisiones de derechos humanos y la acción de inconstitucionalidad*, Porrúa, Mexico City 2007, p. 22.

76 See SCJN P/J31/2011 (9a), *Semanario Judicial de la Federación* 9 (2011), vol. XXXIV, at p. 870.

77 Political Constitution of the United Mexican States, art 113.

The 2011 constitutional reform corrected this situation and expanded the CNDH's powers, allowing the Commission to challenge federal and State laws, as well as laws conflicting with international treaties, that thus violate 'human rights enshrined in this Constitution and in international treaties to which Mexico is a party'.[78] As of 30 September 2019, the Commission has submitted 259 claims for the abstract review of statutes, 10.4 per cent of them against federal norms and 89.6 per cent against local provisions.[79] To date, 575 actions have been filed.[80]

3.3.4. *Criminal and Administrative Complaints*

When conducting an investigation, the CNDH often finds that the accused public officials have not only committed human rights violations but also participated in crimes and/or administrative misconduct. In such cases, the Commission is empowered to file complaints with the criminal and administrative authorities. From 2010 to 2019, the CNDH filed 724 criminal complaints, but only 1.93 per cent of these led to a conviction.[81] This figure reflects the high degree of impunity in the country. During the same period, the Commission filed 830 complaints pertaining to administrative violations.[82]

4. EFFECTIVENESS

The effectiveness of the CNDH can be measured on the basis of various criteria. If one were to consider the number of recommendations issued, in relation to complaints received, less than one per cent of the complaints dealt with by the Commission result in a recommendation. However, such a standard ignores the full scope of the activities, obligations, and functions of the CNDH. Moreover, both the Paris Principles on NHRIs and the Commission's legal framework stipulate that it must first seek conciliation between the parties: that is to say, between authorities and individuals. In this regard, the reports issued annually by the CNDH show that the vast majority of cases are resolved either during the CNDH's processs or through conciliation.

---

78 See Political Constitution of the United Mexican States, art 105.II.g. The respective decree was published on 10 June 2011 in the OGF.

79 See the CNDH's 2019 special report on *acciones de inconstitucionalidad* available at: <https://www.cndh.org.mx/documento/informe-especial-de-acciones-de-inconstitucionalidad>.

80 Information on these actions is available at: <www.cndh.org.mx/tipo/209/accion-de-inconstitucionalidad>.

81 See the CNDH's report of activities from 1 January to 31 December 2019, available at: <https://www.cndh.org.mx/eventos/3662/informe-de-actividades-del-1-de-enero-al-31-de-diciembre-de-2019>.

82 See ibid.

From 2016 to 2019, the CNDH resolved 39,911 complaint files. In that period, it issued 304 ordinary recommendations (0.76 per cent of the cases), 29 recommendations for serious violations (0.07 per cent), and recorded 805 conciliations (2.02 per cent). The CNDH lacked jurisdiction in 56 cases (0.14 per cent), and the complainant desisted or showed no further interest in 310 cases (0.78 per cent). In contrast, 16,263 cases (40.75 per cent) were resolved during the process, thanks to the Commission's intervention. Another 14,387 cases (36.05 per cent) were concluded through legal guidance to the complainant, which usually occurs when the CNDH lacks competence on the issue but can redirect the complainant to the relevant authority: a significant aspect of the CNDH's work is the provision of advice to individuals; this contrasts with the work of NHRIs in many other countries.[83] Finally, in 6,406 cases (16.05 per cent), the Commission did not find elements proving a human rights violation.[84]

With regard to the recommendations issued by the Commission, these have been accepted by the authorities in most cases and to a significant degree. Of the recommendations issued in 2019, about 94 per cent were accepted, although in 86 per cent of cases the submitted evidence of compliance was incomplete. In four per cent of cases, the authorities did not accept the recommendation, while in two per cent of cases the authority has yet to issue a response at the time of writing.

Another criterion used to evaluate the effectiveness of the CNDH refers to the time that elapses between a human rights violation, the Commission's knowledge thereof, and the issuance of the corresponding recommendation. In this regard, some recommendations have been very expeditious, such as in the *Tlatlaya* case, which involved the killings of 22 civilians on 30 June 2014 by members of the military. Here, the CNDH initiated an investigation *ex officio* on 11 July 2014, based on news reports, and its recommendation was issued on 21 October 2014, about three months later.[85] In a similar case, two university students in Monterrey were wrongfully killed by the military on 19 March 2010; the CNDH started investigating on 22 March, and the recommendation was issued on 12 August 2010, less than five months later.[86]

In contrast, the making of other recommendations has been notoriously slow. One example is the *Ayotzinapa* case. 43 students were forcibly 'disappeared' on 27 September 2014; even though an investigation began on the same day, the

83 M. Bullé-Goyri (n 63) p. 1461.

84 See the CNDH's reports of activities of 2016, 2017, 2018, and 2019, available at: <https://www.cndh.org.mx/pagina/informes-anuales-de-actividades>.

85 See Recommendation 51/2014 of the CNDH.

86 See Recommendation 45/2010 of the CNDH.

relevant recommendation was not issued until 28 November 2018.[87] A similar delay was exhibited by a case in which 563 victims, most of them minors, were held captive in an orphanage, in unsanitary conditions, whilst being subjected to mental and sexual abuse, labour exploitation, and other violations. Media outlets reported on the violations on 15 July 2014, and the CNDH initiated an investigation two days later; however, its recommendation was not issued until 31 October 2018, after more than four years.[88]

5. ACCOUNTABILITY

The CNDH is subject to various forms of public scrutiny, both by government and civil society. Since the constitutional reforms of 1999, the Commission has been required to submit an annual report to the three branches of government.[89] The report refers to complaints, work programmes, recommendations, and proposals.[90] This allows the three government branches to issue or amend laws, regulations, and administrative practices and address shortcomings in justice procurement, to more effectively protect human rights.[91] The report has a dual function: on the one hand, it promotes and provides accountability; on the other, it officially informs the branches of government *vis-à-vis* the situation of human rights in Mexico. This second function gives government the opportunity to use its constitutional powers to more effectively promote and protect rights.

The CNDH is also subject to frequent audits by different bodies: the Federal Superior Audit Office, the CNDH's Internal Control Body, and the Ministry of Finance, among others. The Commission is also required to provide information, for the sake of transparency and according to access to information laws. This allows citizens, academia, and the press to request information on CNDH's performance, which subjects the institution to intense scrutiny. For its part, the Commission requests external audits by private companies to make its actions more transparent.

---

87 See Recommendation 15VG/2018 of the CNDH.

88 See Recommendation 14VG/2018 of the CNDH.

89 See Law of the National Commission on Human Rights, art 52.

90 See J. Mena, 'Artículo 53 (Contenido de los informes anuales)' in J. Luis Soberanes, L. García López-Guerrero, and J. Mena (eds.), *Ley de la Comisión Nacional de los Derechos Humanos comentada y concordada* (CNDH, Mexico City 2005) p. 380.

91 See Law of the National Commission on Human Rights, art 53. See also V. Manuel Collí, 'Artículo 52 (Informes anuales)' in J. Luis Soberanes, L. García López-Guerrero, and J. Mena (eds.), *Ley de la Comisión Nacional de los Derechos Humanos comentada y concordada* (CNDH, Mexico City 2005) p. 372.

6. REGIME OF AUTONOMY

The 1999 constitutional reforms gave the CNDH management and budgetary autonomy, legal personality, and its own assets. This implies that it should not be linked or subordinated to any other constitutional organ or state power.[92] It also stipulated that the appointment of the President of the CNDH must be made by the Senate of the Republic, without any exogenous intervention. Civil society, however, will be involved in this process, through a non-binding consultation mechanism.

The Law states that the CNDH shall have financial autonomy and that the federal government will provide it with the material and financial resources for its proper functioning.[93] Despite the CNDH's supposed legal right to these resources, it has recently been affected by austerity criteria imposed by the federal government.[94] Such interference in economic matters could affect the Commission's autonomy.

The President of the CNDH can only be removed through an impeachment process.[95] In this way, the law seeks to guarantee his or her impartiality and the fulfilment of his or her functions, while protecting the institution from political pressure and legal sanctions. The CNDH's recommendations are not subject to judicial review and there is no recourse against them.[96] Moreover, the staff of the Commission are not responsible for the effects of action taken on the basis of their opinions. Management autonomy also means that the CNDH can issue internal criteria: in the form of regulations and guidelines for action and through the creation of programmes, etc. The Commission, as an autonomous constitutional body, has its own legal personality, and in the performance of its duties and exercise of its autonomy, the CNDH must not receive instructions or indications from any authority.[97]

The constitutional reform of 2011 further established that State constitutions must also guarantee the autonomy of State human rights commissions. To date, all constitutions have met this obligation,[98] although several State commissions lack *de facto* autonomy and are controlled by the governors.[99] On the federal

---

[92] See A. Brewer, *Mecanismos nacionales de protección de los derechos humanos* (Instituto Interamericano de Derechos Humanos, San José 2005) p. 279, available at: <https://www.iidh.ed.cr/IIDH/media/1988/mecanismos-nacionales-de-proteccion-2005.pdf>.

[93] See Law of the National Commission on Human Rights, art 75.

[94] See below, section 9.1.

[95] See Political Constitution of the United Mexican States, art 102-B.

[96] See Law of the National Commission on Human Rights, art 47.

[97] See Internal Regulation of the National Human Rights Commission, art 4.

[98] See the CNDH's follow-up platform on the normative harmonisation of human rights, available at: <http://armonizacion.cndh.org.mx/Armonia/Armonizacion>.

[99] J. Carpizo, '¿Es acertada la probable transferencia …' (n 37) p. 325.

level as well, the autonomy of the current President of the CNDH has been seriously questioned due to the interference of the executive power and various irregularities in her appointment, her party militancy, and because of her complacent stance towards the executive power. The critiques have accused the current administration of the CNDH of refraining from condemning human rights violations, particularly in the areas of health, rule of law and criminal policy, and of supporting the executive's controversial initiatives to increase the militarisation of the country and to modify the electoral system.[100]

7. FULFILMENT OF THE PARIS PRINCIPLES

The Mexican state has implemented various measures to fully comply with the Paris Principles on NHRIs. Consequently, it has not only raised the Commission's autonomy to constitutional status but has also instituted legal reforms to strengthen the CNDH's performance and made efforts to provide the Commission with mechanisms to promote compliance with its recommendations.

As a result, in November 2016, the CNDH was re-accredited with A-status by the Global Alliance of National Institutions for the Promotion and Protection of Human Rights (GANHRI).[101] On that occasion, the Sub-Committee on Accreditation (SCA) expressed some concerns, addressed a number of issues, and made recommendations to further improve the CNDH's compliance with the Paris Principles. These recommendations emphasised the need for the CNDH to: implement rigorous and systematic follow-up mechanisms for recommendations contained in annual, special, and thematic reports; establish an independent, clear, objective, and fair dismissal process, in conformity with substantive and procedural requirements; ensure a clear, transparent, and participatory selection and appointment process to promote merit-based selection and ensure diversity to guarantee the independence of and public confidence in the institution; ensure diversity in its membership and staff; carry out the formalisation of its role as National Mechanism for Prevention of Torture; and continue its engagement with the international human rights system.[102]

---

[100] See interview to Luis de la Barrefa Solorzano, available at: <https://cuestione.com/nacional/cndh-organismo-autonomo-sin-autonomia/>; and 'Las críticas a la CNDH por pedir trasformaciones al INE' Reforma, available at: <https://www.reforma.com/las-criticas-a-la-cndh-por-pedir-transformacion-de-ine/ar2495644>.

[101] See generally the Report and Recommendations of the Session of the Sub-Committee on Accreditation, Geneva, 14–18 November 2016, of the Global Alliance of National Human Rights Institutions (GANHRI), available at; <https://nhri.ohchr.org/EN/AboutUs/GANHRIAccreditation/Documents/SCA%20Final%20Report%20-%20Nov%202016%20-%20English.pdf>.

[102] See ibid, para. 2.10.

Some of these recommendations rest in the hands of the legislator; however, on the Commission's side, a series of measures have been undertaken to strengthen its internal mechanisms and overcome the challenges posed by the SCA report. The CNDH's response has included follow-up on the recommendations and proposals made through its special reports, annual reports, general recommendations, etc. In this regard, CNDH has issued a 'Special Report on Claims for the Judicial Review of Statutes'; a 'Special Report on Follow-up to Recommendations'; and the 'Studies on the Compliance and Impact of the CNDH's General Recommendations, Special Reports, and Pronouncements 2001–2017'. The latter is an ambitious work, published in several volumes, which address various topics, such as: children and adolescents; migrant persons; women and gender; the persecution of journalists and civilian defenders; protected natural areas and human rights; human rights in the prison system; discrimination; the procurement and administration of justice; the right to health protection; and rights of individuals, peoples, and indigenous communities.[103]

Regarding other aspects of the SCA recommendations, constitutional provisions which establish the procedure for the dismissal of high-level public servants have not been reformed; however, the process for appointing the President of CNDH has been regulated in more detail and the participation of NGOs in the consultation process has been strengthened.[104] An additional requirement was also incorporated for the appointment of General Inspectors: a minimum of three years' experience in human rights issues.[105] However, a recent reform initiative seeks to remove these and other requirements for such officers. The composition of the CNDH is varied and plural, and there is no *de jure* or *de facto* restriction that allows for the exclusion of or discrimination against any person; on the contrary, the Political Constitution prohibits any kind of discrimination.[106]

In 2017, the Mexican Congress expanded the powers of the CNDH, including among its functions the responsibility of presiding over and ensuring compliance with the powers conferred on the National Mechanism for the Prevention of Torture: through the provisions of the General Law to Prevent, Investigate and Punish Torture and Other Cruel, Inhuman or Degrading

---

103 These reports and studies are available at: <www.cndh.org.mx/pronunciamientos-estudios-informes-especiales>.

104 See Law of the National Commission on Human Rights, art 10. The relevant decree was published on 25 June 2018 in the OGF. Recently, NGOs requested that the SCA conduct a special review of the current A-status of the CNDH. The relevant letter, which is addressed to the SCA, is available at: <http://cmdpdh.org/wp-content/uploads/2019/12/carta-a-sca-ganhri.pdf>.

105 See Law of the National Commission on Human Rights, art 23.III-bis. The respective decree was published on 25 June 2018 in the OGF.

106 See Political Constitution of the United Mexican States, art 1.5.

Treatment or Punishment.[107] The CNDH thus submits reports to relevant treaty bodies; cooperates with various international agencies, both from the universal and regional protection systems; and promotes compliance with international human rights law at the domestic level.

The maintenance of CNDH's A-status accreditation will depend on the Commission's continued compliance with the standards established in the Paris Principles on NHRIs.

8. RELATIONSHIP WITH INTERNATIONAL MONITORING BODIES

The CNDH plays an important role in the implementation of international human rights law in Mexico. This has been the case since its creation in the 1990s. Indeed, the original mandate of the Commission included the promotion of Mexico's compliance with the human rights treaties it had already signed.[108] This was reinforced by the 2011 constitutional amendment, which recognised the hierarchy for human rights established in treaties. Article 1 of the Constitution now states that 'all individuals shall be entitled to the human rights granted by this Constitution and the international treaties signed by the Mexican State, as well as to the guarantees for the protection of these rights'.[109] Because of this provision, there is a clear constitutional mandate for federal and local authorities to exercise their powers and competences with due respect for human rights.

The Supreme Court of Justice has also given the jurisprudence of the IACtHR greater weight, by incorporating the doctrine of 'conventionality control' into the Mexican legal system.[110] This doctrine was created by the IACtHR and requires that all the authorities of the state parties to the ACHR must interpret their domestic law in accordance with the Inter-American *corpus juris* and avoid the enforcement of anti-conventional laws, in cases where no consistent interpretation is legally possible.[111] The Mexican Supreme Court of Justice has declared that all authorities of the state must 'interpret the legal system in light

107 See Law of the National Commission on Human Rights, art 6.XI-bis. The relevant decree was published on 26 June 2017 in the OGF.

108 See Political Constitution of the United Mexican States, art 1.

109 Ibid. See generally M. Carbonell and P. Salazar (eds.), *La reforma constitucional de derechos humanos: un nuevo paradigma* (UNAM, Mexico City 2011).

110 See SCJN file 489/2010 (2010). See also SCJN P/J 293/2011, *Semanario Judicial de la Federación* 10 (2014), vol. I, at 96.

111 See *Almonacid v. Chile*, IACtHR, Judgment, 26 September 2006, Series C Nr. 154, para. 126. See also P. Gonzalez Dominguez, *The Doctrine of Conventionality Control. Between Universality and Legal Pluralism in the Inter-American Human Rights System*, Intersentia, Cambridge 2018, p. 2.

of human rights as protected by the Constitution and in international treaties to which the Mexican State is a party, all times favouring the broadest protection for the person'.[112] It has also considered the decisions of the IACtHR to be binding, in line with the doctrine of conventionality control, at least with respect to those decisions meeting certain requirements. This is true even in cases where Mexico was not a party to the case.[113]

This ample incorporation of human rights standards into the Mexican legal system has bolstered the CNDH's role as a non-jurisdictional bridge, mitigating the perennial conflict between the international and national legal orders.[114] As mentioned above, the Commission issues pronouncements and recommendations against federal and local authorities for actions or omissions that constitute human rights violations; investigates cases of serious human rights violations; and brings actions challenging the constitutionality of general laws. This incorporation of human rights into Mexican law also strengthens the subsidiary implementation of the international system of human rights – both at the regional and universal levels – not only by heightening the protection of victims but also by serving as a mechanism of control of state authorities on the basis of international human rights law.[115]

Furthermore, the CNDH relies on international human rights law to strengthen its own decisions. For instance, in a recent recommendation, the Commission addressed the phenomenon of widespread and systematic kidnapping and killing of migrants, carried out primarily by members of organised criminal groups, in some cases with the direct participation or at least the acquiesce of state authorities. The CNDH reasoned that the obligation of the state to prevent crime is part of its duty to ensure the rights protected by the ACHR. It also discussed the connection that exists between the duty to investigate human rights violations and the rights to access justice and the truth.[116] As these violations have also been addressed by the IACtHR in several decisions, the Commission explicitly quoted some of its decisions.[117] Other recommendations have followed a similar approach.[118]

---

112 SCJN file 489/2010 (2010). See Political Constitution of the United Mexican States, art 1.

113 See SCJN P/J 293/2011, *Semanario Judicial de la Federación* 10 (2014), vol. I, at 96.

114 See S. Garcia Ramírez, 'The Relationship between Inter-American Jurisdiction and States (National Systems): Some Pertinent Questions' (2015) 5/1 *Notre Dame Journal of International & Comparative Law* 115, 124.

115 See P. Carozza, 'The Problematic Applicability of Subsidiarity to International Law and Institutions' (2016) 61/1 *The American Journal of Jurisprudence* 51, 53.

116 See Recommendation 23VG/2019 of the CNDH.

117 See ibid, para. 175. The CNDH referred to the following cases: *Suárez v. Ecuador*, IACtHR, Judgment, 12 November 1997, Series C Nr. 35; *Acosta v. Ecuador*, IACtHR, Judgment, 24 June 2004, Series C Nr. 129; *Tibi v. Ecuador*, IACtHR, Judgment, 7 September 2004, Series C Nr. 114; *García Asto and Ramírez Rojas v. Peru*, IACtHR, Judgment, 25 November 2005, Series C Nr. 137; and *López Álvarez v. Honduras*, IACtHR, Judgment, 1 February 2006, Series C Nr. 141.

118 See Recommendation 92/2019 of the CNDH.

Yet, the relationship of the CNDH with international monitoring bodies is not limited to the control of federal and local authorities on the basis of substantive standards of international human rights law; the Commission is also concerned with Mexico's direct compliance with particular international obligations, which have been agreed upon by the state in some human rights treaties. This is the case when it comes to Article 3 of the Optional Protocol to the Convention against Torture and Other Cruel, Inhuman or Degrading Treatment or Punishment, which establishes that '[e]ach State Party shall set up, designate or maintain at the domestic level one or several visiting bodies for the prevention of torture and other cruel, inhuman or degrading treatment or punishment'.[119] The CNDH was entrusted with carrying out this function by the National Mechanism for the Prevention of Torture, which was itself created by law in compliance with the optional protocol.[120] In conformity with this mechanism, the CNDH visits places of detention and issues reports, observations, and recommendations.[121] The Commission is also responsible for evaluating and monitoring the compliance of gender equality policies; this role is in accordance with the Mexican Law on Equality between Women and Men, which implements the Convention on the Elimination of All Forms of Discrimination against Women.[122]

The CNDH has even participated in some procedures carried out by international monitoring institutions. For example, the Commission has intervened as *amicus curiae* before the IACtHR and has presented relevant information to the Court regarding the compliance of the Mexican state with obligations applicable in a particular case. In recent cases, including *Carvajal et al v. Colombia* and *Herzog v. Brazil*, the CNDH informed the IACtHR about the context of violence and impunity that typically prompts attacks on journalists in the region as well as the chilling effects on press freedom that these attacks produce.[123] In *Castro Rodriguez v. Mexico*, the Commission carried out, upon request, a risk analysis regarding the beneficiary of provisional measures granted by the IACtHR.[124]

---

119 Article 3, Optional Protocol to the Convention against Torture and other Cruel, Inhuman or Degrading Treatment or Punishment, adopted December 2002, entered into force 22 June 2006.

120 See Law of the National Commission on Human Rights, art 6.XI-bis.

121 See the 2017 Annual Activity Report of the CNDH's National Mechanism for the Prevention of Torture, pp. 1–88, available at: <https://www.cndh.org.mx/pagina/informes-anuales-mnpt>.

122 See Law of the National Commission on Human Rights, art 6.XIV-bis. The respective decree was published on 2 August 2006 in the OGF. See also Law on Equality between Women and Men, art 22.

123 See *Carvajal et al v. Colombia*, IACtHR, Judgment, 13 March 2018, Series C Nr. 352, para. 8; and *Herzog v. Brazil*, IACtHR, Judgment, 15 March 2018, Series C Nr. 353, para. 12.

124 See *Castro Rodríguez v. Mexico*, IACtHR, Provisional measures, 14 November 2017, para. 17.

The CNDH also collaborates indirectly with international institutions through the information it produces. This occurs where such information is presented as evidence in specific proceedings. This has happened in several cases before the IACtHR.[125] For instance, in *Radilla v. Mexico*, the Court relied heavily on an investigation carried out by the Commission, which concerned 532 complaints of forced disappearance perpetrated during the so-called 'Dirty War' of the 1970s.[126] By the same token, the IACtHR considered information provided by the CNDH in its decision, in the same case, on the monitoring of compliance with the judgment.[127] Similar situations have occurred at UN monitoring bodies.[128]

The relationship between the CNDH and international institutions is dynamic and serves different purposes. On the one hand, it involves implementing standards of international human rights law through various actions derived from its mandate: the promotion of human rights; the control of federal and local authorities through quasi-jurisdictional mechanisms; and the duty to carry out some international obligations, as determined by human rights treaties and as legislated by national law. On the other hand, the relationship involves the direct and indirect participation of the CNDH in procedures conducted by international monitoring institutions.

9. CURRENT CHALLENGES

For many years, CNDH has been a relevant political and social actor and a very important instrument in the development of Mexican democracy. The Commission has transitioned from being a government office to an autonomous body, invested with constitutional autonomy and operational independence. Although it has faced some criticism in the past for sometimes being too soft on the government or because some of its recommendations might have been influenced by political calculation, the CNDH has still managed to acquire a

125 See *González et al. v. Mexico* (*'Campo algodonero'*), IACtHR, Judgment, 16 November 2009, Series C Nr. 205, para. 116; *Cabrera and Montiel v. Mexico*, IACtHR, Judgment, 26 November 2010, Series C Nr. 220, paras. 74–89; *Women victims of sexual torture in Atenco v. Mexico* IACtHR, Judgment, 28 November 2018, Series C Nr. 371, para. 35; and *Alvarado and others v. México*, IACtHR, Judgment, 28 November 2018, Series C Nr. 371, para. 139.

126 See *Radilla v. Mexico*, IACtHR, Judgment, 23 November 2009, Series C Nr. 209, paras. 132–37. See also Recommendation 26/2001 of the CNDH.

127 See *Radilla v. Mexico*, IACtHR, Monitoring compliance with judgment, 19 May 2011, para. 12.

128 For instance, in his report on extrajudicial, summary, or arbitrary executions, a follow up to his mission to Mexico, the special rapporteur of the HRC relied on the information and conclusions of the CNDH, as presented in several of its recommendations, as evidence to sustain his own conclusions. See UN A/HRC/32/39/Add.2 of 6 May 2016.

solid moral authority and recognition, and it is considered to be one of the most reliable and respected institutions of the Mexican bureaucratic apparatus.

9.1. LOSS OF AUTONOMY AND BUDGETARY CONSTRAINTS

Recent events, however, have shed light on the Commission's fragility. The current political atmosphere, which, after the 2018 election, saw the return of a one-man government and a hegemonic political party, also impacts the CNDH and compromises its stability and regime of autonomy. Political actors have claimed that the 2019 appointment process of the Commission's new President lacked transparency, and they subsequently filed an appeal with the Supreme Court of Justice to overturn her appointment; this is still pending. The Office of the UN High Commissioner for Human Rights (HCHR) issued a press release, emphasising the need to ensure the independence, autonomy, and legitimacy of the CNDH.[129]

The performance of the current President has been further criticised and has proved her critics right. Since her appointment, six members of the Advisory Council have resigned, accusing the new administration of a certain slowness and lack of determination to address urgent issues in the country, such as: the prevention and eradication of torture; the protection of migrants, journalists, and human rights defenders; access to health and the supply of medicines; etc. These concerns should not be taken lightly, especially considering the important role that the CNDH has played in the last three decades. The loss of the Commission's autonomy and efficacy endangers democracy and human rights in Mexico by reducing the checks on government abuses and authoritarian practices.

Another threat to the CNDH's autonomy derives from recent budgetary constraints. In 2019, the Commission's annual budget was cut by 11 per cent.[130] The current administration's so-called 'austerity policy' has led to a decrease in the salaries of CNDH officials. Employment benefits, such as medical and life insurance, productivity bonuses, and the separation fund, have also been cut. This affects the stability of civil servants in their employment, and it might

---

129 See OHCHR Mexico, 'ONU-DH enfatiza la necesidad de asegurar la independencia y autonomía de la Comisión Nacional de los Derechos Humanos' (OHCHR Mexico City 20 November 2019), available at: <http://www.hchr.org.mx/images/Comunicados/2019/20191120_ComPrensa_CNDH.pdf>.

130 In 2018, the budget assigned to CNDH amounted to 2,033,004,229 Mexican pesos (MXN); in 2019, MXN 1,809,400,000; and in 2020, MXN 1,874,207,802. See the 2020 draft budget of the Mexican Federation, available at: <www.ppef.hacienda.gob.mx/work/models/PPEF2020/docs/35/r35_ep.pdf>; see also R. Rueda, 'Presupuesto 2020 "premia" a CNDH y "castiga" al INE e INAI', *El Financiero* (Mexico City, 25 November 2019), available at: <https://elfinanciero.com.mx/nacional/presupuesto-2020-premia-a-cndh-y-castiga-al-ine-e-inai>.

reduce employee loyalty and commitment to the Commission, compromising the quality of the service provided to the public. The overall operating budget has also recently been decreased.

9.2. EFFECTIVENESS

The CNDH's recommendations have a declaratory character.[131] For them to be binding, procedures would have to conform to due process requirements, in the form of strict procedural rules, as required by the rule of law, thus turning the CNDH into a kind of court, which would compromise its authority and nature as well as its effectiveness in the protection of human rights.[132]

Nevertheless, recent efforts have been made to strengthen compliance with the CNDH's recommendations. For instance, the 2011 constitutional reforms established a mechanism that allows the CNDH to request the Senate of the Republic to summon any official who refuses to accept or comply with a recommendation. This power is, however, subject to two levels of discretion or, in other words, it is doubly discretionary: on the one hand, the Commission has to determine whether to make a request to the Senate; on the other, the Senate can, in turn, either follow up on the CNDH's request or choose to ignore it. In a parliament with a one-party majority, as is the case at present, it becomes foreseeable that obstacles will be encountered, at least in situations involving authorities from that same party. In brief, the procedure is not properly regulated, and some adjustments are needed to ensure its impartiality and effectiveness, particularly in complex political contexts.

In light of the claims made by various political actors regarding the proximity of the current President of the CNDH to the government in office, it is particularly necessary to demonstrate the Commission's institutional strength. It must guarantee its impartiality and autonomy, which has been tested when addressing human rights violations committed by the administration as well as when it presents claims for the abstract review of statutes against laws promoted by the ruling party. In that regard, the current administration has proven to side with the federal government – either by action or omission – on crucial matters that have relevant human rights connotations in Mexico. For instance, in October 2022, the CNDH issued a statement supporting a constitutional amendment proposed by the President's Party aimed to deeply transform the Mexican electoral system. This system, although far from perfect, has been a cornerstone of the young Mexican democracy. The proposed amendment

131 See Soberanes (n 57) p. 38.

132 See Carpizo, '¿Es acertada la probable transferencia …' (n 37) p. 322.

was criticised,[133] and its approval would certainly be a step backwards for democracy.

While many human rights violations are committed by federal authorities, a relevant share of transgressions are caused by local authorities, either State or county. Often influenced by political interests, both at the federal and State levels, the collaboration between the CNDH and the 32 State commissions has, at times, been tense. The fragmentation between the different protection bodies inevitably compromises their effectiveness, and the procedure for the CNDH's exercise of the power of attraction is not sufficiently regulated.

As stressed by the UN Special Rapporteur on Extrajudicial, Summary or Arbitrary Executions, the greatest challenge for the Commission's effectiveness remains 'insufficient commitment from the authorities' and the 'unsatisfactory rate of compliance' with its recommendations.[134]

10. CONCLUSION

Mexico faces serious human rights problems. Since the creation of the CNDH, in 1990, much progress has been made in various areas: the strengthening of the CNDH's legal framework through various constitutional reforms; the signing of treaties; the issuance or amendment of laws, regulations, and practices; and the creation of institutions. The sensitivity of the population and the authorities to human rights has also grown, and there is greater awareness of the limits of the state and the need to respect human rights. Although there is still a long way to go, it can be said that the CNDH has contributed significantly to the Mexican rule of law and the common good: by greatly promoting to human rights, as limiters of state action, and by issuing recommendations and reports on sensitive human rights questions.

However, new challenges and difficulties have emerged, including the spread of organised crime, political upheavals and divisions, erosion of democratic institutions and practices, etc. Such developments have important human rights connotations for federal and local authorities; this is particularly true in a country that carries problems from its past, which can easily lead to riots and instability and deepen the existing inequality gap. These exacerbatory problems include deficient training of the authorities to prosecute, procure, and deliver justice; corruption; impunity; a fractured and complex political and social context; and

133 European Commission for Democracy Through Law (Venice Commission). *Opinion on the Draft Constitutional Amendments Concerning the Electoral System.* Approved by the Council for Democratic Elections at its 74th meeting (October 2022), and adopted by the Venice Commission at its 132 Plenary Session (Venice, 21–22 October 2022); available at: <https://www.venice.coe.int/webforms/documents/?pdf=CDL-AD(2022)031-e>.

134 See generally UN Doc. A/HRC/32/39/Add.2 of 6 May 2016.

economic poverty and a lack of basic goods, such as food, housing, education, and infrastructure. In this scenario, it is all the more essential to have a solid, autonomous NHRI, with sufficient moral authority and the operational capacity to face these various challenges. The Mexican state must show clear signs of a genuine commitment to human rights. For this reason, the strengthening of the CNDH is, once again, a matter of urgency: so that the institution can function as a genuine mechanism for limiting power and effectively protecting human rights.

COMMISSION NATIONALE CONSULTATIVE DES DROITS DE L'HOMME (FRANCE)

Emmanuel DECAUX[1]

1. INTRODUCTION

The *Commission nationale consultative des droits de l'homme* (CNCDH), or French National Advisory Commission for Human Rights, is one of the world's oldest NHRIs. Since its inception, the CNDCH has passed through three stages, with different legal bases and mandates.

1.1. THE *ARRÊTÉ MINISTÉRIEL* OF 1947

Established in 1947, by an order of the Minister of Foreign Affairs, as the 'advisory commission for the codification of international law and the definition of the rights and duties of States and human rights', this NHRI was originally composed of 10 eminent members, including Suzanne Bastid (1906–1995), Charles Chaumont (1913–2001), Henri Donnedieu de Vabres (1880–1952), and Georges Scelle (1878–1961), under the leadership of René Cassin (1887–1976).[2] As an administrative commission within the Ministry of Foreign Affairs, its mission was to prepare initiatives and position papers for French diplomats acting within the International Law Commission and the Human Rights Commission of the UN. This first French Commission was particularly instrumental in the

1 The author has been a member of this NHRI from 1992 to 2022; however, the current contribution is presented in his private capacity and reflects his personal views. For a first critical appreciation of the CNCDH, see E. DECAUX, 'Utile Cassandre, du rôle de la Commission nationale consultative des droits de l'Homme' in *Pouvoir et liberté: études offertes à Jacques Mourgeon*, Bruylant, Brussels 1998, p 589.

2 Its original name was *Commission Consultative pour la Codification du droit international et la définition des droits et devoirs des Etats et des droits de l'homme*. See Official Gazette of the French Republic (*Journal Officiel de la République française* (JORF) of 27 March 1947, p. 2849. During this period, the institution was renamed *Commission consultative du droit international*, and later *Commission nationale consultative des droits de l'homme*.

travaux préparatoires of the 1948 Universal Declaration of Human Rights and the 1966 International Covenants on Civil and Political Rights, and Economic, Social and Cultural Rights.[3] Throughout this period, the Commission did not have monitoring functions.

1.2. THE REVISED *DECRET* OF 1984

The CNCDH was re-established in 1984, by a decree of the Prime Minister. This iteration was modelled as an advisory commission for human rights, with more independence from the administration. It was placed under the presidency of Nicole Questiaux, a former minister who was then a member of the *Conseil d'État*, (Council of State). At a time when France was faced with new legal commitments, both at the regional and universal levels, the CNCDH was entrusted with a limited external competence.[4] In 1986, this new entity was attached to a *secrétaire d'État*, an office with inter-ministerial scope, under the aegis of the Prime Minister. It was entrusted with not only a national but also an international mandate, as was reflected in its new name: the National Advisory Commission for Human Rights. Three years later, the Commission was directly attached to the office of the Prime Minister for administrative matters, but it enjoyed full political independence. The CNCDH's members increased, first to about 40 members and eventually to almost 70. In order to reflect all sectors of French society, members included: NGOs; trade-unionists; religious leaders; free-thinkers; magistrates and advocates, or barristers; diplomats and civil servants; physicians; social workers; academics; etc. Under the charismatic chairmanship of Paul Bouchet (1924–2019), a member of the *Conseil d'État*, the CNCDH was highly involved in the creation of an international network of NHRIs and organised, in partnership with the UN Human Rights Secretariat, the so-called Kleber Conference of 1991,[5] where the Paris Principles on NHRIs were adopted.[6] During this time, several administrative reforms periodically revised the decree of 1984, to reinforce the CNCDH's independence, scope of mandate, and efficiency.

---

3 See E. Pateyron, *La contribution française à la rédaction de la Déclaration universelle des droits de l'Homme: René Cassin et la Commission consultative des droits de l'homme*, La Documentation Française, Paris 1998; G-H. Soutou, *La France et la Déclaration universelle des droits de l'homme du 10 décembre 1948*, Les éditions du Diplomate, Paris 2008.

4 See JORF of 1 February 1984, 489. The amended versions of this decree are available at: <https://www.legifrance.gouv.fr/>.

5 Named after the Centre for International Conferences located in Avenue Kleber, Paris.

6 They were subsequently endorsed by the UNGA in 1993. See UN General Assembly Res. 48/134 of 20 December 1993. See also G. Fellous, *Les institutions nationales des droits de l'homme: acteurs de troisième type*, La Documentation Française, Paris 2006.

1.3. THE ACT AND THE DECREE OF 2007

To ensure full compliance with the Paris Principles on NHRIs, the CNCDH was vested with its legislative basis through an act of the French Parliament, in 2007.[7] Due to the distinction between legal competencies and administrative matters made in Articles 34 and 37 of the Constitution of France, the main provisions regulating the CNCDH were still contained in a decree of 2007.[8] As in its former stage of development, the Commission's mandate continued as a three-year term, and the nomination of its President and its body of 64 members continued to be made through an order of the Prime Minister. Due to the fact that appointment of the CNCDH's President is discretionary, in contrast to those of its two Vice-Presidents, who are elected by the institution's members, a conflict of legitimacy has ensued between the head of the Commission and the two representatives of its constituency. Besides this, the appointment process can become complicated and time-consuming, for it involves the consultation of a panel of three 'wise men': the Vice-President of the *Conseil d'État*; the Premier President of the *Cour de cassation* (Court of Cassation); and the President of the *Cour des comptes* (Court of Auditors). There have been gaps in the appointment of the Commission's President, which have affected the continuity and effectiveness of the CNCDH.[9] In 2019, the Sub-Committee on Accreditation (SCA) of the Global Alliance for National Human Rights Institutions (GANHRI) noted that

> the decree is silent on the number of times that a term can be renewed except in the case of the Chairperson and the two deputies whose terms can only be renewed once. In order to promote institutional independence, the SCA is of the view that it would be preferable for all members' terms to be limited to one renewal.[10]

It is not obvious that this recommendation will be a cure to the endemic lack of continuity in respect of the CNCDH's head. On the other hand, the institutional memory of older members is a strong asset for the continuity and consistency of the Commission as a collective independent body. The panel of wise men adopted the same view, encouraging turn-over and seeking to represent the 'diversity of the society'.[11]

---

7 See JORF of 5 March 2007, p. 4215.

8 See JORF of 27 July 2007, p. 12679.

9 This happened, for instance, in 2009, 2012, and 2018. In 2022, there was again a gap of six months before the two mandates, while the secretariat was dealing with current affairs.

10 Report and Recommendations of the Session of the Sub-Committee on Accreditation, Geneva, 11–15 March 2019, of the Global Alliance of National Human Rights Institutions, para. 3.4.

11 JORF of 13 November 2022, advisory opinion of 2 June 2022.

2. OLD AND NEW MANDATES

2.1. GENERAL MANDATE

The CNCDH must promote and protect human rights, both nationally and internationally, by way of advisory opinions, studies, and reports. The Commission has a broad competency, which is at the crossroads of several issues, such as policies that violate constitutional rules or disregard human rights, the domestic implementation of international obligations, diplomatic initiatives, etc. As an independent body, the CNCDH can be seised by the government for any topic and can also act by itself: at least, this has been the case since 1989. While the Commission's drafts and debates are private, to facilitate the free exchanges of views, its final documents are officially published in the annual reports of activities of the *Documentation française* public service publisher and, more recently, under the presidency of Christine Lazerges, in the *Journal officiel de la République française* (JORF). They are also broadly disseminated on the internet, through the CNCDH's website.

2.2. SPECIFIC MANDATES

An Act of 1990, dealing with the fight against racism, antisemitism, and xenophobia, established the CNCDH as a monitoring body, which was now in charge of presenting the Prime Minister with an annual report on 21 March.[12] These reports are duly published by the CNCDH but have continued without a public presentation to the Prime Minister since 2006. These documents combine statistics and opinion polls with the analysis of state agencies, social scientists, and other civil society actors. The reports present general trends and policies and also consider yearly thematic issues, with recommendations made for all relevant stakeholders. In 1996, the scope of the CNCDH's international mandate was increased, as the institution was tasked with acting as the French commission for the application and implementation of international humanitarian law. It performs this role within a network run by the International Committee of the Red Cross.

More recently, new thematic mandates have been entrusted to the CNCDH, as an 'independent rapporteur' across certain topics, including: human trafficking, following the 2014 national plan of action, which responded to the recommendations of the Group of Experts on Action against Trafficking in

12 These reports are available at: <https://www.cncdh.fr/fr/publications>.

Human Beings (GRETA); persons with disabilities, following the Convention on the Rights of Persons with Disabilities (CRPD) and in coordination with the *Défenseur des droits*; discrimination against LGBTI persons, following the 2018 national plan of mobilisation; and the UN Guiding Principles on Business and Human Rights, in response to the 2017 national plan of action. It must be underscored that these new missions, which might imply very specialised competencies, are not linked with new administrative or financial resources and that the CNCDH's framework remains unchanged. In its 2019 report, the SCA declared that it

> acknowledges that the CNCDH has been provided with new legislative responsibilities in relation to human trafficking, business and human rights, and anti-LGBT hate. While these new mandates include responsibilities related to protection, the SCA notes that these are thematic mandates and do not provide an explicit broad protection mandate.[13]

The SCA added that:

> [S]uch functions include monitoring, inquiring, investigating and reporting of human rights violations, and may include individual complaint handling. The SCA encourages the CCDH to continue to broaden its activities in relation to its protection mandate and to advocate for amendments to its enabling law to make its broad protection mandate explicit.[14]

3. THE COMMISSION'S FRAMEWORK

3.1. MEMBERSHIP OF THE CNCDH

The Commission has 64 members, with two colleges of 30 persons: the first includes representatives from civil society and the second is composed of so-called 'qualified persons' in the field of human rights. The four other members of the CNCDH include: a representative from each of the National Assembly, the Senate, and the Economic, Social and Environmental Council; as well as the *Défenseur des droits*, who, as the former *Médiateur de la République*, is an *ex officio* member of the Commission. All of the Commission's members act *pro bono*. Some members are not very effective, such as the two representatives

---

13 Report and Recommendations of the Session of the Sub-Committee on Accreditation, Geneva, 11–15 March 2019, of the Global Alliance of National Human Rights Institutions, para. 3.4.

14 See ibid.

of the French Parliament, whose participation only politicises the debates. Contrary to the claims of a former President of the CNCDH, this NHRI is not a 'little Parliament'; it is a meeting of men and women from all walks of life, inspired by common legal and humanist principles and respect for the pluralism and diversity of society, who are seeking to build a strong consensus on human rights.

As mentioned, the Prime Minister appoints the Commission's President, who can stay in office for two consecutive mandates of three years. Throughout the CNCDH's history, there has been an alternation of three-year and six-year tenures. The bureau is also composed of two Vice-Presidents. At times in the past, these officers were politically appointed, as a means to control and undermine the President, and they were not accountable to the rest of the Commission's members. Since 2009, the two Vice-Presidents have been elected by the CNCDH itself. Although the first election of these officers was decided by consensus, and the President was receptive to the advice of the bureau, the subsequent years have seen highly antagonistic elections, and the relationship between the President, the bureau's other members, and the CNCDH's wider membership has, at times, been quite dysfunctional, with different actors favouring opposing views and differing legitimisations.[15] As a result, a new informal coordinating committee was created to sooth the relationship.

3.2. THE TWO FACES OF THE SECRETARY-GENERAL

Another member of the bureau is the Secretary-General, who has a consultative status at the CNCDH. The Commission's President often does not participate in the international, English-speaking networks of NHRIs. This is where the Secretary-General steps in, as a key element of the CNCDH: not only in terms of its international visibility but also with regard to its domestic continuity. Gérard Fellous, for instance, was a very active Secretary-General. He worked closely with Commission Presidents Paul Bouchet (1989–1996) and Jean Kahn (1996–1999) and was instrumental in the adoption of the Paris Principles, the development of the first network of NHRIs, the creation of the European Information Network on Racism and Xenophobia (RAXEN), and the European Monitoring Centre on Racism and Xenophobia, which is known today as the European Union Agency for Fundamental Rights (FRA). The Secretary-General is now the public face of the CNCDH at international meetings and, thanks to

15 Jean-Marie Delarue, a respected member of the Conseil d'Etat, nominated as president in 2019, presented his resignation a year later.

Michel Forst and Magali Lafourcade, who both chaired the SCA, has a strong involvement in the GANHRI.[16]

The Secretary-General is also the head of a small team of a dozen legal advisers, who, working under his or her administrative direction, assist the members of the CNCDH involved in the various *pôles* (see below section 4.1). These are contractual agents, paid by the French state within its administrative budgetary structures. The responsibility for drafting studies and reports is entrusted to Commission members with a strong legal background and political expertise.

4. ORGANISATION: MATTERS AND MANNERS

4.1. FROM SUB-COMMISSIONS TO WORKING GROUPS

The plenary of the CNCDH is its General Assembly, which used to hold one meeting each month to debate and adopt reports and memoranda of advice prepared by thematic groups. Four or five sub-commissions deal, respectively, with:

- ethics, education, and social issues;
- racism and discrimination;
- legal issues, rule of law, security matters, status of foreigners, and asylum-seekers;
- international issues, with a priority on the UN system and international criminal law but also on regional organisations, such as the European Court of Human Rights; and finally
- humanitarian law and action.

In 2018, a new sub-commission was created for emergency situations in order to be more reactive to humanitarian issues or political topics. Usually, each sub-commission was open to the full participation of the Commission's members and had a monthly meeting, with more meetings for hearings or drafting reports. This trend towards a more specialised membership from generalists with transversal knowledge was reinforced by the multiplication of working groups inside each *pôle*. For example, Sub-Commission D on International and European issues is supervising three working groups: a) on humanitarian international law, dealing also with law of the war and disbarment; b) on Transnational corporations and human rights; and c) on monitoring of treaty bodies and international jurisdictions.

16 See M. Lafourcade, 'Le réseau international des Institutions nationales des droits de l'homme' (2019) 20 *Annuaire français des relations internationales* 917.

4.2. THE OUTPUT OF THE COMMISSION

In the past, the advisory opinions presented by the CNCDH were typically quite short and action-oriented: for the sake of efficiency and follow-up. Furthermore, the Prime Minister used to issue multiple circulars, stressing the importance of timely answers to the recommendations of the Commission. In recent times, however, the link with the government has become weaker, with less official referral and a lack of proper review of the memoranda presented by the CNCDH. Confronted with this situation, the Commission has tried to conduct more general studies, and it has followed the public debates of the French Parliament, so as to introduce amendments to the draft laws being discussed. Generally speaking, the CNCDH's advisory opinions are now much longer, and they are, perhaps, even too scholarly. Being highly technical and containing a lot of academic references, the documents issued by the Commission are difficult for members of the administration to read; they are even more complex from the perspective of civil society. Even though a new policy of communication was adopted six years ago, which promotes the participation of the Commission's President in public debates and the use of new media, the visibility and political impact of the CNCDH are still limited. Communication of a strong but simple message is a continuous challenge for the CNCDH.

In 2016, Dalloz published a book titled *Les grands avis de la Commission nationale consultative des droits de l'homme*; it contained a selection of 34 important opinions issued by the Commission. These were chosen by an editorial team chaired by the Commission's President, Christine Lazerges, and were commented on by external and independent scholars.[17] The full collection of the CNCDH's work, which includes about 20 opinions adopted per year, is accessible on the CNCDH website and in the *Journal Officiel de la République française*.[18] There is a clear difference between declarations of the Commission's President, given in cases of emergency, and more in-depth works, such as studies and reports. The former has the potential to form the starting point for an in-depth opinion, but it is mainly considered an *état des lieux*: a situational analysis written by an external consultant or by a member of the staff under the supervision of a drafting group, which is followed by a set of recommendations. Landmark studies of the CNCDH include evaluations of: the right to asylum in France; human rights in French prisons; diplomacy and human rights; businesses' responsibility for human rights; trafficking and exploitation of

[17] See generally C. Lazerges (ed.), *Les grands avis de la Commission nationale consultative des droits de l'homme*, Dalloz, Paris 2016.

[18] Available at <https://www.journal-officiel.gouv.fr/>.

human beings; and human rights in French overseas territories.[19] The CNCDH also publishes reports on a regular basis: examples being the 2021 annual report on the fight against racism, antisemitism, and xenophobia;[20] and its new report on sexual orientation, gender identity and intersexuality, presented in 2022.[21] As these reports are an important tool for decision-makers and social scientists, *Documentation française* has published them, without interruption, since 1990. In 2009, the CNCDH decided to publish a biennial record of the international monitoring of the human rights situation in France. Available at *Documentation française*, these documents have become more systematic with the release of each new edition.

5. TRAINING, EDUCATION, RESEARCH AND AWARENESS

5.1. TRAINING AND EDUCATION ON HUMAN RIGHTS

Beside its relationship with state authorities, the CNCDH has worked on human rights education in schools and the training of judges and civil servants. In collaboration with the French National Commission for UNESCO, the CNCDH was involved in the 'UN Decade for Human Rights Teaching', a programme that was executed between 1995–2004, pursuant to the suggestion of the World Conference on Human Rights held in Vienna in June 1993. Both an interim report and an action plan were published in relation to this programme. The staff of the CNCDH have also organised regular training sessions with the *École Nationale d'Administration* (ENA) and the *École Nationale de la Magistrature* (ENM); these have focused on different topics, such as the fight against racism and discrimination, etc. The CNCDH has also participated in colloquia or seminars with universities and *grand écoles*, including the Paris Institute of Political Studies, which is better known as *Sciences Po*.

---

19 Available at <https://www.cncdh.fr/fr/publications>. The first studies were published by the *Documentation française* and were titled: *Les conditions d'exercice du droit d'asile en France* (2006); *Les droits de l'homme dans la prison en France* (2007); *Diplomatie et droits de l'homme* (2008); *La responsabilité des entreprises en matière de droits de l'homme* (2009); *La traite et l'exploitation des êtres humains en France* (2010); and *Les droits de l'homme dans les Outre-mers* (2018).

20 CNCDH, *2021 Report on the Fight against Racism, Antisemitism and Xenophobia*, Dalloz, Paris 2022. See <https://www.cncdh.fr/sites/default/files/2022-07/Les%20Essentiels%20Report%20Racism%202021%20EN_0.pdf>.

21 CNCDH, *Orientation sexuelle, identité de genre et intersexuation: de l'égalité à l'effectivité des droits*, Paris 2022. See <https://www.cncdh.fr/actualite/la-cncdh-publie-son-rapport-orientation-sexuelle-identite-de-genre-et-intersexuation-de>.

5.2. RESEARCH AND AWARENESS ON HUMAN RIGHTS

The CNCDH has organised a number of interdisciplinary symposia, including events to recognise landmark occasions, launch thematic initiatives, and commemorate historical events, such as the anniversary of the Universal Declaration of Human Rights. The minutes of this latter symposium were published through *Documentation française*.[22]

5.3. ONE OR TWO HUMAN RIGHTS PRIZES?

The CNCDH used to deliver two set of prizes; however, only one persists. The surviving award is called the *Prix des Droits de l'Homme de la République française – Liberté – Egalité – Fraternité*, through which the French Republic acknowledges the work of individuals and civil society organisations in the protection and promotion of human rights. It is open to applicants from France or abroad, regardless of nationality. Awarded since 1988, the prize is decided upon by an independent jury and focuses on one or two yearly themes chosen by the CNCDH. Each year the five laureates of the prize are invited to Paris for the official ceremony in December, which is presided over by the Prime Minister, the Minister of Foreign Affairs, or the Minister of Justice.[23] The list of winners of the prize is quite impressive, ranging, over its 30 years' history, from grass-roots organisations to human rights defenders. The prize is not only important for the monetary sum awarded, which helps finance concrete projects, but also for the visibility of the laureates, which, in the case of human rights activists abroad, provides an additional layer of protection 'back home'.

The second prize, the *René Cassin Medal for Secondary Schools*, was created by the Ministry of National Education in 1998, and was awarded by a jury chaired by the President of the CNCDH. Initiatives and projects created by teams of pupils from schools in France and its overseas territories, as well as French establishments in foreign countries, were eligible for the prize. Despite

[22] See '*Oui à la justice, non à l'impunité*', 1992 colloquium of Geneva, organised with the International Commission of Jurists; '*Ce racisme qui menace l'Europe*', 1994 colloquium of Strasbourg; '*La Déclaration universelle des droits de l'homme (1948–1998), L'avenir d'un idéal commun?*', 1999 colloquium of Paris.
See also the '*La Déclaration universelle des droits de l'homme (1948–2008), réalité d'un idéal commun?*', 2008 colloquium of Strasbourg; '*De la France libre aux droits de l'homme, l'héritage de René Cassin*', organised with the *Conseil d'État*, 2009 colloquium of Paris. Cf also V. Zuber, E. Decaux and A. Boza (eds.), *Histoire et postérité de la Déclaration universelle des droits de l'homme, nouvelles approches*, Presses universitaires de Rennes, Rennes 2022.

[23] Available at <https://www.cncdh.fr/fr/prix/prix-des-droits-de-lhomme>.

the pedagogical value of the students' outputs and the symbolic importance of the initiative, the Ministry of National Education gradually lost interest in the award – as its focus turned to new priorities, such as sustainable development and climate change; the prize was discontinued in 2018.

6. INTERNATIONAL MONITORING

6.1. THE CNCDH AS A GO-BETWEEN

The CNCDH acts as a bridge between domestic human rights issues and international mechanisms for the promotion and protection of human rights. The Commission contributes to the preparation of France's national reports to UN treaty bodies and to the Universal Periodic Review, and it is vigilant in respect of the follow-up to these procedures. The CNCDH is also a contact point for other human rights bodies, such as: the Office of the High Commissioner for Human Rights (OHCHR); the special rapporteurs of the Human Rights Council; the Commissioner for Human Rights of the Council of Europe; and various thematic mechanisms, including the European Commission against Racism and Intolerance, the European Committee for the Prevention of Torture and Inhuman or Degrading Treatment or Punishment, the High Commissioner on National Minorities of the Organization for Security and Co-operation in Europe, and the Office for Democratic Institutions and Human Rights. The CNCDH's relationship with the European Union Agency for Fundamental Rights (FRA) was formalised by a contract, with a pool of academic bodies, after a public tender.

6.2. THE COMMISSION AND NHRI NETWORKS

Since its beginnings, the CNCDH has been involved in various NHRI networks. It took an active role in the organisation of the International Workshop on National Institutions for the Promotion and Protection of Human Rights, which was held in France, in 1991. A key outcome from this workshop was the Paris Principles on NHRIs. The CNCDH also participated in the World Conference on Human Rights that took place in Vienna in 1993, and the conference held in Tunis, that same year, where the International Coordinating Committee of NHRIs (ICC) was established. The Commission was very active in the development of the biennial international meetings of the ICC.[24] Over time, this

[24] See E. Decaux, 'Le dixième anniversaire des principes directeurs des institutions nationales, dits "Principes de Paris"' (2003) 3 *Droits fondamentaux* 11.

network became more administrative and bureaucratic, and it was linked to the staff of the OHCHR, as the GANHRI is today. Since the birth of the GANHRI, the CNCDH has collaborated actively with the Chairperson of the network as well as with the Sub-Committee on Accreditation (SCA).

Although some of the CNCDH's features were not in complete accordance with the Paris Principles, its accreditation has never been challenged. Historically, the strong independence of the Commission has been protected more by an informal relationship of mutual respect with the French Government than by codified administrative and budgetary rules. However, to ensure full compliance with the Paris Principles, a 2007 law was passed that provided for, amongst other things, more formal consultations regarding Commission membership. Although the CNCDH has no power of decision or sanction, the CNCDH President, Christine Lazerges (2012–2018), made considerable efforts to have the Commission considered an *autorité administrative independante*, or administrative independent authority. This status resulted in the members of the CNCDH being submitted to the control and intrusive monitoring of the *Haute Autorité de la transparence de la vie publique*, or High Authority for the Transparency of Public Life. It is not obvious that this 'transparency' has helped the CNCDH to become more independent. Like other administrative independent authorities, the CNCDH is now exposed to periodic political and administrative challenges.

One of the particularities of the CNCDH is its cohabitation, as an administrative independent authority, with the *Défenseur des droits*. The competence of the *Défenseur des droits* allows it to receive individual communications, as non-contentious equitable remedies in equity, when those of an administrative and judicial nature are unavailable. With the *Conseil d'État* and judiciary being very active in the protection of human rights, along with these remedies in equity, there is no reason to add an individual complaints procedure to the CNCDH's mandate. The CNDH has no administrative staff and does not have the budgetary means to deal with such a competence; moreover, it would also overlap with the work of the *Défenseur des droits*. Instead, the pluralist membership of the CNCDH renders it better suited to collective debate on thematic human rights issues. Furthermore, it should be remembered that the 'individual complaints procedure' competence was stated in the Paris Principles as being optional.[25] Despite this, the CNCDH has presented *amicus curiae* briefs before the European Court of Human Rights: both as part of the European Network of National Human Rights Institutions and, more recently, in its own capacity.

---

25 See generally G. de Beco, *Non-Judicial Mechanisms for the Implementation of Human Rights in European States*, Bruylant, Brussels 2010.

7. EFFECTIVENESS AND CHALLENGES

First created in 1947 and reborn in 1984, the CNCDH used to be a vibrant collective body, with great debates and sometimes passionate votes. Its members were a mix of young activists, religious leaders, trade-unionists, senior civil servants, diplomats, academics, lawyers, and physicians, all inspired by the same principles enshrined in the 1789 Declaration of the Rights of Man and of the Citizen and in the so-called International Bill of Human Rights: composed of the 1948 Universal Declaration of Human Rights and the 1966 International Covenants on Civil and Political Rights and Economic, Social and Cultural Rights and their Optional Protocols. The relevance of the CNCDH's reports and studies is evident at the intellectual level, but their political efficiency and impact is less than obvious. One has to ask whether the considerable output of the CNCDH, including its long documents full of legal and academic references, is still useful within the public debate in this time of tweets and fake news. It is important to stress the principles, to draw the 'red lines', and to alert political institutions and international bodies about gaps in the legal protection of human rights and new trends of systematic violations; however, the CNCDH cannot have the functions of a tribune without democracy. On the contrary, it must become more inclusive, taking all people, especially those deprived of their human rights, into consideration.

7.1. CONTINUITY AND DISCONTINUITY

There are many symptoms of some sort of disconnection between the CNCDH and public authorities. In fact, these are as numerous as they are insidious. The first is the discontinuity in the time frames of the Commission. The CNCDH's President originally served for a two-year period; however, the President now stays in office for three years and, given the possibility of a second term, potentially six. After the 2007 reforms, the appointment process became more complicated, slowing it down and producing some periods of vacancy. For example, while the second mandate of Joël Thoraval ended in September 2008, it was only in April 2009 that a new President was nominated: with the designation of Yves Repiquet by the new Prime Minister, Mr François Fillon. This meant that during the celebration of the 60th anniversary of the adoption of the Universal Declaration of Human Rights, which took place in Paris, there was nobody to speak on behalf of the CNCDH. A similar vacancy occurred again three years later, before the eventual nomination of Professor Christine Lazerges, a former MP. After her two terms in office, Lazerges stepped down in November 2018, and Jean-Marie Delarue succeeded her, but only in April 2019. This time, there was thus no President of the CNCDH for the 70th anniversary of the Universal Declaration. Furthermore, Delarue resigned after less than one year in office, and he was replaced, for the remainder of his tenure, by Jean-Marie Burguburu who was nominated for a new full mandate at the end of 2022. This chronic discontinuity of leadership within a NHRI, in an *État de droit* with a well-organised administration, is worrisome by itself, but it also poses practical problems for the Commission and can even become politically challenging for the state. This situation has been mitigated somewhat by the continuity of the Commission's staff, particularly its Secretary-General: Gerard Fellous, for instance, served between 1986 and 2004 and Michel Forst, his successor, stayed in office, formally, from 2005 to 2016, while his consultative function for international affairs was extended beyond this time.

A second warning sign is the attitude of remoteness held by political authorities towards the Commission's work. Over a 15-year period, the CNCDH had only two opportunities to meet with the Prime Minister: in 2009 and 2012. There was no official installation by the prime Minister of new presidents Delarue or Burguburu. The annual report of the CNCDH on the fight against racism used to be publicly presented to the Prime Minister, but not anymore: it is now a very-low profile affair carried out by officers of the Commission and the Prime Minister's cabinet. In a similar sense, 10 December has historically been a symbolic day for human rights in France, when the '*Prix des Droits de l'Homme de la République française – Liberté – Egalité – Fraternité* ' was delivered in a public ceremony presided over by the Prime Minister, the Minister of Foreign Affairs, or the Minister of Justice. Today, the date is fixed in accordance with the agenda of the minister in charge of the event for that year. While some ministers, such as Bernard Cazeneuve as head of the Home Office, come to hearings or working groups in the CNCDH, this is still an exception. Even the practice of including the plenaries of the Commission's General Assembly within ministries and important institutions is a thing of the past.

7.2. CENTRALITY OR MARGINALISATION?

This political divide is amplified by the CNCDH when it acts in a partisan way, like a 'super-NGO' or a 'little parliament'. Moreover, such activity alters the intrinsic balance of the Commission. Founding fathers of the CNCDH, including René Cassin, were very independently minded lawyers, but, at the same time, they behaved according to the idea of public service and general interest and with a strong sense of state, born of the French Resistance. It is not by chance that four Presidents of the CNCDH were members of the *Conseil d'État*:[26] one was a former First President of the *Cour de cassation*,[27] and

[26] Nicole Questiaux, Paul Bouchet, Alain Bacquet, and Jean-Marie Delarue.
[27] Pierre Truche.

another was a prefect of the Île-de-France region.[28] In contrast, the CNCDH has also had two chairs who were former MPs, with political allegiances: Jean-Pierre Bloch and Christine Lazerges. The other Presidents were lawyers from civil society: such as Jean Kahn, and notably two heads of the Bar Association, Yves Repiquet and Jean-Marie Burguburu. And only two chairwomen, during 40 years.[29]

The need for collective leadership at the CNCDH is even more important, as is a more heterogeneous membership, for parity and diversity purposes. These two changes would lead to a membership made up of fewer 'generalists', who focus on the principles of universality and indivisibility, while including more members who highlight specific priorities and lobby for the inclusion of: (a) particular and important causes, such as the protection of children, women, persons with disabilities, persons in situations of extreme poverty, LGBTI communities, migrants, detainees, etc.; and (b) new challenges, including environmental issues, business and human rights, protection of data, new media, etc. Having said this, the risk of clustering and of over-specialisation is the loss of the global and collective approach of the CNCDH. The participation of the 64 members varies greatly from one to another; some members think that their role is merely honorary, others are disappointed by current affairs, while others consider that, after working on their own topic(s) of interest, they do not need to concern themselves with other issues. The use of quorums and the limitation of substitutes are useful tools to encourage broad and cross-issue participation, as well as the formulation of a core group of like-minded, active, and dedicated members.

Rifts inside the CNCDH are accentuated by the need to find a different mission from that of the *Défenseur des droits*, in order to avoid overlap and sterile competition. As a former, well-known politician, with a constitutional mission, personal visibility, and an administrative staff, the holder of the *Défenseur des droits* office could act as a sort of 'people's advocate' and can be quick and present in all of his or her official functions. In contrast, the CNCDH, even where its President acts alone, can never act as quickly as the *Défenseur des droits*. However, as a collective body, the Commission can work on the basis of legal principles, creating a strong consensus among its members, reaching a broader citizenry, and bridging domestic and international institutions. The CNCDH's legitimacy lies in its independence and pluralistic nature. In order to adequately promote and protect human rights at home and abroad, it must also rely on its openness and inclusivity.

---

28 Joël Thoraval.

29 Nicole Questiaux and Christine Lazerges.

DEFENSORÍA DEL PUEBLO (ARGENTINA, COLOMBIA, AND ECUADOR)

Paola Andrea ACOSTA-ALVARADO*

1. INTRODUCTION

Latin American constitutional systems underwent a strong metamorphosis during the final decades of the twentieth century and have continued to do so during the first part of the twenty-first.[1] One of the main objectives driving this constitutional change has been the desire to overcome the legacies of various conservative political regimes which formerly held power across the region. These regimes fuelled social exclusion and, simultaneously, allowed normative and institutional weaknesses to give rise to a general neglect in the protection of fundamental rights.

The wave of constitutional reforms, termed 'new Latin American constitutionalism'[2] by some and 'neo-constitutionalism'[3] by others, has helped

* The author is grateful for the important research work undertaken by Lina Ballen, a student at the Faculty of Law of Externado University, Bogotá, without whom the writing of this text would have been impossible.

1 There were 388 partial constitutional reforms or amendments, across 18 Latin American countries, between 1978 and 2012. This in addition to the introduction of 16 new constitutions. Among these, the Constitutions of Brazil (1988), Costa Rica (1989), Colombia (1991), Paraguay (1992), Peru (1993), Ecuador (1998; 2008), Venezuela (1999), Bolivia (2009), and the Dominican Republic (2010) can be highlighted. See D. NOLTE, 'Reformas constitucionales en América Latina', paper presented at the international colloquium '*Le constitutionnalisme latino-américain aujourd'hui, entre renouveau juridique et essor démocratique*', 4 April 2013, Center for Legal and Political Philosophy, University of Cergy-Pontoise, France, available at: <https://www.academia.edu/7022280/Reformas_Constitucionales_en_Am%C3%A9rica_Latina>.

2 According to VICIANO and MARTÍNEZ DALMAU, 'the concept of the constitution as merely a limiter of (constituted) power is overcome so that, in addition, it is defined as a way in which the constituent power may express its will.' R. VICIANO PASTOR and R. MARTÍNEZ DALMAU, 'El nuevo constitucionalismo latinoamericano: fundamentos para una construcción doctrinal' (2011) 9 *Revista General de Derecho Público Comparado* 1, 4.

3 Neo-constitutionalism has emerged as a doctrinal stance from the comparative analysis of constitutional texts from the late twentieth and early twenty-first centuries, 'which are not limited to establishing competences or the separation of powers, but which contain high

to bring about significant changes, including: a considerable expansion of the catalogue of legally recognised fundamental rights; the strengthening of institutions responsible for the protection of these rights; the creation of new protection mechanisms; an increased recognition of subjects of special protection (women, children, indigenous peoples, among others); the empowerment of constitutional jurisdiction; and the articulation of constitutional law in keeping with international human rights law, among other significant developments.

In this context, the so-called *defensorías del pueblo* have come to the fore as new institutional figures, which, imported from Europe and adjusted to meet Latin American realities,[4] act as critical tools for the promotion and protection of fundamental rights in the region. The *defensorías del pueblo* were conceived as institutions with an express mandate to work closely with the general public. In performing this role, they constitute a crucial part of multilevel protection systems in which states' national mechanisms for the protection of individuals are closely linked to international mechanisms. It is due to these systems, as well as the work of constitutional judges, that fundamental rights have become a reality for large numbers of people: as theoretical norms have been transformed into concrete practices. Despite such achievements, the *defensorías del pueblo* face a number of normative, institutional, and political challenges, which affect their ability to operate as they were originally intended: as the institutional arm of the public. This chapter provides a comprehensive and comparative look at three *defensorías del pueblo*, those of Argentina, Colombia, and Ecuador, placing emphasis on their respective functional and institutional profiles (section 2). This approach is used to study the advantages brought about by the implementation of these institutions', in accordance with the Paris Principles (section 3), as well as the challenges they face regarding their compliance with these principles (section 4).

The purpose of this document is to offer an analysis based on the cases of Argentina, Colombia and Ecuador, in order to highlight the challenges that still need to be overcome. This author believes that this realistic perspective can help in outlining proposals that will allow for the future improvement of such an important institution for citizens. Thus, first this chapter presents a general overview in section 2 of how it is conceived within the legal system of the three selected States. Then, based on an analysis of the work that has been done in the

---

levels of "material" or substantive norms that condition the action of the State by means of ordering certain aims and objectives'. M. Carbonell, *Teoría del neoconstitucionalismo*, Trotta, Madrid 2007, p. 10.

4 Known as 'ombudsman' in Sweden, 'provider of justice' in Portugal, 'mediator of the Republic' in France, 'civil defender' in Italy, 'public defender' in Spain, and 'parliamentary commissioner' in the United Kingdom.

three cases, an estimate of the scope that they have is made in section 3. And finally, we will examine the future that awaits them in section 4.

2. *DEFENSORÍAS DEL PUEBLO* IN ARGENTINA, COLOMBIA, AND ECUADOR: THE WHAT AND THE HOW

Three different institutions, one common task. This phrase could be applied in summarising the following section; indeed, even though the institutional and functional logics of the three *defensorías del pueblo* vary somewhat from country to country, each was formulated as an institutional tool for the promotion and protection of fundamental rights.

The *defensorías del pueblo* were founded in Argentina, Colombia, and Ecuador, respectively, in 1994, 1991, and 1998. The institutions all derive their powers from their respective national constitutions, and all were conceived as autonomous bodies that hold the primary task of defending human rights. The powers of Argentina's *Defensoría del Pueblo* stem from Article 86 of the Constitution of the Nation, as well as Law Nr. 24,284 of 1993, as amended by Law Nr. 24,379 of 1994.[5] With regard to Colombia, Articles 281–284 of the Political Constitution establish the characteristics, powers, and functions of its *Defensoría del Pueblo*, which is viewed as a projection and development of the concept of the social rule of law. Law Nr. 24 of 1992, amended by Decree Nr. 25 of 2014 of the President of the Republic of Colombia, also pertains to the institution, thereby supplementing the constitutional provisions.[6] Finally, Ecuador's *Defensoría del Pueblo* became part of the state's institutional apparatus through Article 96 of the 1998 Constitution. It is currently regulated by Article 214 of the new Constitution of the Republic of Ecuador, in force since 2008, as well as the Organic Law of the *Defensoría del Pueblo*, of 2019.[7]

In the case of Argentina, emphasis has been placed on the *Defensoría del Pueblo*'s status as a state institution, thereby clarifying that it is not a mere a government agency but an organic part of the broader state structure which oversees public administration. In Colombia, the *Defensoría del Pueblo* is understood as a critical part of the *Ministerio Público*, the Office of the Public Prosecutor. In Ecuador, the *Defensoría del Pueblo* forms part of the state apparatus

---

5 See I. Basaure, 'La ausencia del Defensor del Pueblo en Argentina: siete años sin representación colectiva' (2017) 78 *Derecho PUCP* 199, pp. 202–4.

6 See S. Pérez Portillo, 'La Defensoría del Pueblo' (2008) 21 *Revista Derecho del Estado* 109, pp. 110–13.

7 See V. Figueroa, 'La Defensoría del Pueblo de Ecuador y sus funciones de supervigilancia del debido proceso en el nuevo marco constitucional' (Master's thesis, Simón Bolivar Andean University, Quito, Ecuador) pp. 9–10, 42–48.

that oversees public administration. It performs this role in conjunction with the *Procuraduría General del Estado*, the Office of the Attorney General, and the *Contraloría General el Estado*, the Office of the Comptroller General. Its functions are clearly understood as being decentralised and, unlike its counterparts in Argentina and Colombia, the *Defensoría del Pueblo* of Ecuador has representatives abroad.

2.1. APPOINTMENT OF THE *DEFENSOR DEL PUEBLO*

The heads of each of the three *defensorías* analysed in this chapter are appointed by the corresponding congress, or parliament, in accordance with the conditions established by the constitution of each state. For example, in Argentina, the *Defensor del Pueblo* is appointed by the Congress of the Nation for a period of five years; the appointee may serve a second five-year period but cannot seek a third term and may be removed at any time by the legislative branch, on the basis of a two-thirds vote. The list of potential appointees, which consists of between one and three candidates, is formulated on the basis of proposals made by a bicameral commission, convened by the President of the Argentinian Senate.[8] Should the *Defensor del Pueblo* so require, the bicameral commission may designate *defensores adjuntos* (deputy advocates),

> to assist him or her in performing his or her tasks, being able to provisionally replace him or her in the event of his or her cessation of duties, death, suspension or temporary inability to perform such tasks, in accordance with the conditions determined by the commission during the appointment process.[9]

In Colombia, the *Defensor del Pueblo* is elected for a four-year term by the House of Representatives. The candidate is selected by the House from a shortlist drawn up by the President of the Republic.[10] Conversely, in Ecuador, the *Consejo de Participación Ciudadana y Control Social*, the Council for Citizen Participation and Social Accountability, appoints the *Defensor del Pueblo*, who must assume office before the National Assembly, for a five-year term; this tenure can be extended for a second five-year term 'only once'.[11]

As can be seen, when it comes to the appointment of the heads of the three *defensorías*, the differences are not significant; however, it is important to highlight them, as the appointment procedures may impact how each body functions in practice. For example, although all three appointments are

---

8 See Law Nr. 24,284 of the Republic of Argentina, arts 2, 3.

9 ibid, art 13.

10 See Political Constitution of Colombia, art 281.

11 Organic Law of the *Defensoría del Pueblo* of Ecuador, art 8.

dependent on congress, ratification is required from both houses in Argentina, compared to only one in Colombia. Even though such differences are minimal, it is important to consider that the political-electoral dynamics of the particular Latin American congress or parliament can have an impact on the profile of the appointee and their autonomy and independence.

The issues of autonomy and independence are further reflected in differences between the Colombian system, on the one hand, and the Argentinian and Ecuadorian systems, on the other. In the latter systems, the re-election of the *Defensor* is a decision that, once more, depends on the characteristics of the respective parliament. In this context, the question of guaranteeing the independence of the *Defensor* arises once more. The issue is exacerbated in the Argentinian case, where the Congress of the Nation may also unilaterally remove the incumbent *Defensor* from their post.

Another difference relates to a possibility considered in the Argentinian Constitution: the bicameral commission may, following a proposal submitted by the *Defensor del Pueblo*, name two assistant *defensores* to contribute towards the performance of the *Defensor*'s tasks. These assistants may provisionally replace the *Defensor* in the event that: the *Defensor* ceases his/her duties, dies, is suspended, or is temporarily unable to perform his/her tasks.[12] A similar figure is present in both Colombia and Ecuador, where the position is called the *Vicedefensor del Pueblo* and *Vicedefensor*, respectively.[13]

2.2. FUNCTIONS OF THE *DEFENSORÍAS*

To reiterate, the primary function of the *defensorías* is the promotion and protection of human rights; however, the scope of this function, as well as the way in which each *defensoría* undertakes its work, varies from country to country.

In Argentina, the *Defensor del Pueblo* has the legal standing[14]

> to commence and pursue, *ex officio* or at the request of the interested party, any investigation leading to the clarification of the acts, matters or omissions of public administration and its agents which involve the illegitimate, defective, irregular, abusive, arbitrary, discriminatory, negligent, seriously inconvenient or inopportune exercise of its functions, including those capable of affecting diffuse or collective interests.[15]

---

12 See Law Nr. 24,284 of the Republic of Argentina, art 13.

13 See Decree Nr. 25 2014 of the President of the Republic of Colombia, art 12; Organic Law of the *Defensoría del Pueblo* of Ecuador, arts 15, 16.

14 See Constitution of the Argentine Nation, art 86. See also Basaure (n 5) pp. 204–6.

15 Law Nr. 24,284 of the Republic of Argentina, art 14.

In addition, 'it must pay special attention to behaviour that denotes a systematic and general failure of public administration, ensuring steps are taken to foresee and plan the mechanisms necessary to eliminate or reduce such behaviour'.[16] The notion of public administration includes centralised and decentralised bodies, companies, and private entities of the state, or those in which the state participates, as well as public services in general.[17] The legislative and judicial branches of state power, as well as national defence and security agencies, are, however, excluded from the sphere of influence of the *Defensor* The *Defensoría del Pueblo* has jurisdiction over 'non-state public legal persons who exercise public prerogative powers and private persons who provide public services'.[18] It should be noted that the *Defensoría del Pueblo* may be approached by 'any natural person who considers himself or herself to be affected by the aforementioned acts, matters or omissions', without 'being impeded from doing so on the grounds of nationality, residence, confinement in a prison or detention centre and, in general, any relationship of dependency with the State'.[19]

In Colombia, the *Defensoría del Pueblo* oversees the promotion, safeguarding, and exercise of human rights.[20] Its functions can be grouped into five categories:

- observation, which includes monitoring and complaints;
- dissemination of information;
- a role as legal counsel, to be understood as public legal defence as well as the processing of petitions from the public;[21]
- public policy; and
- mediation.

Given the particular context of the socio-political violence that Colombia has faced over the past five decades, the *Defensoría del Pueblo* assumes a fundamental

16 ibid, art 15.

17 See ibid, art 16.

18 ibid, art 17.

19 ibid, art 18.

20 Political Constitution of Colombia, art 282. The same provision adds: 'for which it shall perform the following functions: 1. Guide and instruct the residents of Colombia and Colombians abroad in the exercise and defence of their rights in relation to the competent authorities or private entities. 2. Promote human rights and recommend policies for the teaching thereof. 3. Invoke the right of habeas corpus and file actions for its protection, without prejudice to the right of the interested parties. 4. Organise and manage the *defensoría pública* in the terms established by the law. 5. File popular actions in matters related to its jurisdiction. 6. Introduce bills on matters related to its jurisdiction. 7. Submit reports to Congress in relation to the performance of its functions. 8. Any other matters as determined by the law'. See Decree Nr. 25 of 2014 of the President of the Republic of Colombia, art 2.

21 Petitions for protection mechanisms are dealt with and processed by the *Defensoría del Pueblo* of Colombia, by means of the so-called *litigio defensorial.*

role with respect to the protection of the civilian population. By means of its powers, the *Defensor del Pueblo* of Colombia employs protection mechanisms which are designed to safeguard human rights that are threatened or violated and provides relevant, case-specific advice, so that interested persons may directly participate in these mechanisms, according to their particular situation and in line with applicable legal norms.

Across the border, the Ecuadorian *Defensoría del Pueblo* is responsible for 'the protection of the rights of the residents of Ecuador and the safeguarding of the rights of Ecuadorians abroad'.[22] In order to perform this task, the institution has been assigned with distinct powers, which can be grouped into the following categories:

- legal counsel, which includes the processing of complaints and notices for the protection of rights as well as legal representation;
- a denunciation making competence; and
- powers relating to public policy.

Two interesting issues are worth noting in the Ecuadorian case: first, it is possible for the *Defensoría del Pueblo* to provide its services to Ecuadorians who are not in Ecuador, a characteristic it shares with its Colombian counterpart, in relation to nationals of Colombia who are abroad; and, second, the Constitution explicitly mentions the duty of the *Defensoría del Pueblo* to respect the rights of nature,[23] as well as what Ecuadorians call '*el buen vivir*', or a understood as the duty of the state to recognise and guarantee respect for the civil, political, economic, social, and cultural rights, which are referred to in Title II of the Constitution of the Republic of Ecuador.

As can be seen, the profiles of the *defensorías del pueblo* vary from country to country. In Colombia and Ecuador, the institutions are designed with a broad mandate and they are vested with various responsibilities, including promotion and monitoring of human rights, and representation, intervention, and mediation. In contrast, the Argentinian *Defensoría* plays a rather restricted role, which is exclusively focused on legal representation.

---

22 Constitution of the Republic of Ecuador, art 215. Accordingly, the primary functions of the *Defensoría del Pueblo* of Ecuador are: '1. Sponsoring, *ex officio* or at the request of the party, actions such as protection, *habeas corpus*, access to public information, *habeas data*, non-compliance, public action and claims in respect of poor quality or improper provision of public or private services. 2. Issue mandatory and immediate measures to ensure the protection of rights, and to request a trial and sanctioning before the competent authority for non-compliance. 3. Investigate and resolve, within the framework of its powers, actions or omissions of natural or legal persons who provide public services. 4. Exercise and promote the due process of law, and prevent and immediately bring an end to torture, cruel, inhuman and degrading treatment in all its forms'.

23 See Organic Law of the *Defensoría del Pueblo* of Ecuador, arts 1, 5.

Regarding the issue of functions, it should be noted that in addition to the powers of the Ombudsmen's Offices, they also have certain duties. Among them, it is worth highlighting their obligation to render accounts periodically. In Argentina, the Ombudsman must report annually to the Chambers of Parliament on the work carried out, in a report to be submitted before 31 May of each year – although, when the seriousness or urgency of the facts make it advisable, a special report may be submitted. In Colombia, the Ombudsman must also submit to the Congress of the Republic an annual report on its activities (with the number and type of complaints received, the measures adopted for their attention and processing, express mention of the reluctant officials or individuals involved, and the administrative and legislative recommendations deemed necessary). Finally, in Ecuador, the Ombudsman's information duties are somewhat different. There, the duty to constantly investigate and report on the situation of human rights and the natural environment, in order to recommend a change in the attitude of the state, is enshrined.

2.3. INSTITUTIONAL STRUCTURE

Concerning the profile of the *defensorías*: the institutional structure of each varies in terms of either a functional or thematic criterion.

In the case of Argentina, the emphasis is thematic. The institution is composed of the *Defensor del Pueblo*, the Secretary-General, the Assistant Secretary-General, and the two assistant *defensores*. The work of the institution concentrates on seven thematic areas:

- identity and citizenship;
- health, social action, education, and culture;
- environment and sustainable development;
- individuals, public works and services;
- social security and work;
- legal and technical advice; and
- vulnerable groups.[24]

In Colombia, the institutional articulation obeys both functional and thematic criteria, which, in addition, are intertwined with a territorial variable. Strictly speaking, the entity is made up of the Ombudsman, its advisory offices, the Office of the Deputy Ombudsman, the Regional Ombudsmen's Offices and the General Secretariat. However, it should be noted that since the organisational reform of 2014, four national directorates

[24] See generally *Defensoría del Pueblo* of Argentina. Available at: <http://www.dpn.gob.ar>.

- promotion and dissemination of human rights;
- attention and processing of complaints;
- resources and legal actions; and
- public defender's office

and 15 offices delegated by thematic criteria;

- guidance and advice to victims of the armed conflict;
- risk prevention and early warning system;
- agrarian and land issues;
- women's rights and gender issues;
- ethnic groups;
- children, youth and the elderly;
- criminal and penitentiary policy;
- right to health and social security;
- constitutional and legal matters;
- rights of the population in human mobility;
- economic, social and cultural rights;
- protection of the right to sports;
- prevention and transformation of social conflict; and
- protection of rights in virtual environments.[25]

Likewise, it is important to clarify that the territorial distribution of the Regional Ombudsmen's offices goes beyond the territorial organisation provided for in the Colombian territorial order to the extent that it has Ombudsmen's Offices in special areas such as Bajo Cauca Antioqueño, Magdalena Medio, Ocaña, the Pacific Region, Soacha, Southern Bolivar, Southern Cordoba, Tumaco, and Urabá-Darién.

The *Defensoría del Pueblo* of Ecuador 'is a decentralised body governed by public law with national jurisdiction' that has 'legal personality and administrative, financial, budgetary and organisational autonomy'.[26] In addition to the *Defensor* and the *Vicedefensor del Pueblo*, its structure includes regional delegations in each province of the country, delegations abroad, and various special commissions, which have been created to assist the institution in carrying out its functions.[27] The provincial and foreign delegations are constituted as missions, and they are tasked with promoting and protecting human rights and the rights of nature as well as ensuring the collection of specialised knowledge through research mandates.[28]

---

25 See Decree Nr. 25, 2014 of the President of the Republic of Colombia.
26 Organic Law of the *Defensoría del Pueblo* of Ecuador, art 2.
27 ibid, arts 16, 17, 18, 20.
28 ibid, art 21.

2.4. INTER-INSTITUTIONAL RELATIONS

To reiterate, the primary characteristics of the *defensoría del pueblo* are its autonomy from other state institutions and its mandate to scrutinise public bodies. Despite this independence, the *defensorías* work in conjunction with, and respond to, a number of other state bodies.

The *Defensoría del Pueblo* of Argentina, for example, is responsible for: coordinating actions with provincial and municipal *defensores*; facilitating the filing of complaints by interested parties through these institutions; organising outreach activities for the institution and activities for the *receptorías del interior*, or national receptions; as well as maintaining permanent relations with Regional Ombudsman organisations.[29]

In Colombia, the *Defensoría del Pueblo* forms part of the *Red Institucional de Apoyo a las Veedurías Ciudadanas*,[30] or Institutional Network of Support for Citizen Oversight. As such, it is responsible, amongst other tasks, for providing legal advice and promoting the monitoring of public management; designing methodologies to enhance management evaluation; and submitting information about plans, programmes, projects, and institutional resources related to public administration.[31]

In conjunction with civil society, the *Defensor del Pueblo* of Ecuador organises the composition of the *Consejos de Defensoras y Defensores de los Derechos Humanos y la Naturaleza*, or Councils of Advocates for Human Rights and Nature.[32] It also ensures, through its delegations, compliance with the right to consular protection and coordinates its work with foreign national human rights institutions and civil society organisations that are operating to protect the rights of persons in situations of human mobility.[33] In order to perform its functions, the *Defensoría del Pueblo* can create special commissions, which 'deal opportunely and effectively with situations that threaten or seriously violate human rights and the rights of nature',[34] and can progressively implement different monitoring and protection mechanisms, relating to torture and other cruel, inhuman, and degrading treatment or punishment; children and young persons; persons with disabilities; violence

---

29 See generally *Defensoría del Pueblo* of Argentina. Available at <http://www.dpn.gob.ar>.

30 Established by Law Nr. 850 of 2003 of the Republic of Colombia.

31 For details about the network see generally the website of the Office of the Comptroller General, available at: <https://www.contraloria.gov.co/web/red-apoyo-veedurias-ciudadanas/-que-es-y-como-funciona->.

32 See Organic Law of the *Defensoría del Pueblo* of Ecuador, arts 9.d, 25.

33 Meaning situations involving migration, refugees and forced displacement. See ibid, arts 18, 19.

34 ibid, art 20.

against women; the rights of nature; and the rights of indigenous peoples, Afro-Ecuadorians, and *Montubios*.[35]

In addition to coordinating activities at the national level, the three *defensorías del pueblo* also work in conjunction with international protection systems. For example, according to the UN General Assembly,[36] and the Paris Principles,[37] the *defensorías del pueblo* should cooperate and coordinate with foreign organisations or bodies, NGOs, and international agencies that work towards the protection of human rights, by coordinating plans, programmes, and other projects aimed at strengthening international cooperation in the human rights sphere.[38]

Thus, the *Defensoría del Pueblo* of Argentina must cooperate by maintaining permanent relations with all UN organisations, in particular the Office of the High Commissioner for Human Rights (OHCHR), and regional bodies working towards state integration in the Americas, including, the OAS and, especially, the Inter-American Commission on Human Rights and Inter-American Court of Human Rights.[39]

In the Colombian case, the Office of International Affairs of the *Defensoría del Pueblo* must develop policies, guidelines, and actions derived from relations with international organisations, within the framework of international cooperation or bilateral relations, including not only matters of human rights but also the concerns of international humanitarian law.[40]

As a final note on international interaction and cooperation, the *defensorías del pueblo* also work in conjunction with collaborative networks, such as: the *Federación Iberoamericana del Ombudsperson* (FIO), or Ibero-American Federation of Ombudspersons; the *Red Iberoamericana de Organismos y Organizaciones contra la Discriminación* (RIOOD), or Ibero-American Network of Organisations against Discrimination; and the *Red de Instituciones Nacionales para la Promoción y Protección de los Derechos Humanos del Continente Americano*, or Network of National Institutions for the Promotion and Protection of Human Rights of the American Continent.

---

35 See ibid, art 22. Afro-Ecuadorians are people of Sub-saharan African decsent, predominantly the descendants of enslaved Africans brought to South America in the 16th century, making up 7.2% of the national population. Montubio describes the mestizo people of the countryside of Coastal Ecuador, making up 7.4% of the national population.

36 See generally A/RES/65/207 of 21 December 2010; A/RES/67/163 of 20 December 2012.

37 See generally the Principles relating to the Status of National Human Rights Institutions. Available at: <https://nhri.ohchr.org/EN/AboutUs/Pages/ParisPrinciples.aspx->.

38 See P. Robledo Silva, 'El rol de las instituciones nacionales de derechos humanos como órganos interamericanos coadyuvantes' in F.J. Matía Portilla and P. Robledo Silva (eds.), *La Corte Interamericana de Derechos Humanos. Mecanismos de cumplimiento e informes nacionales*, Tirant Lo Blanch, Valencia 2020.

39 See generally *Defensoría del Pueblo* of Argentina. Available at: <http://www.dpn.gob.ar>.

40 See generally *Defensoría del Pueblo* of Colombia. Available at: <http://www.defensoria.gov.co/>.

2.5. *DEFENSORÍAS* AND THE GENERAL PUBLIC

The *defensorías del pueblo* are, above all, institutional and representative tools of the general public; as such, they play a special role in the promotion and protection of the rights of public individuals. Consequently, the relationship between these institutions and individuals is critical. The scope and course of this relationship differs, however, according to the functions and powers assigned to each relevant institution.

This section focuses on the two 'types' of interaction that involve direct relations between the general public and the *defensorías*: the first type incorporates interactions that occur during the processing of public complaints; the second includes those that arise in contexts where *defensorías* provide legal representation.

In Argentina, the *Defensor del Pueblo* may commence and pursue, *ex officio* or at the request of the interested party, any investigation that leads to the clarification of acts, or omissions, of the public administration or its agents, which might involve: the illegitimate, defective, irregular, abusive, arbitrary, discriminatory, negligent, seriously inconvenient, or inopportune exercise of their functions. It should be noted that this investigative mandate extends to acts and omissions that are capable of affecting diffuse or collective interests.[41] The institution has no jurisdiction to act in the defence of subjective property rights which correspond to individual legal assets: such actions must be exercised by property owners. The *Defensoría del Pueblo* can, however, act to protect or defend a legal asset that belongs to the entire community, i.e., an asset that is indivisible and to which no exclusion may be permitted. It is clear that the responsibilities of the Argentinian *Defensoría* are broad; essentially, the body must pay close attention to any and all behaviour that indicates a systematic and general failure of public administration.[42]

Natural and legal persons who consider themselves affected by the aforementioned acts or omissions may contact the *Defensoría del Pueblo* of Argentina. This is true regardless of their nationality or place of residence, and this access is not restricted by the person's confinement or imprisonment in a state facility.[43] Complaints must be submitted in writing, within one calendar year of the relevant act or omission. The *Defensoría* must ensure that the case is tailored to the relevant needs of the complainant and that his/her complaint bears the relevant signature. Nevertheless, no further formalities are required, the processing of the case is free of charge, and there is no need for the complainant to be represented by a lawyer.[44]

---

41 See Law Nr. 24,284 of the Republic of Argentina, art 14.
42 See ibid, art 15.
43 See ibid, art 18.
44 See ibid, art 19. See also, art 23.

Legal representation provided by the *Defensor del Pueblo* of Argentina is carried out in such a way as to make use of the institution's procedural legitimacy, which is contemplated in the institution's mandate and allows the *Defensor* to present a case before relevant legal bodies on the grounds of violations of legal rights. However, it should be clarified here that the *Defensor's* primary mission is to act as a critical collaborator, rather than as a litigator; this is emphasised by the institution's ability to avoid the costs and delays that are common in most judicial processes.

When a complaint is filed in Colombia, on the grounds of a human rights violation, the *Defensor del Pueblo* must verify the facts and evaluate the evidence. This process has to occur before the *Defensor* can pass his/her findings on to a competent authority. In the event that the human rights violation is committed by an individual, the body will call upon him/her publicly.[45] In order for it to verify the veracity of the complaints it receives, the *Defensor del Pueblo* 'may visit any public or private body and request all necessary information without any form of opposition or reservation from that body'.[46] The institution may also bring cases that concern human rights before the Constitutional Court, either *ex officio* or at the request of a party. Indeed, the *Defensoría* can bring actions 'before any other court of jurisdiction, public entity or authority'.[47] As such, the Colombian *Defensor del Pueblo* may turn to the Review Chamber of the Constitutional Court and request a review of any verdict on protection that has been excluded by the Court's selection. The *Defensor* can exercise this competence where he/she considers that the Review Chamber can clarify the scope of a right or contribute to the avoidance of serious harm. Any person who has intervened in a protection action, either directly or as an unofficial agent, and any person who is affected by the verdict may request the use of this competence, either themselves or through a representative or agent.[48]

The *Defensoría del Pueblo* of Colombia can also act as a mediator where required, for example, where collective petitions are drawn up against public authorities by civil society or public organisations. It may also mediate in disputes between individuals and public companies, or private companies that provide public services, where it is alleged that rights have been violated.[49]

The *Defensoría del Pueblo* of Ecuador presents various legal and administrative actions. These can be brought *ex officio* or at the request of

---

45 See Decree Nr. 25 of 2014 of the President of the Republic of Colombia, art 26.
46 ibid, art 25.
47 ibid, art 5.
48 See generally Decree 2591 of 1991 of the President of the Republic of Colombia; Agreement 05 of 1992; and Agreement 02 of 2015 of the Constitutional Court of Colombia.
49 See Decree Nr. 25 of 2014 of the President of the Republic of Colombia, art 5.

a party, and include actions relating to: protection; *habeas corpus*; access to public information; *habeas data*; non-compliance; public action; and poor quality or improper provision of public or private services.[50] The institution can also: issue mandatory and immediate measures for the protection of rights; request a trial and sanctioning before competent authorities in cases of non-compliance; and investigate and resolve, within the framework of its powers, actions or omissions of natural or legal persons who provide public services.[51] For these purposes, the *Defensor del Pueblo* exercises 'jurisdictional guarantees, public actions and complaints of poor quality or improper provision of public or private services, with special emphasis on generalised, systematic, or socially relevant cases'.[52]

As can be seen, the three institutions have, at least formally speaking, significant tools which can be employed to build strong relations with the general public and guarantee the rights of their respective citizenries. The following section provides a brief analysis of the work of the *defensorías del pueblo*, as reported in their respective and most recently updated annual reports. The scope of their work is analysed with the Paris Principles in mind.

3. SCOPE OF THE WORK OF THE *DEFENSORÍAS*

Although the concept of the Ombudsman's Office is relatively new in the region, its work has meant a significant change in terms of human rights culture. In order to evaluate the scope of these institutions, perhaps the most appropriate parameter for analysis is the provisions contained in the Paris Principles,[53] which include the objectives and competencies that national human rights institutions must fulfil. In this regard, it is appropriate to recall the provisions of Principle A of Resolution 48/134 of the United Nations General Assembly, where these Principles were adopted in 1993.

In general terms, national human rights institutions – and in this case, the Ombudsmen's Offices – are generally competent in the area of protection and promotion of human rights, particularly insofar as they should have the broadest possible mandate in constitutional or legal terms. However, at least seven specific powers are provided for, which, according to Robledo Silva, can be grouped into four categories: advisory powers, investigative powers, international cooperation powers and, finally, promotional powers.

---

50 See Constitution of the Republic of Ecuador, art 215.

51 See ibid.

52 Organic Law of the *Defensoría del Pueblo* of Ecuador, art 6.a.

53 S. López Escarcena, 'Los principios de París y las instituciones de derechos humanos en América Latina' (2022) 52 *Revista Derecho del Estado* 67–95, https://doi.org/10.18601/01229893.n52.03.

> Within the first we can place all those related to proposing, reviewing and recommending decisions and norms on human rights; in the second all those that involve investigating human rights violations; in the third those that have to do with collaborating with international organizations in the promotion and protection of human rights and finally in the last, those related to education and dissemination of human rights.[54]

Thus, this section will now analyse the scope of the work carried out by the Ombudsman's Offices of Argentina, Colombia and Ecuador in terms of these competencies. To this end, the content of annual reports presented by each of them on their management in different fields will be used.

3.1. ADVISORY POWERS

According to the competencies and powers established in the Paris Principles, the advisory powers include:

> (a) to submit … opinions, recommendations, proposals and reports on all matters relating to the protection and promotion of human rights …
> (b) to promote and ensure that national legislation, regulations and practices are harmonized with the international human rights instruments to which the State is a party, and that their implementation is effective;
> (c) to encourage the ratification of those instruments or accession to those texts and ensure their implementation.

In the Argentine scenario, we find that the Ombudsman's Office exercises an active role in consultative terms insofar as it participates in and supports the legislative procedure. Thus, for example, since 2019, the Ombudsman's Office has contributed to the construction of the Bill on registration of civil status and capacity of persons and maintained an active role in monitoring its legislative process during the following two years.[55] To the same extent, it has monitored the compliance and implementation of various human rights norms such as Bill 26,331 on the protection of native forests and Bill 7,543 on Territorial Planning of Native Forests in the Province of Salta. Along the same lines, it is worth highlighting other efforts initiated earlier. On the one hand, the follow-up advanced with respect to the Sustainable Development Goals through Resolution DP No. 29/14 and the inclusion of the promotion

---

54 See Robledo Silva (n 39), p. 51.

55 See Defensoría del Pueblo de la Nación, *Institución Nacional de Derechos Humanos. Informe Anual 2021*, Buenos Aires 2022, p. 33.

and protection of sexual and reproductive rights as a core competence of the institution, Resolution DP No. 46/16, according to the resolution of the World Health Assembly WHA 55.19.[56]

For its part, the Ombudsman's Office of Colombia has performed its advisory functions in what in recent years has been called moral magistracy, where it includes its participation in the legislative process of laws related to fundamental rights, the preparation of report and opinions, as well as the monitoring of compliance with court rulings. Thus, for example, during 2020, the Ombudsman's Office participated in 40 debates in the Congress of the Republic, held two ombudsman hearings on the right to health and on the humanitarian and environmental crisis in the Pacific Region, prepared 30 ombudsman reports, 34 legal opinions and followed up on 46 court rulings. Among these results, it is worth highlighting the *Defensoria*'s participation in the legislative process of projects related to ethnic issues, rights of children and adolescents, criminal matters, regulation of electronic cigarettes and eradication of illicit crops by aerial spraying.[57]

Finally, in the case of the Ecuadorian Ombudsman's Office, as with its counterparts, it plays an important role in the design, review and monitoring of human rights legislation. In particular, its participation in the state's legislative agenda stands out, seeing for example that in 2021, together with the Asociación de Psiquiatría Núcleo Pichincha, a draft Organic Law on Mental Health was presented with the aim of guaranteeing 'comprehensive mental health care for subjects of priority attention and groups in situations of vulnerability in mental health, under a human rights approach, gender equity, interculturalism and social inclusion'.[58] It also had an impact on Bills related to the right to care in the workplace for women or persons with disabilities, the right to voluntary abortion and the law on transparency and access to information, among others.

3.2. INVESTIGATIVE POWERS

In addition to the above, the Latin American Ombudsman's Offices have the authority to contribute to the preparation of reports that states must submit to United Nations human rights bodies and committees, as well as to regional institutions, in compliance with their treaty obligations.

In the case of Argentina, in recent years, the Ombudsman's Office has played a particularly important role in the preparation of reports that the state must

56 Defensoría del Pueblo de la Nación, *Informe Anual de la Defensoría de la Nación Argentina, 2016*, Buenos Aires 2017.

57 Defensoría del Pueblo de Colombia, *XXVIII Informe del Defensor del Pueblo al Congreso de la República. Parte II. Informe de Gestión 2020*, Bogotá 2020, pp. 26–28.

58 Defensoría del Pueblo Ecuador, *Rendición de cuentas 2021*, Quito 2022, p. 39.

submit to international organisations regarding compliance with its human rights obligations. For example, in 2021, it prepared and submitted the reports requested by: the Expert Mechanism on the Right to Development, in relation to racism and racial discrimination; the United Nations Human Rights Council; the Special Rapporteur on the human rights of migrants; the Special Rapporteur on contemporary forms of racism, racial discrimination, xenophobia and related intolerance; the OHCHR; the Special Rapporteur on the sale and sexual exploitation of children, including child pornography and other child sexual abuse; and the Committee on the Elimination of Discrimination against Women.[59]

Regarding the latter report, it is worth noting that in order to follow up on the General Observations made to Argentina by the Committee on the Elimination of Discrimination against Women (CEDAW), since November 2016 the Femicide Observatory of the National Ombudsman's Office was created, which carries out the registration, systematisation, analysis and communication of cases of femicide. Since then, the Observatory has registered and reported 292 cases in 2017, 281 cases in 2018, 280 cases in 2019, 295 cases in 2020 and 289 cases in 2021.[60]

In the Colombian context, it is worth highlighting especially, beyond the production of reports and responses for international organisations – since this is focused through other state entities –, the work carried out by the Ombudsman's Office in terms of monitoring and follow-up of the human rights situation. In this regard, attention should be drawn to the prevention and protection efforts deployed through the Early Warning System. Six humanitarian missions were deployed in the departments of Nariño, Chocó, Córdoba, Meta, Sucre and La Guajira, 54 early warnings were received, 37 more alerts were followed up and a preventive ombudsman's report was adopted. From this, for example, the Ombudsman's Office was able to identify that 40.7 per cent of the cases involved risks for the population in the reintegration process of former members of FARC-EP, 66 per cent indicated risks derived from the armed conflict for women defenders and leaders, 18.5 per cent involved risks derived from the armed conflict for the population with diverse sexual orientation and gender identity, and 48.1 per cent involved risks for the Afro-Colombian, black and Palenquera population.[61]

For its part, the Ecuadorian Ombudsman's Office deploys its investigative efforts in terms of following up on the recommendations of organisations derived from international treaties. In this regard, it is noteworthy that during the year 2021 the Annual Report on the Human Rights Situation in Ecuador for the year 2020 was prepared, 17 questionnaires and requests

---

59 See n 56, p. 245.
60 ibid, p. 259.
61 See n 58, p. 58.

from international organisations were answered, an alternative report on compliance with the CEDAW was prepared and the Ombudsman participated in the preparation of the annual report of the Ibero-American Federation of Ombudsmen.[62] As part of the efforts deployed for the preparation of these reports, it is necessary to call attention to the monitoring of the granting of administrative measures for the protection of women in compliance with the Organic Law for the Prevention and Eradication of Violence against Women. From it, it was determined that in 2021, 11,351 measures were registered nationwide and 4642 measures were followed up and complied with.

3.3. COOPERATION COMPETENCIES

The third category of competences and powers is related to international cooperation. Specifically, the Paris Principles speak of cooperating with the United Nations and other agencies of the United Nations system, regional institutions and institutions of other countries that are competent in the areas of promotion and protection of human rights.

In general terms, the work of the Ombudsman's Offices in international cooperation can be seen from two angles. On the one hand, there is the active participation by these entities: in scenarios of international cooperation and dialogue, as highlighted by the Argentine Ombudsman's Office, which in 2021 participated in the dialogue between the United Nations High Commissioner for Human Rights and the national human rights institutions of the Americas region on COVID-19, challenges and opportunities; and in the meetings and assemblies of the Network of National Institutions for the Promotion and Protection of Human Rights of the American Continent and the International Ombudsman Institute.[63] And on the other hand, this cooperation is seen through the execution of projects with international funding, as constantly highlighted by the Ombudsman's Office of Colombia, which during 2020 allocated USD $1,593,882 to 48 projects related to ethnic groups, women, children and adolescents, national organisations and collectives, human rights defenders, civilian population, LGTBI community, displaced population, migrant population and victims of the armed conflict.[64]

In a more local context, the Argentine Ombudsman's Office signed during 2021, at least seven cooperation agreements with territorial public entities, local associations and foundations responsible for the defence of human rights. This is the case of the agreements with the municipality of Escobar, the Micaela García 'La Negra' Foundation, the Convoz Civil Association,

62 See n 59, p. 63.
63 ibid.
64 See n 58, p. 120.

the Ombudsman's Offices of the cities of Salta and Viedma, the Argentine Paediatrics Society and the Institute of Public Thought and Policies.[65]

In the Ecuadorian case, the Ombudsman's Office, unlike the Argentine and Colombian cases, emphasises both dimensions of international cooperation, pointing out that the cooperation efforts deployed are aimed at both technical and financial assistance. Thus, for example, during 2021 the Early Warning and Response System Project in the Northern Border – SART – was implemented in cooperation with several agencies and organisations of the United Nations; it trained 58 employees of the Ombudsman's Office through international cooperation courses and spent USD $773,787 through international cooperation.[66] It also participated in the same international dialogue spaces as the Argentinean Ombudsman's Office, as well as in the meetings of the Global Alliance of National Human Rights Institutions.

3.4. POWERS FOR THE PROMOTION, PREVENTION, AND PROTECTION OF HUMAN RIGHTS

Lastly, there is the broadest of the four categories, that of competencies and powers for the promotion of human rights. This category includes at least two specific powers recognised by the Paris Principles:

> (f) to collaborate in the development of programs relating to teaching and research in the field of human rights and to participate in their implementation at the school, university and professional levels; and
>
> (g) to publicize human rights and the fight against all forms of discrimination, in particular racial discrimination, by raising public awareness, in particular through information and education, using all means of communication.

In this regard, the Ombudsman's Office in Argentina carries out different types of workshops, training, diploma courses, seminars, panels, meetings and conferences. Thus, for example, during the year 2021 it held training workshops on the Inter-American SIMORE (the IACHR's online platform) and on the incorporation of SDG16; it participated in the updating of the Protocol of Action for the Protection of Human Rights of Persons in Contexts of Migration and held an international congress on democracy in times of global distrust and uncertainty.[67] With regard to the dissemination of human rights education in Argentina, it is also worth noting that since 1999 the Ombudsman's Office has had a weekly radio programme entitled *La gente y su defensor* (The People and

65 See n 56, p. 280.
66 See n 59, p. 82.
67 See n 56, p. 63.

their Ombudsman). This programme was born as a communication tactic within the operation called 'Federal Dissemination Plan' with the purpose of deepening and publicising the activities carried out by the National Ombudsman, which today has evolved into the podcast 'rights and action'.

Now, within the competencies related to the promotion of human rights, there are also those related to the intervention in judicial proceedings and public defense. Hence, it is worth noting that in the Argentine case, the Ombudsman's Office provided legal and technical advice during the year 2021, processing two judicial processes, among which the process promoted for the collective of native peoples of the province of Chaco stands out, where it was achieved that the Supreme Court of Justice of the Nation adopted a precautionary measure in their favor. It also provided assistance and advice to the victims of obstetric violence so that hospitals and sanatoriums would comply with the obligations derived from Law Nr. 25,929 on Respectful Childbirth for the Prevention, Assistance and Eradication of Obstetric Violence.[68]

For its part, the Colombian Ombudsman's Office developed during 2020 a total of 4751 activities for the promotion and dissemination of human rights at the regional level, reaching more than 9,000 citizens. Of these, about 85 per cent were categorised as subjects of special constitutional protection.[69] Due to national needs and realities, the main themes of these exercises were peacebuilding, economic, social and cultural rights, and the relationship between business and human rights. For example, of the 13 diploma courses offered this year, seven were related to the armed conflict and peacebuilding, three to social control mechanisms, and the remaining three to differential approaches.

Also noteworthy within the promotion, prevention and protection functions of the Colombian Ombudsman's Office is its active participation in the Preliminary Assessment Group (GVP), the Committee for Risk Assessment and Recommendation of Measures (CERREM) and the Technical Committee on Security and Protection for FARC-EP ex-combatants. This is to the extent that the GVP is in charge of determining 'the level of risk and recommending the protection measure to be implemented for the persons evaluated, according to the information provided by the risk analysts of the Technical Body for the Collection and Analysis of Information';[70] CERREM is in charge of validating said recommendations and, based on this, suggesting protection measures; and it is up to the Technical Committee to identify

> the needs in terms of human and physical resources and budget required for the implementation of the Strategic Plan for the Security and Protection of FARC-EP ex-combatants and their families, in order to guarantee the rights to life and personal

68 ibid, p. 208.
69 See n 58, p. 32.
70 ibid, p. 69.

integrity, freedom, mobility and security of these persons, who are the object of the protection programme.[71]

Finally, in the Colombian case, it is worth highlighting the actions taken by the Ombudsman's Office in the defense of human rights before national courts. In this regard, during 2020, the Ombudsman's Office participated in a total of 41,418 judicial processes in different types of actions (compliance actions, group actions, *habeas corpus*, unconstitutionality actions, search mechanisms, nullity actions, popular actions and *tutela* actions in case of breach of fundamental rights). Among the most important and representative processes, the group action regarding the landslide at the *Doña Juana* garbage landfill stands out, where the Ombudsman's Office during 2020 managed to support the resolution of 14,000 appeals by the action's adherents.[72]

Finally, the Ecuadorian Ombudsman's Office, in terms of its functions of promotion and dissemination of human rights, focuses its efforts on carrying out adequate human rights education. Thus, during the year 2021, 67 teaching–learning processes were carried out nationwide, comprising a total of 195 events, in addition to 225 information dissemination processes. In this regard, it is necessary to clarify that 'outreach processes differ from teaching–learning processes because the former seek to disseminate information on certain topics, while the latter aim to train and raise awareness in depth on human rights and nature'.[73] Likewise, the Ombudsman made progress in the creation and certification of the School of Human and Natural Rights, through which it managed to offer nine different education processes on human rights for the training of university students.[74]

4. FUTURE OF THE INSTITUTION

As can be seen, the *Defensorías del Pueblo* of Argentina, Colombia, and Ecuador have achieved their objectives on the basis of agreements and coordinated actions with other bodies working on the promotion and protection of human rights. Moreover, the three *defensorías* have taken steps to create pluralistic and inclusive election and participation procedures in their respective countries – procedures which have come to be seen as an inalienable characteristic of the *defensoría* institution itself. The *defensorías* studied have emphasised the importance of public access to information and of public education on the

71 ibid, p. 71.
72 ibid, p. 85.
73 See n 59, p. 51.
74 ibid, p. 57.

topic of human rights and the procedures that must be followed in order to assert these rights. However, although there have been joint efforts which have involved collaboration with multiple organisations in each of the three countries, various economic and political challenges have impeded the achievement of the *defensorías*' institutional objectives. The primary challenges relate to obstacles which prevent, or restrict, legislative reforms and other projects that might help to further develop the protection of human rights in the field.

It is worth briefly analysing a number of these challenges, as the future of the three *defensorías* depends on their ability to devise responsive strategies which correspond to the issues they face. While several challenges are influenced by the specific context in which each institution operates, as well as the resultant specific priorities imposed upon them, they can be grouped into three general categories: challenges related to guarantees of institutional independence; challenges related to sanctioning powers; and challenges which are particular to the general human rights context of each country.

4.1. INDEPENDENCE

Institutional independence is a critical characteristic of any oversight body; the *Defensorías del pueblo* are no different. In this case, independence refers to autonomy and discretion in the exercise of each *defensorías* functions. The institutions must be able to act freely and objectively, without interference from external powers or coercion that favours individual interests. The fulfilment of this requirement is not an easy task in the current Latin American context. As the *defensorías del pueblo* have become prominent actors in the bureaucratic apparatus of the state, they have, simultaneously, been increasingly influenced by a context in which political parties compete for every single position and post. In addition to the corruption that remains endemic in many of the countries across the region, these institutions must also overcome the challenge of potentially losing their independence.

The constitutional norms which provide legal standing to the three *defensorías* analysed here refer to institutional independence in a similar way. The Constitution of the Argentine Nation, for example, states that the *Defensoría del Pueblo* 'is an independent body [... that shall act with full functional autonomy, receiving instructions from no other authority';[75] the Political Constitution of Colombia states that the *Defensor del Pueblo* 'shall exercise his or her functions in an autonomous manner';[76] while the Constitution of the Republic of

75 Constitution of the Argentine Nation, art 86.

76 Political Constitution of Colombia, art 281.

Ecuador states that the *Defensoría del Pueblo* of that country 'shall be a body of public law with … administrative and financial autonomy'.[77] In the case of the two latter examples, complementary legislation seems to follow Argentina's constitutional example, by adding that the *Defensoría del Pueblo* of Colombia 'has administrative and budgetary autonomy',[78] while the *Defensoría del Pueblo* of Ecuador has 'administrative, financial, budgetary and organisational autonomy' and 'independence'.[79] In the Ecuadorian example, independence is defined as 'the separation from other institutions and functions of the State in order to effectively fulfil its role in the promotion and protection of human rights and nature',[80] and autonomy is defined as 'the ability to self-govern politically and administratively in accordance with its own normative, administrative, financial and organisational processes'.[81]

4.2. SANCTIONING POWERS

In common with other Latin American national human rights institutions, the contexts facing the *defensorías* in Argentina, Colombia, and Ecuador are milieus of normative instability and unequal application of legal rules; therefore, it is vital that their respective authority is based on a platform of social legitimacy.[82] On this point, the compliance plans drawn up by the *defensorías* can, at times, contradict the rulings of judicial organs. This has the capacity to restrict consensus-building on human rights matters and can confound the consistency of human rights messaging and communication, thereby impairing the clear messaging and moral coercion that rulings require to be effective. This restricts the ability of these institutions to fulfil their objectives and has limited the efficacy of the *defensorías*' management. Providing these institutions with *genuine* powers of oversight would give their opinions added weight as well as clear legal priority: clarifying any inconsistent messaging and contributing positively to their efforts to fulfil their human rights objectives.

Due to the current state of play, it is not unusual for the Argentinian *Defensoría* to have to submit recommendations and suggestions to amend shortcomings detected within its own management framework, and state agencies even refuse

77 Constitution of the Republic of Ecuador, art 214.

78 Decree Nr. 25 of 2014 of the President of the Republic of Colombia, art 1.

79 Organic Law of the *Defensoría del Pueblo* of Ecuador, arts 1, 2.

80 ibid, art 4.a.

81 ibid, art 4.b.

82 See T. Pegram, 'Weak Institutions, Rights Claims and Pathways to Compliance: The Transformative Role of the Peruvian Human Rights Ombudsman' (2011) 39/2 *Oxford Development Studies* 229, pp. 245–46.

to implement the *Defensoría*'s findings due to a lack of legal/moral authority. This lack of binding powers of enforcement is also evident in Colombia:

> when the *Defensor* is aware of a situation that affects the exercise of rights ... he or she has the power to denounce it publicly or to encourage the competent bodies to initiate the required steps, but he or she cannot himself or herself initiate a process ... that leads to sanctioning.[83]

Regarding Ecuador, 'all State institutions, their agents or designated parties and related individuals involved in a defence proceeding are obliged to cooperate with the *Defensoría del Pueblo*'.[84] Failure to do so has consequences, since

> [t]he refusal to cooperate in a defence proceeding shall be understood as non-compliance with the decisions of a legitimate and competent authority, when the decision which has not been complied with had been considered final. To this end, the *Defensoría del Pueblo* shall inform the relevant administrative or legal authorities in order that the respective procedures may be initiated.[85]

In addition, the Ecuadorian *Defensoría del Pueblo* issues 'immediate compliance measures in the protection of rights ... and must request a trial and sanctioning before the competent authority on the grounds of non-compliance'.[86]

4.3. PROTECTION OF HUMAN RIGHTS

The *defensores del pueblo* must: gather and disseminate information about mechanisms and means which protect human rights; mobilise public opinion on rights; and actively participate in efforts to provide people with the material means required to exercise their rights, for example, by helping to provide resources to build houses, supply food, and strengthen development, etc. The primary objective of these institutions is to seek a democratic transformation, involving greater participation by the general public in decision-making that shapes their lives and an improved management of public affairs. Both of these factors act as means to improve social, political, and economic conditions; consolidate peace at the national level; and promote increased awareness of human rights.

Achieving this objective is no easy task for Latin American *defensorías del pueblo*, due, in large part, to issues concerning their autonomy and their lack

83 J. Córdoba Triviño, *El Defensor del Pueblo*, Gustavo Ibáñez, Bogotá 1992, p. 274.
84 Organic Law of the *Defensoría del Pueblo* of Ecuador, art 30.
85 ibid, art 32.
86 ibid, art 6.b.

of powers of enforcement. Unfortunately, states in the region have failed to understand the particular needs of their respective populations and have not foreseen the long-term consequences of their decisions. This has made the protection of human rights appear as if it were the least of their priorities.

As Human Rights Watch has noted with respect to Argentina, the human rights situation remains disparate, with long-standing problems 'that include police abuse, poor prison conditions, endemic violence against women, difficulty accessing reproductive services, and obstacles that keep indigenous people from enjoying rights afforded to them by Argentine and international law'. However, the country 'continues to make progress protecting lesbian, gay, bisexual, and transgender (LGBT) rights and prosecuting officials for abuses committed during the "dirty war" (1976–1983), although trials have been subject to worrying delays'.[87] Regarding Colombia, it is among the states which submit the most petitions to the Inter-American Commission on Human Rights,[88] while the Ecuadorian state has been condemned on several occasions by the Inter-American Court of Human Rights.[89]

Consequently, we conclude that the main challenges faced by the *defensorías del pueblo* are no different from the general challenges confronted by other state agencies within twenty-first-century Latin American legal systems. These include: issues of institutional transparency; the expedition of legal processes; protection of constitutional guarantees; efforts to ensure effective reparations; and the ongoing search for convergence between diverse economic interests and respect for fundamental rights. We trust that the academic, political, legal, and economic efforts taken with regard to the *defensores del pueblo* in Latin America will allow these challenges to be overcome. After all, the efficacy of constitutionalism and, above all, the dignified survival of people depend heavily on the emphasis placed on such efforts.

---

87 See generally Human Rights Watch, Argentina. Available at: <https://www.hrw.org/es/americas/argentina>.

88 See generally Inter-American Commission on Human Rights. Available at: <http://www.oas.org/es/cidh/multimedia/estadisticas/estadisticas.html>.

89 See e.g., Editorial, 'Ecuador ha sido condenado en 13 ocasiones por la CIDH', *El Comercio* (Quito, 22 May 2014). Available at: <http://www.elcomercio.com/actualidad/seguridad/ecuador-sido-condenado-13-ocasiones.html>.

DEFENSORÍA DEL PUEBLO (PARAGUAY AND URUGUAY)

Veronika HAÁSZ

1. INTRODUCTION

It is widely known that the Latin American ombudsman model is rooted in the Spanish legal tradition and carries all the core elements of the Swedish ombuds-prototype; this sees it take the form of an independent and autonomous state institution which oversees the public administration and reports to parliament. The Spanish *Defensor del Pueblo* has two additional characteristics: it is empowered to hold laws unconstitutional and plays a role in protecting human rights.[1] The ombuds-institution appeared in Spain in 1978 and in most Latin American systems in the 1980s, during a period of transition from authoritarianism to democracy for these states. Because authoritarian regimes generally distinguish themselves through the systematic abuse of state power, the violation of citizens' rights,[2] and a general lack of mechanisms which provide checks and balances within the state structure,[3] efforts to protect human rights only began to come to the forefront when new state structures were organised in Spain and Latin American countries. The resulting entity was the *Defensoría del Pueblo*, which represents a new institutional model that is able 'to prevent human rights abuses and bureaucracy left behind by the prior regimes'.[4] In Latin America, the authoritarian past had serious consequences. Abusive former regimes had destroyed public trust in state institutions, which placed emerging

[1] See B. MERINO, 'Protecting the People: The Latin American approach to Ombudsmanship' ('Back to Roots: Tracing the Swedish Origin of Ombudsman Institutions' conference, Stockholm, June 2009). Available at: <http://www.theioi.org/downloads/64oj2/Stockholm Conference_28. Back to the Roots_Beatriz Merino.pdf>.

[2] See F. UGGLA, 'The Ombudsman in Latin America' (2004) 36 *J. Lat. Am. Stud.* 423, 424.

[3] See G. O'DONNELL, 'Horizontal Accountability in New Democracies' (1998) 9 *Journal of Democracy* 112, 119.

[4] See T. PEGRAM, 'Diffusion Across Political Systems: The Global Spread of National Human Rights Institutions' (2010) 32 *Hum.Rts.Q.* 729, 736–37.

ombuds-institutions in a disadvantaged position.[5] Beyond restoring public confidence, ombudsmen had to convince public authorities of the benefits their new institutions would bring, all the while waiting until the countries' judiciaries normalised.[6]

The ombudsmen in Latin America had an important role in the consolidation of new democratic states: a role which consisted mostly in hearing the compensation claims of victims of the former dictatorships. Although these authoritarian regimes primarily violated civil and political rights,[7] *defensorías del pueblo* also began to monitor the fulfilment of economic, social, and cultural rights in contexts of inequality, exclusion, and discrimination. It is not surprising, therefore, that one of the fundamental functions of today's Latin American ombudsmen is to promote human rights education, intervene in social conflicts as a mediator and facilitator of dialogue, and supervise public policies in the interest of the most vulnerable members of society.[8]

Despite the similar social and political origins of the *defensorías del pueblo* in Paraguay and Uruguay, the two countries saw state structures rebuilt and transitional justice administered in different ways. This is reflected in the timing and circumstances of the institutions' formation as well as the form and functioning of their ombudsman offices. Each state adopted an institutional variation that best fitted its social and political reality. The Paraguayan *Defensoría del Pueblo* was established in 1995, and it was based on the Swedish and Spanish ombudsman models. The Uruguayan *Institución Nacional de Derechos Humanos y Defensoría del Pueblo* was created in 2008 and, in contrast, combines the ombudsman and institute models.

The following sections study how the laws of Paraguay and Uruguay regulate the status, autonomy, accountability, and functions of these NHRIs as well as their cooperation with other human rights actors.

2. STATUS

Paraguay was headed by General Alfredo Stroessner (1912–2006) from 1954 to 1989. After his dictatorship ended, the 1992 Constitution incorporated

---

5 Interview with Delia Muñoz, Chief of Staff (Peruvian) *Defensoría del Pueblo* (Lima, Peru, 7 December 2016); interview with Elizabeth Flores, Official Advisor of the Human Rights Committee of the (Paraguayan) Ministry of Public Affairs (Asunción, Paraguay, 9 December 2016).

6 See generally J. Luis Maiorano, 'Justice Administration and the Defensor del Pueblo' (1998) *International Ombudsman Institute Occasional Paper* 64. Available at: <http://www.theioi.org/downloads/etrmf/IOI Canada_Occasional Paper 64_Dr. Jorge Maiorana_Justice Administration and the Defensor del Pueblo_1998_EN. Jorge Maiorana_Justice Administration and the Defensor del Pueblo_1998_EN>.

7 See Uggla (n 2) p. 432.

8 See Merino (n 1) p. 7.

the *Defensoría del Pueblo*. Nine years passed before the first ombudsman was appointed by Resolution Nr. 768/2001 of the Chamber of Deputies of Paraguay.[9] Due to budgetary constraints, the office had to wait another year before being set up.[10]

Uruguay was also ruled by a civilian-military regime from 1974 to 1985, headed by Juan María Bordaberry (1928–2011). Unlike that of its neighbour, Uruguay's 1967 Constitution, which has been amended several times, does not include a NHRI within its provisions. The *Institución Nacional de Derechos Humanos* was established in 2008 by Law Nr. 18,446, and was renamed in 2011 by Law Nr. 18,806, as the *Institución Nacional de Derechos Humanos y Defensoría del Pueblo* (INDDHH). According to its constitutive act, the INDDHH is an entity of the legislature, which is aimed at the promotion and protection of those human rights recognised by the Constitution and by international law.[11]

2.1. LEGAL BASIS

The Paraguayan Constitution describes, in Articles 276 to 280, the *Defensor del Pueblo*'s: autonomy; produres for appointment and removal; requirements, incompatibilities and immunities; and duties and powers. These rules are further developed in Law Nr. 631/1995, while Law Nr. 838/1996 vested the *Defensoría del Pueblo* with the additional responsibility of settling compensation claims in respect of victims of human rights violations perpetrated during the 1954–1989 dictatorship. As mentioned, the Uruguayan ombuds-office was not included in the country's Constitution; it was enacted, instead, in Law Nr. 18,446 of 2008, which provides detailed rules on the INDDHH's composition, claims procedure, powers, structure, functioning, and budget. In 2011, Law Nr. 18,806 amended its composition and budget as well as its name.

Both the Paraguayan and Uruguayan NHRIs have drafted their own rules of procedure.[12]

2.2. ORGANISATION

The *Defensoría del Pueblo* and the INDDHH have different organisational structures. The Paraguayan institution is a classical ombuds-office: headed by

---

9 See M. Arenilla (ed.), *Manual de buenas prácticas institucionales de las defensorías de Iberoamérica*, Trama, Madrid 2004, p. 166.

10 See UN HRI/CORE/PRY/2010 of 21 May 2010, para. 178.

11 See Law Nr. 18,446 of the Oriental Republic of Uruguay, art 1.

12 See Internal Rules for Permanent, Hired and Commissioned Officers of the (Paraguayan) *Defensoría del Pueblo*; Rules of the (Uruguayan) *Institución Nacional de Derechos Humanos y Defensoría del Pueblo*.

an ombudsman and a deputy, who can substitute for the latter, if necessary.[13] It has a large number of administrative and operational departments and directorates.[14] The *Defensor del Pueblo* him- or herself, is a parliamentary commissioner, who has no judicial or executive competence and whose functions are to defend human rights, address popular complaints, and protect community interests.[15] The General Directorate of Truth, Justice and Reparation was created in 2009,[16] based on the proposal of the Truth and Justice Commission.[17] Its role is to implement the Truth and Justice Commission's recommendations and carry out the ombudsman's tasks in relation to reparation, as is required by the law.[18]

Being a combination of the institute and ombuds-office models, the Uruguayan NHRI diverges from the traditional Latin American NHRI model.[19] The INDDHH is managed and represented by the Directive Board, a body of five members who are elected by the General Assembly of the Oriental Republic of Uruguay for a period of five years. The members come from different segments of society, thus ensuring pluralism within the institution.[20] The Directive Board appoints one of its members as President of the INDDHH for one year, subject to rotation.[21] Compared to the Paraguayan *Defensoría del Pueblo*, the INDDHH has a considerably smaller apparatus. Beyond the administrative secretariats, it has four main sections, which are responsible for: complaints and investigations; the national preventive mechanism; education; and public relations.[22]

Unlike the INDDHH, the Paraguayan *Defensoría del Pueblo* has regional offices.[23] Its Asunción office provides some assistance to the other offices, but

13 See Law Nr. 631/95 of the Republic of Paraguay, arts 6, 11.

14 See generally *Defensoría del Pueblo* of Paraguay. Available at: <http://www.defensoriadelpueblo.gov.py/organigrama.pdf>.

15 See Constitution of the Republic of Paraguay, art 276; Law Nr. 631/95 of the Republic of Paraguay, art 2.

16 See generally *Defensoría del Pueblo* Res. Nr. 179/09 of 23 January 2009; Dirección General de Verdad, Justicia y Reparación. Available at: <http://atom.ippdh.mercosur.int/index.php/direccion-de-verdad-justicia-y-reparacion-defensoria-del-pueblo>.

17 See generally Final Report of the Truth and Justice Commission of 28 August 2008. Available at: <http://www.derechoshumanos.net/lesahumanidad/informes/paraguay/Informe_Comision_Verdad_y_Justicia_Paraguay_Conclusiones_y_Recomendaciones.pdf>.

18 See L. Roniger *et al*, *Exile, Diaspora, and Return: Changing Cultural Landscapes in Argentina, Chile, Paraguay, and Uruguay*, Oxford University Press, Oxford 2017, p. 133.

19 See K. Linos and T. Pegram, 'The Language of Compromise in International Agreements' (2016) 70 *Int'l Org.* 587, 614.

20 See Law Nr. 18,446 of the Oriental Republic of Uruguay, arts 36, 37.

21 See ibid, art 53.

22 See generally *Institución Nacional de Derechos Humanos y Defensoría del Pueblo* of Uruguay. Available at: <https://www.gub.uy/institucion-nacional-derechos-humanos-uruguay/>.

23 See Constitution of the Republic of Paraguay, art 280. These regional offices are located in: Areguá; Caaguazú; Caazapá; Ciudad del Este; Coronel Oviedo; Encarnación; Itacurubi de la Cordillera;

there are no periodic meetings between headquarters and the regional offices.[24] The ombudsman has complained about the lack of readiness for cooperation on the part of the regional offices.[25]

2.3. SELECTION, APPOINTMENT, AND TENURE

To become *Defensor del Pueblo*, one needs: to hold Paraguayan nationality; to be at least 25 years old; and to enjoy full civil and political rights.[26] In Uruguay, there is no age limit for election as a member of the INDDHH's Directive Board, but Uruguayan citizenship and the full enjoyment of civic rights are necessary requirements. Candidates must also demonstrate high moral authority and have human rights-related experience. Moreover, they must not have held a public appointment over the previous two years.[27]

In Paraguay, the *Defensor del Pueblo* and his or her deputy are elected by a two-thirds majority vote of the Chamber of Deputies, from a list of three candidates submitted by the Senate.[28] During its early years, the NHRI was highly criticised due to a serious delay in the appointment of the first ombudsman. Critics included civil society and international actors, including UN treaty bodies,[29] and the Inter-American Commission on Human Rights (IACHR).[30] Despite the fact that Paraguayan law required the first *Defensor del Pueblo* and his or her deputy to be appointed for the 1993–1998

Itaguá; Pedro Juan Caballero; San Ignacio; San Lorenzo; and Santa Rosa del Aguaray. See generally *Defensoría del Pueblo* of Paraguay. Available at: <http://www.defensoriadelpueblo.gov.py/sedes.html>.

As for the Uruguayan INDDH, even though it has no regional offices, it makes agreements with universities around the country. This allows collaborating academics, who collect data on human rights problems in the different regions of the country, to share vital data with the institution. Interview with Ariela Peralta, former member of the Directive Board of the INDDHH (Montevideo, Uruguay, 17 December 2016).

24 Interview with Elizabeth Flores, Official Advisor of the Human Rights Committee of the (Paraguayan) Ministry of Public Affairs (Asunción, Paraguay, 9 December 2016).

25 Editorial, 'El defensor no encuentra a 21 funcionarios de las sedes', *Ultima Hora* (Asunción, 11 November 2016). Available at: <http://www.ultimahora.com/el-defensor-no-encuentra-21-funcionarios-las-sedes-n1038903.html>.

26 See Law Nr. 631/95 of the Republic of Paraguay, art 7.

27 See Law Nr. 18,446 of the Oriental Republic of Uruguay, art 45.

28 See Constitution of the Republic of Paraguay, art 277; Law Nr. 631/95 of the Republic of Paraguay, arts 4, 11.

29 See e.g. Committee against Torture, CAT/C/SR.425 of 17 May 2000, para. 9; Committee on Economic, Social and Cultural Rights, E/C.12/1/Add.1 of 28 May 1996, para. 19.

30 See 1998 Annual Report of the Inter-American Commission on Human Rights, para. 57; Press Release No. 23/99 of the Inter-American Commission on Human Rights, paras. 31–33.

Congress period,[31] it took nine years for this process to happen. As the IACHR pointed out,

> the special majority of the Chamber of Deputies required by the Paraguayan Constitution to designate the Human Rights Ombudsman is not a valid excuse, especially considering that in the case of other constitutional organs that also require special majorities, the necessary political will has been mustered to make the appointment.[32]

Because Paraguayan legislation does not clarify how to appoint an ombudsman in the case of a vacancy, the Congress had to pass a 2003 law, which established that once the ombudsman's mandate has expired, he or she will continue to exercise his or her functions and powers until a successor takes office.[33] This vague rule made it possible for the first *Defensor del Pueblo* to hold his office for 14 years, until the new ombudsman was elected in 2016.[34] Due to this situation, the NHRI lost significant credibility.[35]

In Uruguay, the selection procedure is rather pluralistic: social organisations may propose candidates for the INDDHH's Directive Board to the General Assembly of Uruguay; parliamentarians receive these proposals and then formulate a list of candidates;[36] the General Assembly designates a special parliamentary commission, with members of all political parties represented, to screen the eligibility of proposed candidates, prepare the list of qualified candidates, and communicate this list to the General Assembly's Presidency;[37] members of the Directive Board are then elected by a two-thirds majority vote of all the members of the General Assembly.[38]

Both the Paraguayan and Uruguayan legislation have rules on incompatibility, which describe the positions or activities that could affect the independence, impartiality, or prestige of the respective NHRI; this excludes some possible candidates from appointment. Exclusionary factors include: engaging in political

---

31 See Law Nr. 631/95 of the Republic of Paraguay, art 32.

32 Third Report on the Situation of Human Rights in Paraguay of the Inter-American Commission on Human Rights, 9 March 2001, Chapter II, H, para. 62. Available at: <http://www.cidh.org/countryrep/Paraguay01eng/chap1.htm>.

33 See Law Nr. 2103/2003 of the Republic of Paraguay.

34 Editorial, 'Diputados designa a Miguel Godoy nuevo Defensor del Pueblo', *Ultima Hora* (Asunción, 1 November 2016). Available at: <http://www.ultimahora.com/diputados-designa-miguel-godoy-nuevo-defensor-del-pueblo-n1036267.html>.

35 Interview with Hugo Oscar Richer, Senator and Head of the Human Rights Committee of the (Paraguayan) Congress (Asunción, Paraguay, 12 December 2016).

36 See Law Nr. 18,446 of the Oriental Republic of Uruguay, art 39.

37 See ibid, art 40.

38 See ibid, art 37.

activity;[39] exercising judicial or executive competence;[40] or holding another remunerated public or private office, with the exception of academic positions.[41] Incompatibility plays a role during the position's candidacy period,[42] while holding the office,[43] and after the termination of the ombuds-mandate.[44] Compatibility must be affirmed, in both countries, by sworn statements upon taking the office.[45]

The *Defensor del Pueblo* in Paraguay and the members of the INDDHH's Directive Board are all elected for a five-year term. In both cases, the respective laws allow for re-election, although in Uruguay this is possible only once, for the subsequent term.[46] Interestingly enough, according to Paraguayan law, the *Defensor del Pueblo*'s five-year term must correspond to that of the Congress. In European legislation, the terms of the ombudsman and the legislature do not typically overlap, at least not fully; thus guaranteeing the independence of the NHRI.

In Paraguay and Uruguay, the position terminates with the expiration of the term of appointment, resignation, death or supervening incapacity.[47] The *Defensor del Pueblo* must leave office by the age of 75.[48] In both Paraguay and Uruguay, a criminal conviction will also terminate the office.[49] While the Paraguayan legislation only provides for termination in cases of poor performance of functions,[50] the Uruguayan law specifies various causes for dismissal, including unworthy behaviour, gross negligence, serious misconduct, and supervening incompatibility.[51]

---

39 See Constitution of the Republic of Paraguay, arts 254, 278; Law Nr. 18,446 of the Oriental Republic of Urguay, art 46.C, D).

40 See Constitution of the Republic of Paraguay, art 276; Law Nr. 631/95 of the Republic of Paraguay, art 3.

41 See Constitution of the Republic of Paraguay, art 254; Law Nr. 18,446 of the Oriental Republic of Uruguay, art 46.B.

42 See Law Nr. 631/95 of the Republic of Paraguay, art 30.

43 See Constitution of the Republic of Paraguay, art 235.3.

44 See Law Nr. 18,446 of the Oriental Republic of Uruguay, art 50.

45 See Law Nr. 631/95 of the Republic of Paraguay, art 29; Law Nr. 18,446 of the Oriental Republic of Uruguay, art 49.

46 See Constitution of the Republic of Paraguay, art 277; Law Nr. 631/95 of the Republic of Paraguay, art 4; Law Nr. 631/95 of the Republic of Paraguay, art 29; Law Nr. 18,446 of the Oriental Republic of Uruguay, art 41.

47 See Law Nr. 631/95 of the Republic of Paraguay, art 5.1–5.3; Law Nr. 18,446 of the Oriental Republic of Uruguay, art 52.A–52.D.

48 See Law Nr. 631/95 of the Republic of Paraguay, art 5.4.

49 See Law Nr. 631/95 of the Republic of Paraguay, art 5.5; Law Nr. 18,446 of the Oriental Republic of Uruguay, art 52.E.

50 See Constitution of the Republic of Paraguay, art 277.

51 See Law Nr. 18,446 of the Oriental Republic of Uruguay, art 52.F.

2.4. COMPLIANCE WITH THE PARIS PRINCIPLES

Both the Paraguayan and Uruguayan NHRIs applied for accreditation some years after their establishment. The *Defensoría del Pueblo* was accredited with A-status in 2008: *ergo*, the International Coordinating Committee of National Institutions for the Promotion and Protection of Human Rights (ICC) considered the Paraguayan ombuds-office to be fully compliant with the Paris Principles.[52] Nevertheless, the Sub-Committee on Accreditation (SCA) of the ICC (since 2016, the Global Alliance of NHRIs – GANHRI) flagged that the salaries of staff members were lower than those of civil servants performing similar tasks in other public institutions; it also encouraged the institution to interact more consistently with the international human rights system and with civil society.[53] As the GANHRI accreditation system works on the basis of a five-year periodic review, the *Defensoría del Pueblo* applied for re-accreditation in 2013. This time, the SCA recommended that the application should be deferred to its next session. The main reason for this decision was the fact that the conclusion of the ombudsman's term, in 2008, had been followed by a subsequent five-year period during which the Paraguayan legislature had failed to appoint a successor.[54] This is a highly sensitive issue within this type of NHRI structure, since '[d]ue to its markedly personal character – which gives its office strong powers over the institutions as such – the appointment of ombudsmen is a potential source of political interference'.[55] The UN Human Rights Committee also expressed its concern about the failure to select a new *Defensor del Pueblo* and 'the lack of clear procedures and criteria for ensuring that the ombudsman's office is fully independent and effective'.[56] A submission from civil society also raised serious concerns about the ombuds-institution's effective performance.[57]

---

52 See generally UN General Assembly Res. 48/134 of 20 December 1993.

53 See the Report and Recommendations of the Session of the Sub-Committee on Accreditation (SCA), Geneva, 3–6 November 2008, of the International Coordinating Committee of National Institutions for the Promotion and Protection of Human Rights (ICC), para. 4.9. Available at: <https://www.ohchr.org/sites/default/files/Documents/Countries/NHRI/GANHRI/2008_November_SCA_Report.pdf>.

54 See the Report and Recommendations of the Session of the SCA, Geneva, 18–22 November 2013, of the ICC, para. 3.6. Available at: <https://www.ohchr.org/sites/default/files/Documents/Countries/NHRI/GANHRI/SCA_NOVEMBER_2013_FINAL_REPORT_ENGLISH.pdf>.

55 Uggla (n 2) p. 434.

56 Concluding observations on the Third Periodic Report of Paraguay, adopted by the UN Human Rights Committee at its 107th session (11–28 March 2013), CCPR/C/PRY/CO/3, 29 April 2013, para. 7.

57 Report and Recommendations of the Session of the SCA (n 54) para. 3.6.

In 2014, the SCA deferred its decision further (once again to the next session) and expressed its continuing concerns about the *Defensoría del Pueblo*'s effectiveness in some areas, which included: making recommendations to the state on a clear and effective mandate; proactively providing assistance to victims of the dictatorship; and advocating for the appointment of a new ombudsman.[58] In its next session, the SCA recommended the suspension of the *Defensoría del Pueblo*'s accreditation status. Instead of providing information on the implementation of the SCA's recommendations, the NHRI withdrew its application for re-accreditation on 10 July 2014.[59] The *Defensoría del Pueblo* has not submitted a subsequent application for re-accreditation, and, as it did not so within one year of its suspension, its accreditation has lapsed as a consequence.[60] According to his own statements, the new Paraguayan ombudsman did not intend to apply for re-accreditation until he solved some issues at home: i.e., working on cases that had been ignored, focusing on public policies, and finishing the accusation procedure he launched against the former *Defensor del Pueblo*, which was an effort intended to make clear his independence from the previous era.[61] In spite of this, the Paraguayan ombuds-office applied for accreditation in 2019, receiving B-status.[62] This time, the SCA expressed concerns regarding the *Defensor*'s selection and appointment process, on the bases that it is not sufficiently broad and transparent and because a right of appeal in respect of the ombudsman's dismissal is lacking. Furthermore, the SCA urged the *Defensor del Pueblo* to advocate for adequate funding and for a broader human rights mandate that includes promoting the ratification of or accession to regional and international human rights instruments. The Paraguayan NHRI was also encouraged to interact more actively with the international human rights system.[63]

Since the INDDHH's establishment, international human rights monitoring bodies have urged it to apply for accreditation.[64] The NHRI applied in 2015,

58 See the Report and Recommendations of the Session of the SCA, Geneva, 17–21 March 2014, of the ICC, para. 3.3. Available at: <https://www.ohchr.org/sites/default/files/Documents/Countries/NHRI/GANHRI/SCA_MARCH_2014_FINAL_REPORT_-_ENGLISH.pdf>.

59 See the Report and Recommendations of the Session of the SCA, Geneva, 27–31 October 2014, of the ICC, para. 3.7. Available at: <https://www.ohchr.org/sites/default/files/Documents/Countries/NHRI/GANHRI/SCA_OCTOBER_2014_FINAL_REPORT_-_ENGLISH.pdf>.

60 See generally GANHRI's Statute. Available at: <https://ganhri.org/wp-content/uploads/2019/11/EN_GANHRI_Statute_adopted_05.03.2019_vf.pdf>.

61 Interview with Miguel Godoy, (Paraguayan) *Defensor del Pueblo* (Asunción, Paraguay, 12 December 2016).

62 See the Report and Recommendations of the Session of the SCA, Geneva, 11–15 March 2019, of the Global Alliance of National Human Rights Institutions (GANHRI), para. 2.2. Available at: <https://www.ohchr.org/sites/default/files/Documents/Countries/NHRI/GANHRI/SCA_Report_March_2019_-_EN_.pdf>.

63 See ibid.

64 See e.g., Concluding Observations on the Third Periodic Report of Uruguay, 10 June 2014, of the UN Committee against Torture, CAT/C/URY/CO/3, para. 15(b); Concluding Observations

but the SCA formulated some particular concerns about the INDDHH and deferred its decision to its next session.[65] One of the primary concerns raised was that more than half of the institution's staff positions were filled by secondment. Such practice stands in contrast to the kind of open, transparent, and merit-based recruitment procedure preferred by the SCA: a preference which fulfils the requirements of pluralism and independence demanded by the Paris Principles on NHRIs. Another concern was the INDDHH's relative lack of state funding. The SCA found that, because non-state donor contributions were significant, the lack of adequate state funding could jeopardise the institution's independence and credibility. Following a 2015 increase in state funding of the INDDHH, it subsequently received an A-status accreditation in 2016.[66] During the recent review of the accredited status of INDDHH, its A-status has been confirmed. Nevertheless, the SCA highlighted three concerns. It noted that the selection process enshrined in the enabling legislation 'is not sufficiently broad and transparent'; in particular, 'it does not require the advertisement of vacancies for members'.[67] The SCA also urged the INDDHH to continue to advocate for legislative amendments protecting its members from criminal and civil liability for their official actions and decisions undertaken in good faith.[68] The SCA encouraged the INDDHH 'to conduct follow-up activities to monitor the extent to which its recommendations have been implemented'.[69]

3. AUTONOMY AND ACCOUNTABILITY

Paraguayan law declares that the *Defensor del Pueblo* is autonomous and irremovable.[70] The same holds for the INDDHH and the members of its Directive Board.[71] This means that neither the institution nor its members are

on the Report Submitted by Uruguay under Article 29, Paragraph 1, of the Convention, adopted by the Committee at its Fourth Session (8–19 April 2013), 8 May 2013, of the UN Committee on Enforced Disappearances, CED/C/URY/CO/1, para. 10.

65 See the Report and Recommendations of the Session of the SCA, Geneva, 16–20 March 2015, of the ICC, para. 5.1. Available at: <https://www.ohchr.org/sites/default/files/Documents/Countries/NHRI/GANHRI/SCA_MARCH_2015_FINAL_REPORT_-_ENGLISH.pdf>.

66 See the Report and Recommendations of the Session of the SCA, Geneva, 9–13 May 2016, of the GANHRI, para. 2.5. Available at: <https://www.ohchr.org/sites/default/files/Documents/Countries/NHRI/GANHRI/SCA_FINAL_REPORT_-_MAY_2016-English.pdf>.

67 See the Report and Recommendations of the Virtual Session of the SCA, 18–29 October 2021, of the GANHRI, para. 1.8. Available at: <https://www.ohchr.org/sites/default/files/2021-12/SCA-Report-October-2021_E.pdf>.

68 See ibid.

69 See ibid.

70 See Constitution of the Republic of Paraguay, art 277; Law Nr. 631/95 of the Republic of Paraguay, art 5.

71 See Law Nr. 18,446 of the Oriental Republic of Uruguay, art 2.

subject to imperative powers and that they will not receive instructions or orders from any authority.[72]

3.1. IMMUNITY

Even though the Paris Principles on NHRIs do not prescribe the functional immunity for members of these institutions, the GANHRI holds the opinion that '[e]xternal parties may seek to influence the independent operation of an NHRI by initiating, or by threatening to initiate legal proceedings against a member of the decision-making body or a staff member of the NHRI';[73] therefore, people representing NHRIs 'should be protected from both criminal and civil liability for [official actions and decisions] undertaken in good faith in their official capacity'.[74]

The *Defensoría del Pueblo* has the same immunities as those enjoyed by Paraguayan judges.[75] Accordingly, he or she may not be accused or interrogated in a judicial manner for opinions formulated while exercising his or her functions. He or she also may not be arrested or detained, except in the case of *in flagrante* crime. In such a case, the arrested person can only be placed in custody in his or her own residence and the intervening authority must communicate this fact immediately to the Supreme Court of Justice, while remitting the prior records to the competent judge.[76] The *Defensor del Pueblo* can be subjected to a political trial for misconduct, for crimes committed in its official capacity, or common crimes. As the SCA recently pointed out, there is no right of appeal for an impeachment, provided an independent and objective dismissal process has been ensured.[77] In this scenario, the Chamber of Deputies formulates the accusation by a majority of two-thirds; the Senate judges the case, in a public trial, by an absolute majority of two-thirds; and, if it declares the *Defensor del Pueblo* guilty, he or she will be removed from office. In cases involving the alleged commission of crimes, the case will be passed on to the ordinary justice system.[78]

Uruguayan law declares that the INDDHH and its members must act in good faith. The violation of this principle implies serious misconduct concerning the

72 See ibid, art 51.

73 General Observations of the SCA, para. 2.3 on 'Guarantee of functional immunity'. See GANHRI Practical Guide to the work of the SCA, p. 21, available at: <https://www.ohchr.org/sites/default/files/Documents/Countries/NHRI/GANHRI/GANHRI_Manual_online.pdf>.

74 See ibid.

75 See Constitution of the Republic of Paraguay, art 278.

76 See ibid, art 255.

77 See Sub-Committee on Accreditation (n 62) para. 2.2.

78 See ibid.

duties inherent to the position. This obligation to act in good faith is not violated where members of the Directive Board issue opinions, recommendations, or proposals in a public way and in a personal capacity: provided the subject-matter falls within a specific competence of the INDDHH and the issuance is made with the Board's prior authorisation.[79]

3.2. FUNDING

Beyond personal autonomy, which is ensured by a fair, transparent, and pluralistic appointment procedure, and functional autonomy, which encompasses immunity and adequate powers, an NHRI's financial autonomy also contributes to its independent operation.

In Paraguay, the *Defensoría del Pueblo* prepares its draft budget annually, the Senate includes it in its state budget proposal, and then presents it to the executive power.[80] According to Uruguayan law, the budget of the INDDHH should be sufficient to guarantee its autonomous operation. This includes guaranteeing the financial resources that are required to secure the infrastructure and staffing necessary for the good performance of the NHRI in all areas of its competence.[81] In this regard, the GANHRI has observed that the adequate funding demanded by the Paris Principles serves the purpose of guaranteeing the institution's independence and its ability to freely determine its priorities and activities.[82] As to procedure, much like the Paraguayan ombuds-office, the Directive Board of the INDDHH prepares the draft budget and submits it to the President of the General Assembly, for inclusion in the budget proposal of the administrative commission of the legislative power.[83] The Chamber of Senators approves the budget, by a vote of at least three-fifths, and notifies the executive power to include the institution's approved budget within the national budget.[84] The INDDHH reports annually to the General Assembly and may propose budgetary modifications.[85]

Despite the fact that the provision of funding to NHRIs is a state responsibility, external funding is also deemed acceptable. Uruguayan legislation allows the INDDHH to obtain resources through assistance and cooperation agreements with international or foreign organisations: provided it gives immediate account

---

79 See Law Nr. 18,446 of the Oriental Republic of Uruguay, art 9.
80 See Law Nr. 631/95 of the Republic of Paraguay, art 28.
81 See Law Nr. 18,446 of the Oriental Republic of Uruguay, art 74.
82 See General Observations of the SCA, para. 1.10.
83 See Law Nr. 18,806 of the Oriental Republic of Uruguay, art 3; Rules of the (Uruguayan) *Institución Nacional de Derechos Humanos y Defensoría del Pueblo*, art 7.
84 See Constitution of the Oriental Republic of Uruguay, art 108.
85 See Law Nr. 18,806 of the Oriental Republic of Uruguay, art 4.

of such arrangements to the General Assembly, the Ministry of Foreign Affairs, and the Office of Planning and Budget. The institution may also receive donations, inheritances, or bequests: again, it must account immediately to the General Assembly for these.[86]

4. FUNCTIONING

The Paraguayan and Uruguayan legislation list a number of duties, competences, and necessary powers of the *Defensoría del Pueblo* and the INDDHH. Both institutions can: investigate complaints related to human rights violations, *ex officio* or on request; advise the government and other public authorities on the adaptation or modification of legal norms and administrative practices; report to the Parliament on an annual basis; file writs of *habeas corpus*; disseminate information on human rights; and provide public human rights education.[87]

The Uruguayan legislation emphasises the INDDHH's compliance with the Paris Principles on NHRIs and international human rights treaties. The institution is expressly mandated to: propose the ratification of international human rights agreements; encourage their implementation; promote the harmonisation of the domestic legal system and state practice with international human rights standards; and issue opinions on state reports addressed to international human rights monitoring bodies.[88]

The internal regulations of the *Defensoría del Pueblo* and the INDDHH also refer to the functioning of these institutions. They give a detailed description of the complaints-handling procedure of the respective NHRIs and are similar to the sets of regulations which are typical of institutions following the classical ombudsman model.[89] While the internal rules of the *Defensoría del Pueblo* govern the labour relations of the office with its permanent staff,[90] those of the INDDHH regulate the institution's structure, attributions, and functioning.[91]

86 See Law Nr. 18,446 of the Oriental Republic of Uruguay, art 77.

87 See Law Nr. 631/95 of the Republic of Paraguay, art 10; Law Nr. 18,446 of the Oriental Republic of Uruguay, art 4.

88 See Law Nr. 18,446 of the Oriental Republic of Uruguay, art 4.A–D.

89 See Law Nr. 631/95 of the Republic of Paraguay, arts 12–27; Law Nr. 18,446 of the Oriental Republic of Uruguay, art 11–34.

90 See Internal Rules for Permanent, Hired and Commissioned Officers of the (Paraguayan) *Defensoría del Pueblo*, art 1.

91 See Rules of the (Uruguayan) *Institución Nacional de Derechos Humanos y Defensoría del Pueblo*, art 1.

4.1. COMPETENCE AND POWERS

The scope of competence of the two NHRIs is rather broad; both have a mandate that covers public bodies and private persons, and thus handle a wide variety of matters.[92] Even though the institutions can investigate complaints of human rights violations, neither the *Defensoría del Pueblo* nor the INDDHH have judicial functions,[93] they cannot investigate matters that are under judicial adjudication, nor can they review a tribunal's decision. This point notwithstanding, if either NHRI identifies systematic administrative malfunctions on the part of the judiciary, they can formulate opinions and reports on the matter. During their investigations, the *Defensoría del Pueblo* and the INDDHH may also request information from public authorities, including the police and judicial organs.[94] In the case of the INDDHH, it may even ask for precautionary measures from the judicial power.[95]

In countries where democracy is not fully consolidated and there is a risk *vis-à-vis* manipulation of elections, some NHRIs are entitled to audit the electoral process to promote and protect the right to vote.[96] In Paraguay, however, the ombuds-office cannot exercise functions that correspond exclusively to those of electoral authorities.[97]

As per the Paris Principles, the NHRIs in Paraguay and Uruguay are allowed to make visits, conduct interviews, examine files, and obtain information for the assessment of a situation under their consideration.[98] They may also enter detention places and can even file criminal complaints to a relevant authority, where it is deemed necessary.[99]

---

92 See Law Nr. 631/95 of the Republic of Paraguay, art 10.6; Law Nr. 18,446 of the Oriental Republic of Uruguay, arts 5, 29; Rules of the (Uruguayan) *Institución Nacional de Derechos Humanos y Defensoría del Pueblo*, art 4.

93 See Law Nr. 631/95 of the Republic of Paraguay, art 3; Law Nr. 18,446 of the Oriental Republic of Uruguay, art 6, 19.

94 See Law Nr. 631/95 of the Republic of Paraguay, art 10.2.

95 See Law Nr. 18,446 of the Oriental Republic of Uruguay, arts 24, 35.D–E.

96 This happens, for example, in El Salvador, through its *Procuraduría para la Defensa de los Derechos Humanos*. See G. Escobar, 'Defensorías del pueblo y democracia' (2005) 13 *Quórum: Revista de Pensamiento Iberoamericano* 72, 80.

97 See T. Pegram, 'National Human Rights Institutions in Latin America: Politics and Institutionalization' in R. Goodman and T. Pegram (eds.), *Human Rights, State Compliance, and Social Change: Assessing National Human Rights Institutions*, Cambridge University Press, Cambridge 2012, p. 232; L. González Volio, 'The Institution of the Ombudsman. The Latin American Experience' (2003) 37 *Revista IIDH* 219, 238.

98 See UN General Assembly Res. 48/134 of 20 December 1993 'Methods of Operation' paras. b, c.

99 See Constitution of the Republic of Paraguay, art 279.2; Law Nr. 631/95 of the Republic of Paraguay, arts 10.2, 23; Law Nr. 18,446 of the Oriental Republic of Uruguay, art 58.

Because the protection offered by an ombudsman could be considered a rather soft compliance tool, it is important to supplement its regulation efforts with legal norms that require state entities to collaborate with the office in its investigations. Paraguayan and Uruguayan laws provide for this. The INDDHH can, and does, include state authorities which fail to cooperate in its annual or special reports, while the *Defensor del Pueblo* can classify the conduct of non-cooperating authorities as an obstruction of the *Defensor's* functions. This constitutes a crime: namely, the failure to obey a lawful order.[100]

After finishing an investigation, the *Defensoría del Pueblo* prepares an individual report in which it communicates the result of the requested action to the claimant.[101] Nevertheless, Paraguayan law remains silent on the effects of the institution's decisions. Those of the INDDHH are characterised as recommendations.[102] Beyond its conclusions relating to the specific complaint, the INDDHH's decisions can even include broader general recommendations, which are aimed at eliminating or preventing similar situations.[103]

It is the right and the duty of the ombuds-office to produce and submit annual reports on its own functioning. The *Defensor del Pueblo* prepares an annual report, which is presented to the two chambers of the Paraguayan Congress at the beginning of each yearly session period.[104] The report describes both rejected and investigated cases and considers the outcomes and obstacles of the cases it accepted. Paraguayan law does not address the question of how the report is to be considered, approved, or rejected by the Congress. Beyond this annual report, the *Defensor* prepares special reports on serious or urgent cases, if he or she considers it to be necessary,[105] as well as disclosure reports on the general human rights situation.[106] In Uruguay, the Directive Board of the INDDHH presents its annual report to the General Assembly, within the first 120 days of each year. The Uruguayan parliament must receive the INDDHH in a special session,[107] and the report is later disseminated nationwide.[108] Beyond its annual reporting, the board may also present special reports to the General Assembly, at any time.[109]

---

100 See Law Nr. 631/95 of the Republic of Paraguay, arts 21, 24; Law Nr. 18,446 of the Oriental Republic of Uruguay, arts 23, 72.
101 See Law Nr. 631/95 of the Republic of Paraguay, art 10.12.c.
102 See Law Nr. 18,446 of the Oriental Republic of Uruguay, art 3.
103 See ibid, art 26.
104 See Law Nr. 631/95 of the Republic of Paraguay, art 10.12.a.
105 See ibid, art 10.12.b.
106 See ibid, art 10.12.d.
107 See Law Nr. 18,446 of the Oriental Republic of Uruguay, art 68.
108 See ibid, art 71.
109 See ibid, art 70.

4.2. NATIONAL PREVENTIVE MECHANISM MANDATE

The 2002 Optional Protocol to the Convention against Torture and other Cruel, Inhuman or Degrading Treatment or Punishment (OPCAT) requires states parties to set up, designate, or maintain one or more visiting bodies, known as national preventive mechanisms (NPMs).[110] The OPCAT also asks state parties to 'give due consideration to the Principles relating to the status of national institutions for the promotion and protection of human rights'.[111] To this effect, states often establish their NPM within their existing NHRI or in connection with it.[112]

Paraguay has designated a specialised institution as its NPM.[113] In Uruguay, the NPM was established as part of the INDDHH.[114] Beyond this, there is a Parliamentary Commissioner of Prisons, who acts as a national mechanism for preventing torture in the adult prison system.[115] Neither the INDDHH nor this commissioner is subject to any form of control by the state: this includes their investigations, reports, and budgets.[116]

5. COOPERATION

NHRIs are well placed to collaborate with a variety of national and international bodies working for the promotion and protection of human rights. Such collaboration is not only a requirement of the Paris Principles, but it is a necessary condition for the effective functioning of an ombuds-office.

5.1. INTERNAL COOPERATION

The relationship between ombudsmen and state organs has already been touched upon. Being bodies established by the state, the Paraguayan and Uruguayan NHRIs cooperate with the countries' respective legislative and

110 See Optional Protocol to the Convention against Torture and Other Cruel, Inhuman or Degrading Treatment or Punishment (OPCAT), art 3.

111 ibid, art 18.4.

112 See A. Müller and F. L. Seidensticker, *The Role of National Human Rights Institutions in the United Nations Treaty Body Process*, German Institute for Human Rights, Berlin 2007, p. 26.

113 See generally *Mecanismo Nacional de Prevención de la Tortura* of Paraguay. Available at: <http://www.mnp.gov.py/>.

114 See Law Nr. 18,446 of the Oriental Republic of Uruguay, art 83.

115 Interview with Juan Miguel Petit, (Uruguayan) Penitentiary Parliamentary Commissioner (Montevideo, Uruguay, 15 December 2016).

116 See UN IHRI/CORE/URY/2016 of 27 December 2016, para. 59.

executive powers – for example, by submitting their annual reports, draft budgets, and opinions in fulfilment of state reporting obligations relating to international actors and mechanisms. The NHRIs also collaborate with the countries' judiciaries and public prosecutors, transferring cases to them where appropriate.

The Paris Principles require NHRIs to 'develop relations with the non-governmental organisations devoted to promoting and protecting human rights'.[117] According to Paraguayan law, the *Defensoría del Pueblo* relies on the participation of NGOs in the implementation of projects and programmes aimed at disseminating knowledge concerning, and promoting the practice of, human rights and human rights protection mechanisms.[118] In practice, there has been little to no cooperation between them.[119] In Paraguay, NGOs mostly bring complaints to the ombuds-office.[120]

The Paraguayan Ministry of Foreign Affairs, together with the Ministry of Justice, have developed a computer-based monitoring device that facilitates the systematisation of recommendations made to Paraguay by the various human rights monitoring mechanisms of the UN and the OAS.[121] It also provides access to updated information on the actions of state organs. The *Defensoría del Pueblo* does not feed information into this system nor does it employ it.[122] The EU Delegation in the country may support the Paraguayan ombuds-office as well, with limited funds dedicated to project cooperation.[123]

The INDDHH also coordinates its functions with other state institutions, including the Parliamentary Commissioner for the Prison System; the *Defensores del Vecino*, which investigate claims related to services provided by the Municipality of Montevideo; the Human Rights Directorate of the Ministry of Education and Culture; and the Directorate of Human Rights and Humanitarian Law of the Ministry of Foreign Affairs.[124] The institution has contact points in

---

117 UN General Assembly (n 98) para g.

118 See Law Nr. 631/95 of the Republic of Paraguay, art 10.10.

119 Interview with Elizabeth Flores, Official Advisor of the Human Rights Committee of the (Paraguayan) Ministry of Public Affairs (Asunción, Paraguay, 9 December 2016); Interview with José Luis Sanchez, First Counsellor and Head of the Political, Press and Information Section, EU Delegation in Paraguay (Asunción, Paraguay, 12 December 2016).

120 Interview with Miguel Godoy, (Paraguayan) *Defensor del Pueblo* (Asunción, Paraguay, 12 December 2016).

121 This device was originally called *Sistema de Monitoreo de Recomendaciones*, or SIMORE. It has subsequently been improved as SIMORE Plus. Available at: <https://www.mre.gov.py/simoreplus/>.

122 Interview with Juan Miguel González Bibolini, Director General, General Human Rights Unit, (Paraguayan) Ministry of Foreign Affairs (Asunción, Paraguay, 13 December 2016).

123 Interview with José Luis Sanchez, First Counsellor and Head of the Political, Press and Information Section, EU Delegation in Paraguay (Asunción, Paraguay, 12 December 2016).

124 See Law Nr. 18,446 of the Oriental Republic of Uruguay, art 10; Law Nr. 18,446 of the Oriental Republic of Uruguay, arts 5, 29; Rules of the (Uruguayan) *Institución Nacional de Derechos Humanos y Defensoría del Pueblo*, art 9.

every ministry to facilitate collaboration, and regularly advises the Ministry of Foreign Affairs on how to comply with recommendations formulated by international human rights bodies.[125] Thus, the Uruguayan institution takes up the classical NHRI role of bridging the national and international levels. Beyond *ad hoc* collaboration, the INDDHH has the power to sign cooperation agreements with, for example, committees and agencies that control the implementation of states' international obligations, human rights NGOs, academic and social organisations, and independent experts.[126]

The INDDHH has established an institutionalised platform for cooperation with other national actors. Within this platform, the Directive Board can convene extraordinary INDDHH sessions, which are known legally as National Assemblies for Human Rights. Social organisations and governmental agencies can participate in these sessions: examples include parliamentary commissions and *Defensores del Vecino*.[127] In this way, the INDDHH is able to inform other actors about its activities; moreover, it can receive their observations and suggestions. The report of each National Assembly for Human Rights is available on the INDDHH's website: it forms part of the annual report presented by the institution to the General Assembly.

5.2. EXTERNAL COOPERATION

NHRIs are good vehicles for the transmission of international debates to the government and general public. According to the Paris Principles, a NHRI can be commissioned to engage with the international human rights system – in particular the Human Rights Council of the UN (HRC) and its mechanisms, including the Universal Periodic Review (UPR) and special procedures – as well as with UN treaty-based bodies.[128] The institutions' participatory rights have evolved immensely, allowing them to engage with these bodies in different ways,[129] which include: providing bodies with written information in the form of shadow reports, briefing papers, etc.; attending HRC sessions; assisting special procedures during country visits; and disseminating and explaining the reports of UN treaty-based bodies.[130]

---

125 Interview with Ariela Peralta, former member of the Directive Board, INDDHH (Montevideo, Uruguay,17 December 2016).

126 See Law Nr. 18,446 of the Oriental Republic of Uruguay, art 35.G.

127 See Law Nr. 18,446 of the Oriental Republic of Uruguay, arts 61–64; Rules of the (Uruguayan) *Institución Nacional de Derechos Humanos y Defensoría del Pueblo*, arts 40–50.

128 See UN General Assembly Res. 48/134 of 20 December 1993 'Competence and Responsabilities' para. 3.

129 See Commission on Human Rights Res. 2005/74 of 20 April 2005.

130 See generally V. Haász, *National Human Rights Institutions in the UN Human Rights Framework*, GRIN Verlag, Munich 2013.

Paraguayan law makes no reference to the cooperation of the *Defensoría del Pueblo* with the international community. The NHRI has only engaged in regional collaboration and is currently a member of the Ibero-American Federation of Ombudspersons: a forum for the cooperation and exchange of experiences of ombuds-offices in Spain, Portugal, and Latin American countries.[131]

Uruguayan law, conversely, gives the INDDHH an express competence to cooperate with regional or international human rights organisations.[132] Accordingly, the INDDHH makes submissions to the UPR,[133] the HRC,[134] and UN treaty-based bodies.[135]

6. CONCLUSION

Despite being neighbours in Latin America and regardless of their similar historical pasts, the Paraguayan *Defensoría del Pueblo* and the Uruguayan INDDHH show different institutional characteristics, levels of efficiency, and social standing. They differ in their legal status (constitutional / non-constitutional), their organisational structure (classical ombudsman / institute), their compliance with Paris Principles (B-status / A-status), and their functioning. The case study reveals that the fact of being established within a constitution does not, in itself, provide a NHRI with what is promised therein. Moreover, it shows that formal design cannot protect an NHRI against political interference.[136]

This can be clearly seen in Paraguay. Despite the *Defensoría del Pueblo* being established after the collapse of an authoritarian regime and despite its enjoyment of constitutional status, delays in the appointment of its first and second *Defensores del Pueblo* and the lapse in its GANHRI accreditation status led the ombuds-office to lose its credibility in the public eye: both in Paraguay and abroad. It is, however, too early to judge the institution's future, especially as the latest ombudsman was only recently appointed. As the experiences of other ombuds-offices have demonstrated, the functioning and effectiveness of this model of NHRI depends largely on the ombudsman's personality, his or her ideas about the mandate, and his or her perception of the role the institution should play.

---

131 See generally *Federación Iberoamericana del Ombudsman*. Available at: <http://www.portalfio.org/>.

132 See Law Nr. 18,446 of the Oriental Republic of Uruguay, art 4.M.

133 See e.g., UN A/HRC/WG.6/18/URY/3 of 7 November 2013.

134 See e.g., UN A/HRC/37/NI/3 of 26 February 2018.

135 See e.g., Committee against Torture, Report by the National Institution of Human Rights and Ombudsman of Uruguay of 11 April 2014.

136 See generally PEGRAM, 'National Human Rights Institutions in Latin America' (n 97).

In Uruguay, the INDDHH is not rooted in the country's constitution; moreover, it is a collective body, with features that differ from those of an ombuds-office. That the INDDHH is inspired by the Paris Principles can be well seen in the wording of its constitutive legislation as well as in the institution's practice. In any case, even if NHRIs face shortcomings from time-to-time, especially in relation to their autonomy, academic studies on the issue repeatedly highlight their value. This value is particularly conspicuous when one considers the achievements of NHRIs in promoting and protecting human rights.[137]

137 See generally E. Moreno and R. Witmer, 'The Power of the Pen: Human Rights Ombudsmen and Personal Integrity Violations in Latin America, 1982–2006' (2016) 17 *Hum. Rts. Rev.* 143; K. Linos and T. Pegram, 'What Works in Human Rights Institutions?' (2017) 112 *AJIL* 1.

DEFENSOR DEL PUEBLO (SPAIN)

José Julio FERNÁNDEZ RODRÍGUEZ

1. INTRODUCTION

The *Defensor del Pueblo* of Spain, or Spanish ombudsperson, is a body created by the 1978 Spanish Constitution. The body has subsequently developed through the Organic Act 3/1981 and the institution's own Structure and Organisation Regulations, of 1983.[1] The first ombudsperson was elected on 28 December 1982 and, from that moment on, the *Defensor del Pueblo* has operated without interruption. At the time of the institution's establishment, there existed a broad consensus regarding the appropriateness of the chosen NHRI 'model' as well as its fit within the Spanish system; indeed, there were hardly any substantial debates on the issue.[2] Being a novel legal concept at the time of its creation, the body's inclusion in the Spanish Constitution strengthened the *Defensor del Pueblo*: reform of the institution requires modification of the Constitution, which is, in itself, a complex process.[3] There are other *defensorías* in Spain, including bodies in most of its *Comunidades Autónomas*, or Autonomous Communities. These

1 See Spanish Constitution, art 54; Organic Act 3/1981 of the Kingdom of Spain; Structure and Organisation Regulations of the Defensor del Pueblo of 6 April 1983. These instruments are available in English at: <https://www.defensordelpueblo.es/en/publications/legal-basis/>. The name *Defensor del Pueblo* comes from the 1977 political programme of the Popular Alliance party, which was accepted by the other Spanish political parties at the time. See A. ARADILLAS, *Todo sobre el Defensor del Pueblo*, Plaza & Janés, Barcelona 1985, p. 117; the *Defensor del Pueblo* has been wrongly linked to other figures from Spanish history, including the Roman *Tribuno Plebis*, the Arab *Sahib-al Mazalim*, and the medieval *Justicia* of Aragon, all of which were created in a very different reality to that of the current Spanish NHRI. See V. FAIRÉN, *Antecedentes aragoneses en los juicios de amparo*, Universidad Nacional Autónoma de México, Mexico City 1971; P. CARBALLO, *El Defensor del Pueblo*, Tecnos, Madrid 1983, p. 124.

2 Perhaps the most important of these issues was the question as to whether regional ombudspersons should be included in the Constitution. This option was eventually ruled out. See P. CARBALLO, *El Defensor del Pueblo*, Tecnos, Madrid 1983, pp. 125 *et seq.*; J. MANUEL VERA, *El Defensor del Pueblo en la Constitución y en los estatutos de autonomía*, Centro de Estudios Políticos y Constitucionales, Madrid 2002, pp. 145 *et seq.*; G. ESCOBAR, 'España' in G. ESCOBAR (ed.), *Defensorías del pueblo en Iberoamérica*, Thomson-Aranzadi, Cizur Menor 2008, p. 167.

3 Only two specific reforms have been made to the Spanish Constitution across its 40-year history: one on foreign citizens' suffrage and the other on budgetary stability.

are similar in their nature to the national *Defensor*, but they were not established by the Constitution. This situation is explained by the decentralised nature of the Spanish political system: whereby there is a central state, which functions as a federal entity, and territorial divisions, which enjoy political autonomy. All in all, the *Defensor del Pueblo* is a relevant body within the architecture of power in Spain; it has, at times, been highly influential in shaping public opinion; however, much like other state entities, it has been affected by a loss of citizen confidence in recent years.

2. OMBUDSPERSONS AS INSTRUMENTS TO IMPROVE DEMOCRATIC QUALITY

To perform its tasks correctly, an ombudsperson must operate according to its institutional design and act with a firm commitment to independence and autonomy.[4] The unique configuration of the ombudsperson is the outcome of its historical evolution, and, in a challenging era for human rights such as the twenty-first Century, the institution's unique flexibility and adaptability can allow it to play a key role in human rights protection and promotion. In adopting the aspirational drive to improve the ombudsperson's effectiveness, this chapter will focus on strategies that increase the democratic quality of the public system. After all, the connection between democracy and human rights is at the core of the ombudsperson's mission. New demands relating to participation underline the role of citizenship in overcoming the crisis of traditional representative democracy.[5] In this sense, the institution of the ombudsperson has great potential: it offers an open door for people's participation in the public process, provides an avenue for resolution of complaints, and makes publicly accessible recommendations. Ombudspersons should promote such participation, thereby strengthening free and equal debate concerning public affairs, opening avenues to examine people's needs, and covering areas that are neglected by other entities.[6]

3. LEGAL NATURE AND POSITION WITHIN THE STATE

The *Defensor del Pueblo* is the high commissioner of the *Cortes Generales* and, by extension, of the Spanish Parliament.[7] The role of *Defensor* is held by a single

4 See generally J.J. Fernández Rodríguez, *Defensorías del pueblo en España: una visión prospectiva*, Universidad de Alcalá, Madrid 2014.

5 See e.g., D. Roussopoulos and G. Benello, *Participatory Democracy: Prospects for Democratizing Democracy*, Black Rose Books, Montréal 2004; J. Luis Martí, *La república deliberativa*, Marcial Pons, Madrid 2006.

6 See Fernández Rodríguez (n 4) pp. 166–67.

7 See Spanish Constitution, art 54; Organic Act 3/1981 of the Kingdom of Spain, art 1.

person, who performs the functions of the role independently and according to his or her own criteria: as Spanish law states, 'he [the *Defensor*] shall not receive instructions from any authority'.[8] The constitutional relevance of the *Defensor del Pueblo* renders it an organ of the global state, in the sense of *Gesamtstaat*, with powers throughout Spanish territory.[9] From a legal perspective, the NHRI has *auctoritas*, as opposed to *potestas*: i.e., it has socially recognised knowledge, or expertise, in its area, rather than legal power in itself. Because of this reality, the ombudsperson's effectiveness relies on the strength of the *Defensor*'s arguments and the power of persuasion that he or she is able to engender. The expression 'persuasion magistracy' or 'magistracy of influence' can certainly be applied to the *Defensor del Pueblo*.[10] As Alvaro Gil Robles expressed with singular plasticity, the ombudsperson's activity, 'rather than [being] repressive or quasi-repressive, must be friendly and persuasively correct':[11] this precise observation reveals the key to the institution's success. The *Defensor del Pueblo* lacks jurisdictional functions; it cannot impose sanctions, nor may it annul agreements or rules. Its work is thus confined to recommendations, reminders, and memoranda of advice, all of which seek to engender publicity in relation to the matter at issue. Consistent with the *auctoritas* nature of its powers, the *Defensor's* decisions are not enforceable, as such. The ombudsperson does, however, have legal standing before the Constitutional Court of Spain.

As a parliamentary commissioner, the ombudsperson regularly attends the *Cortes Generales*, through 'the Speakers of the Congress and the Senate'.[12] In addition, the Spanish Parliament's joint Congress of Deputies–Senate Committee is in charge of engaging with the *Defensor del Pueblo* and of 'reporting' on such consultations 'to their respective Plenums whenever necessary'.[13] This committee meets when the 'speakers of the Congress and the Senate [so decide] and in all cases, in order to propose to the Plenums the candidate or candidates' for the *Defensor del Pueblo*.[14] The decisions of this committee are taken by a simple majority.

The ombudsperson has its own specific legal framework. In this way, the *Defensor del Pueblo* has the traditional prerogatives of parliamentarians: inviolability, immunity, and special jurisdiction. The ombudsperson may only be detained in a case of *flagrante delicto*: in such a case he or she will be tried

8 Organic Act 3/1981 of the Kingdom of Spain, art 6.
9 For contrast, see regional ombudspersons, which lack this feature. See Fernández Rodríguez (n 4) p. 29.
10 A. La Pergola, 'Ombudsman y Defensor del Pueblo. Apuntes para una investigación comparada' (1975) 7 *Revista de Estudios Políticos* 69, 75. See G. Napione, *L'ombudsman: il controllore della pubblica amministrazione*, Giuffrè, Milan 1969, p. 171.
11 Á. Gil Robles, *El control parlamentario de la administración. El ombudsman*, Instituto Nacional de Administración Pública, Madrid 1981, p. 220.
12 Organic Act 3/1981 of the Kingdom of Spain, art 2.1.
13 ibid, art 2.2.
14 ibid, art 2.3.

by the Criminal Chamber of the Supreme Court of Spain.[15] Furthermore, 'he [the *Defensor*] may not be arrested, subjected to disciplinary proceedings, fined, prosecuted or judged on account of opinion he may express or acts he may commit in performing the duties of his office'.[16] These provisions seek to underscore the *Defensor del Pueblo*'s functional independence.

Being an ombudsperson is grounds for ineligibility and incompatibility with respect to the offices respectively of representative and senator in the two parliamentary chambers.[17] The same is true for other elective offices, including those relating to local, regional, or European Parliament elections.[18] Organic Act 3/1981 extends this provision by establishing that the post of *Defensor del Pueblo* is incompatible:

> [W]ith any elected office; with any political position or activities involving political propaganda; with remaining in active service in any Public Administration; with belonging to a political party or performing management duties in a political party or in a trade union, association or foundation, or employment in the service thereof; with practising the professions of judge or prosecutor; and with any liberal profession, or business or working activity.[19]

4. THE *DEFENSOR DEL PUEBLO*'S ORGANISATION

4.1. APPOINTMENT OF THE OMBUDSPERSON

The requirements that must be met by a prospective *Defensor del Pueblo* are simple and have not presented interpretative problems in practice: any citizen of legal age, who enjoys full civil and political rights, may be appointed.[20] He or she is elected by the *Cortes Generales* for a term of five years.[21] Candidate proposals stem from the previously mentioned Congress of Deputies–Senate Committee. Once a proposal has been made, 'a Congressional Plenum shall be held once no less than ten days have elapsed in order to elect him.'[22] To be elected, it is necessary for a candidate to obtain a favourable vote of three-fifths of the members of the Congress of Deputies. Where a vote passes this threshold, the decision must

---

15 ibid, art 6.3.
16 ibid, art 6.2.
17 Spanish Constitution, art 70.1.
18 See Organic Act 5/1985 of the Kingdom of Spain, art 6.
19 Organic Act 3/1981 of the Kingdom of Spain, art 7.1. Part of the Spanish doctrine has considered these incompatibilities to be disproportionate, especially membership in a political party. See e.g. Carballo (n 2) p. 169.
20 Organic Act 3/1981 of the Kingdom of Spain, art 3.
21 ibid, art 2.1.
22 ibid, art 2.4.

be ratified by the same majority of the Senate, within a maximum period of 20 days.[23] If these majorities are not achieved, the Congress of Deputies–Senate Committee must act again to propose a new candidate within a month. In such follow-up cases, the election thresholds are, at least partly, lowered. Although the need for a three-fifths vote remains in the Congress of Deputies, the quorum in the Senate is lowered: an absolute majority will now suffice.[24] In any case, the aim of these qualified majority provisions, as pointed out by Alberto Pérez Calvo, is to prevent the *Defensor del Pueblo* from becoming an instrument of the parliamentary majority: by making sure the elected person brings together a broad parliamentary and social support-base.[25]

The ombudsperson is aided by two deputies, who are proposed by him or her to the Congress of Deputies–Senate Committee, which must give its consent.[26] The legal regime of these deputies is similar to that of the ombudsperson.[27]

4.2. THE OMBUDSPERSON'S MANDATE

As there is no provision to the contrary, it has been assumed that the *Defensor del Pueblo* can be re-elected without limitation. The five-year period of appointment aims to separate the ombudsperson from the ordinary four-year terms of parliamentarians. This feature acts as yet another element strengthening the independence of the *Defensor* post.[28] Organic Act 3/1981 contemplates five causes for the Defensor's termination: resignation, expiry of term in office, death or unexpected incapacity, flagrant negligence in fulfilling the obligations and duties of office, and non-appealable criminal conviction.[29] Due to the difference in nature of the various termination causes, different procedures will occur in the event of termination: in cases of resignation, expiry of the term of office, or in cases of death, the post shall be declared vacant by the Speaker of the Congress of Deputies;[30] in all other cases, a three-fifths majority is required in each house of the Spanish Parliament to cause termination. This vote follows a debate and an audience with the person concerned.

The most problematic of these causes is, undoubtedly, that relating to a charge that the Defensor has been 'acting with negligence'. This is due to the

---

23 ibid.

24 ibid, art 2.5.

25 See A. Pérez Calvo, 'Rasgos esenciales del Defensor del Pueblo según la Constitución y la Ley 3/1981, de 6 de abril' (1981) 11 *Revista de Derecho Político* 67.

26 Organic Act 3/1981 of the Kingdom of Spain, art 2.6.

27 ibid, arts 6.4, 8.4.

28 See J.M. Sánchez Saudinós, 'El control parlamentario indirecto: el Defensor del Pueblo' in A. Palomar and M. Garcés Sanagustín (ed.), *La gestión de los fondos públicos: control y responsabilidad*, Aranzadi, Cizur Menor 2013, pp. 233, 239.

29 Organic Act 3/1981 of the Kingdom of Spain, art 5.1.

30 ibid, art 5.2.

potential that this cause might be used to topple the *Defensor del Pueblo* for political reasons. If such a charge were to occur, there must be a transparent and informed public debate. In the event of termination, it is questionable as to whether the ombudsperson's deputies should be immediately replaced.[31] It would be more logical for the *Defensor del Pueblo* to remain in office temporarily, while a substitute is appointed, instead of a deputy taking over the post: this is due to the deputy holding less legitimacy than the ombudsperson him or herself. The single-person nature of the Ombuds NHRI-model reinforces this argument. In the case of a declaration of judicial incapacity relating to the *Defensor del Pueblo* or of a conviction for an intentional crime, the cessation is not automatic, and the houses of the *Cortes Generales* still have to vote.

4.3. STRUCTURE AND OPERATION OF THE *DEFENSOR DEL PUEBLO*

The ombudsperson has two deputies, first and second, to whom his or her duties may be delegated. In hierarchical order, they will substitute for the ombudsperson in the event of his or her temporary incapacity or dismissal.[32] The NHRI also has a General Secretary, who, among other duties, governs and disciplines all of its personnel. He or she heads the General Secretariat, which is in charge of not only the personnel of the *Defensor del Pueblo* but also its infrastructure, citizens' services, studies, and documentation. The institution also has a Coordination and Internal Regime Board, which, among other functions, regulates matters relating to its personnel and budget. This board is composed by the ombudsperson, his or her deputies, and the General Secretary.

To execute its duties, the *Defensor del Pueblo* must have the appropriate means. In this regard, Organic Act 3/1981 regulates its human and financial resources. The ombudsperson 'may freely appoint the advisers necessary for the execution of his duties, in accordance with the Regulations and within budgetary limits'.[33] Those financial resources deemed necessary for the operation of the institution shall constitute an item of the Spanish parliamentary budget. Because of the economic crisis of 2008, the budget fell from 2008 to 2015; however, it has recently recovered, especially in 2021 and 2022.[34] As of 2022, the staff of the

31 ibid, arts 5.4, 8.1.

32 ibid, art 8.1.

33 ibid, art 34.

34 The 2009 budget was €15,968,468; the 2015 budget was €13,951,700. the 2022 budget is €18,698,200 See the webpage of the *Defensor del Pueblo*, available at: https://www.defensordelpueblo.es/transparencia/informacion-economica-presupuestaria-y-contractual/presupuestos/evolucion-interanual-2009–2022/evolucion-presupuesto/.

Defensor del Pueblo was made up of 172 people. Their areas of action include: local administration; education; taxes; migration; public and essential services; economic activity; interior affairs; employment and social security; equal treatment; social policy; urban planning; administration of justice; correctional facilities; public function and employment; environment; health; and housing.

5. SPAIN'S NHRI COMPETENCE

According to the Spanish Constitution, the *Defensor del Pueblo* has a generic competence: to defend 'the rights contained' in Title I of the Constitution. In doing so, 'he may supervise the activities of the Administration and report thereon to the *Cortes Generales*'.[35] Thus, the Defensor oversees the very general principle of good governance in the Spanish state, focusing on maladministration cases. The *Defensor del Pueblo* has the power to file applications before the Constitutional Court of Spain:[36] in the exercise of this right, the ombudsperson may file the remedies of unconstitutionality (*recurso de inconstitucionalidad*) and protection remedies (*recurso de amparo*).[37] The *Defensor* can also file a writ of *habeas corpus* before the ordinary courts.[38] Through these competences, the ombudsperson assumes a role that analogous institutions typically do not perform in comparative law. As Fernando de Andrés Alonso recalls, the most significant of these is the possibility of presenting a direct application of unconstitutionality, which the *Defensor del Pueblo* may exercise on its own volition or whenever it is requested by a citizen.[39] In this way, the ombudsperson collaborates in the protection of the principle of constitutional supremacy in Spain.

It is also the *Defensor del Pueblo*'s responsibility to prepare and submit an annual report to the *Cortes Generales*. In addition, when the seriousness or urgency of the situation makes it advisable to do so, he or she may submit a

---

35 Spanish Constitution, art 54.
These rights are regulated in arts 10 to 55 of the Constitution.
To this effect, art 9.1 of the Organic Act 3/1981 refers to art 103.1 of the Spanish Constitution, which states that the public administration serves the general interest with objectivity and acts in accordance with the principles of efficiency, hierarchy, decentralisation, de-concentration, and coordination, while being fully subject to justice and the law. Therefore, it could be understood that the Organic Act 3/1981 extends the competence of the *Defensor del Pueblo* by allowing it to audit the administration according to the principles of art103 of the Constitution, although this does not relate to the assurance of rights. As art 1 of the Organic Act 3/1981 declares, the *Defensor del Pueblo* 'shall exercise the functions entrusted to him by the Constitution and this Act'.

36 See Organic Act 3/1981 of the Kingdom of Spain, art 29.

37 See Spanish Constitution, art 162.

38 See Organic Act 6/1984 of the Kingdom of Spain, art 3.

39 See F.L. de Andrés Alonso, *Los defensores del pueblo en España*, Reus, Madrid 2017, p. 124.

special report.[40] Both of these types of report are published. In relation to the annual report, its content must include 'the number and type of complaints filed, of those rejected and the reasons for their rejection, and of those investigations, together with the results of the investigations'.[41] An oral summary of the report shall be presented by the *Defensor del Pueblo* to the plenums of both houses of the Spanish Parliament.[42] Although it is not expressly provided for, it is common for the institution to carry out outreach and learning activities.[43] As from 2009, the ombudsperson has also held the responsibility of performing the duties of the National Preventive Mechanism against Torture: in accordance with the Spanish Constitution, Organic Act 3/1981, and the Optional Protocol to the Convention against Torture and Other Cruel, Inhuman or Degrading Treatment or Punishment. To that end, an Advisory Board was created, which is composed of the ombudsperson's deputies, as *ex officio* members, and a maximum of 10 additional members, who shall be appointed for a four-year period by the *Defensor del Pueblo*.[44]

6. CONTROLLED ENTITIES

As mentioned, the ombudsperson's objects of oversight include the activities of the Spanish 'Administration', without further specification.[45] Organic Act 3/1981 provides a minor clarification, by alluding to the 'Public Administration and its agents regarding citizens'.[46] Likewise, it states that the duties of the *Defensor del Pueblo* also extend to 'the activities of Ministers, administrative authorities, civil servants and any person acting in the service of the Public Administration'.[47] Moreover, the Act specifies that the ombudsperson is to supervise the activities of the autonomous communities.[48] The scope of the entities under the Defensor's oversight is, therefore, very broad. In 2010, The Constitutional Court of Spain offered some clarity, declaring that the 'Administration' referred to in

---

40 See Organic Act 3/1981 of the Kingdom of Spain, art 32.

41 ibid, art 33.1.

42 ibid, art 33.4.

43 These activities can be seen in the social groups section of its webpage.

44 Members are appointed by the General Council of Lawyers of Spain (one); the Medical Association of Spain (one); the General Council of Official Psychology Associations of Spain (one); and the organisations and institutions that concluded collaboration agreements with the *Defensor del Pueblo* to develop the duties of the National Preventive Mechanism (two). The remainder are sourced from candidates submitted to the NHRI, either in a personal capacity or on behalf of organisations or associations representing civil society (five).

45 Spanish Constitution, art 54.

46 Organic Act 3/1981 of the Kingdom of Spain, art 9.1.

47 ibid, art 9.2.

48 ibid, art 12.1.

Article 54 of the Constitution is a *genera* comprising all public powers other than legislative action and the judiciary. This corroborates a broad Constitutional interpretation.[49] The *Defensor*'s practice confirms this understanding, for the entities that it oversees include: the Spanish state's government and administration; the governments and administrations of the Autonomous Communities; local administrations; and concessionary companies that provide public services.

These entities must all collaborate with the *Defensor del Pueblo*: Organic Act 3/1981 leaves no room for doubt when it says that '[a]ll public authorities are obliged to give preferential and urgent assistance to the Ombudsman in his investigations and inspections'.[50] Furthermore, the Spanish Criminal Code provides for the offence of disobedience for 'any civil servant or public authority obstructing an investigation by the *Defensor del Pueblo*', or equivalent organs of an Autonomous Community, 'by refusing to send or unduly delaying the dispatch of reports requested, by hindering access to the administrative records or documents necessary for such investigation'.[51] Regarding judges and courts, the *Defensor del Pueblo* must respect the constitutional principle of judicial independence;[52] therefore, his or her approach needs to be cautious, so to speak, where it is concerned with the judiciary. In this sense, Organic Act 3/1981 restricts its work to the 'functioning of the Administration of Justice' and not to the jurisdictional function proper.[53] Such complaints will be referred to the Public Prosecutor or will be referred to the General Council of the Judiciary.[54] Apart from this, the ombudsperson can refer to such complaints in his or her annual report to the Spanish Parliament.[55] To avoid any undesirable problems in the field of military administration, Organic Act 3/1981 states that the *Defensor del Pueblo*'s action cannot cause interference with the command of National Defence.[56]

7. RECEIVING AND PROCESSING COMPLAINTS

The *Defensor del Pueblo* is a flexible and adaptable NHRI, which has very broad possibilities for action; indeed, it 'may instigate and pursue, *ex officio* or in

49 Constitutional Court of Spain, Judgment 31/2010 of 28 June 2010.
50 Organic Act 3/1981 of the Kingdom of Spain, art 19.1.
51 Criminal Code of the Kingdom of Spain, art 502.2.
52 See Spanish Constitution, art 117.1.
53 Organic Act 3/1981 of the Kingdom of Spain, art 13.
54 ibid.
55 For the sake of respecting judicial independence, the *Defensor del Pueblo* 'shall not investigate individually any complaints that are pending judicial decision, and he shall suspend any investigation already commenced if a claim or appeal is lodged by the person concerned before the ordinary courts or the Constitutional Court'.
ibid, art. 17.2.
56 ibid, art 14.

response to a request from the party concerned, any investigation conducive to clarifying the actions or decisions of the Public Administration and its agents regarding citizens'.[57]

7.1. *LOCUS STANDI*

Consistent with this, 'any individual or legal entity who invokes a legitimate interest may address the Ombudsman, without any restrictions whatsoever'.[58] To emphasise this point, Organic Act 3/1981 adds that nationality; residence; gender; legal issues; legal incapacity; confinement in a penitential institution; or, in general, any special relationship of subordination to, or dependence on, a public administration or authority will *not* be impediments. The possibilities for resorting to the *Defensor del Pueblo* are, thus, broader than those relating to the initiation of an administrative or judicial procedure. In addition to these legitimised individuals and entities, the *Cortes Generales* can also activate the *Defensor del Pueblo*'s procedure in several cases, including where the matter concerns: individual deputies and senators; investigatory committees; committees connected with the general or partial defence of public rights and liberties; and the Congress of Deputies–Senate Committee, which is in charge of relations with the NHRI;[59] however, no administrative authority may present claims before the *Defensor del Pueblo* in matters concerning its own competence.[60]

7.2. THE COMPLAINTS PROCEDURE

It is simple to comply with the requirements for submitting complaints to the *Defensor del Pueblo*; after all, if the situation were otherwise, the ombudsman would not be an easily accessible NHRI. The complainant must: provide his, her, or its name and address on a signed document, written on ordinary paper; state the grounds for the complaint; and file the complaint within a maximum of one year from the time of becoming acquainted with the matters giving rise to it.[61] For some years now, it has also been possible to submit complaints through the website of the *Defensor del Pueblo* or by emailing the following address: registro@defensordelpueblo.es. An important characteristic of the procedure is its cost-free nature: for 'all action by the Ombudsman shall be free

57 ibid, art 9.1.
58 ibid, art 10.
59 See ibid, art 10.2.
60 See ibid, art 10.3.
61 See ibid, art 15.1.

of charge for the party concerned, and attendance by a lawyer or solicitor shall not be compulsory'.[62]

Once the complaint is filed, the admission procedure is opened. In the first phase, the *Defensor del Pueblo* 'shall record and acknowledge receipt of the complaints made, which he shall either proceed with or reject'.[63] Rejections must be justified in writing, stating the reasons for rejection, while also informing the person concerned about the most appropriate channels for further action.[64] The institution rejects anonymous complaints and those in which it perceives bad faith, a lack of grounds, an unfounded claim, or a claim that if investigated might infringe the legitimate rights of a third party.[65] When the complaint is admitted, the ombudsperson will begin the appropriate summary informal investigations to clarify the allegations contained therein. In the second phase of the procedure, the *Defensor del Pueblo* must notify the pertinent administrative agency or office that is the subject of the complaint. The head of that agency must submit a written report in response, within a period of 15 days.[66]

Entities that are subject to the *Defensor*'s oversight have a duty to collaborate with the NHRI. As such, they must submit the information requested by the ombudsperson. Failing to do so may be considered, by the *Defensor del Pueblo*, to be a hostile act which obstructs its functions. A declaration of hostility will be made public immediately and will, later, be incorporated into the annual or special report.[67] During the stages of verifying and investigating a complaint, an agent of the *Defensor* 'may present himself at any establishment of the Public Administration or attached thereto or responsible for a public service, in order to verify any necessary information, hold relevant personal interviews or examine pertinent records and documents'.[68] Organic Act 3/1981 adds that 'in the pursuit of this objective, he may not be denied access to any administrative record or document related to the activity or service under investigation'.[69] These investigations will be conducted in absolute secrecy.[70] If, in the performance of his or her duties, the ombudsperson should obtain knowledge of apparently criminal acts or behaviour, 'he must immediately notify the State Prosecutor-General'.[71]

---

62 ibid, art 15.2.

63 ibid, art 17.1.

64 See ibid.

65 See ibid, art 17.3.

66 See ibid, art 18.1.

67 See ibid, art 18.2.

68 ibid, art 19.2.

69 ibid, art 19.3.

70 See ibid, art 22.2. Access to secret documents may be denied if the Council of Ministers agrees. See ibid, art. 22.1.

71 ibid, art 25.2.

7.3. THE *DEFENSOR DEL PUEBLO*'S DECISION

The third phase of the procedure before the *Defensor del Pueblo* involves the institution's decision, of which there are four types: recommendations; reminders of legal duties; suggestions; and memoranda of advice.[72] Recommendations have a general scope: they propose the interpretive modification of an existing norm or, alternatively, the creation of a new one. Reminders of legal duties are intended to (re)prompt a body or agent's obligation to fulfil certain legal provisions. Suggestions propose concrete actions, which then affect a particular citizen or a specific group. Finally, memoranda of advice communicate the existence of a situation of fact, or a practice, that needs improvement.[73] The content of each decision will be based on the type of subject that has been investigated. When it comes to the content of decisions, Organic Act 3/1981 provides for different options, including: suggested modifications to the criteria employed by public administrative bodies in their issuance of acts and/or decisions; the suggestion of legal reforms to a competent legislative body or the Spanish Administration; and suggestions to relevant and competent administrative authorities for modification, concerning the exercise of powers of inspection and/or sanction.[74]

In any case, the authority receiving the *Defensor del Pueblo*'s decision must respond, in writing, within a one-month period. If there is no response or if adequate measures are not taken, the *Defensor* will notify the highest administrative authority concerned, and,

> [i]f adequate justification is not forthcoming, he shall mention the matter in his annual or special report, together with the names of the authorities or civil servants responsible for this situation, as a case in which, although the Ombudsman thought that a positive solution was possible, it was not however achieved.[75]

Finally, the *Defensor del Pueblo* will inform the person concerned of the results of his or her investigations and operations.

8. INTERNATIONAL OUTREACH AND THE PARIS PRINCIPLES

As the NHRI of Spain, the ombudsperson undertakes a relevant international activity. Indeed, in 2000, it was accredited with A-status by the Sub-Committee

---

72 See ibid, art 30.1.

73 When it comes to the decisions of the ombudspersons of the Autonomous Communities, the gradation is interpreted differently: the recommendation being the most demanding resolution.

74 See Organic Act 3/1981 of the Kingdom of Spain, art 28.

75 ibid, art 30.2.

on Accreditation (SCA) of the International Coordinating Committee of National Institutions for the Promotion and Protection of Human Rights (ICC), now the Global Alliance of National Human Rights Institutions (GANHRI). In all its re-accreditations, the *Defensor del Pueblo* has maintained the same status, which is evidence of its full compliance with the Paris Principles on NHRIs.

The ombudsperson has a specific mandate to adopt follow-up measures in relation to decisions adopted by international human rights mechanisms. In addition, the *Defensor del Pueblo* exercises permanent oversight of Spanish legislation and systematically informs the state about its effects on human rights.[76] As an NHRI, it must also cooperate with the international human rights system, particularly with other NHRIs and regional and supranational protection organisations, by both carrying out joint support tasks and exchanging experiences and good practices. The *Defensor del Pueblo's* annual reports reflect multiple actions at international level from the Office of the UN High Commissioner for Human Rights (OHCHR) and the GANHRI. These reports also document the ombudsperson's interaction with the: Committee against Torture; Committee on the Rights of the Child; Group of Experts on Action against Trafficking in Human Beings of the Council of Europe (GRETA); and Committee on Petitions of the European Parliament. Foreign institutions also visit the *Defensor del Pueblo*; examples include the ombudsmen of Morocco, Moldova, Portugal and Turkey, the *Defensores del Pueblo* of Colombia, Ecuador, Paraguay, Puerto Rico and Peru, and France's *Défenseur des droits*. Beyond this, the ombudsperson has attended many international meetings within the frameworks of the UN system, the Council of Europe, and the European Union and has visited various centres that work on the deprivation of freedom and on humanitarian aid abroad, including institutions located in Rome, Lisbon, Tangier, etc.

The *Defensor del Pueblo* is an active member of the European Network of Ombudsmen, the Association of Mediterranean Ombudsmen, the Ibero-American Federation of Ombudsmen, and the International Ombudsmen Institute.

9. OMBUDSPERSONS OF AUTONOMOUS COMMUNITIES

Spain is a politically decentralised state with 17 Autonomous Communities as well as the Autonomous Cities of Ceuta and Melilla, which are located in Africa. Many of these territorial entities have an ombudsperson, which is

[76] See generally Organic Act 2/2014 of the Kingdom of Spain.

generally formed in the image of the central *Defensor del Pueblo*.[77] Today, nine of these entities have their own ombudsman: Andalusia; Aragon; the Canary Islands; Castilla-León; Catalonia; Galicia; Navarre; the Basque Country; and the Valencian Community. As Gerardo Ruiz-Rico recalls, after the reforms of several Autonomous Community statutes in the twenty-first century, the institutional position of these ombudspersons has been reinforced, expanding their spheres of control and influence.[78]

9.1. A DESCRIPTIVE APPROACH TO REGIONAL OMBUDSPERSONS

Like the *Defensor del Pueblo*, the ombudspersons of the Autonomous Communities are bodies with *auctoritas*, which have been commissioned by their corresponding regional parliament. Their scope of action is limited to the territory of their respective Community. They are given different names: in Andalusia, the ombudsperson is called the *Defensor del Pueblo*; in Aragón, *Justicia*; in the Canary Islands, *Diputado del Común*; in Castilla-León, *Procurador del Común*; in Catalonia, *Síndic de Greuges*; in the Valencian Community, also *Síndic de Greuges*; in Galicia, *Valedor do Pobo*; in Navarre, *Defensor del Pueblo*; and in the Basque Country, *Ararteko*. Between 2011 and 2013, the ombudspersons of Castilla La Mancha, La Rioja, the Principality of Asturias, and the Region of Murcia disappeared, not without controversy, due to the thinning out of public entities in response to the economic crisis. Despite this, their existence remains necessary, as they improve good governance in their respective territories.[79]

---

77 Even though art 54 of the Spanish Constitution makes no allusion to the existence of the position of ombudsperson in the Autonomous Communities, the provision has been interpreted as meaning that the entities are allowed, by virtue of not being prohibited. For this reason, Organic Act 3/1981 expressly contemplated their existence, in art 12.2. The statutes of the Autonomous Communities then began to provide a legal basis for the position; there are also other ombudspersons in Spain, for instance in municipalities and universities. These are problematic because they are not unquestionably independent. This affects the authority of the institution of the ombudsperson.

78 See G. Ruiz-Rico, 'Los derechos sociales estatutarios y los defensores del pueblo autonómicos' in A. Anguita (ed.), *Derechos estatutarios y defensores del pueblo. Teoría y práctica en España e Italia*, Atelier, Los Angeles 2014, pp. 81, 91.
According to art 147 of the Spanish Constitution, these statutes shall constitute the basic institutional rules of each Autonomous Community. The Spanish state shall recognise and protect them as an integral part of its legal order. These statutes must contain: the name of the respective Community, which corresponds most closely to its historic identity; its territorial boundaries; the name, organisation, and seat of its own autonomous institutions; the powers assumed within the framework established by the Spanish Constitution; and the basic conditions for the transfer of the services corresponding to them.

79 See Fernández Rodríguez (n 4) 125.

According to José Agustín González Ares, these institutions respond to real needs, have their own space, and a palpable justification.[80] It should be clarified here that the central *Defensor del Pueblo* cannot answer to the parliaments of the Autonomous Communities: it may only do so before the *Cortes Generales*.

Although lacking its constitutional relevance, regional ombudspersons have been regulated in the mould of the central Spanish *Defensor del Pueblo*. In summing up the different provisions that govern each regional ombudsperson, it can be said that: their election corresponds to the territorial parliaments and requires a qualified majority; the average duration of their mandate is five years; the grounds for termination are similar to those of the *Defensor del Pueblo*; their legal status acts as a guarantee of independence; they have deputies; the respective parliament is closely related to them; and their general competence is to supervise the Administration.

9.2. RELATION BETWEEN THE SPANISH *DEFENSOR DEL PUEBLO* AND OMBUDSPERSON OF AUTONOMOUS COMMUNITIES[81]

The *Defensor del Pueblo* has jurisdiction across Spanish territory, and it can monitor 'the activities of the Autonomous Communities'.[82] This was confirmed by the Constitutional Court of Spain, in 2010.[83] On this point, Organic Act 3/1981 establishes that regional ombudspersons shall coordinate their functions with the *Defensor del Pueblo*, who may request their cooperation.[84] Following this provision, Organic Act 36/1985 was enacted to regulate the regional ombuds-institutions.

Over time, the relationship between the *Defensor del Pueblo* and regional ombudspersons has evolved, from an initial stage in which no one questioned the pre-eminence of the NHRI, to the current situation, where a more egalitarian relationship is promoted between the Spanish and the regional ombudspersons, based on the principles of institutional autonomy, coordination, cooperation, and collaboration.

---

80 See J. Agustín González Ares, *El Valedor do Pobo. Del ombudsman sueco al comisionado parlamentario gallego*, Tirant lo Blanch, Valencia 2005, p. 168.

81 For more on this, see generally J.J. Fernández Rodríguez, 'Defensor del Pueblo y defensorías autonómicas: reflexiones sobre sus relaciones y posición recíproca' (2010) 26 *Teoría y Realidad Constitucional* 259.

82 Organic Act 3/1981 of the Kingdom of Spain, art 12.1.

83 See Constitutional Court of Spain, Judgment 31/2010 of 28 June 2010. In this decision, the exclusive control of the *Generalitat de Catalunya*, or Catalonian administration, by the *Sindic de Greuges*, or Catalonian ombudsperson, was declared unconstitutional. In its ruling, the Constitutional Court held that the work of the *Defensor del Pueblo* covers all Public Administration in Spain.

84 See Organic Act 3/1981 of the Kingdom of Spain, art 12.2.

In practice, the *Defensor del Pueblo* allows regional ombudspersons to freely process the complaints they receive concerning their own territorial and local administration, and usually processes those that it receives, relating to the public sector of an Autonomous Community. However, the risk of overlap and contradiction remains. It is, therefore, necessary to improve, promote, and strengthen the relationships between these bodies, through reform of what are currently imprecise and diffuse regulations.

10. ASSESSING THE *DEFENSOR DEL PUEBLO*'S WORK

It is difficult to summarise the *Defensor del Pueblo*'s 40 years of activity, which is documented in a vast collection of its annual and monographic reports, prepared since 1983, as well as those of the National Mechanism for the Prevention of Torture.[85] Despite being a relevant topic, the history of the NHRI has not been properly studied by Spanish researchers. Instead, the literature tends to focus on aspects of organisation and competency.[86] However, if the excessive judicialisation of Spanish constitutional law is to be mitigated, an analysis of the *Defensor del Pueblo*'s historical proceedings is one of the first steps that should be taken.[87]

Five practice areas are distinguished, as the following divisions outline the ombudsperson's work. The first is the protection of minors, especially unaccompanied minors. The issue of unaccompanied minors is a particularly concerning contemporary phenomenon, especially in light of the increase in migration from Africa to Spain and the exacerbated risks which children, and particularly unaccompanied children, face in such situations. Children and adolescents have always received specific attention from the *Defensor del Pueblo*, especially in its annual reports; moreover, the institution has published several monographic reports and studies concerning children's rights: examples include reports on the criminal responsibility of minors (2002); school violence (2007);[88] centres for the protection of minors with behavioural disorders (2009);

---

85 Available at: <https://www.defensordelpueblo.es/documentacion/>.

86 See G. Escobar, 'Interpretación y garantía de los derechos fundamentales por el Defensor del Pueblo (análisis empírico, reconstrucción dogmática y propuesta del futuro)' (2010) 26 *Teoría y Realidad Constitucional* 229.
For an analysis of its first 25 years, see R. Ramos and J. Gómez Rivas, *El Defensor del Pueblo en una España en cambio: 1982–2007*, Defensor del Pueblo, Madrid 2007.

87 See Escobar (n 2) p. 230.

88 The 2007 report on school violence updated a previous report on the same subject, published in 2000.

the protection of minors in relation to television and internet programming and content (2010); the security and accessibility of children's playgrounds (2015); and brain damage in children (2019).[89]

The second area concerns social rights, for example health, housing, and education. As is commonly observable in comparative law analyses, the public policies that apply and implement social rights are reviewable and actionable matters for the Spanish *Defensor*; however, the rights themselves are not. The *Defensor del Pueblo* has, however, been active in the area of social rights, and the institution has paid them particular attention during periods of economic crisis and resulting budgetary restrictions: periods when social rights are most at risk. As examples, a 2002 monographic report analysed waiting lists in the health system, a 2015 study considered hospital emergencies and patients' rights and guarantees, a 2018 study on economic crisis and inequality, or a 2020 study on the actions against the COVID-19 pandemic.

The *Defensor del Pueblo's* third general practice area concerns its work on specific financial products, including preference shares and subordinated debt, as well as its focus on consumer protection. A good example of output related to this work area is the *Defensor*'s 2017 monographic report on vulnerable consumer protections relating to the supply of electric power.

A fourth field of action relates to persons who have been deprived of their liberty, including those in places of detention. In this area, emphasis has been placed on improving health care; verifying the circumstances of suicide risk; psychological assistance; keeping relatives of the detainee informed; ensuring educational training; and considering the interests of people with mental disabilities. The *Defensor del Pueblo* has also monitored the situation of Spanish prisoners detained abroad; indeed, it prepared a report on the topic in 2015.

The final area of interest concerns the *Defensor del Pueblo*'s efforts to develop a culture of transparency. The *Defensor* made slow progress in building up such a culture in its early years; however, there has been a recent increase in complaints relating to this subject, and, thanks to digital advances, internal transparency has also increased. Autonomous Communities and the enactment of Organic Act 19/2013 have incentivised this change. This issue is highly relevant, as transparency and access to information lead to progress in democratic quality and are vital weapons in the fight against corruption.[90]

89 The reports of the *Defensor del Pueblo* are available at: <https://www.defensordelpueblo.es/informes/>.

90 See J.J. Fernández Rodríguez and D. Neira Barral, 'El papel de las defensorías del pueblo en España en el control de la transparencia y el acceso a la información' (2016) 27 *Revista Estado, Gobierno y Gestión Pública* 89, 114.

11. FUTURE CHALLENGES FOR THIS NHRI?

The recent Spanish economic and institutional crisis has affected the *Defensor del Pueblo* as well as the regional ombudspersons. Recurring surveys, carried out by the Centre for Sociological Research, show that institutional distrust has generally grown in Spain.[91] When it comes to the case of the national *Defensor del Pueblo*, study no. 2657 of October 2006 showed that citizens graded their confidence in the institution at a confidence rating of 5.13 out of a possible 10; in study no. 2853 of November 2010, this confidence rating fell to 4.64; and in study no. 3080 of April 2015, it descended further to 3.96. Like other modern societies, Spain is becoming more aware of, and assertive regarding, its own history, of which all Spaniards want to be a part.[92] Significant challenges for the promotion and protection of human rights are posed by: the second phase of the information society, with its disruptive technologies, new risks, and threats to international security; growing environmental demands; identity-based politics; and the increasingly intercultural nature of society. Both the institutional distrust in Spain and these global challenges demand a renewed effort to update Spanish ombuds-institutions. It is not only their regulations that require modernisation but also their work processes, the criteria they use to shape institutional decisions, their efforts to coordinate with other bodies, and their endeavours to foster the principle of transparency, both internally and externally.[93]

Traditional means and procedures may be insufficient to deal with these challenges. However, much like the Paris Principles on NHRIs, the generic legal regulations of the *Defensor del Pueblo* allow for some necessary adjustments and for the expansion of the institution's activities, which may allow the body to adapt to these new scenarios. This point notwithstanding, the Spanish NHRI requires the assistance of legislative reform to do so properly: to allow the institution to update its capabilities and position itself in the twenty-first Century.

12. CONCLUSION

The *Defensor del Pueblo* is a relevant body in Spain's system of human rights protection. An assessment of its more than 35 years of work allows us to conclude

91 Available at: <www.cis.es>.M. Romero, '¿Cuál es el alcance del descrédito institucional?', *eldiaro.es* (Madrid, 15 April 2008). <https://www.eldiario.es/piedrasdepapel/Instituciones-Confianza-CIS-Caso_Cifuentes_6_761233870.html>.

92 Back in 1983, Pedro Carballo alluded to the fact that public authorities need to continually update their responses to citizens, particularly in societies that have brought up new concerns. In this context, ombudspersons are one of the current legal mechanisms that allow for adequate external control over a growing Administration. See Carballo (n 2) pp. 237, 249, 250.

93 See Fernández Rodríguez (n 4) pp. 63 et seq.

that its endeavours have been intense and positive. It has helped to improve the recognition and protection of human rights, made sure that such protection is not excessively dependent on judges and courts, and generally encouraged good governance in the Spanish state. As Pedro Carballo points out, the institution's success derives, in great part, from its special status as a settler of conflicts, and the significance of this role far surpasses the serious deficiencies of its traditional means of exerting control.[94] Despite this, and much like other public bodies, the *Defensor del Pueblo* has been affected by Spanish society's recent institutional distrust; it will have to work hard to recover public confidence. The Spanish NHRI also needs to improve existing imbalances in terms of its relationships with regional ombuds-institutions. If it acts in an independent, rigorous, credible and flexible manner, the *Defensor del Pueblo* will become stronger, and it will play a role in Spain's democratic consolidation. To do so, technology must be used intensively, allowing for permanent institutional openness and availability, whilst always applying the principle of dynamic transparency. Without its independence and *auctoritas*, the NHRI is meaningless. The near future poses significant challenges for the *Defensor del Pueblo*, which it must face with flexibility, for the benefit of Spanish society.

---

94 See CARBALLO (n 2) p. 250.

DEUTSCHES INSTITUT FÜR MENSCHENRECHTE (GERMANY)

Heiner Bielefeldt, Markus Krajewski,
Michael Krennerich and Beate Rudolf

1. INTRODUCTION

The *Deutsches Institut für Menschenrechte* (DIMR), or German Institute for Human Rights, is still a relatively young institution in the context of NHRIs. The DIMR ('the Institute') was founded in March 2001: this followed a unanimous decision, in December 2000, in which the German Federal Parliament called for the creation of an NHRI.[1] One of the reasons for the comparatively late establishment of such an institution in Germany was the existence of a strong domestic tradition, which has seen basic constitutional rights protected through the German Federal Constitutional Court. This tribunal has the power to annul legislative, administrative, and judicial acts of all state entities, on the basis of individual complaints which successfully claim a violation of the basic constitutional rights enshrined in the German Basic Law (*Grundgesetz*): these rights are viewed as being equivalent to internationally protected human rights.[2]

This chapter is organised as follows: the first substantive section (section 2) introduces the legal and institutional framework of the DIMR, including its legal basis, institutional structure, and main tasks; next, section 3 provides an overview of the DIMR's historic development, including its foundation and establishment, its struggle for a legislative basis, its path to re-accreditation, its current challenges, and future possibilities; the chapter then briefly reflects on the relationship between the DIMR and civil society (section 4); finally, it concludes with some observations on general lessons drawn from the experience of the DIMR (section 5).

---

1 National Human Rights Institute. See below section 3.1.

2 See M. Hailbronner and S. Martini, 'The German Federal Constitutional Court' in A. Jakab, A. Dyeryre, and G. Itzcovich (eds.), *Comparative Constitutional Reasoning*, Cambridge University Press, Cambridge 2017, pp. 362–63. It should be noted that the Basic Law for the Federal Republic of Germany contains predominantly civil and political rights and that the protection of human rights through the Federal Constitutional Court therefore focuses almost exclusively on these rights.

2. LEGAL AND INSTITUTIONAL FRAMEWORK

The DIMR is one of a slowly growing number of NHRIs that are 'institutes', i.e., bodies which undertake research-based work.[3] Its main tasks are observing, reporting, and researching the situation of human rights in Germany and commenting on political developments and proposed legislative acts. While this describes the functional setting of the DIMR, according to German law it is a membership-based and non-profit association, established on the basis of a special parliamentary Act. The institutional structure of the DIMR is shaped by: its Director and Deputy Director, who manage the Institute's day-to-day work; a professional staff of around 80 people, who carry out the main activities of this NHIR; its Board of Trustees, which approves the general policy guidelines and thematic priorities for the DIMR, as proposed by its Board of Directors; and the members of the Institute, which currently include 88 individuals and organisations working in the field of human rights.

2.1. LEGAL BASIS

The legal basis of the DIMR is two-fold: first, its foundation is based on a parliamentary decision, originally a unanimous resolution and later an Act which expresses Germany's will to establish a NHRI; and second, being a membership-based registered association (*eingetragener Verein*) under German law, it enjoys legal and institutional independence from state entities. As such, the DIMR is a non-state actor, and its particular legal foundation can, therefore, be found in the Institute's Articles of Association (*Satzung*).

The double legal basis of the DIMR strengthens its legitimacy and independence (see Table 1). Its parliamentary and legislative foundation legitimatises the DIMR's role and function as an NHRI. As an institution established by a parliamentary Act, the establishment of the DIMR is the expression of the will of a democratically elected legislative body. The Act also maintains the institutional independence of the DIMR from the executive.

The status of the DIMR, as a registered association, is an additional guarantee of its independence from the government, state entities, and other political actors. As such, it exercises the expression of the collective free will of its members,[4] and it is therefore characterised by its distance from the state. Moreover, it reflects the fact that the DIMR is a bearer of the freedom of association: as enshrined in Article 9 of the Basic Law for the Federal Republic of Germany and international

---

[3] For an overview of the different types of NHRIs see V. Aichele, 'National Human Rights Institutions. An Introduction', German Institute for Human Rights, Berlin 2010, p.15.

[4] See W. Höfling, 'Art. 9.2' in M. Sachs (ed.), *Grundgesetz*, C.H. Beck, Munich 2018.

human rights treaties. Hence, the Institute is protected against arbitrary dissolution or other interferences by the executive.

Table 1. Functions of the legal instruments forming the basis of the DIMR

Legal instrument	Function	
	Legitimacy	Independence
DIMR Act	Decision of democratically elected parliament	Legal basis not subject to political will of government
Articles of Association	Freedom of association	Non-state actors as constituent members

Source: Compiled by the authors.

2.1.1. DIMR Act

After a long and difficult journey,[5] the German Federal Parliament unanimously adopted the Act on the Legal Status and Mandate of the DIMR, on 18 June 2015.[6] The DIMR Act was promulgated on 22 July 2015, and it entered into force the next day.[7] The Act provided a legislative basis for the Institute, in accordance with the recommendation of the Sub-Committee on Accreditation (SCA) of the Global Alliance for National Human Rights Institutions (GANHRI), which was itself based on the Paris Principles on NHRIs.[8]

Containing only eight provisions, the DIMR Act is relatively short. Apart from sections 1 and 2, which refer to the legal status and the mandate of the NHRI, most provisions address its institutional structure,[9] including its organs (section 3), the conditions for membership of the association (section 4), the basic rules of its annual General Assembly (section 5), its Board of Trustees (section 6), and the offices of Director and Deputy Director (section 7).

Section 1 of the DIMR Act stipulates the legal status and the financial basis of the NHRI. Paragraph 1 provides:

> The registered association German Institute for Human Rights is the independent national institution of the Federal Republic of Germany to inform the public about the situation of human rights at home and abroad and to promote and protect human rights if and as long as the association fulfils the tasks following the Paris Principles of the United Nations of 1993 as established in Section 2 and meets the conditions of Sections 3 to 7.[10]

---

5 See below section 3.2.
6 The Federal Council had also adopted the Act unanimously.
7 It was subsequently published in the *Bundesgesetzblatt*, or Federal Gazette.
8 See generally UN General Assembly Res. 48/134 of 20 December 1993.
9 For details, see above section 2.
10 DIMR Act, section 1(1) (unofficial translation).

Paragraph 1 of section 1 also establishes that the German Federal Parliament will provide the DIMR with the necessary funds to finance its activities if and as long as the DIMR fulfils the mandate under section 2 following from the Paris Principles and fulfils the requirements under sections 3 to 7.[11]

Section 1 of the DIMR Act therefore clarifies that the Institute which already existed upon the adoption of the Act maintains the functions of an NHRI, provided it continues to follow the Paris Principles. That is to say, even though the DIMR Act cannot directly mandate the Institute to fulfil the Paris Principles because the DIMR is an independent association, if it no longer adheres to the Principles it will lose its legal status as the NHRI of Germany.

This provision seems to maintain and respect the non-state status and the independence of the DIMR as a registered association; however, it also contains a potential political threat to the Institute: should a majority of the German Federal Parliament deem that the DIMR no longer follows the Paris Principles, it could instead confer the status of NHRI upon another entity. As this could allow for unacceptable political pressure to be placed on the Institute, section 1 of the DIMR Act needs to be interpreted in light of the institutional framework of the Paris Principles on NHRIs. A determination as to whether the DIMR still complies with these principles can only be made by the SCA, to the exclusion of all other entities: that is to say, it is only where the SCA rejects the re-accreditation of the DIMR's A-status that the German Federal Parliament could withdraw the institution's designation as an NHRI; any other approach of the German state aimed at rescinding the DIMR's status would be a violation of the DIMR Act.

The DIMR Act also protects the Institute against activities of its own governing bodies that would result in moving the Institute away from the Paris Principles on NRHIs. Should its Director, Deputy Director, Board of Trustees, or General Assembly adopt measures or policies contradicting these principles, such activities would violate the DIMR Act and would, therefore, be deemed illegal.

Section 2 of the DIMR Act contains the mandate as well as the main tasks and functions of the NHRI. Paragraph 1 reiterates that the Institute should not only inform the public about the situation of human rights at home and abroad, but it should also promote and protect those rights. Furthermore, the provision maintains that the DIMR acts independently of any requirements or directives of the Federal Government or any other public or private entity. The DIMR either acts on its own initiative or can opt to follow a request made by the Federal Government or Federal Parliament. While the government and the parliament may request the DIMR to act, the Institute remains free to follow or reject such a request. Furthermore, parliamentary or governmental requests may not pre-empt the outcome of an activity of the Institute. If the DIMR acts

11 ibid.

on the basis of a request, it may use its resources at its own discretion. The latter qualification protects the Institute against requests by the political branches of the government that could unduly limit or restrain its resources and, therefore, endanger its independence.

In its decision to re-accredit the DIMR with A-status in November 2015,[12] the SCA noted that the statutory mandate of the Institute pointed to what it perceived as a narrow set of tasks. In particular, the SCA stated that the 'protection mandate appears to be somewhat limited'.[13] The SCA recalled that protection activities address and seek to prevent actual human rights violations and that measures to achieve this should include monitoring, inquiries, investigations and, reporting of/into/on such violations. While the SCA acknowledged that the DIMR interprets its protection mandate broadly and undertakes specific protection activities, it encouraged the Institute 'to advocate amendments to its enabling law that would clarify and strengthen its protection mandate'.[14]

The concern of the SCA is understandable, but it seemed to focus too heavily on a literal interpretation of the DIMR Act. The mandate of the DIMR is not only determined by this Law but also the more elaborate Articles of Association, which offer an important additional legal basis for the Institute.[15] These Articles further concretise its tasks and contain a solid legal basis for its protection mandate.[16]

2.1.2. Articles of Association

As pointed out, the DIMR's second legal basis is its Articles of Association. The original version of these Articles dates back to 2001, when the Institute was founded. The Articles of Association were amended, subsequent to and as a reaction to the adoption of the DIMR Act, in 2015. The most recent version of the Articles was adopted in December 2020.[17]

The Articles of Association specify the Institute's mandate and institutional structure, and therefore supplement the DIMR Act. As it is easier to amend the Articles than the Act, the Articles should be considered the more up-to-date

---

12 For current NHRIs' accreditation status (as at April 2023), see the Chart at: <https://www.ohchr.org/sites/default/files/Documents/Countries/NHRI/StatusAccreditationChartNHRIs.pdf>.

13 Report and Recommendations of the Session of the Sub-Committee on Accreditation, Geneva, 16–20 November 2015, of the International Coordinating Committee of National Institutions for the Promotion and Protection of Human Rights, para. 3.1(3), p. 16. <https://www.ohchr.org/sites/default/files/Documents/Countries/NHRI/GANHRI/SCA_FINAL_REPORT_-_NOVEMBER_2015-English.pdf>.

14 ibid.

15 See below section 2.1.2.

16 See also below section 3.3.

17 The German version is available at: <https://www.institut-fuer-menschenrechte.de/das-institut/auftrag/rechtliche-grundlagen/>.

legal basis for the Institute. Even though the Articles of Association rank below the DIMR Act in a formal legal sense, as the Act itself is now the legal framework from which they cannot deviate, both sources mutually depend on each other, and both are directly linked to the Paris Principles on NHRIs (see Figure 1 below).

The Preamble to the Articles of Association stipulates that they are a reaction to the requirements of the DIMR Act. As the establishment of these Articles is an expression of the freedom of association, as enshrined in Article 9 of the German Basic Law, a legislative Act can only limit their contents and effects within constitutional boundaries. It is therefore important that the Articles of Association explicitly refer to the DIMR Act, as this indicates that the members of the association (the General Assembly of the Institute) freely determined their intention that the Institute would continue to perform its role as Germany's NHRI, based on the DIMR Act.

Figure 1. The relationship between the legal instruments that form the basis of the DIMR

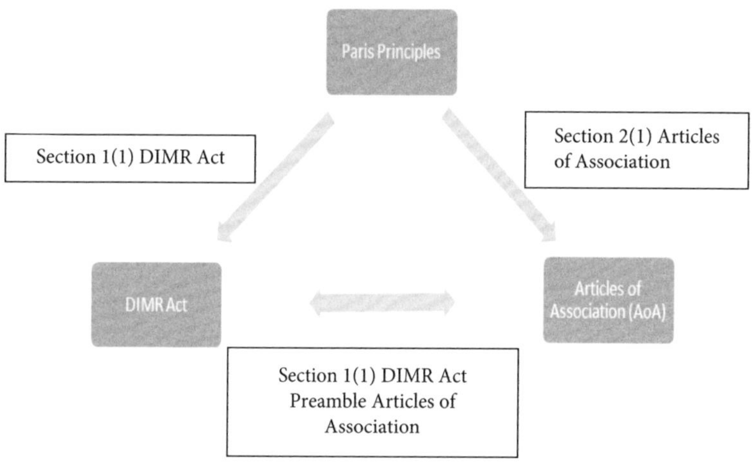

Source: Produced by the authors.

The close connection between the DIMR Act and the Articles of Association is further realised in section 2 of the Articles, which refers to the mandate of the Institute. This provision repeats the general description of the mandate of the NHRI, as prescribed in the DIMR Act; however, it adds that the Institute shall also 'contribute to the prevention of human rights violations'.[18] This is an important element which addresses the SCA's concerns in relation to the mandate of the DIMR:[19] as 'prevention' forms an essential part of the protection mandate of an NHRI.

18 Articles of Association of the DIMR, section 2.

19 See above section 2.1.1.

Section 3 of the Articles of Association reaffirms the independent status of the DIMR; it repeats the language of section 2 of the DIMR Act but adds that '[t]he majority of members of its governing bodies will be representatives of civil society', which is an important institutional guarantee of the Institute's independence.[20] The governing bodies must reflect the plurality of views of governmental and non-governmental agencies concerned with human rights issues, as well as the DIMR's comprehensive range of tasks. As a consequence, the governing bodies of the Institute should always include individuals and groups representing persons with disabilities: due to the DIMR's function as the monitoring body of the Convention on the Rights of Persons with Disabilities (CRPD).[21] Furthermore, actors with expertise concerning women's human rights, gender and sexual orientation, migrants and refugees, racist discrimination, and children should also be represented, due to the special relevance of related human rights issues in Germany.

2.2. INSTITUTIONAL STRUCTURE

In accordance with the DIMR Act and the Articles of Association, the institutional structure of the DIMR consists of three organs: its General Assembly, Board of Trustees, and Board of Directors (see Figure 2).

2.2.1. General Assembly and Membership

The German Civil Code stipulates that a registered association needs at least two governing bodies: a General Assembly of its members and a Board of Directors.[22] Usually, the General Assembly is the highest decision-making body of an association, as it has the power to change the Articles of Association, while the Board of Directors represents the association legally and determines its day-to-day business.

The General Assembly of the DIMR meets at least once a year and has four main institutional tasks:[23] first, it can change its Articles of Association, by a majority of three-quarters of the members present and half of all members; second, it confirms the membership of those newly admitted by the Board of Trustees; third, it elects six of the 18 members of the Board of Trustees, which has a significant bearing on the composition of this body; and fourth, it accepts the financial statements and annual reports and relieves the Board of Directors of their personal financial accountability at the end of each fiscal year.

---

20 Articles of Association of the DIMR, section 3.

21 See below section 2.3.

22 See *Bürgerliches Gesetzbuch*, or German Civil Code, sections 26 and 31.

23 For a full list of the General Assembly's tasks see Articles of Association of the DIMR, section 12.

Section 8 of the Articles of Association lays down the conditions for membership. Only individuals and legal entities that have shown special expertise and undertaken activities to protect and promote human rights can become members of the DIMR. Applications for membership are reviewed and decided upon by the Board of Trustees: by a special majority of two-thirds of the board's voting, rights-holding members. The General Assembly needs to confirm any decision to accept membership applications. In December 2016, the Board of Trustees and the General Assembly jointly adopted guidelines for the consideration of applications for membership. These clarify that, in accordance with the Paris Principles on NHRIs, an individual or legal entity wishing to become a member needs to be a recognised expert in a particular field.

Pluralist representation of the many social forces of civilian society involved in the protection and promotion of human rights is ensured by the Board of Trustees and the General Assembly. So far, the goal to ensure pluralism has been achieved. In December 2020, the membership of the DIMR consisted of 37 individuals and 51 organisations. The individuals are mostly recognised human rights activists, academics, or former politicians who have actively promoted human rights. The organisations include those with a broad and general mandate to protect human rights, such as the German branches of Amnesty International, Human Rights Watch, the International Society for Human Rights, and the Nuremberg Human Rights Centre as well as political, religious, or humanitarian groups that work in the interests of human rights, such as the relief works by Christian churches and issue-specific NGOs and interest groups, which focus more on the specific rights of people in vulnerable situations, including FoodFirst Information and Action Network (FIAN), the Federal Network of Immigrant Organisations, and the Lesbian and Gay Association.[24]

2.2.2. Board of Trustees

The Board of Trustees is made up of 18 members with voting rights and nine members without voting rights: the former include members of human rights organisations, individual experts, respected human rights defenders, academics, and members of parliament; the latter are representatives of various ministries and government agencies in charge of different aspects relating to human rights policy, such as the Federal Foreign Office, the Ministry of Justice, the Ministry of Development Cooperation, and the Government's Representative for Persons with Disabilities.

The 18 members with voting rights are selected or appointed by various institutions and bodies: the DIMR's General Assembly elects six of its members

24 A complete list of the DIMR's members is available at: <https://www.institut-fuer-menschenrechte.de/das-institut/gremien/mitglieder-des-vereins/>.

to become trustees; *Forum Menschenrechte*, the network of human rights civil society organisations in Germany,[25] elects three members; the German National Coalition for Persons with Disabilities nominates one member; and the Federal Parliament elects six members, three from academic institutions and three from civil society organisations. In addition, two members of the Federal Parliament's Committee on Human Rights and Humanitarian Affairs are also elected as members of the Board of Trustees.

In its most recent decision to re-accredit the DIMR, the SCA criticised the significant presence of government representatives, including parliamentarians, on the Board of Trustees. Even if the majority of these representatives are trustees without voting rights, the SCA was of the opinion that the mere presence of these representatives could have a negative effect on the independence of the DIMR. The SCA held that:

> The Paris Principles require that a NHRI be independent of government in its composition, operation and decision-making. It must be constituted and empowered to consider and determine its strategic priorities and activities based solely on its determination of the human rights priorities in the country, free from political interference.
>
> For these reasons, government representatives and members of parliament should not be members of, nor participate in the decision-making of, organs of a NHRI. Their membership of, and participation in, the decision-making body of the NHRI has the potential to impact on both the real and perceived independence of the NHRI.[26]

Based on this, the SCA was of the following opinion:

> Where government representatives or members of parliament are included in the decision-making body, they should be excluded from attending parts of the meeting where final deliberations and strategic decisions are made, and they should not be able to vote on these matters.[27]

While the Institute cannot fully exclude these members of the Board of Trustees from any deliberation, because the DIMR Act does not allow this, the General Assembly incorporated in the Articles of Association the possibility to exclude non-voting members from certain deliberations. This addresses the concerns of the SCA, without formally amending the DIMR Act.

---

25 See below section 4.

26 Report and Recommendations of the Session of the Sub-Committee on Accreditation, Geneva, 16–20 November 2015, of the Global Alliance of National Human Rights Institutions, para. 3.1(2), p. 15.

27 ibid, p 16.

The SCA also criticised the selection process for the filling of vacant seats on the Board of Trustees, due to its lack of transparency and inclusivity. It encouraged the DIMR:

> [T]o advocate for the formalization and application of a consistent process that includes requirements to:
>
> a) Publicize vacancies broadly;
> b) Maximize the number of potential candidates from a wide range of societal groups and educational qualifications;
> c) Promote broad consultation and/or participation in the application, screening, selection and appointment process;
> d) Assess applicants on the basis of pre-determined, objective and publicly-available criteria; and
> e) Select members to serve in their individual capacity rather than on behalf of the organization they represent.[28]

The Institute subsequently addressed these concerns within its Articles of Association and shared the SCA's requirements with all bodies that elect or appoint members of the Board of Trustees.

The Board of Trustees has five main functions: these relate either to the institutional structure of the DIMR or to its activities and tasks. Regarding its institutional structure, the Board of Trustees appoints or reappoints the Director and the Deputy Director, oversees their work, and admits new members to the association. Concerning the activities and tasks of the DIMR, the Board of Trustees approves guidelines for the activities of the Institute and its long-term planning, as proposed by the Board of Directors. In practice, the Board of Trustees has limited itself to reviews, which determine whether the drafts submitted by the Board of Directors reflect existing human rights challenges, but it has not replaced its priorities, thus protecting the DIMR from political pressure. Furthermore, the Board of Trustees approves the budget of the Institute, based on a proposal of the Director and Deputy Director, and accepts their annual financial statement and reports.

2.2.3. Board of Directors

The DIMR is led by its Board of Directors, composed of its Director and Deputy Director. Both are appointed by the Board of Trustees for a period of four years, which can be renewed. The Articles of Association specify that only one of the two should have a legal background and at least one should be a woman.

---

28 ibid, para. 3.1(1), p. 15.

Figure 2. Governance Structure of the DIMR

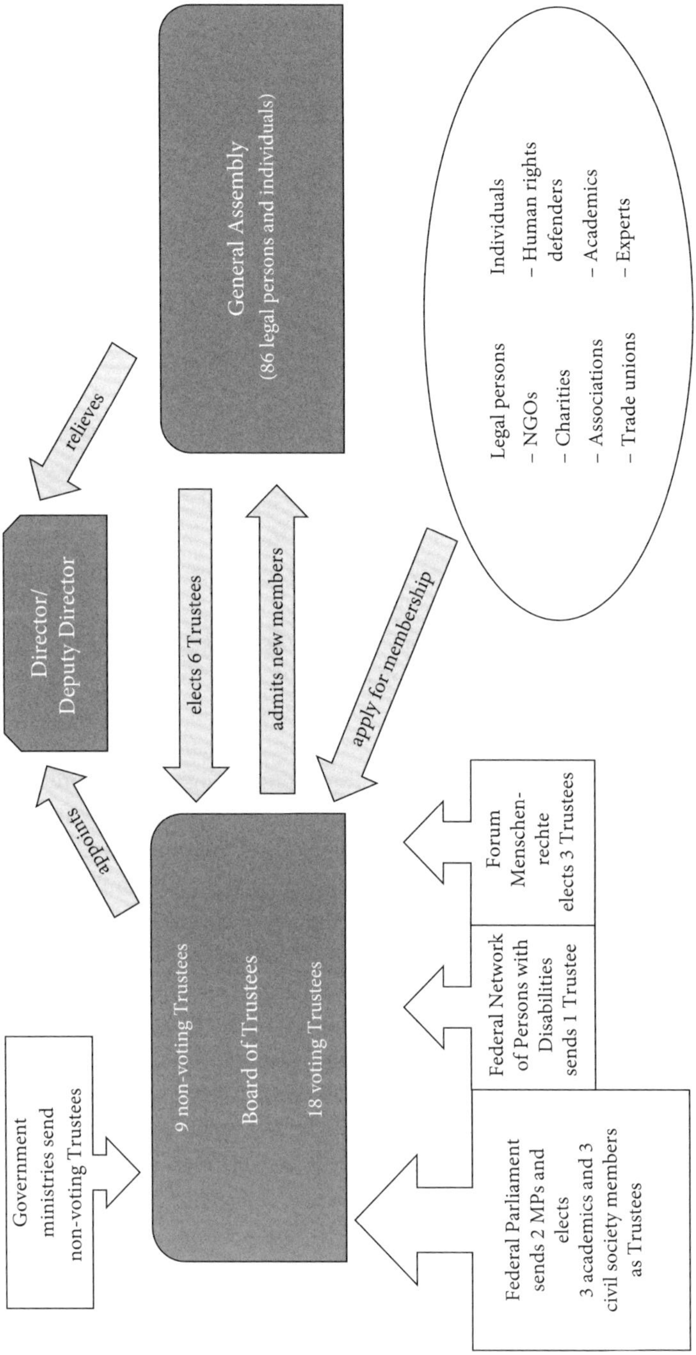

Source: Produced by the authors.

The Director and Deputy Director lead the DIMR's daily work: they hire staff, decide on the draft budget, and make decisions regarding the thematic issues and topics of the Institute's work. While the Board of Directors is formally accountable to the Board of Trustees and General Assembly, they enjoy a high degree of autonomy as well as national and international visibility. The Director and Deputy Director are the faces of the DIMR *vis-à-vis* politicians, government agencies, the media, and civil society; therefore, they need to be both nationally and internationally recognised human rights experts, must show leadership, and must have significant management skills.

2.3. TASKS AND COMPETENCES

As mentioned, the main tasks and competences of the Institute are laid down in the DIMR Act and the Articles of Association. Some of these tasks go beyond the Paris Principles, reflecting subsequent international developments. There are also some activities that are not expressly laid down in the two legal bases of the Institute. The following tasks are worth special mention.

2.3.1. Monitoring Body for the Convention on the Rights of Persons with Disabilities and the Convention on the Rights of the Child

With the entering into force of the CRPD in Germany in 2009, the DIMR assumed the role of independent monitoring mechanism, in accordance with Article 33.2 of the treaty. The monitoring mechanism is a department within the DIMR. Apart from broadening the thematic expertise in an important area of human rights work, this also offered the legislature an opportunity to strengthen the formal status of the DIMR under German law.[29] The monitoring function of the DIMR, under the CRPD, is now recognised in section 1(2) and section 2(4) of the DIMR Act as well as section 2 of the Articles of Association.

The Institute also established a monitoring body for the UN Convention on the Rights of the Child (CRC). According to the CRC, the German

29 In 2008, the Institute had been unsuccessful in its advocacy for the creation of an analogous formal monitoring function under the Optional Protocol to the Convention against Torture and Other Cruel, Inhuman or Degrading Treatment or Punishment. Instead, the competence to run the National Preventative Mechanism was vested in a small, newly founded committee of experts working in an honorary capacity. The National Agency for the Prevention of Torture is composed of 10 members: eight in the Joint Commission of the States and two in the Federal Agency. The entity has few support-staff and is based in Wiesbaden. See *Nationale Stelle zur Verhütung von Folter*. Available at: <https://www.nationale-stelle.de/en/home.html>.

monitoring body's mandate is to monitor, on an independent basis, Germany's implementation of the treaty.[30] However, unlike the example of the CRPD, the DIMR's role as monitoring entity for the CRC is not an express part of its legal mandate, and therefore it does not enjoy the same security as the mechanism relating to the CRPD.[31] It took seven years until the Federal Parliament decided, in 2022, to transfer the project budget of the CRC monitoring body into the permanent budget of the DIMR, thus ensuring permanent fulfilment of this task.[32]

2.3.2. Interaction with International Human Rights Monitoring Bodies and Domestic Courts

The DIMR collaborates closely with the human rights bodies of the United Nations, the Council of Europe, and the European Union. It also prepares submissions to international and domestic courts as well as other international human rights bodies (section 2(2) No. 5 DIMR Act).

Even though the DIMR has no explicit mandate to file *amici curiae*, it follows the practice of many other NHRIs and submits such briefs in selected court cases dealing with human rights.[33] This is noteworthy, because the instrument of *amicus curiae* is generally not known in German legal practice. An example of the practice is a statement addressing the human rights aspects of gender identity, which was filed by the DIMR in a 2017 case before the Federal Constitutional Court: it concerned the right of persons not to associate themselves with a masculine or feminine gender.[34] The Institute's statement was recognised by the Court, and it may have contributed to its finding that the exclusive use of masculine and feminine genders in German law violated the constitutional right of free development of one's personality.[35]

---

30 This does not follow explicitly from the CRC but from the interpretation of the CRC by the CRC Committee. See e.g., Committee on the Rights of the Child, Concluding observations on the combined third and fourth periodic reports of Germany, CRC/C/DEU/CO/3-4 (2014), para. 18.

31 This was criticised by the Committee on the Rights of the Child, Concluding observations on the combined fifth and sixth periodic reports of Germany, CRC/C/DEU/CO/5-6 (2022), para. 11(a).

32 German Federal Parliament (*Deutscher Bundestag*), Decision recommended by the Budget Committee (*Beschlussempfehlung des Haushaltsausschusses*), BT – Drucksache 20/3502 (14 November 2022) p. 5.

33 This is considered part of the Institute's advisory functions.

34 See *Amicus-Curiae-Stellungnahme des DIMR im BVerfG – Verfahren zum Geschlechtseintrag.* Available at: <http://www.institut-fuer-menschenrechte.de/publikationen/show/amicus-curiae-stellungnahme-des-dimr-im-bverfg-verfahren-zum-geschlechtseintrag/>.

35 Federal Constitutional Court, Order of the First Senate of 10 October 2017, 1 BvR 2019/16, paras. 22 and 43.

2.3.3. *Annual Report to the Federal Parliament*

In line with the Paris Principles, the DIMR Act also introduced the provision that the DIMR must report annually to the Federal Parliament on the Institute's work and the human rights situation in Germany.[36] As this obligation is statutory in nature, the reports are of significant public importance. They are usually discussed both within the Parliamentary Committee on Human Rights and in a plenary session of the Federal Parliament. Because the DIMR often comments critically on laws and policies, the parliamentary debates based on the reports are sometimes quite controversial. Beyond the official relevance of the DIMR's annual reports, the documents play a broader, unofficial role, as their contents are given considerable attention by the media, academia, and civil society.

2.3.4. *Information, Research and Political Advice*

Much of the daily work of the Institute concerns information sharing, the giving of political advice, and the carrying out of research. As stipulated in section 2(2) of the DIMR Act, its tasks include informing the public of the human rights situation in Germany and abroad, in particular, through the establishment and maintenance of a specialised library; the publication of information material and statements; and the undertaking of human-rights related educational work. The DIMR supports the efforts of educational stakeholders to anchor human rights in education and training programmes for sensitive occupations, i.e., in schools, etc.

Another important function of the DIMR is to carry out interdisciplinary and application-oriented research on human rights. This relates to its mandate to monitor the human rights situation in Germany. Based on this research, the DIMR advises political decision-makers at the federal and State level, courts and the legal profession in general, the business sector, and civil society, on matters relating to the implementation of international human rights conventions. The DIMR Act explicitly mandates the Institute to bring a comparative perspective to its analyses, if appropriate.

Section 2(3) of the DIMR Act and Article 2 of the Articles of Association stipulate that the Institute may also support the Federal Government by analysing the effects of European and German policies, especially in the field of development policy. This is a function that may only be fulfilled if additional financing is provided.

---

36 See below section 2.3.4. The Institute publishes the report in two parts. The annual reports of the DIMR on the human rights situation in Germany are available at: <https://www.institut-fuer-menschenrechte.de/menschenrechtsschutz/berichterstattung/menschenrechtsbericht/>. The annual activity reports are available at: <https://www.institut-fuer-menschenrechte.de/menschenrechtsschutz/jahresbericht/>.

Moreover, the DIMR Act entrusts the Institute with the examination of the continued human rights effects of totalitarian dictatorships as well as of armed conflict and post-conflict situations. Although the DIMR engages in these activities, they are not, currently, primary areas of focus. Because these areas are not mandated by the Paris Principles on NHRIs, their reduced relevance does not seem to be a problem from an international human rights law perspective.

3. HISTORICAL DEVELOPMENT

The DIMR is a relatively young organisation. It was founded in 2001, as a result of the then Federal Government's efforts to strengthen the institutional human rights landscape in Germany. Its foundation, however, was not based on a formal legislative Act but on a parliamentary resolution. As such, after its formative years, the DIMR's development was dominated by its struggle to attain a formal legislative basis. Currently, the German NHRI is seeking to increase its personnel and budget, to meet the expectations of its broad mandate.

3.1. ESTABLISHMENT AND FORMATIVE YEARS

The plan to create an independent NHRI was part of the 1998 coalition agreement between the Social Democratic Party and the Green Party, which allowed the Federal Government to form.[37] In conjunction with other structural changes – such as the upgrade of the previous Subcommittee on Human Rights of the Federal Parliament to a full parliamentary committee as well as the nomination of a Human Rights Commissioner located in the Federal Foreign Office – the creation of a specialised national human rights agency was intended to symbolise the new government's commitment to strengthening the protection and promotion of human rights, both domestically and abroad. In order to secure broad agreement across the party spectrum, parliamentary preparations and negotiations lasted more than two years. At the time, the international accreditation system was not yet in existence; hence, the Paris Principles on NHRIs did not play an important role in the domestic debate. This is reflected in the language of the parliamentary resolution and the DIMR's Articles of Association.

---

37 See generally the Coalition Agreement between the Social Democratic Party of Germany and the Alliance 90/The Greens of 20 October 1998. Available at: <https://www.spd.de/fileadmin/Dokumente/Beschluesse/Bundesparteitag/koalitionsvertrag_bundesparteitag_bonn_1998.pdf>.

3.1.1. Parliamentary Resolution of 2000

On 7 December 2000, the Federal Parliament unanimously voted for the establishment of the DIMR.[38] As such, the Institute received formal support from all parties represented in Parliament at the time: the Christian Democratic Union, including its Bavarian sister, the Christian Social Union; the Social Democratic Party; the liberal Free Democratic Party; the Green Party; and the Party of Democratic Socialism (today known as the Left). This broad political endorsement proved important for the DIMR's work, which naturally included the tackling of sensitive political issues.

Based on the DIMR resolution of the Federal Parliament, the Institute was formally founded in March 2001: in the form of a membership-based, registered association under German law. In subsequent years, this proved to be problematic. While the status of a registered association guaranteed independence from the state, it deviated from the Paris Principles on NHRIs, which, *inter alia*, prescribe that a NHRI must have a formal legal basis.[39] The problematic nature of the DIMR's legal structure centred around the fact that a parliamentary resolution does not amount to formal law or a formal legal basis for an entity. Despite this, as early as 2002 the DIMR received an A-status from the SCA of the International Coordinating Committee of National Institutions for the Promotion and Protection of Human Rights (ICC), now GANHRI: the A-status attested to the DIMR's full compliance with the Paris Principles on NHRIs, and in its assessment, the SCA emphasised that the DIMR functioned independently and effectively.[40] The (then) ICC's move to require periodic re-accreditation of NHRIs began in 2006 and eventually became a major incentive for the DIMR to secure a solid legal basis, in full conformity with the Paris Principles.[41] Otherwise, in the long run, the DIMR would have risked losing its full accreditation status within the global network of NHRIs: this would have had far-reaching negative implications, for both its domestic authority and international outreach.

3.1.2. Structural Challenges

Even after its formal establishment, the DIMR still had to strive to find its place within German society and abroad. In the face of a complex landscape of civil

---

38 See generally the German Federal Parliament, motion by the Social Democratic Party of Germany, Christian Democratic Union of Germany and the Christian Social Union in Bavaria, Alliance 90/The Greens and Free Democratic Party, Establishment of a German Institute for Human Rights, 28 November 2000, BT – Drucksache 14/4801.

39 See UN General Assembly Res. 48/134 of 20 December 1993, para. 2.

40 See the Report and Recommendations of the Session of the Sub-Committee on Accreditation (SCA), Geneva, 3–6 November 2008, of the International Coordinating Committee of National Institutions for the Promotion and Protection of Human Rights (ICC), para. 4.3.

41 See above section 2.

society organisations and given the traditionally strong role of the Federal Constitutional Court in securing individual rights, the added value of the newly-created DIMR was far from obvious: its value still had to be developed and publicly demonstrated. On the surface, the relationship between the DIMR and German civil society seemed uncomplicated; throughout the 1990s, human rights NGOs in Germany had actively and, ultimately, successfully campaigned for the creation of an independent NHRI. From the beginning, therefore, the DIMR enjoyed a warm reception and broad approval among NGOs. Nevertheless, the question of how to cooperate, in a spirit of mutual respect for the various entities' different roles, still had to be tackled. This was the first structural challenge faced during the DIMR's early years.

A second structural challenge originated from the enormous reputation that the Federal Constitutional Court enjoyed, and continues to enjoy, in Germany. The flipside of the unusually strong role of this court, was the very limited German interest in regional and international human rights protection systems.[42] Geographic realities notwithstanding, the distance between Karlsruhe, the seat of the Federal Constitutional Court, and Strasbourg, the seat of the European Court of Human Rights, often seemed to be further than that between Vienna, or some other European capital, and the Alsatian city. Moreover, the Geneva-based system of treaty body monitoring was even further removed from the interests of German legal and political minds, and thus received even less attention. While it enjoyed general and gradually increasing political support, the UN human rights system was by and large ignored, if not openly rejected, when it came to considering the potential of the system to assess the human rights situation in Germany. In this context, it is worth mentioning that many politicians, including those generally supportive of the DIMR, expressed surprise upon learning that the Institute saw a strong role for itself in the domestic sphere: this reaction evidenced a widespread and predominantly implicit assumption that human rights politics should be oriented primarily towards 'third-world issues', or foreign affairs more broadly, and should not waste too much energy on domestic matters, at least not in the domestic politics of a liberal democratic society like Germany. Such scepticism became particularly strong when, in the wake of 11 September 2001 and during the early days of the fight against terrorism, the DIMR issued a number of critical comments on policies of internal security and other delicate domestic issues.

---

42 For an analysis of the relevance of global human rights treaties and the UN human rights system in the case-law of German courts, see generally M. Krajewski, 'Schmückendes Beiwerk oder echte Ergänzung? Zur Wirkung der Menschenrechte im innerstaatlichen Recht' (2017) (1) *Zeitschrift für Menschenrechte* 8.

3.1.3. *Establishing the Role of the DIMR in the Context of the UN Treaty Body Reporting System*

An illustrative example as to how the DIMR dealt with these interconnected challenges during its early years was the role it adopted within the UN treaty body reporting cycle. In the interests of preserving a clear and visible distance from the Federal Government and thus demonstrating political independence, the DIMR could not participate in the drafting of official state reports: including the reports which the German government was, and is, obliged to submit periodically to relevant treaty bodies. A more complicated question was whether and, if so, how it should contribute to the elaboration of alternative reports, which are often known as 'parallel' or 'shadow' reports.[43] In order for the DMIR to appreciate the experience that had been gained by NGOs concerning parallel reporting to UN treaty bodies, the Institute decided to take a more indirect role: rather than submitting its own parallel reports, the Institute facilitated NGO reporting, by providing structural information and coordination.[44]

In contrast to this, mainly indirect, facilitative function, the DIMR took a much stronger role in follow-up processes relating to treaty body recommendations. Whenever a treaty body, or a similar international institution, issued a Germany-specific list of recommendations, the Institute invited representatives of the affected ministries, relevant civil society organisations, academic experts, and others to a one-day roundtable conference, with the objective of exploring what steps to take in response to the recommendations. From early on, many NGOs showed a keen interest in participating in these roundtable meetings. The attitude within the Federal Government was mixed: while the Federal Foreign Office and the Ministry of Justice were particularly supportive, other parts of the government, particularly the Ministry of the Interior, showed, at least initially, a more reluctant attitude. Over the course of the first few years, this changed; protocol notes of the roundtables, containing major results and projects, were sent back to the treaty bodies, to illustrate to them the ways in which their findings had been received domestically. This type of systematic follow-up to the recommendations of treaty bodies had not existed previously in Germany.

The DIMR's specific approach to treaty body reporting is typical of the way the Institute positioned itself within the existing political landscape, especially in its first years of operation. The approach had a number of practical advantages.

First, the DIMR successfully avoided a danger with which most NHRIs must cope: the risk of antagonising civil society organisations by starting unfair

43 See S. Joseph, 'Committees: Human Rights Bodies' in H. Ruiz Fabri (ed.), *Max Planck Encyclopedia of International Procedural Law*, Oxford University Press, Oxford 2019, para. 27.

44 After the introduction of the Universal Periodic Review, the DIMR began to write its own alternative reports.

competition in the area of parallel reporting. There were a few rare occasions, however, where representatives of the German government indicated that they would prefer to deal mainly with the Institute, as a 'more solid' alternative to NGOs. By taking on a facilitative role, the DIMR managed to preserve and cherish the trusting relationships it had built with civil society organisations. In turn, these organisations appreciated the specific expertise provided by the Institute as well as its open and public support of their own work.

Second, the DIMR functioned as a systematic link between international human rights protection efforts and the domestic human rights discourse. When their work is viewed from an international perspective, NHRIs can be seen to play a general role in domestic human rights protection and promotion: this is indicated by the very name used to refer to them. In contrast, when viewed from a national perspective, their role can be perceived as being somewhat reversed: NHRIs can actually appear to be representatives of international or regional human rights protection regimes; after all, they do operate in close collaboration with Geneva and Strasbourg, respectively. No systematic link between national and international human rights work had existed in Germany prior to the establishment of the DIMR. It was thus able to demonstrate its added value by filling an obvious gap.

Third, the strong focus placed on treaty body recommendations as well as the recommendations of similar mechanisms allowed the DIMR to deliver thematic statements on a broad variety of political issues: all with the explicit backing of the broader international human rights protection system. The thematic contributions included, *inter alia*: the absolute prohibition of torture;[45] the need to combat all forms of racism;[46] human rights concerns arising in the context of counter-terrorism;[47] migration and refugees; as well as emerging and complicated issues relating to the intersectionality between multiculturalism and gender issues, such as forced marriage.[48] At the same time, consistent references

---

45 See e.g., P. Follmar, W.S. Heinz, and B. Schulz, 'Zur aktuellen Folterdebatte in Deutschland' (2003) 1 *DIMR Policy Paper*; H. Bielefeldt, 'Das Folterverbot im Rechtsstaat' (2004) 4 *DIMR Policy Paper*; H. Bielefeldt, 'Menschenwürde und Folterverbot' (2007) 6 *DIMR Essay*.

46 See e.g., D.N. Addy, 'Diskriminierung und Rassismus. Internationale Verpflichtungen und nationale Herausforderungen für die Menschenrechtsarbeit in Deutschland' (2005) *DIMR Study*.

47 See e.g., W.S. Heinz, S. Schlitt, and A. Würth, 'Internationale Terrorismusbekämpfung und Menschenrechte (Oktober 2001–April 2003)', (2004) *DIMR Analysis*; W.S. Heinz and J.-M. Arend, 'Internationale Terrorismusbekämpfung und Menschenrechte. Entwicklungen 2003/2004' (2005) *DIMR Study*; W.S. Heinz and J.-M. Arend, 'The International Fight against Terrorism and the Protection of Human Rights – With Recommendations to the German Government and Parliament' (2005) *DIMR Study*.

48 See e.g., H. Bielefeldt, 'Zwangsheirat und multikulturelle Gesellschaft. Anmerkungen zur aktuellen Debatte' (2005) 2 *DIMR Essay*. See also the collection of contributions by T. Mirbach *et al*, *Zwangsverheiratung in Deutschland – Anzahl und Analyse von Beratungsfällen*, Verlag Barbara Budrich, Leverkusen 2011.

to international norms were supposed to familiarise the German audience with the specificities and relevance of international human rights protections. The DIMR's role within treaty body reporting exemplifies the understanding of its more general role as an institution which facilitates cooperation and broad communication.

3.1.4. Human Rights Education

When it comes to human rights education, the DIMR began by mapping the expertise that already existed in the area. It did so in order to gather and appreciate the know-how that had already been built up by various actors as well as to identify potential weak points or gaps in existing human rights education programmes. In response, the Institute took on a strong role in facilitating more effective human rights education, primarily by improving the conditions for information and knowledge exchange and through fostering synergies between programmes and actors. Accordingly, a focus was placed on 'training the trainers'. In 2004, the DIMR started an annual intensive course, which gave a broad overview on human rights standards and mechanisms. The format resembled a summer school, but it was called the 'Autumn Academy', because it usually took place in September. Members of the DIMR's staff taught all of the Academy's courses, thus guaranteeing a high degree of coordination and consistency. Beyond its purely educational aspects, the 'Autumn Academy' also provided opportunities for recruitment and networking.

One of the primary gaps identified within the context of human rights education concerned specific training programmes for German police forces.[49] As a response to this gap, the DIMR embarked on a long-term programme, which was co-chaired by its head of human rights education and an ex-police officer. In order to better understand the specific challenges of police work, the programme incorporated professionals who taught in various police academies as well as the police trade union. Cooperation with police practitioners proved particularly important when it came to dealing with public controversies involving security issues, especially as they emerged in the context of counter-terrorism measures. In response to the occasional criticism, that 'human rights people' allegedly propagate a lofty idealism that is remote from reality, the DIMR could consistently point to its close collaboration with practitioners in the field and thus gain additional credibility. Stakeholders working in international development cooperation were identified by the DIMR as another important target group for specific human rights education. The purpose of such training was to anchor development cooperation to a human

[49] See G. Schlicht, 'Menschenrechtsbildung für die Polizei' (2007) *DIMR Study*.

rights-based approach, overcoming traditional notions of 'mere charity work' in the process.[50]

3.1.5. *European and International Network of National Human Rights Institutions*

As already mentioned, the DIMR succeeded in obtaining its A-status from the SCA in 2002, the year following its establishment. From then on, the DIMR participated in the international NHRI network and, particularly, in the European regional sub-group. As a member of the European Coordinating Group (a sub-body composed of four NHRIs), the DIMR organised a 2004 meeting of the entire regional group, held in Berlin. As one of the leaders of the European group, the DIMR also participated actively in the management of the global network of NHRIs. In 2006, the DIMR was elected to chair the SCA. It assumed this sensitive function at a particularly critical juncture: at the commencement of the policy of periodic re-accreditation, which was supposed to enhance the credibility of NHRIs as a group. The SCA adopted a policy to strengthen the Paris Principles on NHRIs, by adopting stricter interpretations of the Principles themselves. This created a paradoxical situation: the DIMR, which enjoyed a legal status that was arguably not in full conformity with the Principles, due to its lack of a formal legislative basis, had to prepare recommendations, together with other members of the SCA, on the re-accreditation of other NHRIs. The need to strengthen the DIMR's legal basis, to bring it in full conformity with the Paris Principles, became more urgent in light of this somewhat awkward paradox; indeed, it became a matter of the DIMR's international credibility.

3.2. THE STRUGGLE FOR A LEGISLATIVE BASIS

In the DIMR's first re-accreditation, which occurred in 2008, the SCA expressed:

> its concern that the GIHR [i.e., the German Institute for Human Rights] is founded by a Motion of the Bundestag (Motion 14/4801). Notwithstanding the fact that the Motion was unanimously adopted and that the GIHR is functioning independently and effectively under this arrangement, the Sub-Committee reiterates the need for an NHRI to be established in a constitutional or legal text and therefore recommends the adoption of a stronger legal basis for the Institute.[51]

---

50 For an analysis, see S. Crawford and A. Würth, *Training on Human Rights-Based Approaches to Development: Experiences and Materials 2006*, Deutsche Gesellschaft für Technische Zusammenarbeit, Bonn 2007.

51 Report and Recommendations of the Session of the SCA, Geneva, 3–6 November 2008, of the ICC, para. 4.3.

As a result of the SCA's observations, it became a top priority for the DIMR's leadership to advocate domestically for a legislative basis, and the effort to secure such a basis ramped up after the 2009 federal elections. Despite intensive engagement with all parties in the Federal Parliament as well as relevant ministries, it proved impossible to overcome a political blockade that stood against the proposal. This impediment was created and supported by small, but influential, conservative elements of the then coalition government between the Christian Democratic Union and the Free Democratic Party. A number of parliamentarians rejected the need for an independent German NHRI, arguing that there were no human rights problems in the country at all or that they were insignificant when compared with human rights situations elsewhere. Finally, as a result of the DIMR's four years of advocacy, a coalition agreement, concluded between the Christian Democrats and the Social Democrats after the federal elections of December 2013, contained a commitment to provide the DIMR with a 'stable basis'.[52] It was high time for such a commitment, as the DIMR's re-accreditation procedure had already commenced, in November 2013, and the SCA had already granted a one-year deferral in view of the change of German government.

3.2.1. The Decisive Six Months

In September 2014, an opposition party applied public pressure, introducing a motion in the Federal Parliament which called upon the Federal Government majority to ensure a legislative basis for the DIMR.[53] Since the summer of 2014, the Ministry of Justice had been drafting a law on the matter, and by autumn it had reached an agreement with different ministries and other political actors. The plan was to have the Federal Government adopt the draft for submission to Parliament in October; however, the process was put on hold by some influential members of the Federal Parliament who claimed that they should have been involved in the process. Negotiations now shifted to a group of parliamentarians from the government's coalition parties, with the Ministry of Justice providing technical support and the DIMR leadership explaining the requirements of the Paris Principles on NHRIs, as interpreted by the SCA. It transpired that there was a counterproposal on the table, which sought to replace the existing structure of the DIMR, place it under the supervision of the Federal Foreign Office, and re-direct its work to human rights situations abroad. This proposal would have

---

52 Coalition Agreement 'Shaping Germany's Future' between Christian Democratic Union of Germany and the Christian Social Union in Bavaria, and the Social Democratic Party of Germany of 16 December 2013, p. 125. Available at: <https://www.cdu.de/sites/default/files/media/dokumente/koalitionsvertrag.pdf>.

53 See generally German Federal Parliament, motion by the Alliance 90/The Greens, 23 September 2014, BT – Drucksache. 18/2618.

turned the DIMR from a NHRI into a government-controlled think-tank for external human rights policy.

In October 2014, the Minister of Justice notified the SCA about the ongoing negotiations and assured it of the Federal Government's firm intention to provide the DIMR with a legislative basis in time for the next SCA session. On this basis, the SCA granted a further deferral until March 2015. This was generally understood as being the last possible deferral:[54] if the DIMR did not obtain a legislative foundation in March 2015, the SCA would be left with no choice but to notify the DIMR of its intention to downgrade it to B-status; the Institute would then have one year to show its continued compliance with the Paris Principles on NHRIs, and, in the meantime, it would maintain its participation rights within the UN. Nevertheless, the SCA's mere notice of an intention to downgrade the DMIR would have seriously damaged Germany's international reputation as a champion of human rights and staunch promoter of NHRIs, particularly as the sponsor of the biannual General Assembly resolution on these institutions.

The urgency to introduce a draft Bill was recognised by relevant members of the Federal Parliament, although it was not taken seriously by some. The urgency was also recognised at the Federal Foreign Office and the Ministry of Justice as well as within civil society. Given the proposals on the table, there was little room for negotiation, especially considering the fact that the counterproposal amounted to abolishing the NHRI, as such. In response to the situation, the DIMR leadership, with the support of the Board of Trustees and the Institute's General Assembly, made it clear that no law would be preferable to a bad law. In both alternatives, the DIMR would lose its A-status; however, a no-law situation could at least be remedied by a Paris Principles-compliant law at some stage in the future. In contrast, a bad law would mean that the struggle for a German NHRI would need to start from scratch, and, as a result, the DIMR's experienced staff, institutional knowledge, and domestic, European, and international interconnectedness would have been lost.

Negotiations continued behind closed doors but without much progress. In light of the limited room to negotiate, the DIMR leadership advised its supporters in politics and civil society not to intervene publicly, so as to preserve the chances of a face-saving solution for all: in other words, a solution which might be suitable for unanimous support within the Federal Parliament. In mid-December, however, the issue became widely known to the general public, through a critical article published in an influential conservative newspaper.[55]

---

54 At the time, the SCA considered 18 months to be the maximum time within which to carry out an accreditation. This rule was provided for in the SCA Rules of Procedure and related to special reviews; however, it was also applied to ordinary re-accreditations. For the change see n 60 below.

55 E. Lohse, 'Unter der Fuchtel', *Frankfurter Allgemeine Zeitung* (Frankfurt, 12 December 2014) 3.

In early February 2015, opposition parties used the parliamentary question time to grill the Federal Government about the status of negotiations and the timing envisaged for the draft law.[56] With the Institute's downgrade looming, one opposition party introduced its own draft law, which translated the core provisions of the DIMR Articles of Association into law.[57]

Around the same time, many public statements appeared and letters were written to the German Chancellor and ministers calling for a legal basis that would preserve the DIMR and its existing structure and mandate. The broad range of supporters of the Institute was impressive, including not only human rights organisations belonging to the *Forum Menschenrechte*[58] and organisations working for the interests of persons with disabilities,[59] but also the two big Christian churches of Germany (Catholics and Evangelists), the Association of Lesbians and Gays, associations representing religious or other minorities, individual scholars, as well as organisations of judges and lawyers. Not a single civil society actor came forward publicly in favour of the fundamental changes proposed by the counterproposal.

Pressure on the government increased even more when the German Minister of Foreign Affairs, accompanied by members of the Federal Parliament, paid an official visit to Geneva to meet with the UN Human Rights Council (HRC), the UN High Commissioner for Human Rights (HCHR), and other human rights bodies and organisations. According to participants, the interlocutors in all meetings raised the DIMR's lack of legislative basis and the reputational damage that would be done to Germany if the DIMR were to lose its A-status. The fact that Germany had just assumed the presidency of the HRC exacerbated the negative impact that might be expected if A-status were lost. It thus became clear to every participant that preserving the DIMR's accreditation status was of the highest public interest for Germany. A few days after the visit to Geneva, a breakthrough was reached in negotiations, and on the morning of 18 March 2015, the Federal Government adopted the draft law on the DIMR. The letter of the Minister of Justice, which informed the SCA of the draft law's adoption, arrived just in time: before the SCA's afternoon session, which was the very session scheduled for the review of the DIMR's re-accreditation. As the law had not yet been adopted by the legislature, the SCA could not make a final decision; however, thanks to a change in the SCA's

---

56 See generally German Federal Parliament, minutes of the 84th meeting, 5 February 2015, Plenarprotokoll 18/84, 7983-91.

57 See generally German Federal Parliament, Draft Law on the Legal Status and Mandate of the DIMR, motion by the Alliance 90/The Greens, 24 February 2015, BT – Drucksache 18/4089.

58 The *Forum Menschenrechte* is the preeminent German network of human rights NGOs. It elects three members to the DIMR's Board of Trustees, see above section 2.2.2 and below section 4.

59 Since 2009, the DIMR has fulfilled the mandate of monitoring the implementation of the CRPD in Germany, pursuant to art 33.2 of the CRPD. See above at section 2.3.1.

practice, which had been brought about by a prior challenge (by another NHRI) to its procedures,[60] the sub-committee was in a position to decide on a further deferral, this time until November 2015.

On 24 March 2015, the coalition parliamentarians introduced the Federal Government's draft law as an initiative in the Federal Parliament, so as to speed up the legislative procedure.[61] At the first reading, the opposition parties criticised the fact that the coalition had not asked them to join as sponsors; nevertheless, they announced that they would support the law.[62] As a show of support, they introduced an identical draft law.[63] The Federal Government formally submitted its identical legislative proposal, once the first reading had shown the support from the coalition parliamentarians.[64] Although the second reading did not bring about a merger of all three proposals, the Parliamentary Human Rights Committee was unanimous in recommending the adoption of the merged draft laws of the coalition parties and the government,[65] with a few minor changes.[66] Two days later, the Federal Parliament adopted the draft law unanimously.[67] During the accompanying debate, all political parties expressed their support for the DIMR, and there was broad praise for its work. In its last session before the summer break, the Federal Council assented to the draft law unanimously, and in mid-July the Federal President signed the draft into law.

---

60 The SCA changed its practice following an advisory opinion of the legal counsel of the (then) ICC. In 2019, the GANHRI Statute was amended. The new art 14.1 provides for a limitation of deferrals to two years, with the possibility of a longer deferral in exceptional circumstances, not exceeding five years.

61 See generally German Federal Parliament, Draft Law on the Legal Status and Duties of the DIMR, motion by the Christian Democratic Union of Germany and the Christian Social Union in Bavaria, and the Social Democratic Party, 24 March 2015, BT – Drucksache 18/4421.

62 See German Federal Parliament, minutes of the 98th Meeting, 27 March 2015, Plenarprotokoll 18/98, 9359–73. The 2000 parliamentary motion was sponsored by all political parties at the time, with the exception of *Die Linke*, or The Left. Until the present day, neither the Christian Democratic Union nor the Christian Social Union undertake joint parliamentary initiatives with *Die Linke*, on the grounds that it is the successor of the former German Democratic Republic state-party, which was called the Socialist Unity Party of Germany.

63 German Federal Parliament, Draft Law on the Legal Status and Duties of the DIMR, motion by The Left and Alliance 90/The Greens, 5 May 2015, BT – Drucksache 18/4798.

64 German Federal Government, Bill on the Legal Status and Tasks of the DIMR, 13 May 2015, BT – Drucksache 18/4893.

65 See German Federal Parliament, Recommendation for Decision and Report of the Committee on Human Rights and Humanitarian Aid, 16 June 2015, BT – Drucksache 18/5198, 9–10.

66 See German Federal Parliament, Committee on Human Rights and Humanitarian Aid, Ausschussdrucksache 18(17)88. These changes clarified that the DIMR's budget would also cover the additional task of submitting an annual report to the Federal Parliament on the human rights situation in Germany. A few years later, the DIMR's budget was increased to cover an increase of 50% in staff numbers.

67 See German Federal Parliament, minutes of the 112th Meeting, 18 June 2015, Plenarprotokoll 18/112, 10833–39.

3.2.2. *Assessment*

When looking back at the DIMR's history, five critical factors can be identified that have led to the successful adoption of the necessary legal basis:

(1) its recognition of the Paris Principles on NHRIs as the international standards which drive its work, including the Principles' authoritative interpretation by the SCA;
(2) the Institute's broad support from civil society;
(3) its international support, especially that offered by the UN OHCHR;
(4) its efforts, along with its supporters, to impress on interested stakeholders, especially the Federal Parliament, that a downgrade of the DIMR's accreditation status would reflect negatively, not only on the Institute but also on the Federal Government and the country itself; and finally,
(5) the firm position, held by its Board of Directors, Board of Trustees, and Membership Assembly, which rejected any fundamental changes to the structure and mandate of the Institute that might endanger its compliance with the Paris Principles.

In the end, these factors all hinged on the reputation and recognition that the Institute enjoyed domestically and internationally; it was only because the DIMR had proved to be an independent actor, which produced high-quality work in line with the Paris Principles, that all of its defenders held, adamantly, that any new law must uphold the existing structure and mandate of the Institute. For that same reason, opponents of the DIMR were not able to muster support for their proposals.

The long struggle for a legislative foundation for the DIMR is a stark reminder that the acceptance of an independent NHRI cannot be taken for granted, not even in a developed democracy. With respect to Germany, the state of affairs was all the more surprising, as the Institute has significantly fewer powers than most of its sister institutions in Europe.[68] Opposition to an NHRI reflects an unwillingness on the part of some politicians to be reminded of the limits that constitutional and international human rights set on state power, and thus on their own room to manoeuvre. This insight points to an unwritten precondition for the effective promotion and protection of human rights by an NHRI: responsiveness by state authorities to its findings and advice. It is for this reason that the unanimous adoption of the DIMR Act was particularly important; it made clear that the existence of the NHRI was a non-partisan undertaking and that all parties represented in the Federal Parliament needed to commit to respecting the role of the NHRI into the future.

68 See below section 5.

The experience of the DIMR illustrates a conundrum which the SCA must often face in re-accreditation procedures: is it appropriate to downgrade a NHRI when its corresponding parliament or government is responsible for non-fulfilment of the Paris Principles? This aporia is frequently considered by observers and stakeholders. Some argue that downgrading a NHRI in such circumstances would be unfair, as it punishes the NHRI for the actions or inactions of other actors, over which it has no power. Even if a NHRI lives up to international standards in the course of its everyday work, it cannot force the government or parliament to ensure that their share of the responsibility, when it comes to upholding the requirements of the Paris Principles, is fulfilled; however, the accreditation system must consider all elements of the Paris Principles that are within the state's exclusive purview. This conclusion is warranted, as A-status accreditation is the precondition for enjoying participation rights within UN human rights bodies, processes, and mechanisms. The worldwide community of NHRIs, and the very NHRI concept itself, would suffer if the mandate, powers, and independence of any one NHRI were not ensured and protected, as is required by the Paris Principles. What incentive would a state have to fulfil the Principles if their breach was not taken seriously? Would it not, in such a situation, be tempted to create and maintain a weak and non-critical institution? The accreditation system, which serves to strengthen NHRIs worldwide, would achieve the very opposite if NHRIs were given A-status accreditation despite state failures, or even bad-faith in government behaviour *vis-à-vis* their obligations under the Paris Principles; therefore, downgrading a NHRI to B-status in such situations serves to protect NHRIs in general and helps strengthen the NHRI concerned, albeit in the longer run.

The DIMR's struggle for a legislative basis teaches an important lesson. In both the domestic and international arenas, this lesson and its message must be made clear: the fulfilment of the Paris Principles by an NHRI is first and foremost a responsibility of the state and, as a result, so too is the responsibility of ensuring an NHRI's ongoing A-status accreditation. Governments and parliaments must understand their roles as guarantors of the independence, broad mandate, and powers of NHRIs, and they must also ensure that all state actors are ready to listen to criticism by the NHRI and engage constructively with it.

3.3. RE-ACCREDITATION

In its November session of 2015, the SCA concluded its review of the DIMR's accreditation status and recommended its re-accreditation with A-status.[69]

69 See Report and Recommendations of the Session of the SCA, Geneva, 16–20 November 2015, of the ICC, para. 3.1, p. 14.

Unsurprisingly, however, the sub-committee raised a number of concerns, which it will examine in the next re-accreditation round.[70] As the DIMR leadership had warned during the negotiations for its legislative basis, the participation of two members of the Federal Parliament on the Board of Trustees remained problematic for the SCA. The SCA also reiterated its concerns about the presence, albeit without voting rights, of representatives of ministries and government departments. That the number of representatives from governmental bodies had increased, due to the new DIMR Act, exacerbated such concerns.[71] The SCA emphasised that a mechanism should be put in place to exclude government representatives from discussions about strategic decisions and from decision-making processes.[72] It also called for a transparent appointment process regarding the members of the DIMR's Board of Trustees.[73] Moreover, it underlined that the Institute must be provided with adequate funding, to ensure that it can carry out the new tasks it has been mandated with by the DIMR Act.[74] While the SCA commended the Institute for interpreting its protection mandate in a broad and purposive manner, it encouraged advocacy for a stronger protective mandate and stressed that time-limited funding of mandates, such as for the CRC monitoring body, is insufficient.[75] It is worth noting that the Commissioner for Human Rights of the Council of Europe had raised the same five concerns only a few weeks before.[76]

What the SCA did not take up in 2015, was its 2008 recommendation that the protection mandate of the DIMR should be strengthened by vesting the Institute with a complaints-handling function.[77] This change reflects the more

---

70 In view of its workload, the SCA postponed the DIMR's re-accreditation review for a year; it had originally been scheduled for autumn 2020, but due to the COVID 19 pandemic, the review was re-scheduled to begin in 2022. Germany's status is due to be reviewed in the second SCA session of 2023.

71 See above section 2.2.2.

72 See Report and Recommendations of the Session of the SCA, Geneva, 16–20 November 2015, of the ICC, para. 3.1(2), pp. 15–16. The SCA referred to General Observation 1.9 of the SCA, of 21 February 2018, on political representatives on NHRIs.

73 See ibid. The SCA referred to General Observation 1.8 of the SCA, of 21 February 2018, on selection and appointment of the decision-making body of NHRIs.

74 See ibid. The SCA referred to General Observation 1.10 of the SCA, of 21 February 2018, on adequate funding of NHRIs.

75 See ibid. The SCA referred to General Observation 1.2 of the SCA, of 21 February 2018, on human rights mandate.

76 See Report by N. Muižnieks, Commissioner for Human Rights of the Council of Europe following his visit to Germany on 24 April and from 4 to 8 May 2015, CommDH(2015)20 of 1 October 2015, para. 67.

77 See Report and Recommendations of the Session of the SCA, Geneva, 3–6 November 2008, of the ICC, para. 4.3. At the time of the 2015 SCA recommendation, the CRC and the Committee on Economic, Social, and Cultural Rights (CESCR) had already recommended that the German state entrust the DIMR with such functions. See CESCR E/C.12/DEU/CO/5 of 20 May 2011, para. 8; CRC/C/DEU/CO/3-4 of 31 January 2014, para. 18. It should be noted that the CESCR did not repeat its recommendation in its concluding observations

nuanced understanding of NHRIs' protection mandates, which had subsequently been developed by the SCA. The SCA's updated interpretation reflects the fact that complaints handling is not considered a core NHRI function, according to the Paris Principles; indeed, it is an optional competence. By 2015, the SCA had developed a new definition of 'protection', which it applied to the DIMR. According to this updated view, protection is defined as 'addressing and seeking to prevent actual human rights violations' and NHRIs carry out their protective role through 'monitoring, inquiring, investigating and reporting on human rights violations, and may include individual complaint handling'.[78] Based on this understanding, the SCA was satisfied that the DIMR had fulfilled its protection mandate. On this point, the SCA noted that the DIMR had submitted *amicus curiae* briefs to courts; monitored the human rights situation in Germany for the EU Agency for Fundamental Rights; and been entrusted with monitoring functions as Germany's CRPD-mandated National Monitoring Mechanism, pursuant to Article 33(2) of the CRPD. The SCA did, however, call for a clarification and strengthening of the DIMR's protection mandate within its legislative basis.[79]

3.4. CURRENT CHALLENGES AND FUTURE POSSIBILITIES

In light of the arduous path to establishing the DIMR's legislative basis, the implementation of the SCA recommendations remains an ongoing challenge. A top priority is to strengthen the monitoring functions of the Institute. This was achieved with respect to the CRC monitoring body through a transfer of the project budget into the institutional budget of the DIMR, thus permitting the permanent fulfilment of this task.[80] The CRPD monitoring body, on the other hand, has continuously engaged with the *Länder*, or States of the Federal Republic of Germany, to help them implement the Convention on the Rights of Persons with Disabilities in areas under their jurisdiction and assist in monitoring the progress made. Until now, however, only three of the 16 *Länder* have entrusted the DIMR with a formal monitoring mandate,[81] despite a 2015 recommendation made to this effect by the Committee on the Rights of Persons

of 2018. See CESCR E/C.12/DEU/CO/6 of 12 October 2018. During the Universal Periodic Review of that year, Germany received three recommendations – from Denmark, the Philippines, and Mali – to expand the DIMR's mandate to include complaints handling. See Report of the Working Group on the Universal Periodic Review: Germany A/HRC/39/9 of 11 July 2018, paras 155.26–28. These were simply noted by the German Government. See Report of the Working Group on the Universal Periodic Review: Germany A/HRC/39/9/Add.1 of 11 September 2018.

78 General Observation 1.2 of the SCA, of 21 February 2018.

79 Report and Recommendations of the Session of the SCA, Geneva, 16–20 November 2015, of the ICC, para. 3.1(3), p. 16.

80 See supra 2.3.a.

81 These are Berlin, North-Rhine-Westphalia and Saarland.

with Disabilities.[82] Furthermore, in 2021, one *Land* (Hesse) entrusted the DIMR with monitoring the CRC. In early 2020, after in-depth consultations with the DIMR, the Federal Ministry for Family Affairs, Senior Citizens, Women and Youth announced its intention to provide the DIMR with a mandate to monitor the implementation of the Council of Europe Convention on Preventing and Combating Violence against Women and Domestic Violence, also known as the 'Istanbul Convention', and the pertinent Council of Europe and European Union standards on preventing and combatting human trafficking in Germany. A preparatory phase relating to this mandate began immediately,[83] and two years later, in November 2022, the DIMR was formally entrusted with these mandates, albeit as projects only, with the government expressing its intention to work towards a specific legal basis.[84] These positive developments can be attributed to insight regarding the need for independent monitoring in these respective areas and support from civil society. The recommendations of the SCA did not play a decisive role in these contexts.

A further challenge is to cope with the manifold expectations of the German federal and State governments and parliaments, courts, civil society, and the European and international human rights bodies. These expectations have increased considerably, due to: the growing recognition of both the DIMR's value and the role that NHRIs can play in regional and international organisations; and the reputation of the Institute in both the international and domestic arenas. On the international plane, NHRIs are expected to contribute to the monitoring processes of UN treaty bodies. This includes contributions at the various stages of the state reporting procedure, during which NHRIs can, in particular, submit their own parallel reports. Domestically, the DIMR faces the constantly increasing challenge of dealing with the rising number of governmental or parliamentary invitations to comment on draft laws. These deal with an ever-broader array of human rights issues and have ever-shorter deadlines. This is particularly the case in the areas of asylum and migration and security and anti-terrorism issues. The pressure in this context has been compounded by initiatives instituted by populist politicians and parties, which, *inter alia*, promote hatred and discrimination; undermine the equality of all human beings and thus of

---

82 See Concluding Observations on the First State Report of Germany CRPD/C/DEU/CO/1 of 13 April 2015, para. 58.

83 Federal Ministry of Family Affairs, Senior Citizens, Women and Youth, 'Construction of the Monitoring Centre against Violence to Women Started', press release of 31 January 2020. Available at: <https://www.bmfsfj.de/bmfsfj/aufbau-der-monitoringstelle-gegen-gewalt-an-frauen-gestartet/147466>.

84 Federal Ministry of Family Affairs, Senior Citizens, Women and Youth, 'Construction of the Monitoring Centre against Violence to Women Started', press releases of 18 November 2022 (trafficking) and of 25 November 2022 (violence against women). Available at: <https://www.bmfsfj.de/bmfsfj/aktuelles/alle-meldungen/bundesregierung-verstaerkt-kampf-gegen-menschenhandel-205132/>, and at <https://www.bmfsfj.de/bmfsfj/aktuelles/alle-meldungen/deutschland-setzt-verpflichtungen-aus-der-istanbul-konvention-um-205292/>.

human rights; distort definitions of human rights, especially the freedom of expression; intimidate their critics; and disparage the democratic process. As is the task of every NHRI and especially those with a strong focus on application-oriented research, the DIMR has had to strike a balance between responding to such situations at short notice and pursuing long-term issues, so as to be able to also draw political attention to insufficiently recognised human rights issues.

In light of its limited budget and the long-term lack of political will for a sizeable budgetary increase,[85] the DIMR has been promoting human rights-based research by other actors and continues to do so. For example, it cooperates with the German Youth Institute in the development of children's rights indicators and advises the Federal Government on the design of reports it commissions, such as those on the participation of persons with disabilities and on poverty and wealth in Germany. So far, the DIMR has only cooperated with universities on an *ad hoc* basis. As the 2019–2023 DIMR strategic plan identifies new human rights challenges – i.e., societal distortions caused by growing inequalities, social exclusion, climate change, and the globalisation of economies, trade, and the finance sector; and the need to shape changes brought about by digitalisation and artificial intelligence in a way that respects human rights – new forms of interdisciplinary cooperation will have to be developed as well.

New challenges also call for a critical re-assessment of the powers of the DIMR. In the words of the Commissioner for Human Rights of the Council of Europe:

> While the provision of a legal basis for the GIHR [i.e., the German Institute for Human Rights] represents clear progress, in the Commissioner's view, the authorities could have been more ambitious and taken the opportunity of the legislative reform to increase the powers and resources of the GIHR. The Commissioner notes, for instance, that the Institute still has very limited investigation powers (no right to access official documents and places or power to compel testimony from any authority, for instance), which would permit it to better fulfill its monitoring mandate, in particular its obligation to report to parliament. In addition, the Commissioner recalls the State's obligation to match the increase in tasks of a national human rights Institution by an increase in financial resources. The Commissioner finally notes that the GIHR cannot bring complaints before the Federal Constitutional Court to check the constitutionality of a law in light of Germany's international human rights obligations.[86]

---

85 In 2022, and in line with the coalition agreement between the Social Democratic Party of Germany, Alliance 90/The Greens, and the Free Democratic Party of 24 November 2021 (available at: <https://www.fdp.de/sites/default/files/2021-11/Koalitionsvertrag%202021-2025_0.pdf/>, p. 146), the DIMR saw its budget considerably increased in two steps (for the 2022 and the 2023 budgets), see German Federal Parliament, Decision recommended by the Budget Committee (*Beschlussempfehlung des Haushaltsausschusses*), BT – Drucksache 20/1602 (19 May 2022), p. 2, and fn. 31.

86 Report by N. Muižnieks, Commissioner for Human Rights of the Council of Europe following his visit to Germany on 24 April and from 4 to 8 May 2015, CommDH(2015)20 of 1 October 2015, para. 25.

Further powers could certainly be conceived of: for example, some NHRIs can submit draft laws to parliament, while others are *ex officio* called upon to present their views on draft laws in parliament, irrespective of a request. More than 20 years after the DIMR was founded, it is high time for a debate concerning such powers. Compared to its sister institutions in many countries, including those in Europe, the DIMR has few powers. While the core of an NHRI's influence is found within its words, specific investigatory powers would amplify and further strengthen the influence of the DIMR's voice, boosting its impact in courts and in the Federal Parliament and enhancing its weight and prospects of successfully influencing powerbrokers. Human rights are the substantive component of the rule of law, and, as developments all over the world sadly demonstrate, a democracy requires strong independent institutions to uphold and defend human rights – as the very basis of the state and its ultimate objective.

4. CIVIL SOCIETY AND THE DIMR

Germany features an active, vocal, and diverse scene of civil society organisations that focus on various human rights issues. Many organisations work on specific issues, often with a local or regional specialisation. There are also larger groups and organisations which address multiple issues and enjoy national recognition.

Following the 1993 World Conference on Human Rights, German NGOs established (in 1994) the *Forum Menschenrechte* as a nationwide network committed to better and more comprehensive protection of human rights. By 2022, the forum consisted of about 50 NGOs, engaged in critically observing and addressing the domestic and international policies of the Federal Government and Parliament from a human rights perspective.[87] Today, the *Forum Menschenrechte* is the institutionalised platform of and for civil society organisations that have a human rights focus in Germany.

This forum is linked to the DIMR in many ways: as already pointed out, the DIMR Act mandates that the *Forum Menschenrechte* elects three of its members to the Board of Trustees;[88] in addition, many forum members are also part of the DIMR itself, and therefore participate in the activities and functions of its General Assembly. It is also a well-established good practice that the DIMR Director and the Deputy Director attend the annual plenary meeting of the *Forum Menschenrechte*. Furthermore, DIMR staff are frequent guests and speakers at NGO events, while NGO representatives are often invited to contribute to activities of the DIMR. This being said, unlike the DIMR's former approach,

---

87 See generally *Forum Menschenrechte*. Available at: <https://www.forum-menschenrechte.de/english-summary/>.

88 See above 2.2.3.

taken during its early years of operation,[89] it now only seldom facilitates the drafting of parallel reports within the context of treaty body monitoring or the Universal Period Reviews. Instead, parallel reports are now drafted by permanent or *ad hoc* NGO networks.

In general, exchanges and collaborations between the DIMR and civil society organisations are frequent, and they cover a variety of issues. The DIMR staff who make up the CRPD and CRC monitoring bodies[90] cooperate closely with NGOs working on the rights of persons with disabilities and children's rights, respectively. Another area of intensive partnership – this time between NGOs, the DIMR, and academia – concerns human rights education. Many contacts and exchanges are informal and *ad hoc*, and they concern a variety of issues addressed by the DIMR, such as care for older persons, human trafficking, women's rights, and anti-racism. In its publications and annual reports to the Federal Parliament,[91] the DIMR takes up many issues of concern for civil society organisations, including poverty, homelessness, labour exploitation, business and human rights, arms exports, the human rights of refugees, human rights violations in psychiatric institutions, and the rights of persons with disabilities. There are many substantive overlaps, even if the political demands of NGOs and the DIMR do not always coincide.

While NGOs and the DIMR often share the same long-term goals, they may advocate different means as they strive to reach them. Even though civil society groups and the Institute are aware of, and keen on, preserving their distinctive functions, roles, and approaches, they seem to complement each other well. NGOs sometimes focus on one particular aspect of an issue and also criticise the government in a more outspoken manner: in part, because they perceive their role as being one of opposition to state actors. On the contrary, the DIMR often makes efforts to voice a more balanced view and, at times, also seeks to mediate between different positions, without compromising on specific positions. As a rule, the DIMR refrains from joining NGO-sponsored public calls and open letters, so as to keep their distinct functions and roles apart. Furthermore, NGOs often have their own contacts and communication avenues to ministries, politicians, or other political actors.

In sum, civil society views the DIMR as an important ally in its goals to promote the indivisibility of human rights and the compliance of German politics with human rights. NGOs and the DIMR share the aim of strengthening guarantees of civil and political rights and of economic, social, and cultural rights, both inside and outside of Germany. They also critically reflect on and influence the human rights policies of the Federal Government and Parliament. Nevertheless, both civil society organisations and the DIMR maintain distinct

---

89 See above 3.1.3.

90 See above 2.3.1.

91 See above 2.3.3.

roles and may, at times, pursue different strategies and avenues to achieve their common goals.

5. CONCLUSION

More than 20 years after its foundation, the DIMR has established itself as a key player for the protection and promotion of human rights at both the national and international levels. During its formative years, the DIMR was viewed with scepticism by many political actors, who did not see the case for an additional institution tasked with assessing conformity with and respect for human rights in Germany, especially in light of the dominant role of the Federal Constitutional Court. However, the Institute has shown that it can deal with many structural and systemic issues which the Constitutional Court would never have been able to address. The DIMR is now an important partner both of the Federal Government and Parliament and civil society, and it is highly respected by state and non-state actors.

The development of the DIMR since its foundation indicates that the struggle for an independent NHRI can be won if a number of conditions are fulfilled. First, it is vital that the NHRI is supported by civil society actors and at least some weighty political actors. While the decision to establish the DIMR was based on a unanimous parliamentary resolution, the path towards this resolution, and especially its subsequent legislative basis, depended very much on civil society input and pressure. Second, the international NHRI framework, especially GANHRI and the SCA, is important. A threat to downgrade a NHRI can work as a catalyst for domestic change, especially where the national government fears that it may lose its international credibility. Third, once established, the further development of a NHRI depends on its leadership and senior staff. If they act as convincing advocates in promoting the institution's cause, they may contribute to securing and broadening the body's mandate. In this context, close working relations between the NHRI and civil society organisations as well as efforts to enhance the NHRI's international visibility and credibility – through interaction with other NHRIs and regional and global human rights frameworks, such as the Council of Europe or the UN – are vital. Active civil society, international support, and institutional credibility propagated through the work of the NHRI's representatives are the interrelated and mutually supportive key factors for any successful NHRI. Above all, however, it is the responsiveness of state actors to the recommendations of the NHRI that is key to the institution's success in promoting and protecting human rights.

INSTITUTO NACIONAL DE DERECHOS HUMANOS (CHILE)

Manuel Núñez Poblete and Sebastián Donoso

1. INTRODUCTION

On 10 December 2009, Law Nr. 20,405 created the *Instituto Nacional de Derechos Humanos* (INDH or the Institute) in Chile: this followed four years of discussion and negotiation in the country's National Congress. President Ricardo Lagos had introduced the original Bill concerning the National Human Rights Institute back in 2005. It was based on the recommendations of several national and international organisations. Initially, the process included general comments and observations received since the 1990s from distinct treaty bodies, which acknowledged the important role that NHRIs can play in monitoring specific human rights instruments.[1] At the regional level, the Organization of American States (OAS) had been promoting the strengthening of these institutions since 2005.[2] Domestically, following an initial announcement by President Lagos in his annual address to the nation, the National Commission on Political Imprisonment and Torture recommended the creation of an NHRI in 2005.[3]

---

1 See generally, Committee on Economic, Social and Cultural Rights, General Comment Nr. 10 of 10 December 1998; Committee on the Elimination of Racial Discrimination, General Recommendation Nr. XVII of 15 December 1993; Committee on the Rights of the Child, General Comment Nr. 2 of 15 November 2002.

2 OAS General Assembly Res. 2132 (XXXV-O/05) of 7 June 2005; OAS General Assembly Res. 2221 (XXXVI-O/06) of 6 June 2006; OAS General Assembly Res. 2345 (XXXVII-O/07) of 5 June 2007; OAS General Assembly Res. 2411 (XXXVIII-O/08) of 3 June 2008.

3 This commission held that:

'In order to protect and promote respect for the rights of individuals and to ensure the implementation of such rights and of new measures to ensure the promotion thereof, the Commission considers it essential to support the initiative of the President of the Republic to establish a National Human Rights Institute. This Institute should be a public body that assists Chilean society to reflect on and study in depth the lessons of the past, to drive initiatives that contribute to building a coexistence based on the respect of the rights of individuals, and to remain vigilant to possible situations of discrimination or violations of these rights. The Institute should also contribute to continuing the work of understanding the truth about past human rights violations and to bring about justice accordingly. Furthermore, it should promote the study and execution of best practices in the dissemination and promotion

Consequently, Law Nr. 20,405 reflected the broader institutional fabric that had begun to be woven throughout the Chilean state following the return of democracy, which, in terms of distinct Transitional Justice measures or decrees, had led to the creation of the National Commission for Truth and Reconciliation[4] as well as the aforementioned National Commission on Political Imprisonment and Torture.[5] The 2005 Law abandoned the paradigm of temporary institutions, replacing it with a permanent NHRI. In this context, the establishment of the INDH was an important step:[6] 18 years had passed since President Patricio Aylwin (1918–2016) had introduced an, ultimately unsuccessful, Bill in the National Congress calling for an ombuds office.[7]

Although incipient, the creation of the INDH marked the beginning of a process of consolidation that would be deepened through 2016 reforms to the Ministry of Justice, which was renamed as the Ministry of Justice and Human Rights, and the subsequent creation of the National Preventive Mechanism against Torture, which was established within the Institute itself. As such, the establishment of the INDH moved Chilean institutions away from the previous comparative models and opened up a new horizon centred around the Institute, which is now over 13 years old.

Table 1. Human rights institutions: key stages

Stage	Institution
Stage 1: memory construction and design of reparations policy	National Commission for Truth and Reconciliation (1990); National Office of Returnees (1990); and National Commission on Political Imprisonment and Torture (2003)

(continued)

of human rights, as well as in the peaceful resolution of disputes. Finally, it should follow up on the implementation of the measures proposed by this Commission.' 2005 report of the National Commission on Political Imprisonment and Torture. Available at: <https://bibliotecadigital.indh.cl/handle/123456789/455>.

4 See Supreme Decree Nr. 3,555 of 25 April 1990, published on 9 May 1990 in the Official Gazette (OG). Chilean legislation concerning the Chilean national reparations policy ran until 2004. Among the most significant Acts are Law Nr. 19,568 (on restitution or compensation for confiscated property); Law Nr. 19,123 (which created the National Corporation for Reparation and Reconciliation and established associated benefits); and Law Nr. 18,994 (which created the National Office of Returnees). For subsequent regulations, see Law Nr. 19,980 (on basic state pensions). On this particular piece of legislation, see E. Lira, 'The Reparations Policy for Human Rights Violations in Chile' in P. de Greiff (ed.), *The Handbook of Reparations*, Oxford University Press, Oxford 2008, pp. 57–94. See generally E. Lira and B. Loveman, *Políticas de reparación. Chile 1990–2004*, LOM, Santiago 2005.

5 See Supreme Decree Nr. 1,040 of 26 September 2003, published on 11 November 2003 in the OG; Supreme Decree Nr. 1,086 of 3 November 2004, published on 17 March 2005 in the OG.

6 Although the Act creating the INDH was enacted in December 2009, the Institute was not established until mid-2010, when the last of its Council members was officially appointed. Its first Council session was held at the National Library of Chile, on 20 July 2010.

7 See President of the Republic of Chile, official provision Nr. 333-07 of 9 April 1991.

Table 1 *continued*

Stage	Institution
Stage 2: institutional consolidation	National Human Rights Institute (2009) and its international accreditation with A-status (2012)
Stage 3: deepening of institutional consolidation	Undersecretary of Human Rights (2016); *Defensoría de la Niñez*, or Children's Ombuds Office (2018); and National Preventive Mechanism against Torture (2019)

Source: Compiled by the authors.

This chapter attempts to explain the composition and main powers of the INDH, emphasising its consultative, autonomous, and collegial character. Subsequently, it seeks to outline what we contend are the primary short-term challenges facing the Institute: i.e., generating a broad and pluralistic understanding of human rights in Chile; positioning the INDH as an agent of change in its field; and strengthening its institutional management.

2. CONSULTATIVE, AUTONOMOUS, AND COLLEGIAL CHARACTER OF THE INDH

According to its organic law, the INDH is 'an autonomous corporation under public law, with legal personality and its own assets'.[8] Its senior management is constituted by a council composed of 11 members, who are appointed as follows:

Table 2. Composition of INDH Council

Number of Council members	Appointment process
2	By the President of the Republic of Chile
2	By the Senate of the Republic of Chile
2	By the Chamber of Deputies of Chile
4	By organisations linked to the defence and promotion of human rights
1	By the deans of the faculties of law of Chilean universities

Source: Compiled by the authors.

From an administrative perspective, the INDH is a collegial and de-centralised body run under the auspices of state administration.[9] From the perspective of Law Nr. 18,575, or Constitutional Organic Act on the General Bases of State

8 Law Nr. 20,405 of the Republic of Chile, art 1.

9 See Office of the Comptroller General of the Republic of Chile, Res. Nr. 38,427 of 18 June 2013.

Administration, the Institute is a 'public service created for the fulfilment of administrative roles'.[10] According to the Office of the General Comptroller of the Republic, the INDH is obliged to submit a declaration of interests and assets,[11] in addition to adhering to state accounting standards.[12] Moreover, by virtue of its organic rules, all state regulations on probity apply to the Institute.[13]

The INDH's consultative nature, autonomy, and collegiality are three key features that characterise the NHRI, and all require a detailed analysis.

2.1. CONSULTATIVE CHARACTER OF THE INDH

By analysing the Institute's powers, it can easily be concluded that the INDH is a primarily advisory or opinion-making body. Aside from its custody of specific archives and its participation in certain judicial proceedings, the vast majority of the INDH's powers are constituted by what the legal doctrine refers to as consultative roles. According to the Institute's Act, these include, *inter alia*:

- preparing an annual report on its own activities and the human rights situation in Chile, which must be submitted to the President of the Republic, National Congress, and the President of the Supreme Court of Justice, and must also be made public to everyone in the country;
- making recommendations, as it deems necessary, for the promotion and protection of human rights;
- communicating to the Chilean government and distinct state bodies, as and where it considers appropriate, its opinion on the human rights situation in any part of the country;
- proposing to state organs those measures that are necessary to respect all human rights in Chile;
- promoting the harmonisation of national legislation, regulations, and practices with international human rights treaties, which have been ratified by Chile and which are currently in force, to ensure their effective implementation;
- collaborating with the Ministry of Foreign Affairs and other related public services in the preparation of reports that the state is required to submit to specialised bodies and committees of the UN and the OAS as well as other regional institutions;

---

10 Office of the Comptroller General of the Republic, Res. Nr. 51,013 of 21 August 2012.

11 See Office of the Comptroller General of the Republic, Res. Nr. 37,866 of 29 May 2014.

12 See Office of the Comptroller General of the Republic, Res. Nr. 79,692 of 22 December 2011.

13 See Law Nr. 20,405 of the Republic of Chile, art 12. Law Nr. 20,880 also requires all Council members to make a declaration of their interests and assets.

- encouraging the dissemination of human rights information and teaching at all levels of the educational system, as well as to the armed forces and the police; and
- providing advice and technical support to public and private organisations that request it on matters that fall within its remit.[14]

Therefore, both legally and politically, the INDH possesses *auctoritas* rather than *potestas*. In other words, the Institute has a socially recognised knowledge in its field, rather than proper power as such. From the multiple options available to the Chilean legislator at the moment of shaping the INDH, a consultative body was chosen over an institution that could receive complaints. Hence, the initial challenge for the INDH was to build its own social legitimacy, which would allow its decisions to be surrounded by 'a certain amount of discursive coercion'.[15] In view of the practice followed during its initial two-year period, the INDH's impartiality was justly criticised by the Chilean legal community, which also highlighted the substantive differences between the Institute and human rights NGOs.[16] This issue had its roots in the previous 40 years of Chilean history: for decades, the discourse on human rights had revolved around political repression and the crimes committed during the dictatorship of Augusto Pinochet (1915–2006). Given this history of concentrating solely on one part of the political spectrum, the pluralistic construction of the INDH's institutional agenda rendered its task difficult, at least initially.

The pre-eminence of *auctoritas* over *potestas* is best and most clearly exhibited in the collectively expressed INDH opinions, memoranda of advice, and recommendations, which are made and delivered according to Law Nr. 20,405. In Chile, the decisions of multi-person administrative bodies 'are called agreements and are carried out by means of resolutions from the executive authority of the corresponding entity'.[17] Thus, in line with the logic of the INDH's Act, it is the Institute's Council that adopts agreements and its Director who executes them. Building a collective opinion requires dialogue within the main deliberative body of the INDH: its Council. Clearly, this process is not easy. Urgent situations are often tragic, such as the first one that confronted the INDH, in December 2010, when a fire in the San Miguel Prison in Santiago claimed the lives of 81 inmates. Such situations require the Institute to intervene quickly, usually through its Director. The media may also generate internal tensions in the INDH Council, making it difficult to reach a consensus.

---

14 See Law Nr. 20,405 of the Republic of Chile, art 3.

15 R. Letelier, 'El Instituto Nacional de Derechos Humanos y la gestión de su *auctoritas*' in J. Couso (ed.), *Anuario de Derecho Público 2011*, Ediciones UDP, Santiago 2011, p. 158.

16 See S. Verdugo and J. Francisco Garcia, 'Radiografía al Instituto Nacional de DD.HH.: entre la política y el Derecho' (2012) 26 *Actualidad Jurídica* 193–252.

17 Law Nr. 19,880 of the Republic of Chile, art 3.7.

The annual report is the main manifestation of the INDH's consultative role. This report is prepared on the basis of an agenda, which is agreed upon by the Council of the INDH and which occupies a significant portion of the work undertaken every year by the Research Unit and its external consultants. The identification of themes to be included in the annual report depends on the consensus reached that year. An attempt was made during the INDH's first five years to maintain a structure that would provide for thematic continuity, while simultaneously allowing the incorporation of unforeseen contingent topics.

From a methodological point of view, the annual report combines qualitative and quantitative analysis, although the former usually dominates the latter. There is a constant effort to support the opinions offered in the report with data. An interesting example can be found in the 2017 report, which provides an account of the national perception of discrimination. Further examples include: the publication, in 2012, of the 'Indicators on Economic, Social and Cultural Rights: The Right to Health and the Right to Work'; the 2013 publication of the 'Indicators on Economic, Social and Cultural Rights'; and the publication, also in 2013, of a report titled 'Monitoring Social Policies to Overcome Poverty and Achieve Equality'. While these publications did not correspond to Council agreements, they stood out in an era characterised by a scarcity of regional studies on human rights methodologies.[18] Unfortunately, this approach is not prevalent within the broader catalogue of INDH reports: a tension has always existed between rigorous data-backed opinions and the drive for activism, which can lead the Institute to make declarations based merely on appearances or assumptions that are deduced from the sole perspective of the alleged victim.

The annual report has been published on 10 occasions; the first report was characterised as report 'Zero', because it was the starting point for a recently constituted NHRI, which had spent its initial months consolidating the process of its own inception. The drive to provide the document with a sense of continuity existed during the 2010–2016 period. In 2017, however, the structure of the report was modified in favour of thematic analyses, followed by recommendations. The main themes covered by each of the 10 reports published thus far were:

---

18 On these regional studies, see D. Vásquez, *Fundamentos teóricos para la metodología aplicada a los derechos humanos*, Comisión de Derechos Humanos del Distrito Federal, Mexico City 2012; Secretaría de Acción Social and Oficina del Alto Comisionado de las Naciones Unidas para los Derechos Humanos, *Indicadores de derechos humanos vinculados a los programas sociales de la Secretaría de Acción Social*, Secretaría de Acción Social, Santiago 2017. Beyond Latin America, the literature is broader. See T. Landman, *Studying Human Rights*, Routledge, Abingdon 2006; J. Asher, D. Banks, and F. Scheuren (eds.), *Statistical Methods for Human Rights*, Springer, New York 2008; F. Coomans, F. Grünfeld, and M. Kamminga (eds.), *Methods of Human Rights Research*, Intersentia, Cambridge 2009; T. Landman and E. Carvalho, *Measuring Human Rights*, Routledge, Abingdon 2009; N. Denzin and M. Giardina (eds.), *Qualitative Inquiry and Human Rights*, Routledge, Abingdon 2010.

Table 3. Themes addressed in Annual Reports

Year	Themes	Recs[19]
2010	Equality and non-discrimination: women; indigenous peoples; sexual diversities; prison population; refugees. Management report.	20
2011	Publicly significant circumstances of the year: prisoners; indigenous peoples; right to education; right to protest. Access to justice: *habeas corpus* and writs of protection; military justice; terrorism; access to justice; women. Economic, social, and cultural rights: labour; health; environment. Equality and non-discrimination: people with special needs; older adults; migrants, children; sexual diversities. Massive, systematic, and institutionalised violations of human rights 1973–1990: right to truth; access to justice; reparation measures.	66
2012	Demands for deepening democracy: democratic security; right to education; indigenous peoples. Democratic institutions: prevention of torture; Undersecretariat for Human Rights; Legal Assistance Corporation; *Defensoría del Pueblo* or Ombuds Office; Law Nr. 20,500; Anti-Discrimination Act; lobbying and reform of the National Service for Minors. Exercise of rights without discrimination: women prisoners; migrants; human trafficking; older adults; persons with disabilities. Economic, social, and cultural rights: health; work; social security; environment; adequate housing. Violations of human rights 1973–1990: truth and memory; access to justice; reparations and compensation. Human rights education. Media and human rights.	77
2013	Demands for deepening democracy: self-determination and self-government of indigenous peoples; land and human rights; right to participation. Access to justice: judicial reforms. Violence and human rights: torture; children; women. Exercise of rights without discrimination: prisoners and social reintegration; young persons; indigenous peoples in urban contexts; migrants and trans persons. Economic, social, and cultural rights: business and human rights; adequate housing; water; quality education. Media and human rights: treatment in the news. Violations of human rights 1973–1990.	50
2014	Challenges of deepening democracy: Constitution and human rights; democratic institutions; natural disasters and emergencies. Access to justice: pretrial detention. Exercise of rights without discrimination: unpaid work in the domestic sphere; autonomy of persons with mental disabilities; Afro-Chileans; child victims and witnesses in legal proceedings; religious freedom. Economic, social, and cultural rights: right to education and freedom of teaching in educational reform; health and maternity; right to work; industrial tribunals. Land and human rights: indigenous peoples; territories and prior consultation; environment; sacrifice zones; environmental institutions. Human rights violations 1973–1990: access to public information; archives; access to justice.	71

(continued)

[19] Recommendations.

Table 3 *continued*

Year	Themes	Recs
2015	Democratic institutions and human rights: corruption and democratic institutions. Economic, social, and cultural rights: poverty and human rights; right to work; right to education. Civil and political rights: public service; right to protection of the family. Exercise of rights without discrimination: prostitution and human rights. Land and human rights: environment; intercultural relations. Violations of human rights 1973–1990: access to justice.	84
2016	Challenges of deepening democracy: democratic institutions and human rights. Equality and non-discrimination: migration and nationality; persons with disabilities. Civil and political rights: NGOs linked to the protection of democracy and human rights; democratic security and human rights; children. Land and human rights: environment; right to health in Chilean regions. Economic, social, and cultural rights: social security and the pension system; obstetric violence; right to education; prisoners. Massive, systematic, and institutionalised violations 1973–1990: exile.	77
2017	Manifestations of racial discrimination. Culture of arbitrary discrimination against women. Trans and intersex children and young persons in health and educational contexts. Torture, cruel, inhuman, and degrading treatment: living conditions in long-term psychiatric units; young persons in state-run detention centres; state-run residential centres for vulnerable children and young persons. Protection of biodiversity, climate change, and human rights. Transitional justice and reparations.	44
2018	Violence against rural indigenous and non-indigenous women: invisible and marginalised. Rights of migrants and the new immigration policy. Memorial sites and their contribution to non-repetition. Natural resources, businesses, and human rights: Impact of industrial activities on natural resources and the environment. Rights of older persons and obligations of the state: care provision in long-term care facilities. Solutions to waiting lists in the public health system. Technological innovation, protection of personal data and human rights.	45
2019	Social crisis of October 2019.[20]	22
2020	Health crisis and COVID 19 pandemic Search for victims of enforced disappearance during dictatorship.	30
2021	The right of peaceful assembly Violence in neighborhoods Women and migrant rights under pandemic Migrant people Transitional justice	36

(continued)

[20] As a result of the civil unrest that began in October 2019, the Council agreed, at its meeting held on 13 November of that year, that this last annual report would concentrate exclusively on violations that occurred during that period.

Table 3 *continued*

Year	Themes	Recs
2022	Human rights victims in democracy Human rights in rural territories Water, climate change and sustainable development Religious freedom, intolerance and hate speech Elder people rights Child rights in school after pandemic Enforced disappearance	111

Source: Compiled by the authors.

As can be seen, these themes are varied and accurately encapsulate the Chilean social and political history of the last decade: from crisis in the educational, prison, environmental, immigration, and children's systems, to the political crisis of 2019 and the pandemic of 2020-2021. The persistence of problems associated with Transitional Justice should also be noted, in addition to the emergence of less publicised but no less important issues, such as the situation of vulnerable rural groups or technological progress. Naturally, the INDH Council also tends to provide space for issues that reflect the broad plurality of its members, including those of indigenous peoples, children, constitutional change, NGOs, and religious freedom.

From a quantitative perspective, the total number of recommendations made in the INDH's annual reports generally exceeds 500. This figure does not take account of the fact that the INDH also approves sectorial reports, which involves a process that requires the generation of further recommendations throughout the year. It is undoubtedly a huge challenge for the INDH to implement follow-up processes for its recommendations: due to their sheer number as well as a high rate of non-compliance, they run the risk of being devalued or simply forgotten.

2.2. AUTONOMOUS CHARACTER OF THE INDH

This particular characteristic was deliberately attributed to the, as yet non-existent, institution, via the presidential message that subsequently became law:

> It is an entity autonomous of the government and therefore not subject to hierarchical control, supervision or oversight. The text expressly stresses that it is an 'autonomous corporation'. In order to guarantee its autonomy, it is provided with its own legal personality. Thus, it does not require recourse to the legal personality of the State in order to act in the legal sphere. This is reinforced by its legal personality under public law, which is granted by the legislative branch and cannot be revoked by administrative authorities or the courts.[21]

[21] President of the Republic of Chile (Michelle Bachelet), official provision 3878-17 of 19 May 2005.

The institutional autonomy of the INDH has a dual nature: both national and international.[22] This institutional characteristic can be understood in a number of different ways, for example, as independence or as administrative autonomy.

Independence or legal autonomy is a special attribute assigned to the administrative organisation of a constituted entity. In Chile, autonomous public law organisations, such as the INDH, are not common; however, this was the form chosen for the INDH, on the basis that it best suited the various roles that were to be played by the Institute.[23] As the Paris Principles on NHRIs expressly state, as interpreted by the Sub-Committee of Accreditation (SCA) of the Global Alliance of National Human Rights Institutions (GANHRI),[24] an NHRI is required 'to be independent from government in its structure, composition, decision-making and method of operation'.[25] Furthermore, '[i]t must be constituted and empowered to consider and determine the strategic priorities and activities of the NHRI based solely on its determination of the human rights priorities in the country, free from political interference'.[26] If independence is the organic expression of autonomy, the power to self-regulate is its rules-based equivalent. Administrative autonomy unambiguously resides in the INDH Council. Law Nr. 20,405 explicitly granted statutory and internal autonomy to it, declaring that it is the responsibility of the INDH Council to enact its statutes and modifications as well as all its internal rules for operation, including those related to its organisation.[27] In fact, the only limitation placed on the autonomy of the INDH Council is the requirement that all of its statutes must be approved by the President of the Republic, by means of a supreme decree. This normative autonomy is a manifestation of the collegial nature of the Institute.[28] In the

---

22 See Law Nr. 20,405 of the Republic of Chile, art 2.

23 See Letelier (n 15) p. 157.

24 GANHRI was formerly known as the International Coordinating Committee of National Institutions for the Promotion and Protection of Human Rights (ICC). The ICC was formally established at an international conference, held in Tunis in 1993, which was aimed at coordinating NHRI activities worldwide. Since changing its name to GANHRI in 2016, the main mission of the network has focused on the accreditation and re-accreditation of NHRIs, according to their level of compliance with the Paris Principles. Even though GANHRI is a private law organisation, incorporated under Swiss law, it administers this international peer review-system, which allows accredited NHRIs to access the Human Rights Council and other UN treaty bodies. See G. de Beco, 'Compliance with the Paris Principle and the ICC Sub-Committee on Accreditation' in J. Wouters and K. Meuwissen (eds.), *National Human Rights Institutions in Europe. Comparative, European and International Perspectives*, Intersentia, Cambridge 2013, pp. 248–62.

25 General Observation 1.9 of the SCA, of 21 February 2018. Available at: <https://nhri.ohchr.org/EN/AboutUs/GANHRIAccreditation/General%20Observations%201/EN_GeneralObservations_Revisions_adopted_21.02.2018_vf.pdf>.

26 ibid.

27 See Law Nr. 20,405 of the Republic of Chile, arts 8.1, 8.9.

28 See J. Valero, *Los órganos colegiados: análisis histórico de la colegialidad en la organización pública española y régimen jurídico-administrativo vigente*, Instituto Nacional de Administración Pública, Madrid 2002, p. 491.

exercise of its powers, as expressly assigned to it by Law Nr. 20,405, the INDH Council has issued regulations on the following institutional issues: personnel, internal structure, order, hygiene, and security, among others.[29]

2.3. COLLEGIAL CHARACTER OF THE INDH

According to Manfred Nowak, there are three distinct types of NHRI: multi-person commissions; single-person ombudsmen; and research and documentation institutions, also known as the Danish model.[30] The INDH clearly belongs to the first category, which Thomas Pegram classifies as being among the varied group of human rights commissions.[31] It is in this commission-type configuration that the INDH is included as one of the collegial bodies that constitute the Chilean state administration. In contrast to bodies employing a single-person or monocratic institutional design, the collegial nature of the INDH facilitates relationships of equality, horizontal alignment, and *pari* or *equi* status across its council members.[32] This multi-person or collegial structure is, according to Guido Corso, characteristic of consultative bodies and entities which operate on the basis of political representation.[33]

In accordance with Law Nr. 18,575, which established the Constitutional Organic Act on the General Bases of State Administration, collegiality is not the general rule in Chile. As this Act states, '[i]n exceptional circumstances, law may establish collegial councils or bodies in line with the structure of the public services with such powers that the law may specify, including the senior management of the service'.[34] The INDH is precisely one such case, albeit uncommon, in which the law directly and expressly entrusts its Council with the 'Senior Management' of the institution.[35] The INDH Director is, on

---

29 The minutes of the INDH Council are available at: <https://bibliotecadigital.indh.cl/handle/123456789/1195>.

30 See M. Nowak, 'National Human Rights Institutions in Europe: Comparative, European and International Perspectives' in J. Wouters and K. Meuwissen (eds.), *National Human Rights Institutions in Europe. Comparative, European and International Perspectives*, Intersentia, Cambridge 2013, pp. 15–16.

31 See T. Pegram, 'Diffusion across Political Systems: The Global Spread of National Human Rights Institutions' (2010) 32/2 *Hum.Rts.Q.* 729, 735.

32 See G. Pepe, 'La posizione giuridica del Presidente negli organi collegiali político-asambleari' (2015) 1 *Nomos. Le attualità nel diritto* 1, 2; J. Alfonso Santamaría, *Fundamentos de derecho administrativo*, Centro de Estudios Ramón Areces, Madrid 1991, p. 860. See generally E. Carbonell, *Los órganos colegiados: organización, funcionamiento, procedimiento y régimen jurídico de sus actos*, Centro de Estudios Políticos y Constitucionales, Madrid 1999; J.J. Menuret and C. Reiplinger (eds.), *La collégialité, valeurs et significations en droit public*, Bruylant, Brussels 2012.

33 See G. Corso, *Manuale di diritto amministrativo*, Giappichelli, Turin 2017, p. 14.

34 Law Nr. 18,575 of the Republic of Chile, art 31.

35 Law Nr. 20,405 of the Republic of Chile, art 6.

the other hand, endowed with the administrative and executive management responsibilities entrusted to him or her by the Council.[36] It is important to stress this, because the decision to alter the collegiality of the body does not vest in the INDH itself, or even the judicial branch, but, instead, in the Chilean legislator.[37]

Another consequence of the Institute's collegiality is the application of the principle of majority, as expressed in the INDH's Act.[38] This principle reinforces the need to attain agreements within the Council, in order to exercise all of the Institute's powers.[39] As a final note on the Institute's collegial nature, it is the Council itself that is tasked with electing and removing the Institute's Director: this occurs where an absolute majority is reached by the Council's members.[40]

2.4. WORKING GUARANTEES

In terms of composition, the INDH is a pluralistic body. It combines the expert approach of Council members appointed by universities and civil society, with the political input of those elected by the Senate, the Chamber of Deputies, and the President of the Republic. In accordance with the Paris Principles on NHRIs, nominees to the INDH Council do not act on behalf of those who appointed or elected them and are in no way accountable to these institutions. On the contrary, members of the Institute's Council act in a purely personal capacity and maintain no kind of relationship of dependence with the appointing or electing authority.

In 2012, the SCA observed two sensitive issues concerning the INDH Council: the legal immunity of its Council members and its funding. With regard to the former, Chilean law establishes certain guarantees in cases of the removal of Council members from their position, but it lacks a concrete provision to protect them from legal liability for actions performed in their Institutional capacity.[41] As to its budget, the SCA stressed that the INDH should have sufficient funding

---

36 See Law Nr. 20,405 of the Republic of Chile, art 9.

37 For example, this is the position that the National Congress took with regard to the National Sports Institute, when it modified, in Law Nr. 20,686, the body's original collegial structure, which had been previously enshrined in Law Nr. 19,787. Due to the changes introduced by the Act, this Institute was transformed from a collegial to a single-member entity.

38 See Law Nr. 20,405 of the Republic of Chile, art 6.

39 See Law Nr. 20,405 of the Republic of Chile, art 3.

40 See Law Nr. 20,405 of the Republic of Chile, art 6.3. In 1998, the INDH's Director was removed by the Council. This situation led to a judgment of the Supreme Court of Justice, in which it ruled that the removal of an individual by the Institute's Council from the position of Director is not equivalent to the removal of an individual from the position of Council member. In other words, as *primus inter pares*, the Director can be removed by an absolute majority among the Council members, but he or she will continue in their role as a member of the Council. See Supreme Court of Justice, *Branislav Marelic v. INDH and others*, Judgment, 24 September 2018, Case Nr. 8,135-2,018.

41 See Law Nr. 20,405 of the Republic of Chile, art 7. The SCA noted that 'the independence of the INDH and its members is promoted, and the possibility of outside interference is

to reasonably ensure the fulfilment of its mandate.[42] This observation is highly significant, given the fact that the Institute's competence is both general – i.e., it can be contrasted with a body that is limited to a particular subject – and national, which has potentially significant budgetary implications: purely due to the fact that the INDH's mandate covers a significant and complex territory, in terms of both land area and the peculiar fact that the Chilean territory is several thousand kilometers long, from a North-South perspective.

It is also worth pointing out that Chilean law expressly entitles the INDH to request information from police authorities and conduct visits to detention facilities.[43] Unfortunately, there are no sanctions for those who fail to provide information to the INDH or for those who deny INDH agents access to detention facilities.[44] These deficiencies are not merely theoretical: state officials have frequently perceived the INDH as a nuisance and, far from assisting it in its work, have even impeded the Institute's activities.

3. MANDATE OF THE INDH

In general terms, there is full concordance between the type of NHRI mandate expected by the Paris Principles and the powers bestowed concretely upon the INDH under Law Nr. 20,405. When comparing these two instruments, it is possible to observe a broad resemblance:

Table 4. Paris Principles and powers of the INDH

Paris Principles	Law 20,405
To promote and protect human rights	✓ However, the INDH cannot receive formal complaints

(continued)

reduced, by means of the inclusion of a clear provision in the legislative basis of an NHRI to protect members of the governing body from legal liability for actions taken in their official capacity'. Report and Recommendations of the Session of the Sub-Committee on Accreditation, Geneva, 19–23 November 2012, of the Global Alliance of National Human Rights Institutions, para. 2.3.

42 See ibid.

43 The INDH's act provides that '[i]n order to exercise its powers, the Institute may request the cooperation of State bodies. It may also receive all testimony and obtain all information and documentation necessary for the examination of situations coming under its sphere of influence. Similarly, it may commission one or more Council members, the Director or his/her staff to enter public premises where a person is or may be deprived of liberty'. Law Nr. 20.405 of the Republic of Chile, art 4.

44 It should be noted that during the INDH's first years of operation, the police refused to include their own institutional vehicles under the definition of premises or detention spaces. This

Table 4 *continued*

Paris Principles	Law 20,405
To provide advice	✓
To promote and ensure the harmonisation of national legislation regulations and practices	✓
To encourage the ratification of international human rights instruments	✓
To contribute to the reports required by UN bodies and committees, and those of regional institutions	✓
To cooperate with the UN and any other organisation in the UN system, regional institutions, and national institutions of other countries that are competent in the areas of the promotion and protection of human rights	✓
To assist in the formulation of programmes for the teaching of, and research into, human rights and to take part in their execution in schools, universities, and professional circles	✓
To publicise human rights and efforts to combat all forms of discrimination	✓

Source: Compiled by the authors.

As will be explained further, these functions have evolved over time.

3.1. THE CONSULTATIVE ROLE OF THE INDH

The Institute's annual report is the main product of its consultative role: a power that is framed by constitutional and legal norms, international treaties in force in Chile, and even general principles of law.[45] This regulatory scheme exceeds

created serious problems of accountability, since police vehicles are frequently used as places of detention for protesters, often for several hours, during demonstrations. To secure access to these vehicles, the INDH was required to seek a ruling from the Office of the Comptroller General of the Republic of Chile, who declared that police cars, vans, and other vehicles were, in fact, detention spaces and that the police could not, therefore, deny INDH officials access to such spaces. As the Office of the Comptroller General then stated:

'Accordingly, the concept of a public premises in which a person is or may be deprived of liberty, referred to in Law 20,405, article 4.2 must be interpreted in a such a way that enables the fulfilment of the objectives of the INDH and which acts in harmony with the provisions of the international treaties, being useful to specify that in this context the sense of being "under the care of" that the forgoing legal precept contemplates is that, by means of this provision, the Institute obtains the necessary background information to exercise the powers granted thereto under article 3 of the foregoing law, among which is the power to bring legal proceedings before the courts .... In accordance with the foregoing, it should be understood that it is applicable in law for the INDH to commission the persons referred to in the aforementioned paragraph 2 of article 4 to enter any area of spatial confinement under the care of public officials where a deprivation of liberty may occur, in order to obtain the necessary background information required for the fulfilment of the powers of that entity, which is the regulatory hypothesis in the case of police vehicles.'

Office of the Comptroller General of the Republic, Res. Nr. 58,070 of 21 September 2012.

45 See Law Nr. 20,405 of the Republic of Chile, art 2.

simple notions of individual or collective political opinion. However, the sources of international human rights law are multiple, and they sometimes contradict each other; there is also a natural tension between what is stipulated domestically and internationally in this regard. This conflict tends to be irrelevant when the corresponding domestic rule is situated in an ordinary law, but it becomes potentially problematic and may lead to a conflict of laws when the rule forms part of the Political Constitution of the Republic of Chile. In such cases, the INDH Council must debate the matter and select the most favourable regulation. When making this choice, the Institute inevitably follows the criteria advanced by the Chilean Constitutional Court which deal with conflicts between international and constitutional rules.[46] Nevertheless, if the relevant issue is viewed from the perspective of the Paris Principles on NHRIs, an argument in favour of the treaty emerges.[47]

Within this consultative role, and perhaps as a symptomatic result of an observable devaluation of the domestic constitutional rule in Chile,[48] international law has acquired a significant relevance in the country. In this respect, two phenomena can be observed. Firstly, when the rights at issue before the INDH Council were neatly defined for recommendation purposes, agreement among the Council was easily reached: with a focus placed on the treaties in force at the time, rather than on the Political Constitution. This

---

46 See Political Constitution of the Republic of Chile, art 5.2. See also Constitutional Court of Chile, *Estatuto de Roma de la Corte Penal Internacional*, Judgment, 8 April 2002, Case Nr. 346-2002; Constitutional Court of Chile, *Artículo 1°, numerales 20,3, letra c) y 48 del Proyecto que modifica la Ley N° 18.892, General de Pesca y Acuicultura*, Judgment, 23 January 2013, Case Nr. 2387-2012. Like art 5 of the Chilean Constitution, art 2 of Law Nr. 20,405 includes open-ended formulas, which are based on references to 'the essential rights that derive from human nature' or 'general principles of law', while simultaneously limiting referral to 'international treaties ratified by Chile and currently in force'.

47 See UN General Assembly Res. 48/134 of 20 December 1993, para. 3.d.

48 The relationship between the Political Constitution and international human rights bodies has never been straightforward. As is widely documented, the UN viewed the Constitution, from its inception in 1980, as an instrument drafted with a lack of public participation, with flaws that allowed for 'interference with human rights and fundamental freedoms'. (UN General Assembly Res. A/RES/36/157 of 16 December 1981, preamble.)
This reproach remained more or less intact in its relevance until the end of the 1980s, since 'the institutional and legal framework that makes human rights violations possible [had] remained unchanged'. (UN General Assembly Res. A/RES/43/158 of 8 December 1988; UN General Assembly Res. A/RES/44/166 of 15 December 1989.)
The UN General Assembly has passed 16 resolutions on Chile, since 1974: all during the dictatorship of Augusto Pinochet. The Chilean situation in these years even led to the formation of the first *ad hoc* working group of the former UN Commission on Human Rights, in 1975, which subsequently became a special rapporteur four years later. In addition, the Inter-American Commission on Human Rights (IACHR) held a severe view of the human rights situation in the country as well as in the Political Constitution, especially its transitional article XXIV, which characterised the regime as an 'emergency' administration. See e.g., OEA/Ser. L/V/II.50 of 2 October 1980; OEA/Ser. L/V/II.57 of 20 September 1982; OEA/Ser. L./V/II.63 of 28 September 1984.

explains why, even to the present day, a significant number of the economic rights that are constitutionally enshrined in Chile, but which have no immediate correlation with any rule of international human rights law (for example, the right to carry out any economic activity), have been left out of the INDH's annual reports. Secondly, the Institute operates as something of a 'conveyor belt', not only between civil society and the state[49] but also between the domestic legal system and international law. With regard to the latter, the INDH has promoted the so-called 'spill-over' effect, through which international standards enter into the domestic sphere.[50] This effect can be seen in the everyday language used by the Institute's authorities, who constantly resort to the so-called 'international standards', as well as in its reports. It is no exaggeration to say that the current working method within the INDH is essentially based on international case-law and the doctrine of human rights treaty bodies. In this context, it is easy for the Institute to defer entirely to a wide range of international sources, ranging from case-law, to recommendations, to national reports, and those of special rapporteurs, etc. In the process, the body could be charged with reserving all of its critical approaches for domestic proceedings. Unfortunately, it is not uncommon for human rights lawyers to yield to activism.[51] Because these professionals are part of, or at least provide advice to, some civil society groups, which only accept pronouncements from the INDH, this puts added pressure on its work.

3.2. THE INDH AS A LEGAL ACTOR

The ability to intervene in legal proceedings is outlined in the Institute's act, which grants it the power to:

> [p]resent legal proceedings that fall within its remit before the courts of justice. In the exercise of this power, in addition to presenting complaints in relation to acts of the nature of the crime of genocide, crimes against humanity or war crimes, torture,

---

49 The description used here is based on the statement of the UN High Commissioner for Human Rights, Navanethem Pillay, on the 10th International Conference of NHRIs held in Edinburgh, UK, on 8–10 October 2010. Available at: <https://www.ohchr.org/Documents/Issues/Business/HC_NHRIConference08102010.pdf>.

50 See K. Meuwissen and J. Wouters, 'Conclusion: Towards a Better Understanding of European NHRIs in a Multi-Layered Human Rights System' in J. Wouters and K. Meuwissen (eds.), *National Human Rights Institutions in Europe. Comparative, European and International Perspectives*, Intersentia, Cambridge 2013, p. 305. See also K. Roberts, 'National Human Rights Institutions as Diplomacy Actors' in M. O'Flaherty, K. Zdzislaw, A. Müller, and G. Ulrich (eds.), *Human Rights Diplomacy: Contemporary Perspectives*, Martinus Nijhoff, Leiden 2011, pp. 243–44.

51 See F. Coomans, F. Grünfeld, and M. Kamminga, 'A primer' in F. Coomans, F. Grünfeld, and M. Kamminga (eds.), *Methods of Human Rights Research*. Intersentia, Cambridge 2009, p. 14.

> forced disappearances, illicit trafficking of migrants or trafficking in persons, it may also present the writs of protection and habeas corpus enshrined in articles 20 and 21 of the Constitution, respectively, in areas that fall within its remit.[52]

Although this provision has been interpreted as being restrictive, for instance where other entities intervene in criminal proceedings on behalf of the state, this has not prevented the INDH from exercising its consultative role at the courts by submitting *amicus curiae* briefs.

At a legal level, the objective of the procedural legitimacy granted to the INDH goes far beyond the actual resolution of a particular case: it also involves the formation of precedents for subsequent cases. For example, during the second year of the INDH's operation, the Supreme Court of Justice ruled on a case filed by the Institute; it resulted in a devastating decision, which limited the role of writs of protection in cases related to the use of force by Chilean police.[53] Fortunately, this judicial doctrine has changed over time, not only for writs of protection but also for writs of *habeas corpus*, many of which are filed by the INDH. *Amicus curiae* briefs, which are common in international proceedings, had a less than enthusiastic reception in Chilean courts. In the first months of the INDH's operations, tribunals were reluctant to receive *amicus curiae* briefs from the Institute, and they were even less willing to accept the Institute's lawyers at hearings.[54] Perhaps due to a lack of education on international human rights law, Chilean judges of the time had limited knowledge of the theory and practice of such briefs, and some were even suspicious of them. It was therefore necessary for the INDH to hold meetings with higher-court judges, to explain to them the Institute's role and the purely consultative nature of *amici curiae*.[55] The

---

52 Law Nr. 20,405 of the Republic of Chile, art 3.

53 See Supreme Court of Justice, *INDH v. Carabineros de Chile*, Judgment, 17 July 2012, Case Nr. 4.143-2012.

54 In response to a request to admit an *amicus curiae* brief from the INDH, the Supreme Court of Justice responded with the *acuerdo*, or agreement, of 15 November 2013, which stated that:

> '[T]he institution of *amicus curiae* lacks legal recognition in the Chilean legal system, with the exception of environmental matters, and it is not possible to determine its origin in light of the procedural rules that regulate third parties who can present at legal hearings, since their application is restricted to cases expressly provided for by legislators … [T]he intervention of the National Human Rights Institute in human rights trials may take the form of a writ presented in those cases provided for by law, or as an intervener, or adviser, at the request of the court. Any other intervention or presentation other than those aforementioned must be resolved by the court in which the claim is made, which must determine its origin according to the merit and purpose of the process thereof. Consequently, in the opinion of the Supreme Court, it is not appropriate to pass general instruction to the national courts regarding this matter.'

(See Supreme Court of Justice, Memorandum of 26 November 2013.).

55 It was not until 2012, with the enactment of Law Nr. 20,417, that Chilean legislation expressly recognised the legal standing of *amici curiae*.

INDH Council also discussed internally how its views, which are institutional in nature, should always be agreed upon by a majority, before any exercise of the Institute's role as a legal actor.[56]

3.3. THE INDH'S ROLE AS OFFICIAL ARCHIVE CUSTODIAN

According to its Act, the INDH must safeguard and protect the records compiled by: the National Commission for Truth and Reconciliation; the National Corporation for Reparation and Reconciliation; the Human Rights Programme; and the National Commission on Political Imprisonment and Torture.[57] Keeping custody of these archives and of others that were brought to the offices of the INDH, such as those related to the *Colonia Dignidad* case, generated a subsequent problem for the Institute: that of deciding whether to provide or deny access to the information contained therein, both to interested parties and third parties. The conflict between the confidentiality of the records and the rights of those requesting access was the subject of a debate which was eventually included in the Institute's 2014 annual report.[58]

3.4. COLLABORATION WITH THE GOVERNMENT, THE UN AND REGIONAL HUMAN RIGHTS INSTITUTIONS

The Institute acts as a focal point and communicator of both legal standards and civil society expectations, with the aim of bringing about the institutional transformations required of the Chilean state.[59] The A-status that was awarded to the INDH by the SCA in 2012 has enabled the Institute to maintain a free-flowing relationship with the UN Human Rights Committee. Similarly, since 2010, the INDH has cooperated in the preparation of all Chilean periodic reports to the various UN treaty bodies, and it has participated in various organs of the Inter-American System for the protection of human rights. Within this sphere and despite the fact that the presence of the INDH is virtually non-existent within the pronouncements of the IACHR relating to Chile – i.e., reports on

56 For illustrative purposes, see the minutes of the 101st session, of 25 June 2012; the 139th session, of 21 January 2013; and the 16th session, of 15 November 2010. The minutes of the INDH Council are available at: <https://www.portaltransparencia.cl/PortalPdT/pdtta/-/ta/CO001>.

57 See Law Nr. 20,405 of the Republic of Chile, art 3.c.

58 See INDH, *Situación de los derechos humanos en Chile. Informe anual 2014*, INDH, Santiago 2014, pp. 273–89.

59 See J-W. Koo and F. Ramírez, 'National Incorporation of Global Human Rights: Worldwide Expansion of National Human Rights Institutions, 1966–2004' (2009) 87/3 *Social Forces* 1321, 1324.

admissibility and on the merits – there are certain cases in which the Institute has been involved, for example, in proposals aimed at Chilean compliance with recommendations included in the IACHR's documents.[60] With regard to the Inter-American Court of Human Rights (IACtHR), when adjudicating cases against Chile, from 2010 onwards, the opinion of the INDH has not been relevant to the positions taken by the parties, nor has it been deemed pertinent within the decisions of the Court.[61] However, in a compliance monitoring judgment, the IACtHR noted that an *amicus curiae* brief tendered by the INDH had provided 'other information' which was distinct from that submitted by the state.[62] The process of building the authority and international standing of the INDH is gradual, and its consolidation will, necessarily, take some time.

3.5. EDUCATION AND PROMOTION OF HUMAN RIGHTS

The INDH is responsible for: disseminating knowledge about human rights; encouraging the teaching of human rights at all levels of the educational system, including the training of police and the armed forces; and promoting human rights research.[63] This role is based on the preamble to the Universal Declaration of Human Rights, the Vienna Declaration and Programme of Action, and the majority of human rights treaties, which all emphasise the importance of publicising information about the human rights treaty obligations of states.[64] This competence also lines up with the approach of the World Programme for Human Rights Education, which has been in place since 2005.[65] In this respect, the INDH has performed an important task since its inception: although its work has yet to yield profound outcomes across the Chilean state, or Chilean society at large, its efforts have been reflected in distinct post-graduate and diploma courses, collaborative activities with universities, and the training of public officials. One particularly critical area has been the Institute's work with armed and police forces.

60 See e.g., OEA/Ser. L./V/II.159 of 29 November 2016 para. 2.

61 See *Órdenes and others v. Chile*, IACtHR, Judgment, 29 November 2018, Series C Nr. 372; *Poblete and others v. Chile*, IACtHR, Judgment, 8 March 2018, Series C Nr. 349; *Norín and others ('Dirigentes, miembros y activista del pueblo indígena Mapuche') v. Chile*, IACtHR, Judgment, 29 May 2014, Series C Nr. 279; *Garcia Lucero and others v. Chile*, IACtHR, Judgment, 28 August 2013, Series C Nr. 267; *Atala and girls v. Chile*, IACtHR, Judgment, 24 February 2012, Series C Nr. 239.

62 *Palamara v. Chile*, IACtHR, Monitoring compliance with judgment, 1 September 2006, para. 4.

63 See Law Nr. 20,405 of the Republic of Chile, art 3.9.

64 See G. de Beco and R. Murray, *A Commentary on the Paris Principles on Human Rights Institutions*, Cambridge University Press, Cambridge 2015, p. 46.

65 See UN General Assembly Res. 59/113 A of 17 February 2005. See also Human Rights Council Res. 15/11 of 30 September 2010, which approved the adoption of the plan of action for the Programme's second stage.

3.6. NATIONAL PREVENTIVE MECHANISM AGAINST TORTURE

In 2019, the INDH was designated as the Chilean National Preventive Mechanism against Torture and other Cruel, Inhuman or Degrading Treatment or Punishment.[66] To fulfil its role as this mechanism, the INDH 'shall act exclusively through the Committee for the Prevention of Torture'.[67] From an administrative perspective, a second collegial body – referred to here as the national torture prevention mechanism, or NTPM – has been created, with the specific power to submit opinions and act on matters related to torture. This is interesting, as the NTPM corresponds, in terms of its nature, to an internal body within the INDH; however, despite being created by the INDH Council, the mechanism is free from its tutelage or supervision. In other words, the INDH Council intervened, in conjunction with the civil service, in the creation of the NTPM, but since its installation, the new body has had all of the independence necessary for the fulfilment of its duties.[68] The autonomy of the NTPM committee is, however, limited in exceptional circumstances: when it is required to act through the INDH[69] or when it is required to submit recommendations to the Institute.[70] In such cases, the NTPM's power is placed under the control of the INDH Council.

4. INSTITUTIONAL CHALLENGES[71]

The INDH's 13-year existence has coincided with the creation of additional national bodies which perform essential work in what is today a comprehensive institutional framework for the protection and promotion of human rights in Chile. Such bodies include: the Undersecretariat for Human Rights, operating under the Ministry of Justice and Human Rights; the Office for the Protection of Children, established as an independent entity of the INDH; and the aforementioned National Preventive Mechanism against Torture and Other Cruel, Inhuman or Degrading Treatment or Punishment. In terms of public policy, this institutional framework has been strengthened by the adoption of the first National Human Rights Plan, for the four-year period 2018–2021, and

66 See Law Nr. 21,154 of the Republic of Chile.

67 ibid, art 1.

68 This is manifested through the use of the adverb 'exclusively' in art 1 of this Committee's Act.

69 See Law Nr. 21,154 of the Republic of Chile, art 3.l.

70 See ibid, art 3.i.

71 Some of the challenges described in this section were faced in the constitutional proposal of 2022. The text proposed by the Convention replaced the INDH with a *Defensoría del Pueblo* led by a single authority elected by the Congress. The *Defensoría de la Niñez* was also included in the proposal as an autonomous institution. In the referendum of 4 September 2022, the Chilean voters rejected overwhelmingly the constitutional proposal, consequently the INDH remained unmodified.

the drafting of the first National Business and Human Rights Action Plan, for the three-year period 2017–2019, among other measures.

In this context, there are three main challenges faced by the INDH: first, issues relating to the Institute's efforts to fulfil its mandate and mission, in line with the Institute's act; second, making sure not to deviate from the guidelines provided by the Paris Principles; and third, cooperating with other institutions to achieve the shared objective of promoting and protecting human rights.

All of these challenges are reflected, in some way or other, in the INDH's Strategic Plan for 2018–2023. In this plan, the INDH is described as the specialised state agency that contributes to the consolidation of a democratic culture which respects human rights. According to this plan, the Institute's threefold mission is defined as: promoting a culture of respect for human rights in an autonomous and pluralistic manner; monitoring the state's work on the basis of human rights standards; and protecting the dignity of people living in Chile.[72] The INDH's pillars or 'strategic themes' for the 2018–2023 period are consistent with this mission, and they seek to: generate a broad and pluralistic understanding of human rights in the country; position the INDH as an agent of change in the field of human rights; and strengthen its institutional management.[73]

4.1. GENERATE A BROAD AND PLURALISTIC UNDERSTANDING OF HUMAN RIGHTS IN CHILE

If the first challenge faced by the INDH was to provide historical continuity to the human rights discourse, by building bridges between a painful recent past in Chile and current problems, the second task was to broaden this discourse, to include all human rights, particularly in the fields of non-discrimination and economic, social, and cultural rights.[74] Although the Institute undertook important human rights education and training work in its early years, particularly in relation to public officials, the task remains unfinished. On one hand, it has proven quite difficult to combat biased views of human rights in Chile, which are bound to traumatic experiences from the country's highly-politicised recent past. On the other hand, a portion of Chilean society feels that the INDH does not understand them and considers the Institute to be a biased entity that represents merely a partial view of human rights. Furthermore, social and political movements are emerging in Chile that question basic assumptions of the international human rights system, such as those that advocate for so-called 'penal populism'. All these situations put a strain on the INDH, which,

72 See ibid.

73 See ibid.

74 See L. Fries, 'El Instituto Nacional de Derechos Humanos 2010–2016: recapitulación y proyecciones' (2015) 10 *Cuadernos de Difusión* 21, 25.

like any other NHRI, must ensure the pluralist representation of all social forces within its membership, without making concessions to ideologies that relativise the universal value of human rights.

To overcome the view that human rights are exclusively or primarily related to civil and political rights, and particularly those violated in Chile during the 1973–1990 period, the INDH has periodically conducted the National Human Rights Survey. The survey has documented that economic, social, and cultural rights have a consistent standing within the general public. In the fourth survey, carried out in 2018, responses to the question: 'which rights are you most aware of?' indicated that economic, social, and cultural rights are at the forefront of Chilean minds: the four most common responses to the question correspond to the rights to health, education, housing, and work, respectively.[75] Beyond this, the INDH is constantly addressing global social and political trends that have an impact on how human rights are perceived. This is not an easy task, as it requires the INDH to exhibit a willingness to listen to and genuinely enquire about the concerns that underpin these trends, such as resistance to immigration, while also affirming the universal value of the rights involved. The pluralist composition of the Institute's senior management body, its Council, is certainly an institutional strength when it comes to meeting this challenge. As Manfred Nowak has stated:

> In general, multi-member human rights commissions appear to meet the minimum standards of the Paris Principles better than one-person ombudsman institutions and human rights research institutes. First of all, the requirement of pluralism, which includes fair representation of different civil society actors (NGOs, professional organizations, universities, religious organizations, etc.), can be undertaken far more easily in a multi-member commission than in a one-person institution.[76]

In spite of this, the most visible face of the INDH is that of its Director, who, as its spokesperson, periodically issues statements in accordance with the Institute's legal mandate. Given the fact that the Director is the only member of the INDH Council who exclusively dedicates his or her time to institutional tasks, and whose main role is to execute the Council's agreements, this role makes sense. However, there are also particular disadvantages associated with the Director's prominent role. First, it is common for a spokesperson to react to issues as and when they arise. In the case of the INDH, this can mean that the Director's reactions may not necessarily reflect the Council's views. Second, if all spokesperson-related responsibilities are placed on the shoulders of a

---

75 The results are similar in terms of the surveyed population's perceptions of the most violated rights. See INDH, National Human Rights Survey 2018. Available at: <https://www.indh.cl/destacados-2/encuesta-ddhh/>.

76 Nowak (n 30) p. 25.

single person, it can cause tension, especially given the collegial nature of the institution. Third, when the Director refers to a matter that is not the subject of a consensus position in the INDH Council, the concentration of power within his or her position prevents the Council's diversity of opinions from being heard. It could be argued that, in these situations, the INDH Council may issue public statements and that Council members should be able to express their opinions in a personal capacity.

There is a further challenge regarding pluralism at the INDH. According to its legal mandate, the Institute must periodically issue particular documents. Although the INDH Council defines their content and approves their final version, the documents themselves are prepared by a team of professionals working at the INDH. Consequently, and as is the case within the Council, the composition of the Institute's staff must reflect the main political, social, and economic views that exist in Chilean civil society: so that, in turn, the institutional documents exhibit a pluralistic perspective on the subject at issue. As Nowak warns, 'the effective monitoring of human rights is a very politically sensitive task that requires a particularly high level of professionalism'.[77] In an NHRI, this professionalism is required at all levels.

4.2. POSITIONING THE INDH AS AN AGENT OF CHANGE IN THE FIELD OF HUMAN RIGHTS

The INDH's latest Strategic Plan highlights the active role that the institution must play in guiding concrete actions that are aimed at modifying relevant human rights situations in favour of the inhabitants of Chile. Being an agent of change requires the INDH to get involved in the legislative and regulatory spheres. An example of such action can be seen in the marked role that the INDH played, in October 2018, in dealing with the fall-out from the crisis linked to the murder of the Mapuche community member Camilo Catrillanca by the police. The Institute contributed significantly to both clarification of the facts of the case and, in coordination with other state institutions working on the case, the protection of the human rights of those involved, including the rights of the minor who was accompanying Catrillanca at the time of the murder.

The challenge of acting as an agent for change is not exempt from ideological debate. According to the fourth National Human Rights Survey of 2018, 40.1 per cent of respondents replied that the INDH protects the human rights of all people in Chile; however, only 19.7 per cent believed that the Institute defends all people. Worse still, almost 13 per cent think that the INDH is 'an institution that defends the interests of a few', that 'it is an institution of the left' which

[77] ibid, 26.

defends prisoners and terrorists, or 'that it is useless'.[78] These opinions are linked to the recent history of the country, but they also reveal contrasting views regarding the scope of human rights, and therefore the mission of Chile's NHRI. However, the main ideological debate tends to be sparked by recommendations issued by human rights treaty bodies, particularly those that go beyond the express text of their corresponding convention. For some, these recommendations are not binding *stricto sensu*; for others, the principle of the progressive realisation of human rights requires them to be so. In conformity with the Paris Principles, NHRIs should have the power '[t]o promote and ensure the harmonisation of national legislation, regulations and practices with the international human rights instruments to which the State is a party' as well as 'encourage ratification of the above-mentioned instruments or accession to those instruments, and to ensure their implementation'.[79] From this perspective, it is evident that both powers refer to the international agreements to which the state is a party and not the recommendations that emanate from treaty bodies.

Somewhat related to this problem, is the question of how to gauge the impact of the INDH's recommendations. One of the INDH's tasks is to monitor and measure the impact of these recommendations on the actions of state organs and beyond. At the time of writing, the INDH has issued 10 annual reports; these contain over 500 recommendations issued to the different branches of government. Apart from certain cases wherein the effectiveness of its recommendations is concretely demonstrated – for example, by the enactment of laws or the creation of state programmes – there is generally no information available as to the level of compliance with the recommendations of the annual reports. Consequently, the INDH has recently instigated efforts to monitor compliance by means of an internal follow-up tool; although a positive development, the tool is limited and only allows users to identify the INDH's recommendations according to certain search criteria.[80] This resource must continue to be developed, on a permanent and systematic basis, to enable the Institute to have an objective assessment of its recommendations' influence and to propose specific actions to enhance their impact.

As an agent of change, the INDH faces another challenge. Under the prevailing paradigm, its work is restricted to considerations of the acts and omissions of state agents that may constitute human rights violations. Despite the emergence of new realities and views within human rights discourses, this state-centric lens has shown particular resilience. As far back as 2015, the

---

78 INDH, National Human Rights Survey 2018. It should be noted that the question was asked in such a way as to allow for multiple spontaneous responses.

79 UN General Assembly Res. 48/134 of 20 December 1993, para. 3.c.

80 Following a second stage of development, users will be able to monitor levels of compliance with each recommendation. The tool is called '*Recomendaciones*' and is available at: <www.recomendaciones.indh.cl/>.

INDH's first Director spoke about the new challenges and projections of the INDH, and placed particular emphasis on the need to 'begin a debate on the horizontal effect of human rights', adding that 'a debate is already underway at the global level on the responsibility that private entities/individuals may have in this regard'.[81] A pertinent example of non-state actors that influence human rights issues can be found in the key role played by companies; companies are increasingly recognised as 'specialised bodies of society' that hold a responsibility to respect human rights. Internationally, the UN Guiding Principles on Business and Human Rights endorsed this view in 2011.[82] At the domestic level, this debate encompasses several stark realities, such as the situations of violence that have affected individuals, indigenous peoples and the state for a number of years in the central-southern regions of Chile. As is the case with other similar examples, albeit in distinct contexts, these considerations constitute a powerful interpellation into the predominant paradigm: one which obliges all stakeholders to rethink the borders that determine when and where human rights protection becomes relevant. This is a pertinent question for the INDH; in order to confront the new challenges of today's society, it must always consider novel paradigms and nascent ideas in the field of human rights.

4.3. STRENGTHENING THE MANAGEMENT OF THE INSTITUTE

The challenge of strengthening the INDH's institutional management can be addressed by applying four perspectives: decision-making, regional expansion, funding, and responsibilities. Regarding the first standpoint, the task refers to the institutional consolidation of the INDH as a collegial and autonomous body. In this regard, strengthening the INDH Council remains high on the list of institutional priorities. As to the second perspective, the INDH needed to establish regional offices around the country, to transform the institution into a genuinely national entity. This task was completed in 2019. The following table shows the progress made by the INDH over the past few years, in terms of its regional expansion:

Table 5. Establishment of regional offices

Regional office	Year established
Valparaiso Region	2015
Los Lagos Region	2015
Antofagasta Region	2015

(continued)

81 Fries (n 73) p. 27.
82 See Human Rights Council Res. 17/4 of 16 June 2011, which endorsed these principles.

Table 5 *continued*

Regional office	Year established
La Araucanía Region	2015
Arica and Parinacota Region	2015
Biobio Region	2015
Coquimbo Region	2016
Magallanes Region	2016
Tarapacá Region	2016
Los Ríos Region	2016
Metropolitan Region	2017
Atacama Region	2017
Maule Region	2017
Aysen Region	2017
O'Higgins Region	2018
Ñuble Region	2019

Source: Compiled by the authors.

Although the INDH's regional expansion has been adequate, ensuring consistency throughout the country, by ensuring its collegial nature in all regions, remains a pending task: this task is not easy to achieve, due to the physical distance between the INDH's regional offices and its seat of centralised institutional decision-making as well as the urgency that surrounds many of the human rights situations that it must respond to.

In terms of the third point of view, it is vital that the INDH is able to secure an adequate allocation of resources, so as to enable the Institute to fulfil its mandate: this includes the resources necessary for the running of its regional offices. Finally, as to the fourth perspective, the creation of thematic rapporteur-ships constitutes a major challenge for the INDH. A number of alternatives are possible here, all of which present their own problems. For instance, the creation of new agencies with parallel responsibilities to those of the INDH raises questions of harmonisation, coordination, and cooperation with and between each of these entities. An example of this alternative in action, is the newly created *Defensoría de la Niñez*, or Ombuds Office for the Protection of Children: a body which is external to the INDH.[83] Another possibility is housing such rapporteur-ships within the INDH's institutional structure; this would require a deployment of the new sub-entities, within the broader Institute, in a manner that is harmonious, coordinated, and cooperative *vis-à-vis* the execution of the Institute's roles. The

83 See Law Nr. 21,067 of the Republic of Chile.

National Preventive Mechanism against Torture and Other Cruel, Inhuman or Degrading Treatment or Punishment is a good example of this alternative. In either case, an evaluation of all experiences which have been accumulated since the inception of these entities should be a key factor in guiding future legislative discussion on the creation of new thematic rapporteur-ships.

NATIONAL INSTITUTIONS AT THE SERVICE OF INTERNATIONAL HUMAN RIGHTS LAW

Conclusions

Sebastián López Escarcena, Manuel Núñez Poblete and Jan Wouters

The Paris Principles are the benchmark against which all NHRIs are generally measured in the important accreditation process managed by the international network that groups them today. These principles, as construed and applied by GANHRI's SCA, are a good example of how international law can bring the rule of law into municipal law. Because of their origin, the Paris Principles favour the human rights commission as an institutional model over the ombuds-institute and the human rights institute, and focus on the creation of NHRIs, rather than in their subsequent operation. These two aspects constitute a limitation of these principles. Even though the first of these problems has been solved in practice, the second one remains a reality that requires identifying efficiency criteria going beyond institutional design and guiding NHRIs in the effective fulfilment of their functions.

From a comparative perspective, NHRIs are a common tool of constitutional law for the promotion and protection of human rights. As this book has shown, this is particularly true for Latin American NHRIs, where the figure of the ombuds tends to take precedence over commissions or institutes. With few exceptions, the vast majority of these NHRIs enjoy a legal status that allows us to describe them as constitutional institutions, aimed at fulfilling that critical role. NHRIs' relevance has been recently highlighted by the UN, the Council of Europe and the OAS. In 2017, the UNGA promoted the existence of independent NHRIs as an indicator for Sustainable Development Goal 16 of Agenda 2030 – that of promoting just, peaceful and inclusive societies;[1] it reiterated the significance of NHRIs during the COVID-19 pandemic.[2] Three years later, the UN Human

1 A/RES/71/313, para. 16.a.1, 6 July 2017.
2 A/RES/72/186, 19 December 2017.

Rights Council also recognised 'the important role of national human rights institutions in highlighting the human rights implications of the COVID-19 pandemic',[3] thus renewing the global call for increased awareness about these institutions and their work.

Regionally, the Committee of Ministers of the Council of Europe adopted in 2021 a recommendation on the development and strengthening of NHRIs,[4] which follows on from its important 1997 recommendation on the original establishment of these institutions.[5] The 2021 recommendation of the Committee of Ministers focuses not only on individual NHRIs, but also on the ENNHRI and GANHRI, bolstering them, respectively, as a regional promoter of technical assistance and as a global network. This is an important endorsement, given the essentially cooperative nature of NHRIs and the proven need to exchange institutional experiences. On the other side of the Atlantic Ocean, the IACHR included NHRIs among the core elements of its 2017–2021 Strategic Plan,[6] which in 2018 led to the signing of a Declaration of Commitment for Technical Cooperation and the creation of a Mechanism of Points of Contact that, to date, comprises a dozen NHRI members.[7] Although this mechanism is nascent, it is a necessary companion to the as yet precarious cooperation that exists within the Network of National Institutions for the Promotion and Protection of Human Rights in the American Continent (RINDHCA),[8] which currently has 18 members, 15 of which have been accredited with 'A-status' and three with 'B-status' by GANHRI. In its 2023–2027 Strategic Plan, the IACHR mentioned following up on the Declaration of Commitment for Technical Cooperation as one of its lines of action, emphasising the need to continue expanding, diversifying, and deepening civil society participation in the activities of NHRIs.[9]

1. INSTITUTIONAL CHALLENGES IN THE AMERICAS

The NHRIs reviewed in this book are far from having reached full institutional maturity. As explained in the chapters in Part 2 by Paola Acosta (Chapter 8), Manuel Núñez Poblete and Sebastián Donoso (Chapter 12), Veronika Haasz

---

3 A/HRC/45/L.20, 30 September 2020.

4 CM/Rec (2021)1, 31 March 2021, on the Development and Strengthening of Effective, Pluralist and Independent National Human Rights Institutions.

5 Recommendation No. R (97) 14, 30 September 1997, on the Establishment of Independent National Institutions for the Promotion and Protection of Human Rights.

6 Available at: <https://www.oas.org/en/iachr/mandate/StrategicPlan2017/docs/StrategicPlan2017-2021.pdf>.

7 <https://www.oas.org/en/iachr/media_center/PReleases/2018/246.asp>.

8 For its name in Spanish: *Red de Instituciones Nacionales para la Promoción y Protección de los Derechos Humanos del Continente Americano.* <https://www.rindhca.org>.

9 <https://www.oas.org/en/iachr/mandate/strategicplan/2023/StrategicPlan2023-2027.pdf>.

(Chapter 9), and Emilio Maus and Pablo González Domínguez (Chapter 6), there are several factors that hinder Latin American NHRIs from exercising their powers. Among these, specific phenomena have been identified, which include:

- delays in the appointment of the most senior officials (Paraguay and the Dominican Republic);
- the lengthy period of time spent without appointing an ombudsman (Argentina);
- a closeness to or excessive leniency with governments (Mexico);
- legal disputes regarding appointments or removals of a Chair or Director (Chile and Mexico);
- the removal of ombudsmen (Panama and Ecuador); and
- the extensive appropriation by third parties of a building belonging to a NHRI (Chile).

Although they may seem anecdotal, such incidents often cause significant damage to the prestige, trust or, at the very least, the continuity of NHRIs. Beyond these particular setbacks, there are a number of cross-cutting challenges that have been identified in this book, including threats to institutional independence and the effectiveness of their recommendations, as noted by Acosta with regard to Colombia (Chapter 8), and the insufficiency of constitutional norms to guarantee autonomy on their own, as explained by Haasz in her chapter on Paraguay and Uruguay (Chapter 9). Budgetary design; accountability; guarantees of investigative powers, including immunity of members; and necessary interrelations with civil society are additional aspects that should be strengthened in Latin American NHRIs. All these are known as formal institutional design safeguards,[10] the lack of which severely affects the authority and effectiveness of NHRIs. Some of them are reflected in the latest GANHRI SCA reports.[11]

The chapters by Haasz (Chapter 9), and Núñez Póblete and Donoso (Chapter 12) warn us of an even more intractable issue: the excessive dependence of institutional performance on the personal characteristics or agendas of the individual person in charge of the relevant NHRI. This is an institutional challenge in itself, since it is germane to the very essence of an institution of this kind not to depend, to a disproportionate degree, on the personalities of those serving there. In a continent scarred by dictatorships, where the very concept of human rights was, for a long time, associated with certain experiences and particular forms of victimisation that may have sometimes been the focus of

10 See K. Linos and T. Pegram, 'What Works in Human Rights Institutions?' (2017) 111/3 *AJIL* 628, 630.

11 Available at: <https://ganhri.org/accreditation/sca-reports/>.

institutional agendas, this is all the more difficult. Such a cultural factor certainly impacts on the performance of NHRIs, as does the constitutional identity of the political system in which they are embedded. The latter is the case regarding Bolivia and Ecuador, reviewed in the chapter by Núñez Poblete (Chapter 4), whose NHRIs' mandates are complemented by a new category of rights hitherto unknown in the American and European constitutional tradition: the rights of nature. Although it remains too early to draw conclusions about the way in which these mandates – which extend to non-human rights – may influence the design and performance of NHRIs in the Americas, the emergence of the rights of nature shines a new spotlight on those institutions that are moving beyond the traditional anthropocentric conception of human rights.

In addition to the rights of nature, the collective rights of indigenous peoples in Latin America should be added to the list of challenges that NHRIs in this region face. Elsewhere, in New Zealand for instance, the promotion and protection of indigenous peoples' rights has led to the creation of an Indigenous Rights Commissioner that can operate separately from, or in an integrated manner with, traditional NHRIs. Conversely, indigenous rights in Latin America have remained under the mandate of traditional ombuds offices, leaving specialised agencies for criminal law purposes only. In this regard, certain Latin American NHRIs have played a valuable role as mediators in conflicts that have involved indigenous communities and their states.[12] This mediating function, which the Paris Principles include among the quasi-jurisdictional competences of NHRIs, goes beyond the field of indigenous populations, considering the intensity that some of these conflicts have reached in different states of the region.

Another feature that should be noted with regard to Latin American NHRIs concerns the international standards they are expected to promote and protect domestically. Much like the constitutional identity of these states, which conditions the institutional features of their NHRIs, the Inter-American System of human rights has also had an impact on the design and performance of such institutions. The development by the IACtHR of the conventionality control doctrine is an example of this.[13] The conventionality control has had a powerful effect in the region by requiring, in IACtHR judicial decisions and advisory opinions, a review of conformity or compatibility between, on the one hand, their respective municipal law and, on the other hand, the interpretation given by the Court to the ACHR and other treaties of the Inter-American System conferring jurisdiction on the Court. For this reason, RINDHCA has urged Latin American

---

[12] See J. Aylwin, 'Los Ombudsman y los derechos de los pueblos indígenas en América Latina' in M. Berraondo (ed.), *Pueblos indígenas y derechos humanos*, Publicaciones de la Universidad de Deusto, Bilbao 2006, p. 349.

[13] See generally P. González Domínguez, *The Doctrine of Conventionality Control. Between Uniformity and Legal Pluralism in the Inter-American Human Rights System*, Intersentia, Cambridge 2018.

NHRIs to incorporate the standard within the scope of their powers, and to foster its implementation by the corresponding national executive, judicial and legislative branches.[14]

Lastly, the general crisis of trust in public institutions is also a huge challenge for every NHRI. As public institutions, NHRIs require strong legitimation to persuade and influence state organs and civil society. In the Americas, there are some negative trends which are already having detrimental effects on NHRIs.[15] For example, according the 2020 National Human Rights Survey of the Chilean *Instituto Nacional de Derechos Humanos* (National Institute of Human Rights),[16] people in that country were more willing to trust the police force than this human rights institute. Even if the surveys are made with different methodologies, offering divergent outcomes, the need to boost trust in NHRIs will persist.

2. INSTITUTIONAL CHALLENGES IN EUROPE

Several chapters have highlighted institutional challenges for NHRIs in Europe, including:

- the shrinking space for democracy and the rule of law in various European countries, which complicates the independent and effective work of NHRIs;
- the rise of populism and negative human rights discourses, which often target minority groups and restrict the space for actors – such as NHRIs – which speak up for the rights of individuals belonging to such groups;
- the fact that national decision-makers ultimately are not bound by NHRI recommendations and may ignore their findings; and
- the reduction in resources allocated to human rights and to NHRIs as a result of successive recent crises, such as the financial and austerity crises, COVID-19, the war against Ukraine and its economic impacts.

As Katrien Meuwissen notes in Chapter 2, tight resources and increasing human rights challenges pose important challenges for all European NHRIs. To this

14 See generally its Declaration on the Challenges of the Implementation of the Constitutional Bloc and the Conventionality Control in Ibero-America, of 17 November 2020. Available at: <https://www.rindhca.org/images/declaraciones_pronunciamientos/DECLARACION_FIO_RINDHCA_CONTROL_CONVENCIONALIDAD.pdf>.

15 See generally A. ESTELLA, 'Confianza institucional en América Latina: Un análisis comparado' (2020) 34 *Documentos de Trabajo*. Available at: <https://www.fundacioncarolina.es/wp-content/uploads/2020/05/DT_FC_34.pdf>.
This article compares the Latin American and European experiences, showing some interesting differences of patterns between both regions.

16 Available at: <https://www.ciperchile.cl/wp-content/uploads/Encuesta-Nacional-DDHH.pdf>.

may be added that NHRIs are, in many countries, relatively new players that need to find their place in an often densely populated human rights landscape and that face toweringly high expectations from public authorities at all levels as well as from civil society. In some cases, as narrated by Emmanuel Decaux for the *Commission nationale consultative des droits de l'homme* in France in Chapter 7, there have been painful disconnects with the authorities. Moreover, the European mechanisms dedicated to the protection of human rights typically pre-dated the emergence of NHRIs and are therefore often not specifically adapted to accommodate effective engagement with the latter. Nevertheless, especially in the internal and external policies of the EU, one sees a remarkable rise of the importance attached to NHRIs in recent years.

3. COMMON INSTITUTIONAL CHALLENGES

This book has identified a number of common challenges for all NHRIs, despite the diversity of their institutional designs and of their historical and political backgrounds. Such challenges include:

- delays in their establishment;
- non-renewal of their membership by the state;
- dissimilar institutionalisation of autonomy;
- budgetary problems;
- persistent obstacles to pluralism;
- difficulties in assessing their effectiveness;
- disparate cooperation networks;
- complexities in building legitimacy and public awareness; and
- inter-institutional competition for resources with new agencies specialised in non-discrimination, child rights, personal data, torture, or other areas.

In terms of budgetary issues, the adequacy of the funding allocated to NHRIs and the setbacks experienced during recent economic and health crises are highlighted in the chapter by José Julio Fernández (Chapter 10), with regard to the Spanish *Defensor del Pueblo*. These issues extend even further, reaching budgetary autonomy in certain institutions. This has been the case in Brazil, where the budget of the *Conselho Nacional dos Direitos Humanos* (National Human Rights Council) remains closely linked to the executive branch – a situation which the IACHR has urged should be improved.[17] Beyond the worrisome lack of autonomy in the use of their resources, the political perception

[17] Report on the Situation of Human Rights in Brazil of the IACHR, OAS/ Ser.L/V/II. Doc. 9, rev.12, February, 2012, para. 433.

that the functions of NHRIs are dispensable, or at least can be reduced, may be an indication of a broader undermining of certain values associated with the rule of law. This is a major hindrance for national institutions aimed at fostering the rule of law by helping states to comply with their international obligations, most notably the human rights commitments of these states, as Sebastián López Escarcena shows in Chapter 1.

Inter-institutional competition with new specialised agencies has taken place in both regions, in a rather inverse manner. In Latin America, unlike in several European states, thematic agencies appeared after NHRIs were established, and began to compete with them on quantitative issues, including budget, human resources and territorial reach, as well as on qualitative aspects, such as citizenry awareness and linkage with public authorities. For the moment, there cannot be said to be any winners or losers emerging from this contest. At any rate, institutional fragmentation and dispersion of limited resources is not good news for states, particularly for poor ones. Exceptionally in Europe, the prior existence of specialised agencies continues to delay the creation of NHRIs with a general mandate in some states. This is the case in Italy, where the creation of a *Commissione Nazionale per la Promozione dei Diritti Umani Fondamentali* (National Commission for the Promotion of Fundamental Human Rights), in line with the commitment made by the Italian government in the 2019 Universal Periodic Review, remains pending.[18]

As for effectiveness and mandate extensions, the chapters on the Chilean and German NHRIs display the contrasting experience of institutions that lack the power to receive complaints, as part of their correspondent mandates. As Heiner Bielefeldt, Markus Krajewski, Michael Krennerich and Beate Rudolf noted in Chapter 11, this circumstance did not appear to pose a problem for the re-accreditation of the *Deutsches Institut für Menschenrechte* in 2015. In fact, this institution has been further consolidated over time. Similarly, this was not an issue for the Chilean *Instituto Nacional de Derechos Humanos* in its 2021 re-accreditation. However, as informed by Núñez Poblete and Donoso in Chapter 12, this NHRI has slowly achieved an institutional consolidation, nuancing the assessment of Katerina Lino and Tom Pegram regarding the impact of the 'lack of complaint-handling powers' within the protective function of the institution.[19] Effectiveness would thus depend less on the ability to receive complaints than on the authority to issue opinions.

---

18 Report of the Working Group on the Universal Periodic Review: Italy, A/HRC/43/4, 27 December 2019, para. 6.

19 See Linos and Pegram, 'What Works in Human Rights Institutions?' (n 10) p. 651.

INDEX